President Wilson's State Papers and Addresses

© Harris & Ewing

WOODROW WILSON

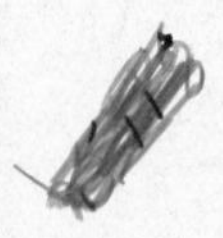

PRESIDENT WILSON'S STATE PAPERS AND ADDRESSES

WITH EDITORIAL NOTES
A BIOGRAPHICAL SKETCH
AN INTRODUCTION AND
AN ANALYTICAL INDEX

NEW YORK
THE REVIEW OF REVIEWS COMPANY
1918

INTRODUCTION

Under our form of government, the President occupies place that has no exact parallel in the government of any ther important country. In the last analysis we are govrned by public opinion, of which the President is chief xponent. He is the country's spokesman, not merely by ustom but by express Constitutional provision and manate. He is directed to inform Congress from time to time oncerning the vital interests of the United States. He is lso made the spokesman of the country in its dealings with oreign governments.

The President's Messages to Congress are not merely a orm of communication between the executive and the lawıaking authority, but they are intended to give information nd guidance to the citizenship. Thus we have a surprising uantity of important historical and governmental material f an authoritative kind in the unbroken series of Presidenial messages and addresses, beginning with the first inugural of George Washington and coming down to the atest official utterance of Woodrow Wilson.

All of our Presidents have been fully responsive to the uty of giving information to Congress and the country oncerning the carrying-on of the government and the ublic concerns of the nation. Not one of them in the ist has come seriously short in this regard, although ome of them have been more conspicuous than others in oint of literary or oratorical ability.

Perhaps no other President has, relatively speaking, ccomplished as much of his work through the successful use of written and spoken appeals to Congress, to America citizens, and to the public opinion of the world, as ha Woodrow Wilson. His utterances have shaped events, no only in the current sense but in the larger aspects of his tory. His Messages to Congress have been unusual in thei frequency, vital in their relation to policies, and notabl in the fact that he has appeared in person to present them All of these Messages are published in this little volume

Besides these Messages to Congress, however, he ha made many important addresses of a semi-official natur since assuming the Presidency, while he has been the autho of a series of diplomatic notes and of proclamations relatin to international affairs that constitute state papers of th highest significance. These documents also are include in the present volume, together with much material o Presidential authorship relating to the conduct of the wa and to the policies of the Government.

The remarkable literary quality of Mr. Wilson's ad dresses is only eclipsed by their statesmanlike character i relation to public affairs of great moment. His sentence and paragraphs, in their discussion of world affairs, hav helped to crystallize the vague longings of right-thinkin men in all nations into something like definite policies fo permanent peace on the basis of democracy and interna tional justice. This collection of state papers and Presi dential utterances is not, therefore, of transitory interes and importance, but of permanent value; and it ought t be in the home and at the hand of every intelligent citizen

ALBERT SHAW.

CONTENTS

CONTENTS—(*Continued*)

CONTENTS—(*Continued*)

CONTENTS—(*Continued*)

CONTENTS—(*Continued*)

CONTENTS—(*Continued*)

CAREER OF WOODROW WILSON

Twenty-eighth President of the United States

[*Vice-President, two terms, Thomas R. Marshall*]

The return of the Democratic party to power was made certain by the feeling of the country that the Payne-Aldrich tariff, enacted by the Republicans early in Mr. Taft's term, did not properly meet the pledge that the tariff should be thoroughly revised and substantially reduced by those responsible for the protective policy. In 1910, the Democrats elected a majority of the new Congress. In 1912, they carried the Presidential election as well as the Congressional. For the first time, the plan of popular primaries was used by the parties in the selection of candidates.

The Democratic primaries showed Champ Clark (Speaker of the House) to be a plurality favorite, while the Republican primaries showed a clear preference for Theodore Roosevelt. But the effort to secure a second term for Taft gave him control of the Republican convention at Chicago, with the result that the larger half of the Republican party supported Roosevelt on a separate ticket. Woodrow Wilson, Governor of New Jersey, had been a prominent Democratic candidate, and through the influence of Mr. Bryan, Wilson prevailed over Clark in the Democratic convention at Baltimore. Apart from the fact that it was logically a Democratic year, the split in the Republican party made Democratic victory quite inevitable.

Woodrow Wilson had not been in active politics, but he had long been a distinguished citizen and an eminent authority in the field of American history, government, and public policy. From his youth he had excelled in oratory, and his life study had been in the fields of jurisprudence and politics. After graduation from Princeton in 1879, he had studied law at the University of Virginia and had for a short time practiced law at Atlanta, Ga. His birthplace was Staunton, Va., and his boyhood had been spent in the States farther south. In 1883 he had entered upon special studies at Johns Hopkins University, where in 1886 he received the degree of Doctor of Philosophy.

He had not only obtained recognition at that time as an accomplished student in history, economics, and the science of government, but he had completed what has always held place as a very notable book, entitled "Congressional Government," which deals with the American national system in contrast with the British. After some years of teaching elsewhere, Wilson returned to Princeton as professor, and in due time became president of that institution, having devoted himself constantly to work in the field of American history, comparative politics, and the principles of constitutional law and government.

The headship of an American educational institution is analagous, in the character of its executive authority, to the governorship of a State or the presidency of the Union. In 1910 he was made Governor of the State of New Jersey, and at once attracted notice throughout the country as a probable President of the United States. He was still Governor when elected to the Presidency.

Wilson's first term was notable for the vigor and success with which he led his party in the revision of the tariff, the important reconstruction of the country's banking and currency system, and in various other policies which were favorably received regardless of party divisions. The principal foreign situation with which he had to deal in the early part of his term was caused by the chaotic condition of Mexico. Later, however, and before he had been in the presidential chair a full year and a half, the great war in Europe began and his attention was absorbed by the problems due to the neutral position of the United States as among the most powerful commercial nations of the world which were now opposing each other in two belligerent groups.

President Wilson's renomination, in the summer of 1916, was unanimously accorded by the Democratic party. The Republicans nominated Charles E. Hughes (formerly Governor of the State of New York), who had for six years been an Associate Justice of the United States Supreme Court. The election was very close, and turned finally upon the count of votes in the State of California. Mr. Wilson's reëlection was, however, fully conceded by his opponents and accepted with characteristic good will by the entire country.

The most serious situation of the latter part of his first term had to do with his diplomatic controversy with Germany over the ruthless and illegal use of submarines against the world's merchant shipping in the North Sea and in waters adjacent to the British, French, and Italian coasts. The principal slogan used by the Democrats, particularly in the West and South, in reëlecting Mr. Wilson was found in the phrase: "He kept us out of war." But just a month after his second inauguration he led the country into war, with the support of a Democratic Congress and the very general endorsement, regardless of party, of the entire country. This apparent change in his attitude was due to the resumption by Germany, on a far greater scale than two years previous, of reprisal methods in the form of unrestricted use of floating mines and submarine torpedoes in what the Germans denominated a "blockade" of England, France, and Italy—this policy being in violation of the rights of neutrals.

Mr. Wilson's leadership—his country having supported him in the great decision—was fully accepted at home and highly respected abroad. His object, which was to "make the world safe for democracy," was acclaimed by the European Allies who were fighting Germany; and his official views were felt as strengthening movement for popular government everywhere in the world. He was visited by important commissions from the governments of France, Great Britain, Italy, Russia, Japan, and several other countries; and his attitude toward these countries, and toward the support of the war against German aggression, secured in every case the confidence and admiration of these official visitors. His leadership in creating a National Army and in obtaining financial support for his war measures upon a scale of unparalleled magnitude, had resulted within six months after war was declared on April 6, 1917, in measures that were at once transforming a considerable part of the human energies and material resources of the country into effective agencies for the carrying-on of war.

Born, Staunton, Va., Dec. 28, 1856. Graduated, Princeton, 1879. Graduated in law, University of Virginia, 1881. Practised law at Atlanta, Ga., 1882-3. Post-graduate work at Johns Hopkins, 1883-5. Ph. D., 1886. Associate Professor of History and Political Economy, Bryn Mawr College, 1885-8; Professor of History and Political Economy, Wesleyan University; 1888-90; Professor of Jurisprudence and Political Economy, Princeton University, 1890-95; Professor of Jurisprudence, Princeton, 1895-7; Professor of Jurisprudence and Politics, Princeton, 1897-1910; President of Princeton University, 1902-10. Governor of New Jersey, January 17, 1911-March 1, 1912. Nominated for President of the United States, Democratic National Convention, Baltimore, 1912. Elected on Nov. 4, 1912, receiving 435 electoral votes, against 88 for Theodore Roosevelt, Progressive, and 8 for William Howard Taft, Republican. (Wilson's popular vote was 2,450,000 less than that of all other candidates combined.) Nominated for second term by the Democratic National Convention at St. Louis, June, 1916, and elected on Nov. 7, 1916 receiving 276 electoral votes against 255 for Charles E. Hughes, Republican, wilh a popular plurality of about 400,000. Author of: "Congressional Government, A Study in American Politics" (1885); "The State—Elements of Historical and Practical Politics" (1889); "Division and Reunion, 1829-1889" (1893); "An Old Master, and Other Political Essays" (1893); "Mere Literature, and Other Essays" (1893); "George Washington" (1896); "A History of the American People" (1902); "Constitutional Government in the United States" (1908); "Free Life" (1913); "The New Freedom" (1913); "When a Man Comes to Himself" (1915).

WOODROW WILSON'S INAUGURAL ADDRESS

There has been a change of government. It began two years ago, when the House of Representatives became Democratic by a decisive majority. It has now been completed. The Senate about to assemble will also be Democratic. The offices of President and Vice-President have been put into the hands of Democrats. What does the change mean? That is the question that is uppermost in our minds to-day. That is the question I am going to try to answer, in order, if I may, to interpret the occasion.

It means much more than the mere success of a party. The success of a party means little except when the Nation is using that party for a large and definite purpose. No one can mistake the purpose for which the Nation now seeks to use the Democratic Party. It seeks to use it to interpret a change in its own plans and point of view. Some old things with which we had grown familiar, and which had begun to creep into the very habit of our thought and of our lives, have altered their aspect as we have latterly looked critically upon them, with fresh, awakened eyes; have dropped their disguises and shown themselves alien and sinister. Some new things, as we look frankly upon them, willing to comprehend their real character, have come to assume the aspect of things long believed in and familiar, stuff of our own convictions. We have been refreshed by a new insight into our own life.

We see that in many things that life is very great. It is incomparably great in its material aspects, in its body of wealth, in the diversity and sweep of its energy, in the industries which have been built up by the genius of individual men and the limitless enterprise of groups of men. It is great, also, very great, in its moral force. We have built up, moreover, a great system of government, which has stood through a long age as in many respects a model for those who seek to set liberty upon foundations that will endure against fortuitous change, against storm and accident.

But the evil has come with the good, and much fine gold has been corroded. With riches has come inexcusable waste. We have squandered a great part of what we might have used, and have not stopped to conserve the exceeding bounty of nature, without which our genius for enterprise would have been worthless and impotent, scorning to be careful, shamefully prodigal as well as admirably efficient. We have been proud of our industrial achievements, but we have not hitherto stopped thoughtfully enough to count the human cost, the cost of lives snuffed out, of energies overtaxed and broken, the fearful physical and spiritual cost to the men and women and children upon whom the dead weight and burden of it all has fallen pitilessly the years through. The groans and agony of it all had not yet reached our ears, the solemn, moving undertone of our life, coming up out of the mines and factories and out of every home where the struggle had its intimate and familiar seat. With the great Government went many deep secret things which we too long delayed to look into and scrutinize with candid, fearless eyes. The great Government we loved has too often been made use of for private and selfish purposes, and those who used it had forgotten the people.

At last a vision has been vouchsafed us of our life as a whole. We see the bad with the good, the debased and decadent with the sound and vital. With this vision we approach new affairs. Our duty is to cleanse, to reconsider, to restore, to correct the evil without impairing the good, to purify and humanize every process of our common life without weakening or sentimentalizing it. There has been something crude and heartless and unfeeling in our haste to succeed and be great. Our thought has been "Let every man look out for himself, let every generation look out for itself," while we reared giant machinery which made it impossible that any but those who stood at the levers of control should have a chance to look out for themselves. We had not forgotten our morals. We remembered well enough that we had set up a policy which was meant to serve the humblest as well as the most powerful, with an eye single to the standards of justice and fair play, and remembered it with pride. But we were very heedless and in a hurry to be great.

We have come now to the sober second thought. The scales of heedlessness have fallen from our eyes. We have made up our minds to square every process of our national life again with the standard we so proudly set up at the beginning and have always carried at our hearts. Our work is a work of restoration.

We have itemized with some degree of particularity the things that ought to be altered and here are some of the chief items: A tariff which cuts us off from our proper part in the commerce of the world, violates the just principles of taxation, and makes the Government a facile instrument in the hands of private interests; a banking and currency system based upon the necessity of the Government to sell its bonds fifty years ago and perfectly adapted to concentrating cash and restricting credits; an industrial system which, take it on all its sides, financial as well as administrative, holds capital in leading strings, restricts the liberties and limits the opportunities of labor, and exploits without renewing or conserving the natural resources of the country; a body of agricultural activities never yet given the efficiency of great business undertakings or served as it should be through the instrumentality of science taken directly to the farm, or afforded the facilities of credit best suited to its practical needs; watercourses undeveloped, waste places unreclaimed, forests untended, fast disappearing without plan or prospect of renewal, unregarded waste heaps at every mine. We have studied as perhaps no other nation has the most effective means of production, but we have not studied cost or economy as we should either as organizers of industry, as statesmen, or as individuals.

Nor have we studied and perfected the means by which government may be put at the service of humanity, in safeguarding the health of the Nation, the health of its men and its women and its children, as well as their rights in the struggle for existence. This is no sentimental duty. The firm basis of government is justice, not pity. These are matters of justice. There can be no equality or opportunity, the first essential of justice in the body politic, if men and women and children be not shielded in their lives, their very vitality, from the consequences of great industrial and social processes which they can not alter, control, or singly cope with. Society must see to it that it does not itself crush or weaken or damage its own constituent parts. The first duty of law is to keep sound the society it serves. Sanitary laws, pure food laws, and laws determining conditions of labor which individuals are powerless to determine for themselves are intimate parts of the very business of justice and legal efficiency.

These are some of the things we ought to do, and not leave the others undone, the old-fashioned, never-to-be-neglected, fundamental safeguarding of property and of individual right. This is the high enterprise of the new day: To lift everything that concerns our life as a Nation to the light that shines from the hearthfire of every man's conscience and vision of the right. It is inconceivable that we should do this as partisans; it is inconceivable we should do it in ignorance of the facts as they are or in blind haste. We shall restore, not destroy. We shall deal with our economic system as it is and as it may be modified, not as it might be if we had a clean sheet of paper to write upon; and step by step we shall make it what it should be, in the spirit of those who question their own wisdom and seek counsel and knowledge, not shallow self-satisfaction or the excitement of excursions whither they can not tell. Justice, and only justice, shall always be our motto.

And yet it will be no cool process of mere science. The Nation has been deeply stirred, stirred by a solemn passion, stirred by the knowledge of wrong, of ideals lost, of government too often debauched and made an instrument of evil. The feelings with which we face this new age of right and opportunity sweep across our heartstrings like some air out of God's own presence, where justice and mercy are reconciled and the judge and the brother are one. We know our task to be no mere task of politics but a task which shall search us through and through, whether we be able to understand our time and the need of our people, whether we be indeed their spokesmen and interpreters, whether we have the pure heart to comprehend and the rectified will to choose our high course of action.

This is not a day of triumph; it is a day of dedication. Here muster, not the forces of party, but the forces of humanity. Men's hearts wait upon us; men's lives hang in the balance; men's hopes call upon us to say what we will do. Who shall live up to the great trust? Who dares fail to try? I summon all honest men, all patriotic, all forward-looking men, to my side. God helping me, I will not fail them, if they will but counsel and sustain me!

WASHINGTON, March 4, 1913.

WOODROW WILSON'S FIRST SPECIAL ADDRESS TO CONGRESS CALLING FOR IMMEDIATE TARIFF REVISION

(Delivered before Congress in Joint Session, April 8, 1913.)

[EDITORIAL NOTE: *The two first Presidents, George Washington and John Adams, delivered their annual addresses "On the State of the Union" in person. Thomas Jefferson, the third President, introduced the written form of communication. His successors followed the precedent. Woodrow Wilson returned to the original custom and ap-*

peared before the Congress to deliver not only the Annual Message, but also many special Messages.

Tariff revision downward had been one of the uncompromising issues on which he and his party had won the campaign. When he delivered this Address, the new tariff bill (the Underwood Bill), already had been definitely formulated and approved by him. Its big features were free wool (the famous Schedule K), and the income tax provision, passed under the Sixteenth Amendment to the Constitution. Such an Amendment had been urged repeatedly by Roosevelt in order to make income tax legislation possible, after the United States Supreme Court had declared the first income tax provision unconstitutional. The Underwood Bill was signed by the President in October, 1913.]

Mr. Speaker, Mr. President, gentlemen of the Congress, I am very glad indeed to have this opportunity to address the two Houses directly and to verify for myself the impression that the President of the United States is a person, not a mere department of the Government hailing Congress from some isolated island of jealous power, sending messages, not speaking naturally and with his own voice—that he is a human being trying to co-operate with other human beings in a common service. After this pleasant experience I shall feel quite normal in all our dealings with one another.

I have called the Congress together in extraordinary session because a duty was laid upon the party now in power at the recent elections which it ought to perform promptly, in order that the burden carried by the people under existing law may be lightened as soon as possible, and in order, also, that the business interests of the country may not be kept too long in suspense as to what the fiscal changes are to be to which they will be required to adjust themselves. It is clear to the whole country that the tariff duties must be altered. They must be changed to meet the radical alteration in the conditions of our economic life which the country has witnessed within the last generation. While the whole face and method of our industrial and commercial life were being changed beyond recognition the tariff schedules have remained what they were before the change began, or have moved in the direction they were given when no large circumstance of our industrial development was what it is to-day. Our task is to square them with the actual facts. The sooner that is done the sooner we shall escape from suffering from the facts and the sooner our men of business will be free to thrive by the law of nature—the nature of free business—instead of by the law of legislation and artificial arrangement.

We have seen tariff legislation wander very far afield in our day—very far indeed from the field in which our prosperity might have had a normal growth and stimulation. No one who looks the facts squarely in the face or knows anything that lies beneath the surface of action can fail to perceive the principles upon which recent tariff legislation has been based. We long ago passed beyond the modest notion of "protecting" the industries of the country and moved boldly forward to the idea that they were entitled to the direct patronage of the Government. For a long time—a time so long that the men now active in public policy hardly remember the conditions that preceded it—we have sought in our tariff schedules to give each group of manufacturers or producers what they themselves thought that they needed in order to maintain a practically exclusive market as against the rest of the world. Consciously or unconsciously, we have built up a set of privileges and exemptions from competition behind which it was easy by any, even the crudest, forms of combination to organize monopoly; until at last nothing is normal, nothing is obliged to stand the tests of efficiency and economy, in our world of big business, but everything thrives by concerted arrangement. Only new principles of action will save us from a final hard crystallization of monopoly and a complete loss of the influences that quicken enterprise and keep independent energy alive.

It is plain what those principles must be. We must abolish everything that bears even the semblance of privilege or of any kind of artificial advantage, and put our business men and producers under the stimulation of a constant necessity to be efficient, economical, and enterprising, masters of competitive supremacy, better workers and merchants than any in the world. Aside from the duties laid upon articles which we do not, and probably can not, produce, therefore, and the duties laid upon luxuries and merely for the sake of the revenues they yield, the object of the tariff duties henceforth laid must be effective competition, the whetting of American wits by contest with the wits of the rest of the world.

It would be unwise to move toward this end headlong, with reckless haste, or with strokes that cut at the very roots of what has grown up amongst us by long process and at our own invitation. It does not alter a thing to upset it and break it and deprive it of a chance to change. It destroys it. We must make changes in our fiscal laws, in our fiscal system, whose object is development, a more free and wholesome development, not revolution or upset or confusion. We must build up trade, especially foreign trade. We need the outlet and the enlarged field of energy more than we ever did before. We must build up industry as well, and must adopt freedom in the place of artificial stimulation only so far as it will build, not pull down. In dealing with the tariff the method by which this may be done will be a matter of judgment exercised item by item. To some not accustomed to the excitements and responsibilities of greater freedom our methods may in some respects and at some points seem heroic but remedies may be heroic and yet be remedies. It is our business to make sure that they are genuine remedies. Our object is clear. If our motive is above just challenge and only an occasional error of judgment is chargeable against us, we shall be fortunate.

We are called upon to render the country a great service in more matters than one. Our responsibility should be met and our methods should be thorough, as thorough as moderate and well considered, based upon the facts as they are, and not worked out as if we were beginners. We are to deal with the facts of our own day, with the facts of no other and to make laws which square with those facts. It is best, indeed it is necessary, to begin with the tariff. I will urge nothing upon you now at the opening of your session which can obscure that first object or divert our energies from that clearly defined duty. At a later time I may take the liberty of calling your attention to reforms which should press close upon the heels of the tariff changes, if not accompany them, of which the chief is the reform of our banking and currency laws; but just now I refrain. For the present, I put these matters on one side and think only of this one thing—of the changes in our fiscal system which may best serve to open once more the free channels of prosperity to a great people whom we would serve to the utmost and throughout both rank and file.

Wilson Attacks "Lobby" Engaged in Influencing Congress on Tariff Schedules

[On May 26, 1913, the President gave out for publication the following statement:]

I think that the public ought to know the extraordinary exertions being made by the lobby in Washington to gain recognition for certain alterations of the Tariff bill. Washington has seldom seen so numerous, so industrious or so insidious a lobby. The newspapers are being filled with paid advertisements calculated to mislead the judgment of public men not only, but also the public opinion of the country itself. There is every evidence that money without limit is being spent to sustain this lobby and to create an appearance of a pressure of opinion antagonistic to some of the chief items of the Tariff bill.

It is of serious interest to the country that the people at large should have no lobby and be voiceless in these matters, while great bodies of astute men seek to create an artificial opinion and to overcome the interests of the public for their private profit. It is thoroughly worth the while of the people of this country to take knowledge of this matter. Only public opinion can check and destroy it.

The Government in all its branches ought to be relieved from this intolerable burden and this constant interruption to the calm progress of debate. I know that in this I am speaking for the members of the two houses, who would rejoice as much as I would to be released from this unbearable situation.

[It was plainly understood that the statement was aimed particularly at the "wool lobby" and the "sugar lobby." A Senate investigation followed and disclosed the names of many men who had busied themselves in attempting to influence Congress. The effect of the appeal to the public was to clear away very suddenly all secret machinations in regard to the new tariff act.]

Wilson Urges Currency Legislation

(Address delivered before Congress in Joint Session, June 23, 1913.)

[Editorial Note: *At the time of this Address, the country's finance was under the operation of the Aldrich-Vreeland Currency Law, passed in 1908, which provided for the issue by the Treasury Department of emergency currency to the banks whenever necessary. The bill passed in response to Wilson's Address was the Glass-Owen Federal Reserve Banking Law, which provided for Federal Reserve centers throughout the United States under mixed government and private control.*]

Mr. Speaker, Mr. President, gentlemen of the Congress, it is under the compulsion of what seems to me a clear and imperative duty that I have a second time this session sought the privilege of addressing you in person. I know, of course, that the heated season of the year is upon us, that work in these Chambers and in the committee rooms in likely to become a burden as the season lengthens, and that every consideration of personal convenience and personal comfort, perhaps, in the cases of some of us, considerations of personal health even, dictate an early conclusion of the deliberations of the session; but there are occasions of public duty when these things which touch us privately seem very small; when the work to be done is so pressing and so fraught with big consequence that we know that we are not at liberty to weigh against it any point of personal sacrifice. We are now in the presence of such an occasion. It is absolutely imperative that we should give the business men of this country a banking and currency system by means of which they can make use of the freedom of enterprise and of individual initiative which we are about to bestow upon them.

We are about to set them free; we must not leave them without the tools of action when they are free. We are about to set them free by removing the trammels of the protective tariff. Ever since the Civil War they have waited for this emancipation and for the free opportunities it will bring with it. It has been reserved for us to give it to them. Some fell in love, indeed, with the slothful security of their dependence upon the Government; some took advantage of the shelter of the nursery to set up a mimic mastery of their own within its walls. Now both the tonic and the discipline of liberty and maturity are to ensue. There will be some readjustments of purpose and point of view. There will follow a period of expansion and new enterprise, freshly conceived. It is for us to determine now whether it shall be rapid and facile and of easy accomplishment. This it can not be unless the resourceful business men who are to deal with the new circumstances are to have at hand and ready for use the instrumentalities and conveniences of free enterprise which independent men need when acting on their own initiative.

It is not enough to strike the shackles from business. The duty of statesmanship is not negative merely. It is constructive also. We must show that we understand what business needs and that we know how to supply it. No man, however casual and superficial his observation of the conditions now prevailing in the country, can fail to see that one of the chief things business needs now and will need increasingly as it gains in scope and vigor in the years immediatelly ahead of us is the proper means by which readily to vitalize its credit, corporate and individual, and its originative brains. What will it profit us to be free if we are not to have the best and most accessible instrumentalities of commerce and enterprise? What will it profit us to be quit of one kind of monopoly if we are to remain in the grip of another and more effective kind? How are we to gain and keep the confidence of the business community unless we show that we know how both to aid and to protect it? What shall we say if we make fresh enterprise necessary and also make it very difficult by leaving all else except the tariff just as we found it? The tyrannies of business, big and little, lie within the field of credit. We know that. Shall we not act upon the knowledge? Do we not know how to act upon it? If a man can not make his assets available at pleasure, his assets of capacity and character and resource, what satisfaction is it to him to see opportunity beckoning to him on every hand when others have the keys of credit in their pockets and treat them as all but their own private possession? It is perfectly clear that it is our duty to supply the new banking and currency system the country needs, and it will need it immediately more than it has ever needed it before.

The only question is, When shall we supply it—now or later, after the demands shall have become reproaches that we were so dull and so slow? Shall we hasten to change the tariff laws and then be laggards about making it possible and easy for the country to take advantage of the change? There can be only one answer to that question. We must act now, at whatever sacrifice to ourselves. It is a duty which the circumstances forbid us to postpone. I should be recreant to my deepest convictions of public obligation did I not press it upon you with solemn and urgent insistence.

The principles upon which we should act are also clear. The country has sought and seen its path in this matter within the last few years—sees it more clearly now than it ever saw it before—much more clearly than when the last legislative proposals on the subject were made. We must have a currency, not rigid as now, but readily, elastically responsive to sound credit, the expanding and contracting credits of everyday transactions, the normal ebb and flow of personal and corporate dealings. Our banking laws must mobilize reserves; must not permit the concentration anywhere in a few hands of the monetary resources of the country or their use for speculative purposes in such volume as to hinder or impede or stand in the way of other more legitimate, more fruitful uses. And the control of the system of banking and of issue which our new laws are to set up must be public, not private, must be vested in the Government itself, so that the banks may be the instruments, not the masters, of business and of individual enterprise and initiative.

The committees of the Congress to which legislation of this character is referred have devoted careful and dispassionate study to the means of accomplishing these objects. They have honored me by consulting me. They are ready to suggest action. I have come to you, as the head of the Government and the responsible leader of the party in power, to urge action now, while there is time to serve the country deliberately and as we should, in a clear air of common counsel. I appeal to you with a deep conviction of duty. I believe that you share this conviction. I therefore appeal to you with confidence. I am at your service without reserve to play my part in any way you may call upon me to play it in this great enterprise of exigent reform which it will dignify and distinguish us to perform and discredit us to neglect.

Wilson's Address at Gettysburg, Before G. A. R. and Confederate Veterans, upon Occasion of Fiftieth Anniversary Reunion, July 4, 1913

[In the President's audience on this occasion were several thousand survivors of the Gettysburg battle, who had gone back to the scene of the conflict—with other veterans of the armies of the North and the South—to commemorate the fiftieth anniversary of "the high-water mark of the Confederacy."]

Friends and Fellow-Citizens:

I need not tell you what the battle of Gettysburg meant. These gallant men in blue and gray sit all about us here. Many of them met upon this ground in grim and deadly struggle. Upon these famous fields and hillsides their comrades died about them. In their presence it were an impertinence to discourse upon how the battle went, how it ended, what it signified! But fifty years have gone by since then, and I crave the privilege of speaking to you for a few minutes of what those fifty years have meant.

What *have* they meant? They have meant peace and union and vigour, and the maturity and might of a great nation. How wholesome and healing the peace has been! We have found one another again as brothers and comrades in arms, enemies no longer, generous friends rather, our battles long past, the quarrel forgotten—except that we shall not forget the splendid valour, the manly devotion of the men then arrayed against one another, now grasping hands and smiling into each other's eyes. How complete the union has become and how dear to all of us, how unquestioned, how benign and majestic, as State after State has been added to this our great family of free men! How handsome the vigour, the maturity, the might of the great Nation we love with undivided hearts; how full of large and confident promise that a life will be wrought out that will crown its strength with gracious justice and with a happy welfare that will touch all alike with deep contentment! We are debtors to those fifty crowded years; they have made us heirs to a mighty heritage.

But do we deem the Nation complete and finished? These venerable men crowding here to this famous field have set us a great example of devotion and utter sacrifice. They were willing to die that the people might live. But their task is done. Their day is turned into evening. They look to us to perfect what they established. Their work is handed on to us, to be done in another way but not in another spirit. Our day is not over; it is upon us in full tide.

Have affairs paused? Does the Nation stand still? Is what the fifty years have wrought since those days of battle finished, rounded out, and completed? Here is a great people, great with every force that has ever beaten in the lifeblood of mankind. And it is secure. There is no one within its borders, there is no power among the nations of the earth, to make it afraid. But has it yet squared itself with its own great standards set up at its birth, when it made that first noble, naive appeal to the moral judgment of mankind to take notice that a government had now at last been established which was to serve men, not masters? It is secure in everything except the satisfaction that its life is right, adjusted to the uttermost to the standards of righteousness and humanity. The days of sacrifice and cleansing are not closed. We have harder things to do than were done in the heroic days of war, because harder to see clearly, requiring more vision, more calm balance of judgment, a more candid searching of the very springs of right.

Look around you upon the field of Gettysburg! Picture the array, the fierce heats and agony of battle, column hurled against column, battery bellowing to battery! Valour? Yes! Greater no man shall see in war; and self-sacrifice, and loss to the uttermost; the high recklessness of exalted devotion which does not count the cost. We are made by these tragic, epic things to know what it costs to make a nation—the blood and sacrifice of multitudes of unknown men lifted to a great stature in the view of all generations by knowing no limit to their manly willingness to serve. In armies thus marshaled from the ranks of free men you will see, as it were, a nation embattled, the leaders and the led, and may know, if you will, how little except in form its action differs in days of peace from its action in days of war.

May we break camp now and be at ease? Are the forces that fight for the Nation dispersed, disbanded, gone to their homes forgetful of the common cause? Are our forces disorganized, without constituted leaders and the might of men consciously united because we contend, not with armies, but with principalities and powers and wickedness in high places. Are we content to lie still? Does our union mean sympathy, our peace contentment, our vigour right action, our maturity self-comprehension and a clear confidence in choosing what we shall do? War fitted us for action, and action never ceases.

I have been chosen the leader of the Nation. I cannot justify the choice by any qualities of my own, but so it has come about, and here I stand. Whom do I command? The ghostly hosts who fought upon these battle fields long ago and are gone? These gallant gentlemen stricken in years whose fighting days are over, their glory won? What are the orders for them, and who rallies them? I have in my mind another host, whom these set free of civil strife in order that they might work out in days of peace and settled order the life of a great Nation. That host is the people themselves, the great and the small, without class or difference of kind or race or origin; and undivided in interest, if we have but the vision to guide and direct them and order their lives aright in what we do. Our constitutions are their articles of enlistment. The orders of the day are the laws upon our statute books. What we strive for is their freedom, their right to lift themselves from day to day and behold the things they have hoped for, and so make way for still better days for those whom they love who are to come after them. The recruits are the little children crowding in. The quartermaster's stores are in the mines and forests and fields, in the shops and factories. Every day something must be done to push the campaign forward; and it must be done by plan and with an eye to some great destiny.

How shall we hold such thoughts in our hearts and not be moved? I would not have you live even to-day wholly in the past, but would wish to stand with you in the light that streams upon us now out of that great day gone by. Here is the nation God has builded by our hands. What shall we do with it? Who stands ready to act again and always in the spirit of this day of reunion and hope and patriotic fervor? The day of our country's life has but broadened into morning. Do not put uniforms by. Put the harness of the present on. Lift your eyes to the great tracts of life yet to be conquered in the interest of righteous peace, of that prosperity which lies in a people's hearts and outlasts all wars and errors of men. Come, let us be comrades and soldiers yet to serve our fellow men in quiet counsel, where the blare of trumpets is neither heard nor heeded and where the things are done which make blessed the nations of the world in peace and righteousness and love.

Wilson's Special Message on Mexico

(Delivered before Congress in Joint Session, August 27, 1913)

[Editorial Note: *General Huerta had been proclaimed Provisional President on February 18, 1913, by the rebelling troops under his control. On February 19 a hastily assembled Congress elected him Provisional President. On February 22, 1913, Francisco Madero and Pino Suarez, deposed President and Vice-President, were shot dead "while attempting to escape." President Wilson had refused to recognize Huerta; and for a year following this message he remained steadfast. Huerta then resigned.*]

Gentlemen of the Congress:

It is clearly my duty to lay before you, very fully and without reservation, the facts concerning our present relations with the Republic of Mexico. The deplorable posture of affairs in Mexico I need not describe, but I deem it my duty to speak very frankly of what this Government has done and should seek to do in fulfillment of its obligation to Mexico herself, as a friend and neighbor, and to American citizens whose lives and vital interests are daily affected by the distressing conditions which now obtain beyond our southern border.

Those conditions touch us very nearly. Not merely because they lie at our very doors. That, of course, makes us more vividly and more constantly conscious of them, and every instinct of neighborly interest and sympathy is aroused and quickened by them; but that is only one element in the determination of our duty. We are glad to call ourselves the friend of Mexico, and we shall, I hope, have many an occasion, in happier times as well as in these days of trouble and confusion, to show that our friendship is genuine and disinterested, capable of sacrifice and every generous manifestation. The peace, prosperity, and con-

f her own peace, and not for any other purpose whatever. The
Government of the United States would deem itself discredited if
t had any selfish or ulterior purpose in transactions where the
peace, happiness, and prosperity of a whole people are involved.
t is acting as its friendship for Mexico, not as any selfish interest,
lictates.

The present situation in Mexico is incompatible with the fulfill-
nent of international obligations on the part of Mexico, with the
ivilized development of Mexico herself, and with the maintenance
f tolerable political and economic conditions in Central America.
t is upon no common occasion, therefore, that the United States
ffers her counsel and assistance. All America cries out for a
ettlement.

A satisfactory settlement seems to us to be conditioned on—

(*a*) An immediate cessation of fighting throughout Mexico, a
lefinite armistice solemnly entered into and scrupulously observed;

(*b*) Security given for an early and free election in which all
will agree to take part;

(*c*) The consent of Gen. Huerta to bind himself not to be a
candidate for election as President of the Republic at this election;
and

(*d*) The agreement of all parties to abide by the results of the
election and co-operate in the most loyal way in organizing and
supporting the new administration.

The Government of the United States will be glad to play any
part in this settlement or in its carrying out which it can play
honorably and consistently with international right. It pledges
itself to recognize and in every way possible and proper to assist
the administration chosen and set up in Mexico in the way and
on the conditions suggested.

Taking all the existing conditions into consideration, the Government of the United States can conceive of no reasons sufficient to
justify those who are now attempting to shape the policy or exercise the authority of Mexico in declining the offices of friendship
thus offered. Can Mexico give the civilized world a satisfactory
reason for rejecting our good offices? If Mexico can suggest any
better way in which to show our friendship, serve the people of
Mexico, and meet our international obligations, we are more than
willing to consider the suggestion.

Mr. Lind executed his delicate and difficult mission with
singular tact, firmness, and good judgment, and made clear
to the authorities at the City of Mexico not only the purpose of his visit but also the spirit in which it had been
undertaken. But the proposals he submitted were rejected,
in a note the full text of which I take the liberty of laying
before you.

[The Mexican note was addressed to Mr. Lind and signed by Senor F. Gamboa, Secretary for Foreign Affairs. Its salient parts were:

The imputation that no progress has been made toward establishing a Government that may enjoy the obedience of the Mexican people is unfounded. In contradiction with their gross imputation, which is not supported by any proofs, principally because there are none, it affords me pleasure to refer, Mr. Confidential Agent, to the following facts which abound in evidence and which to a certain extent must be known to you by direct observation. The Mexican Republic, Mr. Confidential Agent, is formed by 27 States, 3 Territories, and 1 Federal District, in which the supreme power of the Republic has its seat. Of these 27 States, 18 of them, the 3 Territories, and the Federal District (making a total of 22 political entities) are under the absolute control of the present Government, which, aside from the above, exercises its authority over almost every port in the Republic and, consequently, over the custom houses therein established. Its southern frontier is open and at peace. Moreover, my Government has an army of 80,000 men in the field, with no other purpose than to insure complete peace in the Republic, the only national aspiration and solemn promise of the present provisional President. . . .

Inasmuch as the Government of the United States is willing to act in the most disinterested friendship, it will be difficult for it to find a more propitious opportunity than the following: If it should only watch that no material and monetary assistance is given to rebels who find refuge, conspire, and provide themselves with arms and food on the other side of the border; if it should demand from its minor and local authorities the strictest observance of the neutrality laws, I assure you, Mr. Confidential Agent, that the complete pacification of this Republic would be accomplished within a relatively short time. . . .

His Excellency Mr. Wilson is laboring under a serious delusion when he declares that the present situation of Mexico is incompatible with the compliance of her international obligations and with the required maintenance of conditions tolerable in Central America. No charge has been made by any foreign Government accusing us of the above lack of compliance, we are punctually meeting all of our credits, we are still maintaining diplomatic missions cordially accepted in almost all the countries of the world. With regard to our interior development, a contract has just been signed with Belgian capitalists which means to Mexico the construction of something like 5,000 kilometers of railway. In conclusion, we fail to see the evil results, which are prejudicial only to ourselves, felt in Central America by our present domestic war. . . . With reference to the rebels who style themselves "Constitutionalists," one of the representatives of whom has been given an ear by Members of the United States Senate, what could there be more gratifying to us than if, convinced of the precipice to which we are being dragged by the resentment of their defeat, in a moment of reaction they would depose their rancor and add their strength to ours so that all together we would undertake the great and urgent task of national reconstruction? Unfortunately they do not avail themselves of the amnesty law enacted by the provisional government. . . .

The request that General Victoriano Huerta should agree not to appear as a candidate for the Presidency of the Republic in the coming election cannot be taken into consideration, because, aside from its strange and unwarranted character, there is a risk that the same might be interpreted as a matter of personal dislike. . . . The legality of the government of General Huerta cannot be disputed. Article 85 of our political constitution provides:

If at the beginning of a constitutional term neither the President nor the Vice-President elected present themselves, the President whose term has expired will cease in his functions, and the secretary for foreign affairs shall immediately take charge of the Executive power in the capacity of provisional President; and if there should be no secretary for foreign affairs, the Presidency shall devolve on one of the other secretaries pursuant to the order provided by the law.

Now, then, the facts which occurred are the following: The resignation of Francisco I. Madero, constitutional President, and Jose Maria Pino Suarez, constitutional Vice-President of the Republic. These resignations having been accepted, Pedro Lascurain, Minister for Foreign Affairs, took charge by law of the vacant executive power, appointing, as he had the power to do, Gen. Victoriano Huerta to the post of Minister of the Interior. As Mr. Lascurain soon afterwards resigned, and as his resignation was immediately accepted by Congress, Gen. Victoriano Huerta took charge of the executive power, also by operation of law, with the provisional character and under the constitutional promise already complied with to issue a call for special elections. As will be seen, the point of issue is exclusively one of constitutional law in which no foreign nation, no matter how powerful and respectable it may be, should mediate in the least. . . .

With reference to the final part of the instructions of President Wilson, which I beg to include herewith and say, "If Mexico can suggest any better way in which to show our friendship, serve the people of Mexico, and meet our international obligations, we are more than willing to consider the suggestion," that final part causes me to propose the following equally decorous arrangement: One, that our ambassador be received in Washington; two, that the United States of America send us a new ambassador without previous conditions.

And all this threatening and distressing situation will have reached a happy conclusion; mention will not be made of the causes which might carry us, if the tension persists, to no one knows what incalculable extremities for two peoples who have the unavoidable obligation to continue being friends, provided, of course, that this friendship is based upon mutual respect, which is indispensable between two sovereign entities wholly equal before law and justice.]

I am led to believe that they were rejected partly because the authorities at Mexico City had been grossly misinformed and misled upon two points. They did not realize the spirit of the American people in this matter, their earnest friendliness and yet sober determination that some just solution be found for the Mexican difficulties; and they did not believe that the present administration spoke through Mr. Lind, for the people of the United States. The effect of this unfortunate misunderstanding on their part is to leave them singularly isolated and without friends who can effectually aid them. So long as the misunderstanding continues we can only await the time of their awakening to a realization of the actual facts. We can not thrust our good offices upon them. The situation must be given a little more time to work itself out in the new circumstances; and I believe that only a little while will be necessary. For the circumstances are new. The rejection of our friendship makes them new and will inevitably bring its own alterations in the whole aspect of affairs. The actual situation of the authorities at Mexico City will presently be revealed.

Meanwhile, what is it our duty to do? Clearly, everything that we do must be rooted in patience and done with calm and disinterested deliberation. Impatience on our part would be childish, and would be fraught with every risk of wrong and folly. We can afford to exercise the self-restraint of a really great nation which realizes its own strength and scorns to misuse it. It was our duty to offer our active assistance. It is now our duty to show what true neutrality will do to enable the people of Mexico to set their affairs in order again and wait for a further opportunity to offer our friendly counsels. The door is not closed against the resumption, either upon the initiative of Mexico or upon our own, of the effort to bring order out of the confusion by friendly co-operative action, should fortunate occasion offer.

While we wait, the contest of the rival forces will undoubtedly for a little while be sharper than ever, just because it will be plain that an end must be made of the existing situation, and that very promptly; and with the increased activity of the contending factions will come, it is to be feared, increased danger to the noncombatants in Mexico as well as to those actually in the field of battle. The position of outsiders is always particularly trying and full of hazard where there is civil strife and a whole country is upset. We should earnestly urge all Americans to leave Mexico at once, and should assist them to get away in every way possible—not because we would mean to slacken in the least our efforts to safeguard their lives and their interests, but because it is imperative that they should take no unnecessary risks when it is physically possible for them to leave the country. We should let every one who assumes to exercise authority in any part of Mexico know in the most unequivocal way that we shall vigilantly watch the fortunes of those Americans who can not get away, and shall hold those responsible for their sufferings and losses to a definite reckoning. That can be and will be made plain beyond the possibility of a misunderstanding.

For the rest, I deem it my duty to exercise the authority conferred upon me by the law of March 14, 1912, to see to it that neither side to the struggle now going on in Mexico receive any assistance from this side the border. I shall follow the best practice of nations in the matter of neutrality by forbidding the exportation of arms or munitions of war of any kind from the United States to any part of the Republic of Mexico—a policy suggested by several interesting precedents and certainly dictated by many manifest considerations of practical expediency. We can not in the circumstances be the partisans of either party to the contest that now distracts Mexico, or constitute ourselves the virtual umpire between them.

I am happy to say that several of the great Governments of the world have given this Government their generous moral support in urging upon the provisional authorities at the City of Mexico the acceptance of our proffered good offices in the spirit in which they were made. We have not acted in this matter under the ordinary principles of international obligation. All the world expects us in such circumstances to act as Mexico's nearest friend and intimate adviser. This is our immemorial relation towards her. There is nowhere any serious question that we have the moral right in the case or that we are acting in the interest of a fair settlement and of good government, not for the promotion of some selfish interest of our own. If further motive were necessary than our own good will towards a sister Republic and our own deep concern to see peace and order prevail in Central America, this consent of mankind to what we are attempting, this attitude of the great nations of the world towards what we may attempt in dealing with this distressed people at our doors, should make us feel the more solemnly bound to go to the utmost length of patience and forbearance in this painful and anxious business. The steady pressure of moral force will before many days break the barriers of pride and prejudice down, and we shall triumph as Mexico's friends sooner than we could trimph as her enemies—and how much more handsomely, with how much higher and finer satisfactions of conscience and of honor!

Wilson's Address on Occasion of the Rededication and Restoration of Congress Hall, Philadelphia, October 25, 1913

Your Honor, Mr. Chairman, Ladies, and Gentlemen:

No American could stand in this place to-day and think of the circumstances which we are come together to celebrate without being most profoundly stirred. There has come over me since I sat down here a sense of deep solemnity, because it has seemed to me that I saw ghosts crowding—a great assemblage of spirits no longer visible, but whose influence we still feel as we feel the molding power of history itself. The men who sat in this hall, to whom we now look back with a touch of deep sentiment, were men of flesh and blood, face to face with extremely difficult problems. The population of the United States then was hardly three times the present population of the city of Philadelphia, and yet that was a Nation as this is a Nation, and the men who spoke for it were setting their hands to work which was to last, not only that their people might be happy, but that an example might be lifted up for the instruction of the rest of the world.

I like to read the quaint old accounts such as Mr. Day has read to us this afternoon. Strangers came then to America to see what the young people that had sprung up here were like, and they found men in counsel who knew how to construct governments. They found men deliberating here who had none of the appearance of novices, none of the hesitation of men who did not know whether the work they were doing was going to last or not; men who addressed themselves to a problem of construction as familiarly as we attempt to carry out the traditions of a Government established these 137 years.

I feel to-day the compulsion of these men, the compulsion of examples which were set up in this place. And of what do their examples remind us? They remind us not merely of public service but of public service shot through with principle and honor. . . .

Politics, ladies and gentlemen, is made up in just about equal parts of comprehension and sympathy. No man ought to go into politics who does not comprehend the task that he is going to attack. He may comprehend it so completely that it daunts him, that he doubts whether his own spirit is stout enough and his own mind able enough to attempt its great undertakings, but unless he comprehend it he ought not to enter it. After he has comprehended it, there should come into his mind those profound impulses of sympathy which connect him with the rest of mankind, for politics is a business of interpretation, and no men are fit for it who do not see and seek more than their own advantage and interest.

We have stumbled upon many unhappy circumstances in the hundred years that have gone by since the event that we are celebrating. Almost all of them have come from self-centered men, men who saw in their own interest the interest of the country, and who did not have vision enough to read it in wider terms, in the universal terms of equity and justice and the rights of mankind. I hear a great many people at Fourth of July celebrations laud the Declaration of Independence who in between Julys shiver at the plain language of our bills of rights. The Declaration of Independence was, indeed, the first audible breath of liberty, but the substance of liberty is written in such documents as the declaration of rights attached, for example, to the first constitution of Virginia which was a model for the similar documents read elsewhere into our great fundamental charters. That document speaks in very plain terms. The men of that generation did not hesitate to say that every people has a right to choose its own forms of government—not once, but as often as it pleases—and to accommodate those forms of government to its existing interests and circumstances. Not only to establish but to alter is the fundamental principle of self-government.

We are just as much under compulsion to study the particular circumstances of our own day as the gentlemen were who sat in this hall and set us precedents, not of what to do but of how to do it. Liberty inheres in the circumstances of the day. Human happiness consists in the life which human beings are leading at the time that they live. I can feed my memory as happily upon the circumstances of the revolutionary and constitutional period as you can, but I can not feed all my purposes with them in Washington now. Every day problems arise which wear some new phase and aspect, and I must fall back, if I would serve my conscience, upon those things which are fundamental rather than upon those things which are superficial, and ask myself this question, How are you going to assist in some small part to give the American people and, by example, the peoples of the world more liberty, more happiness, more substantial prosperity; and how are you going to make that prosperity a common heritage instead of a selfish possession? . . .

The men of the day which we now celebrate had a very great advantage over us, ladies and gentlemen, in this one particular: Life was simple in America then. All men shared the same circumstances in almost equal degree. We think of Washington, for example, as an aristocrat, as a man separated by training, separated by family and neighborhood tradition, from the ordinary people of the rank and file of the country. Have you forgotten the personal history of George Washington? Do you not know that he struggled as poor boys now struggle for a meager and imperfect education; that he worked at his surveyor's tasks in the lonely forests; that he knew all the roughness, all the hardships, all the adventure, all the variety of the common life of that day; and that if he stood a little stiffly in this place, if he looked a little aloof, it was because life had dealt hardly with him? All his sinews had been stiffened by the rough work of making America. He was a man of the people, whose touch had been with them since the day he saw the light first in the old Dominion of Virginia. And the men who came after him, men, some of whom had drunk deep at the sources of philosophy and of study, were, nevertheless, also men who on this side of the water knew no complicated life but the simple life of primitive neighborhoods. Our task is very much more difficult. That sympathy which alone interprets public duty is more difficult for a public man to acquire now than it was then, because we live in the midst of circumstances and conditions infinitely complex.

No man can boast that he understands America. No man can boast that he has lived the life of America, as almost every man who sat in this hall in those days could boast. No man can pretend that except by common counsel he can gather into his consciousness what the varied life of this people is. The duty that we have to keep open eyes and open hearts and accessible understandings is a very much more difficult duty to perform than it was in their day. Yet how much more important that it should be performed, for fear we make infinite and irreparable blunders. The city of Washington is in some respects self-contained, and it is easy there to forget what the rest of the United States is thinking about. I count it a fortunate circumstance that almost all the windows of the White House and its offices open upon unoccupied spaces that stretch to the banks of the Potomac and then out into Virginia and on to the heavens themselves, and that as I sit there I can constantly forget Washington and remember the United States. Not that I would intimate that all of the United States lies south of Washington, but there is a serious thing back of my thought. If you think too much about being re-elected, it is very difficult to be worth re-electing. You are so apt to forget that the comparatively small number of persons, numerous as they seem to be when they swarm, who come to Washington to ask for things, do not constitute an important proportion of the population of the country, that it is constantly necessary to come away from Washington and renew one's contact with the people who do not swarm there, who do not ask for anything, but who do trust you without their personal counsel to do your duty. Unless a man gets these contacts he grows weaker and weaker. He needs them as Hercules needed the touch of mother earth. If you lift him up too high or he lifts himself too high, he loses the contact and therefore loses the inspiration.

I love to think of those plain men, however far from plain their dress sometimes was, who assembled in this hall. One is startled to think of the variety of costume and color which would now occur if we were let loose upon the fashions of that age. Men's lack of taste is largely concealed now by the limitations of fashion. Yet these men, who sometimes dressed like the peacock, were, nevertheless, of the ordinary flight of their time. They were birds of a feather; they were birds come from a very simple breeding; they were much in the open heaven. They were beginning, when there was so little to distract their attention, to show that they could live upon fundamental principles of government. We talk those principles, but we have not time to absorb them. We have not time to let them into our blood, and thence have them translated into the plain mandates of action.

The very smallness of this room, the very simplicity of it all, all the suggestions which come from its restoration, are reassuring things—things which it becomes a man to realize. Therefore my theme here to-day, my only thought, is a very simple one. Do not let us go back to the annals of those sessions of Congress to find out what to do, because we live in another age and the circumstances are absolutely different; but let us be men of that kind; let us feel at every turn the compulsions of principle and of honor which they felt; let us free our vision from temporary circumstances and look abroad at the horizon and take into our lungs the great air of freedom which has blown through this country and stolen across the seas and blessed people everywhere; and, looking east and west and north and south, let us remind ourselves that we are the custodians, in some degree, of the principles which have made men free and governments just.

Wilson's Address Before the Southern Commercial Congress at Mobile, Ala., October 27, 1913

[The Panama Canal was approaching completion—the President himself, two weeks earlier, having touched a button in the White House and set off an explosive which blasted away the last barrier separating the waters of the Atlantic and the Pacific.]

Your Excellency, Mr. Chairman:

It is with unaffected pleasure that I find myself here to-day. I once before had the pleasure, in another southern city, of addressing the Southern Commercial Congress. I then spoke of what the future seemed to hold in store for this region, which so many of us love and toward the future of which we all look forward with so much confidence and hope. But another theme directed me here this time. I do not need to speak of the South. She has, perhaps, acquired the gift of speaking for herself. I come because I want to speak of our present and prospective relations with our neighbors to the south. I deemed it a public duty, as well as a personal pleasure, to be here to express for myself and for the Government I represent the welcome we all feel to those who represent the Latin American States.

The future, ladies and gentlemen, is going to be very different for this hemisphere from the past. These States lying to the south of us, which have always been our neighbors, will now be drawn closer to us by innumerable ties, and, I hope, chief of all, by the tie of a common understanding of each other. Interest does not tie nations together; it sometimes separates them. But sympathy and understanding does unite them, and I believe that by the new route that is just about to be opened, while we physically cut two continents asunder, we spiritually unite them. It is a spiritual union which we seek.

I wonder if you realize, I wonder if your imaginations have been filled with the significance of the tides of commerce. Your governor alluded in very fit and striking terms to the voyage of Columbus, but Columbus took his voyage under compulsion of circumstances. Constantinople had been captured by the Turks and all the routes of trade with the East had been suddenly closed. If there was not a way across the Atlantic to open those routes again, they were closed forever, and Columbus set out not to discover America, for he did not know that it existed, but to discover the eastern shores of Asia. He set sail for Cathay and stumbled upon America. With that change in the outlook of the world, what happened? England, that had been at the back of Europe with an unknown sea behind her, found that all things had turned as if upon a pivot and she was at the front of Europe; and since then all the tides of energy and enterprise that have issued out of Europe have seemed to be turned westward across the Atlantic. But you will notice that they have turned westward chiefly north of the Equator and that it is the northern half of the globe that has seemed to be filled with the media of intercourse and of sympathy and of common understanding.

Do you not see now what is about to happen? These great tides which have been running along parallels of latitude will now swing southward athwart parallels of latitude, and that opening gate at the Isthmus of Panama will open the world to a commerce that she has not known before, a commerce of intelligence, of thought and sympathy between North and South. The Latin American States, which, to their disadvantage, have been off the main lines, will now be on the main lines. I feel that these gentlemen honoring us with their presence to-day will presently find that some part, at any rate, of the center of gravity of the world has shifted. Do you realize that New York, for example, will be nearer the western coast of South America than she is now to the eastern coast of South America? Do you realize that a line drawn northward parallel with the greater part of the western coast of South America will run only about 150 miles west of New York? The great bulk of South America, if you will look at your globes (not at your Mercator's projection), lies eastward of the continent of North America. You will realize that when you realize that the canal will run southeast, not southwest, and that when you get into the Pacific you will be farther east than you were when you left the Gulf of Mexico. These things are significant, therefore, of this, that we are closing one chapter in the history of the world and are opening another, of great, unimaginable significance.

There is one peculiarity about the history of the Latin American States which I am sure they are keenly aware of. You hear of "concessions" to foreign capitalists in Latin America. You do not hear of concessions to foreign capitalists in the United States. They are not granted concessions. They are invited to make investments. The work is ours, though they are welcome to invest in it. We do not ask them to supply the capital and do the work. It is an invitation, not a privilege; and States that are obliged, because their territory does not lie within the main field of modern enterprise and action, to grant concessions are in this condition, that foreign interests are apt to dominate their domestic affairs, a condition of affairs always dangerous and apt to become intolerable. What these States are going to see, therefore, is an emancipation from the subordination, which has been inevitable, to foreign enterprise and an assertion of the splendid character which, in spite of these difficulties, they have again and again been able to demonstrate. The dignity, the courage, the self-possession, the self-respect of the Latin American States, their achievements in the face of all these adverse circumstances, deserve nothing but the admiration and applause of the world. They have had harder bargains driven with them in the matter of loans than any other peoples in the world. Interest has been exacted of them that was not exacted of anybody else, because the risk was said to be greater; and then securities were taken that destroyed the risk—an admirable arrangement for those who were forcing the terms! I rejoice in nothing so much as in the prospect that they will now be emancipated from these conditions, and we ought to be the first to take part in assisting in that emancipation. I think some of these gentlemen have already had occasion to bear witness that the Department of State in recent months has tried to serve them in that wise. In the future they will draw closer and closer to us because of circumstances of which I wish to speak with moderation and, I hope, without indiscretion.

We must prove ourselves their friends, and champions upon terms of equality and honor. You can not be friends upon any other terms than upon the terms of equality. You can not be friends at all except upon the terms of honor. We must show ourselves friends by comprehending their interest whether it squares with our own interest or not. It is a very perilous thing to determine the foreign policy of a nation in the terms of material interest. It not only is unfair to those with whom you are dealing, but it is degrading as regards your own actions.

Comprehension must be the soil in which shall grow all the fruits of friendship, and there is a reason and a compulsion lying behind all this which is dearer than anything else to the thoughtful men of America. I mean the development of constitutional liberty in the world. Human rights, national integrity, and opportunity as against material interests—that, ladies and gentlemen, is the issue which we now have to face. I want to take this occasion to say that the United States will never again seek one additional foot of territory by conquest. She will devote herself to showing that she knows how to make honorable and fruitful use of the territory she has, and she must regard it as one of the duties of friendship to see that from no quarter are material interests made superior to human liberty and national opportunity. I say this, not with a single thought that anyone will gainsay it, but merely to fix in our consciousness what our real relationship with the rest of America is. It is the relationship of a family of mankind devoted to the development of true constitutional liberty. We know that that is the soil out of which the best enterprise springs. We know that this is a cause which we are making in common with our neighbors, because we have had to make it for ourselves. . . .

I know what the response of the thought and heart of America will be to the program I have outlined, because America was created to realize a program like that. This is not America because it is rich. This is America because it has set up for a great population great opportunities of material prosperity. America is a name which sounds in the ears of men everywhere as a synonym with individual opportunity because a synonym of individual liberty. I would rather belong to a poor nation that was free than to a rich nation that had ceased to be in love with liberty. But we shall not be poor if we love liberty, because the nation that loves liberty truly sets every man free to do his best and be his best, and that means the release of all the splendid energies of a great people who think for themselves. . . .

In emphasizing the points which must unite us in sympathy and in spiritual interest with the Latin American peoples we are only emphasizing the points of our own life, and we should prove ourselves untrue to our own traditions if we proved ourselves untrue friends to them. . . .

Wilson's First Annual Message

(Delivered before Congress in Joint Session, December 2, 1913)

[The custom of including departmental reports in the President's annual message is here abandoned by Mr. Wilson; and this message is therefore noticeably shorter than those of his predecessors.]

Mr. Speaker, Mr. President, Gentlemen of the Congress:

In pursuance of my constitutional duty to "give to the Congress information of the state of the Union," I take the liberty of addressing you on several matters which ought, as it seems to me, particularly to engage the attention of your honorable bodies, as of all who study the welfare and progress of the Nation.

I shall ask your indulgence if I venture to depart in some degree from the usual custom of setting before you in formal review the many matters which have engaged the attention and called for the action of the several departments of the Government or which look to them for early treatment in the future, because the list is long, very long, and would suffer in the abbreviation to which I should have to subject it. I shall submit to you the reports of the heads of the several departments, in which these subjects are set forth in careful detail, and beg that they may receive the thoughtful attention of your committees and of all Members of the Congress who may have the leisure to study them. Their obvious importance, as constituting the very substance of the business of the Government, makes comment and emphasis on my part unnecessary.

The country, I am thankful to say, is at peace with all the world, and many happy manifestations multiply about us of a growing cordiality and sense of community of interest among the nations, foreshadowing an age of settled peace and good will. More and more readily each decade do the nations manifest their willingness to bind themselves by solemn treaty to the processes of peace, the processes of frankness and fair concession. So far the United States has stood at the front of such negotiations. She will, I earnestly hope and confidently believe, give fresh proof of her sincere adherence to the cause of international friendship by ratifying the several treaties of arbitration awaiting renewal by the Senate. In addition to these, it has been the privilege of the Department of State to gain the assent, in principle, of no less than 31 nations, representing four-fifths of the population of the world, to the negotiation of treaties by which it shall be agreed that whenever differences of interest or of policy arise which can not be resolved by the ordinary processes of diplomacy they shall be publicly analyzed, discussed, and reported upon by a tribunal chosen by the parties before either nation determines its course of action.

There is only one possible standard by which to determine controversies between the United States and other nations, and that is compounded of these two elements: Our own honor and our obligations to the peace of the world. A test so compounded ought easily to be made to govern both the establishment of new treaty obligations and the interpretation of those already assumed.

There is but one cloud upon our horizon. That has shown itself to the south of us, and hangs over Mexico. There can be no certain prospect of peace in America until General Huerta has surrendered his usurped authority in Mexico; until it is understood on all hands, indeed, that such pretended governments will not be countenanced or dealt with by the Government of the United States. We are the friends of constitutional government in America; we are more than its friends, we are its champions; because in no other way can our neighbors, to whom we would wish in every way to make proof of our friendship, work out their own development in peace and liberty. Mexico has no Government. The attempt to maintain one at the City of

Mexico has broken down, and a mere miltary despotism has been set up which has hardly more than the semblance of national authority. It originated in the usurpation of Victoriano Huerta, who, after a brief attempt to play the part of constitutional President, has at last cast aside even the pretense of legal right and declared himself dictator. As a consequence, a condition of affairs now exists in Mexico which has made it doubtful whether even the most elementary and fundamental rights either of her own people or of the citizens of other countries resident within her territory can long be successfully safeguarded, and which threatens, if long continued, to imperil the interests of peace, order, and tolerable life in the lands immediately to the south of us. Even if the usurper had succeeded in his purposes, in despite of the constitution of the Republic and the rights of its people, he would have set up nothing but a precarious and hateful power, which could have lasted but a little while, and whose eventual downfall would have left the country in a more deplorable condition than ever. But he has not succeeded. He has forfeited the respect and the moral support even of those who were at one time willing to see him succeed. Little by little he has been completely isolated. By a little every day his power and prestige are crumbling and the collapse is not far away. We shall not, I believe, be obliged to alter our policy of watchful waiting. And then, when the end comes, we shall hope to see constitutional order restored in distressed Mexico by the concert and energy of such of her leaders as prefer the liberty of their people to their own ambitions.

I turn to matters of domestic concern. You already have under consideration a bill for the reform of our system of banking and currency, for which the country waits with impatience, as for something fundamental to its whole business life and necessary to set credit free from arbitrary and artificial restraints. I need not say how earnestly I hope for its early enactment into law. I take leave to beg that the whole energy and attention of the Senate be concentrated upon it till the matter is successfully disposed of. And yet I feel that the request is not needed—that the Members of that great House need no urging in this service to the country.

I present to you, in addition, the urgent necessity that special provision be made also for facilitating the credits needed by the farmers of the country. The pending currency bill does the farmers a great service. It puts them upon an equal footing with other business men and masters of enterprise, as it should; and upon its passage they will find themselves quit of many of the difficulties which now hamper them in the field of credit. The farmers, of course, ask and should be given no special privilege, such as extending to them the credit of the Government itself What they need and should obtain is legislation which will make their own abundant and substantial credit resources available as a foundation for joint, concerted local action in their own behalf in getting the capital they must use It is to this we should now address ourselves.

It has, singularly enough, come to pass that we have allowed the industry of our farms to lag behind the other activities of the country in its development. I need not stop to tell you how fundamental to the life of the Nation is the production of its food. Our thoughts may ordinarily be concentrated upon the cities and the hives of industry upon the cries of the crowded market place and the clangor of the factory, but it is from the quiet interspaces of the open valleys and the free hillsides that we draw the sources of life and of prosperity, from the farm and the ranch, from the forest and the mine. Without these every street would be silent, every office deserted, every factory fallen into disrepair. And yet the farmer does not stand upon the same footing with the forester and the miner in the market of credit. He is the servant of the seasons Nature determines how long he must wait for his crops and will not be hurried in her processes. He may give his note, but the season of its maturity depends upon the season when his crop matures, lies at the gates of the market where his products are sold. And the security he gives is of a character not known in the broker's office or as familiarly as it might be on the counter of the banker.

The Agricultural Department of the Government is seeking to assist as never before to make farming an efficient business, of wide cooperative effort, in quick touch with the markets for foodstuffs. The farmers and the Government will henceforth work together as real partners in this field, where we now begin to see our way very clearly and where many intelligent plans are already being put into execution. The Treasury of the United States has, by a timely and well-considered distribution of its deposits, facilitated the moving of the crops in the present season and prevented the scarcity of available funds too often experienced at such times. But we must not allow ourselves to depend upon extraordinary expedients. We must add the means by which the farmer may make his credit constantly and easily available and command when he will the capital by which to support and expand his business. We lag behind many other great countries of the modern world in attempting to do this. Systems of rural credit have been studied and developed on the other side of the water while we left our farmers to shift for themselves in the ordinary money market. You have but to look about you in any rural district to see the result, the handicap and embarrassment which have been put upon those who produce our food.

Conscious of this backwardness and neglect on our part, the Congress recently authorized the creation of a special commission to study the various systems of rural credit which have been put into operation in Europe, and this commission is already prepared to report. Its report ought to make it easier for us to determine what methods will be best suited to our own farmers. I hope and believe that the committees of the Senate and House will address themselves to this matter with the most fruitful results, and I believe that the studies and recently formed plans of the Department of Agriculture may be made to serve them very greatly in their work of framing appropriate and adequate legislation. It would be indiscreet and presumptuous in anyone to dogmatize upon so great and many-sided a question, but I feel confident that common counsel will produce the results we must all desire.

Turn from the farm to the world of business which centers in the city and in the factory, and I think that all thoughtful observers will agree that the immediate service we owe the business communities of the country is to prevent private monopoly more effectually than it has yet been prevented. I think it will be easily agreed that we should let the Sherman antitrust law stand, unaltered, as it is, with its debatable ground about it, but that we should as much as possible reduce the area of that debatable ground by further and more explicit legislation; and should also supplement that great act by legislation which will not only clarify it but also facilitate its administration and make it fairer to all concerned. No doubt we shall all wish, and the country will expect, this to be the central subject of our deliberations during the present session; but it is a subject so many-sided and so deserving of careful and discriminating discussion that I shall take the liberty of addressing you upon it in a special message at a later date than this. It is of capital importance that the business men of this country should be relieved of all uncertainties of law with regard to their enterprises and investments and a clear path indicated which they can travel without anxiety. It is as important that they should be relieved of embarrassment and set free to prosper as that private monopoly should be destroyed. The ways of action should be thrown wide open.

I turn to a subject which I hope can be handled promptly and without serious controversy of any kind. I mean the method of selecting nominees for the Presidency of the United States. I feel confident that I do not misinterpret the wishes or the expectations of the country when I urge the prompt enactment of legislation which will provide for primary elections throughout the country at which the voters of the several parties may choose their nominees for the Presidency without the intervention of nominating conventions. I venture the suggestion that this legislation should provide for the retention of party conventions, but only for the purpose of declaring and accepting the verdict of the primaries and formulating the platforms of the parties; and I suggest that these conventions should consist not of delegates chosen for this single purpose, but of the nominees for Congress, the nominees for vacant seats in the Senate of the United States, the Senators whose terms have not yet closed, the national committees, and the candidates for the Presidency themselves, in order that platforms may be framed by those responsible to the people for carrying them into effect.

These are all matters of vital domestic concern, and besides them, outside the charmed circle of our own national life in which our affections command us, as well as our consciences, there stand out our obligations toward our territories oversea. Here we are trustees. Porto Rico, Hawaii, the Philippines, are ours, indeed, but not ours to do what we please with. Such territories, once regarded as mere possessions, are no longer to be selfishly exploited; they are part of the domain of public conscience and of serviceable and enlightened statesmanship. We must administer them for the people who live in them and with the same sense of responsibility to them as toward our own people in our domestic affairs. No doubt we shall successfully enough bind Porto Rico and the Hawaiian Islands to ourselves by ties of justice and interest and affection, but the performance of our duty toward the Philippines is a more difficult and debatable matter. We can satisfy the obligations of generous justice toward the people of Porto Rico by giving them the ample and familiar rights and privileges accorded our own citizens in our own territories and our obligations toward the people of Hawaii by perfecting the provisions for self-government already granted them, but in the Philippines we must go further. We must hold steadily in view their ultimate independence, and we must move toward the time of that independence as steadily as the way can be cleared and the foundations thoughtfully and permanently laid.

Acting under the authority conferred upon the President by Congress, I have already accorded the people of the islands a majority in both houses of their legislative body by appointing five instead of four native citizens to the membership of the commission. I believe that in this way we shall make proof of their capacity in counsel and their sense of responsibility in the exercise of political power, and that the success of this step will be sure to clear our view for the steps which are to follow. Step by step we should extend and perfect the system of self-government in the islands, making test of them and modifying them as experience discloses their successes and their failures; that we should more and more put under the control of the native citizens of the archipelago the essential instruments of their life, their local instrumentalities of government, their schools, all the common interest of their communities, and so by counsel and experience set up a government which all the world will see to be suitable to a people whose affairs are under their own control. At last, I hope and believe, we are beginning to gain the confidence of the Filipino peoples. By their counsel and experience, rather than by our own, we shall learn how best to serve them and how soon it will be possible and wise to withdraw our supervision. Let us once find the path and set out with firm and confident tread upon it and we shall not wander from it or linger upon it.

A duty faces us with regard to Alaska which seems to me very pressing and very imperative; perhaps I should say a double duty, for it concerns both the political and the material development of the Territory. The people of Alaska should be given the full Territorial form of government, and Alaska, as a storehouse, should be unlocked. One key to it is a system of railways. These the Government should itself build and administer, and the ports and terminals it should itself control in the interest of all who wish to use them for the service and development of the country and its people.

But the construction of railways is only the first step; is only thrusting in the key to the storehouse and throwing back the lock and opening the door. How the tempting resources of the country are to be exploited is another matter, to which I shall take the liberty of from time to time calling your attention, for it is a policy which must be worked out by well-considered stages, not upon theory, but upon lines of practical expediency. It is part of our general problem of conservation. We have a freer hand in working out the problem in Alaska than in the States of the Union; and yet the principle and object are the same, wherever we touch it. We must use the resources of the country, not lock them up. There need be no conflict or jealousy as between State and Federal authorities, for there can be no essential difference of purpose between them. The resources in question must be used, but not destroyed or wasted; used, but not monopolized upon any narrow idea of individual rights as against the abiding interests of communities. That a policy can be worked out by conference and concession which will release these resources and yet not jeopard or dissipate them, I for one have no doubt; and it can be done on lines of regulation which need be no less acceptable to the people and governments of the States concerned than to the people and Government of the Nation at large, whose heritage these resources are. We must bend our counsels to this end. A common purpose ought to make agreement easy.

Three or four matters of special importance and significance I beg that you will permit me to mention in closing.

Our Bureau of Mines ought to be equipped and empowered to render even more effectual service than it renders now in improving the conditions of mine labor and making the mines more economically productive as well as more safe. This is an all-important part of the work of conservation; and the conservation of human life and energy lies even nearer to our interest than the preservation from waste of our material resources.

We owe it, in mere justice to the railway employees of the country, to provide for them a fair and effective employers' liability act; and a law that we can stand by in this matter will be no less to the advantage of those who administer the railroads of the country than to the advantage of those whom they employ. The experience of a large number of the States abundantly proves that.

We ought to devote ourselves to meeting pressing demands of plain justice like this as earnestly as to the accomplishment of political and economic reforms. Social justice comes first. Law is the machinery for its realization and is vital only as it expresses and embodies it.

An international congress for the discussion of all questions that affect safety at sea is now sitting in London at the suggestion of our own Government. So soon as the conclusions of that congress can be learned and considered we ought to address ourselves, among other things, to the prompt alleviation of the very unsafe, unjust, and burdensome conditions which now surround the employment of sailors and render it extremely difficult to obtain the services of spirited and competent men such as every ship needs if it is to be safely handled and brought to port.

May I not express the very real pleasure I have experienced in cooperating with this Congress and sharing with it the labors of common service to which it has devoted itself so unreservedly during the past seven months of uncomplaining concentration upon the business of legislation? Surely it is a proper and pertinent part of my report on "the state of the Union" to express my admiration for the diligence, the good temper, and the full comprehension of public duty which has already been manifested by both the Houses; and I hope that it may not be deemed an impertinent intrusion of myself into the picture if I say with how much and how constant satisfaction I have availed myself of the privilege of putting my time and energy at their disposal alike in counsel and in action.

Wilson's Special Message on Trusts and Monopolies

(Delivered before Congress in Joint Session January 20, 1914)

[Editorial Note: *Wilson's views on trust legislation were fairly well known, having been embodied in the famous New Jersey laws which became noted as "The Seven Sisters" while he still was Governor of that State. This Message formulated the following definite laws: (1) Prohibition of interlocking directorates, (2) government supervision of railway financing, (3) exact definition of the meaning of the Sherman anti-trust law, (4) an interstate trade commission to direct and shape corrective processes and inform the public, (5) legislation to reach individuals responsible for corporate wrong-doing.*

Bills had already been prepared, under the direction of Henry D. Clayton of Alabama, Chairman of the Judiciary Committee of the House, who had declined nomination to the Senate on Wilson's public request that he remain in the House to formulate this legislation.

The bills, known first as the "Five Brothers," finally were merged into one bill, the Clayton anti-trust bill, and passed in October, 1914. The Federal Trade Commission law was passed September, 1914.]

Mr. Speaker, Mr. President, gentlemen of the Congress, in my report "on the state of the Union," which I had the privilege of reading to you on the 2d of December last, I ventured to reserve for discussion at a later date the subject of additional legislation regarding the very difficult and intricate matter of trusts and monopolies. The time now seems opportune to turn to that great question, not only because the currency legislation, which absorbed your attention and the attention of the country in December, is now disposed of, but also because opinion seems to be clearing about us with singular rapidity in this other great field of action. In the matter of the currency it cleared suddenly and very happily after the much-debated act was passed; in respect of the monopolies which have multiplied about us and in regard to the various means by which they have been organized and maintained, it seems to be coming to a clear and all but universal agreement in anticipation of our action, as if by way of preparation, making the way easier to see and easier to set out upon with confidence and without confusion of counsel.

Legislation has its atmosphere like everything else, and the atmosphere of accommodation and mutual understanding which we now breathe with so much refreshment is matter of sincere congratulation. It ought to make our task very much less difficult and embarrassing than it would have been had we been obliged to continue to act amidst the atmosphere of suspicion and antagonism which has so long made it impossible to approach such questions with dispassionate fairness. Constructive legislation, when successful, is always the embodiment of convincing experience and of the mature public opinion which finally springs out of that experience. Legislation is a business of interpreta tion, not of origination; and it is now plain what the opinion is to which we must give effect in this matter. It is not recent or hasty opinion. It springs out of the experience of a whole generation. It has clarified itself by long contest, and those who for a long time battled with it and sought to change it are now frankly and honorably yielding to it and seeking to conform their actions to it.

The great business men who organized and financed monopoly and those who administered it in actual everyday transactions have, year after year until now, either denied its existence or justified it as necessary for the effective maintenance and development of the vast business processes of the country in the modern circumstances of trade and manufacture and finance; but all the while opinion has made head against them. The average business man is convinced that the ways of liberty are also the ways of peace and the ways of success as well; and at last the masters of business on the great scale have begun to yield their preference and purpose, perhaps their judgment also, in honorable surrender.

What we are purposing to do, therefore, is, happily, not to hamper or interfere with business as enlightened business men prefer to do it, or in any sense to put it under the ban. The antagonism between business and Government is over. We are now about to give expression to the best business judgment of America, to what we know to be the business conscience and honor of the land. The Government and business men are ready to meet each other halfway in a common effort to square business methods with both public opinion and the law. The best-informed men of the business world condemn the methods and processes and consequences of monopoly as we condemn them, and the instinctive judgment of the vast majority of business men everywhere goes with them. We shall now be their spokesmen. That is the strength of our position and the sure prophecy of what will ensue when our reasonable work is done.

When serious contest ends, when men unite in opinion and purpose, those who are to change their ways of business joining with those who ask for the change, it is possible to effect it in the way in which prudent and thoughtful and patriotic men would wish to see it brought about, with as few, as slight, as easy and simple business readjustments as possible in the circumstances, nothing essential disturbed, nothing torn up by the roots, no parts rent asunder which can be left in wholesome combination. Fortunately, no measures of sweeping or novel change are necessary. It will be understood that our object is *not* to unsettle business or anywhere seriously to break its established courses athwart. On the contrary, we desire the laws we are now about to pass to be the bulwarks and safeguards of industry against the forces who have disturbed it. What we have to do can be done in a new spirit, in thoughtful moderation, without revolution of any untoward kind.

We are all agreed that "private monopoly is indefensible and intolerable," and our program is founded upon that conviction. It will be a comprehensive but not a radical or unacceptable program and these are its items, the changes which opinion deliberately sanctions and for which business waits:

It waits with acquiescence, in the first place, for laws which will effectually prohibit and prevent such interlockings of the *personnel* of the directorates of great corporations—banks and railroads, industrial, commercial, and public service bodies—as in effect result in making those who borrow and those who lend practically one and the same, those who sell and those who buy but the same persons trading with one another under different names and in different combinations, and those who affect to compete in fact partners and masters of some whole field of business. Sufficient time should be allowed, of course, in which to effect these changes of organization without inconvenience or confusion.

Such a prohibition will work much more than a mere negative good by correcting the serious evils which have arisen because, for example, the men who have been the directing spirits of the great investment banks have usurped the place which belongs to independent industrial management working in its own behoof. It will bring new men, new energies, a new spirit of initiative, new blood, into the management of our great business enterprises. It will open the field of industrial development and origination to scores of men who have been obliged to serve when their abilities entitled them to direct. It will immensely hearten the young men coming on and will greatly enrich the business activities of the whole country.

In the second place, business men as well as those who direct public affairs now recognize, and recognize with painful clearness, the great harm and injustice which has been done to many, if not all, of the great railroad systems of the country by the way in which they have been financed and their own distinctive interests subordinated to the interests of the men who financed them and of other business enterprises which those men wished to promote. The country is ready, therefore, to accept, and accept with relief as well as approval, a law which will confer upon the Interstate Commerce Commission the power to superintend and regulate the financial operations by which the railroads are henceforth to be supplied with the money they need for their proper development to meet the rapidly growing requirements of the country for increased and improved facilities of transportation. We can not postpone action in this matter without leaving the railroads exposed to many serious handicaps and hazards; and the prosperity of the railroads and the prosperity of the country are inseparably connected. Upon this question those who are chiefly responsible for the actual management and operation of the railroads have spoken very plainly and very earnestly, with a purpose we ought to be quick to accept. It will be one step, and a very important one, toward the necessary separation of the business of production from the business of transportation.

The business of the country awaits also, has long awaited and has suffered because it could not obtain, further and more explicit legislative definition of the policy and meaning of the existing antitrust law. Nothing hampers business like uncertainty. Nothing daunts or discourages it like the necessity to take chances, to run the risk of falling under the condemnation of the law before it can make sure just what the law is. Surely we are sufficiently familiar with the actual processes and methods of monopoly and of the many hurtful restraints of trade to make definition possible, at any rate up to the limits of what experience has disclosed. These practices, being now abundantly disclosed, can be explicitly and item by item forbidden by statute in such terms as will practically eliminate uncertainty, the law itself and the penalty being made equally plain.

And the business men of the country desire something more than that the menace of legal process in these matters be made explicit and intelligible. They desire the advice, the definite guidance, and information which can be supplied by an administrative body, an interstate trade commission.

The opinion of the country would instantly approve of such a commission. It would not wish to see it empowered to make terms with monopoly or in any sort to assume control of business, as if the Government made itself responsible. It demands such a commission only as an indispensable instrument of information and publicity, as a clearing house for the facts by which both the public mind and the managers of great business undertakings should be guided, and as an instrumentality for doing justice to business where the processes of the courts or the natural forces of correction outside the courts are inadequate to adjust the remedy to the wrong in a way that will meet all the equities and circumstances of the case.

Producing industries, for example, which have passed the point up to which combination may be consistent with the public interest and the freedom of trade, can not always be dissected into their component units as readily as railroad companies or similar organizations can be. Their dissolution by ordinary legal process may oftentimes involve financial consequences likely to overwhelm the security market and bring upon it breakdown and confusion. There ought to be an administrative commission capable of directing and shaping such commission capable of directing and shaping such corrective processes, not only in aid of the courts but also by independent suggestion, if necessary.

Inasmuch as our object and the spirit of our action in these matters is to meet business half way in its processes of self-correction and disturb its legitimate course as little as possible, we ought to see to it, and the judgment of practical and sagacious men of affairs everywhere would applaud us if we did see to it, that penalties and punishments should fall not upon business itself, to its confusion and interruption, but upon the individuals who use the instrumentalities of business to do things which public policy and sound business practice condemn. Every act of business is done at the command or upon the initiative of some ascertainable person or group of persons. These should be held individually responsible and the punishment should fall upon them, not upon the business organization of which they make illegal use. It should be one of the main objects of our legislation to divest such persons of their corporate cloak and deal with them as with those who do not represent their corporations, but merely by deliberate intention break the law. Business men the country through would, I am sure, applaud us if we were to take effectual steps to see that the officers and directors of great business bodies were prevented from bringing them and the business of the country into disrepute and danger.

Other questions remain which will need very thoughtful and practical treatment. Enterprises in these modern days of great individual fortunes are oftentimes interlocked, not by being under the control of the same directors but by the fact that the greater part of their corporate stock is owned by a single person or group of persons who are in some way intimately related in interest. We are agreed, I take it, that holding *companies* should be prohibited, but what of the controlling private ownership of individuals or actually co-operative groups of individuals? Shall the private owners of capital stock be suffered to be themselves in effect holding companies? We do not wish, I suppose, to forbid the purchase of stocks by any person who pleases to buy them in such quantities as he can afford, or in any way arbitrarily to limit the sale of stocks to bona fide purchasers. Shall we require the owners of stock, when their voting power in several companies which ought to be independent of one another would constitute actual control, to make election in which of them they will exercise their right to vote? This question I venture for your consideration.

There is another matter in which imperative considerations of justice and fair play suggest thoughtful remedial action. Not only do many of the combinations effected or sought to be effected in the industrial world work an injustice upon the public in general; they also directly and seriously injure the individuals who are put out of business in one unfair way or another by the many dislodging and exterminating forces of combination. I hope that we shall agree in giving private individuals who claim to have been injured by theses processes the right to found their suits for redress upon the facts and judgments proved and entered in suits by the Government where the Government has upon its own initiative sued the combinations complained of and won its suit, and that the statute of limitations shall be suffered to run against such litigants only from the date of the conclusion of the Government's action. It is not fair that the private litigant should be obliged to set up and establish again the facts which the Government has proved. He can not afford, he has not the power, to make use of such processes of inquiry as the Government has command of. Thus shall individual justice be done while the processes of business are rectified and squared with the general conscience.

I have laid the case before you, no doubt, as it lies in your own mind, as it lies in the thought of the country. What must every candid man say of the suggestions I have laid before you, of the plain obligations of which I have reminded you? That these are new things for which the country is not prepared? No; but that they are old things, now familiar, and must of course be undertaken if we are to square our laws with the thought and desire of the country. Until these things are done, conscientious business men the country over will be unsatisfied. They are in these things our mentors and colleagues. We are now about to write the additional articles of our constitution of peace, the peace that is honor and freedom and prosperity.

The Two Proclamations Concerning the Shipment of Arms into Mexico

Whereas, by a proclamation of the President issued on March 14, 1912, under a Joint Resolution of Congress approved by the President on the same day, it was declared that there existed in Mexico conditions of domestic violence which were promoted by the use of arms or munitions of war procured from the United States; and

Whereas, by the Joint Resolution above mentioned it thereupon became unlawful to export arms or munitions of war to Mexico except under such limitations and exceptions as the President should prescribe:

Now, therefore, I, Woodrow Wilson, President of the United States of America, hereby proclaim that, as the conditions on which the Proclamation of March 14, 1912, was based have essentially changed, and as it is desirable to place the United States with reference to the exportation of arms or munitions of war to Mexico in the same position as other Powers, the said Proclamation is hereby revoked.

Done at the City of Washington this third day of February, in the year of our Lord one thousand nine hundred and fourteen, and of the Independence of the United States the one hundred and thirty-eighth.

Woodrow Wilson.

By the President:

W. J. Bryan, *Secretary of State.*

Whereas, a Joint Resolution of Congress, approved March 14, 1912, provides: "That whenever the President shall find that in any American country conditions of domestic violence exist which are promoted by the use of arms or munitions of war procured from the United States, and shall make proclamation thereof, it shall be unlawful to export except under such limitations as the President shall prescribe any arms or munitions of war from the United States to such country until otherwise ordered by the President or by Congress";

Now, therefore, I, Woodrow Wilson, President of the United States of America, do hereby proclaim that I have found that there exist in Mexico such conditions of domestic violence promoted by the use of arms or munitions of war procured from the United States as contemplated by the said Joint Resolution; and I do hereby admonish all citizens of the United States and every person to abstain from every violation of the provisions of the Joint Resolution above set forth, hereby made applicable to Mexico, and I do hereby warn them that all violations of such provisions will be rigorously prosecuted. And I do hereby enjoin upon all officers of the United States, charged with the execution of the laws thereof, the utmost diligence in preventing violations of the said Joint Resolution and this my Proclamation issued thereunder, and in bringing to trial and punishment any offenders against the same.

Done at the city of Washington this nineteenth day of October in the year of our Lord one thousand nine hundred and fifteen and of the Independence of the United States of America the one hundred and fortieth.

WOODROW WILSON.

By the President:

ROBERT LANSING, *Secretary of State.*

[On the same day (October 19) the President ordered that an exception be made in favor of the Carranza de facto government, by permitting arms shipments into the territory under that government's control.]

WILSON URGES REPEAL OF LAW GIVING AMERICAN COASTWISE SHIPS FREEDOM FROM PANAMA TOLLS

(Delivered before Congress, Joint Session, March 5, 1914.)

[EDITORIAL NOTE: *The Panama Canal Act had granted passage of the canal to American coastwise ships free of tolls. The question of whether or not this was a violation of the treaty with Great Britain was vehemently debated in the United States, but the debate was, on the whole, based more on differing National instincts and opinions than on clearly understood facts. The history of Anglo-American treaties and negotiations over Central American canal projects is highly involved and only a few specialists in diplomatic history and international law could really assert authoritative knowledge. As nearly as the temper of so huge a population as ours could be gauged, it seems correct to say that the majority favored a repeal of the act on the ground that it was better for American justice to surrender a possible right than to commit a possible injustice. Congress responded favorably to the Message.*]

Gentlemen of the Congress:

I have come to you upon an errand which can be very briefly performed, but I beg that you will not measure its importance by the number of sentences in which I state it. No communication I have addressed to the Congress carried with it graver or more far-reaching implications as to the interest of the country, and I come now to speak upon a matter with regard to which I am charged in a peculiar degree, by the Constitution itself, with personal responsibility.

I have come to ask you for the repeal of that provision of the Panama Canal Act of August 24, 1912, which exempts vessels engaged in the coastwise trade of the United States from payment of tolls, and to urge upon you the justice, the wisdom, and the large policy of such a repeal with the utmost earnestness of which I am capable.

In my own judgment, very fully considered and maturely formed, that exemption constitutes a mistaken economic policy from every point of view, and is, moreover, in plain contravention of the treaty with Great Britain concerning the canal concluded on November 18, 1901. But I have not come to urge upon you my personal views. I have come to state to you a fact and a situation. Whatever may be our own differences of opinion concerning this much debated measure, its meaning is not debated outside the United States. Everywhere else the language of the treaty is given but one interpretation, and that interpretation precludes the exemption I am asking you to repeal. We consented to the treaty; its language we accepted, if we did not originate it; and we are too big, too powerful, too self-respecting a nation to interpret with a too strained or refined reading the words of our own promises just because we have power enough to give us leave to read them as we please. The large thing to do is the only thing we can afford to do, a voluntary withdrawal from a position everywhere questioned and misunderstood. We ought to reverse our action without raising the question whether we were right or wrong, and so once more deserve our reputation for generosity and for the redemption of every obligation without quibble or hesitation.

I ask this of you in support of the foreign policy of the administration. I shall not know how to deal with other matters of even greater delicacy and nearer consequence if you do not grant it to me in ungrudging measure.

Wilson's Special Message on the Tampico Affair

(Delivered before Congress in Joint Session April 20, 1914.)

Gentlemen of the Congress:

It is my duty to call your attention to a situation which has arisen in our dealings with Gen. Victoriano Huerta at Mexico City which calls for action, and to ask your advice and co-operation.

On April 9 a Paymaster of the U. S. S. *Dolphin* landed at the Iturbide bridge landing at Tampico with a whaleboat and boat's crew to take off certain supplies for his ship, and while engaged in loading the boat was arrested by an officer and squad of men of the army of General Huerta. Neither the Paymaster nor any one of the crew was armed. Two of the men were in the boat when the arrest was made, and were obliged to leave it and submit to be taken into custody, notwithstanding that the boat carried, both at her bow and her stern, the flag of the United States. The officer who made the arrest was proceeding up one of the streets of the town with his prisoners when met by an officer of higher authority, who ordered him to return to the landing and await orders, and within an hour and a half from the time of the arrest, orders were received from the commander of the Huertista forces at Tampico for the release of the Paymaster and his men. The release was followed by apologies from the commander and also by an expression of regret by General Huerta himself. General Huerta urged that martial law obtained at the time at Tampico, that orders had been issued that no one should be allowed to land at the Iturbide bridge, and that our sailors had no right to land there. Our naval commanders at the port had not been notified of any such prohibition, and, even if they had been, the only justifiable course open to the local authorities would have been to request the Paymaster and his crew to withdraw and to lodge a protest with the commanding officer of the fleet. Admiral Mayo regarded the arrest as so serious an affront that he was not satisfied with the apologies offered, but demanded that the flag of the United States be saluted with special ceremony by the military commander of the port.

The incident can not be regarded as a trivial one, especially as two of the men arrested were taken from the boat itself—that is to say, from the territory of the United States; but had it stood by itself, it might have been attributed to the ignorance or arrogance of a single officer.

Unfortunately, it was not an isolated case. A series of incidents have recently occurred which can not but create the impression that the representatives of General Huerta were willing to go out of their way to show disregard for the dignity and rights of this Government, and felt perfectly safe in doing what they pleased, making free to show in many ways their irritation and contempt.

A few days after the incident at Tampico an orderly from the U. S. S. *Minnesota* was arrested at Vera Cruz while ashore in uniform to obtain the ship's mail, and was for a time thrown into jail. An official dispatch from this Government to its embassy at Mexico City was withheld by the authorities of the telegraphic service until peremptorily demanded by our *Chargé d' Affaires* in person.

So far as I can learn, such wrong and annoyances have been suffered to occur only against representatives of the United States. I have heard of no complaints from other governments of similar treatment. Subsequent explanations and formal apologies did not and could not alter the popular impression, which it is possible it had been the object of the Huertista authorities to create, that the Government of the United States was being singled out, and might be singled out with impunity, for slights and affronts in retaliation for its refusal to recognize the pretensions of General Huerta to be regarded as the Constitutional Provisional President of the Republic of Mexico.

The manifest danger of such a situation was that such offenses might grow from bad to worse until something happened of so gross and intolerable a sort as to lead directly and inevitably to armed conflict. It was necessary that the apologies of General Huerta and his representatives should go much further, that they should be such as to attract the attention of the whole population to their significance, and such as to impress upon General Huerta himself the necessity of seeing to it that no further occasion for explanations and professed regrets should arise. I, therefore, felt it my duty to sustain Admiral Mayo in the whole of his demand and to insist that the flag of the United States should be saluted in such a way as to indicate a new spirit and attitude on the part of the Huertistas.

Such a salute General Huerta has refused, and I have come to ask your approval and support in the course I now purpose to pursue.

This Government can, I earnestly hope, in no circumstances be forced into war with the people of Mexico. Mexico is torn by civil strife. If we are to accept the tests of its own Constitution, it has no government. General Huerta has set his power up in the City of Mexico, such as it is, without right and by methods for which there can be no justification. Only part of the country is under his control.

If armed conflict should unhappily come as a result of his attitude of personal resentment toward this Government, we should be fighting only General Huerta and those who adhere to him and give him their support, and our object would be only to restore to the people of the distracted republic the opportunity to set up again their own laws and their own government.

But I earnestly hope that war is not now in question. I believe that I speak for the American people when I say that we do not desire to control in any degree the affairs of our sister republic. Our feeling for the people of Mexico is one of deep and genuine friendship, and everything that we have so far done or refrained from doing has proceeded from our desire to help them, not to hinder or embarrass them. We would not wish even to exercise the good offices of friendship without their welcome and consent.

The people of Mexico are entitled to settle their own domestic affairs in their own way, and we sincerely desire to respect their right. The present situation need have none of the grave complications of interference if we deal with it promptly, firmly, and wisely.

No doubt I could do what is necessary in the circumstances to enforce respect for our Government without recourse to the Congress, and yet not exceed my constitutional power as President; but I do not wish to act in a matter possibly of so grave consequence except in close conference and co-operation with both the Senate and House. I therefore come to ask your approval that I should use the armed forces of the United States in such ways and to such an extent as may be necessary to obtain from General Huerta and his adherents the fullest recognition of the rights and dignity of the United States, even amid the distressing conditions now unhappily obtaining in Mexico.

There can in what we do be no thought of aggression or of selfish aggrandizement. We seek to maintain the dignity and authority of the United States only because we wish always to keep our great influence unimpaired for the uses of liberty, both in the United States and wherever else it may be employed for the benefit of mankind.

[The important event that had led up to this incident was the continued refusal to recognize Huerta. A popular election had been set in Mexico for October 26, 1913, to elect a Constitutional President. On October 10 Huerta sent a strong force of soldiers to the Parliament House in Mexico City and arrested 110 members of the lower chamber, making himself supreme and rendering the election farcical. Congress gave President Wilson the approval for which he asked, by passing a joint resolution that the President was justified in using the armed forces of the United States to enforce demands on Huerta for unequivocal amends to the United States. This resolution was adopted April 22 1914.]

Wilson Orders Dissolution of New England Railroad Mergers

[Editorial Note: *As a result of sensational disclosures in New England relating to monopoly of transportation acquired by the New York, New Haven and Hartford Railroad as a principal, the Federal Government, in order to save the interests of stock-holders and of the public, proposed to the controlling financiers a systematic process of correcting the objectionable practices and of dissolving the unlawful combinations. After long negotiations the United States Attorney-General, J. C. McReynolds, was obliged to inform the President that the directors of the N. Y., N. H. and H. R. R. had failed to comply with the terms of settlement. The President thereupon gave the Attorney-General the following written instruction:*]

Their final decision in this matter causes me the deepest surprise and regret. Their failure upon so slight a pretext to carry out an agreement deliberately and solemnly entered into, and which was manifestly in the common interest, is to me inexplicable and entirely without justification.

You have been kind enough to keep me informed of every step the Department took in this matter and the action of the Department has, throughout, met with my entire approval. It was just, reasonable and efficient. It should have resulted in avoiding what must now be done.

In the circumstances the course you propose is the only one the Government can pursue. I therefore request and direct that a proceeding in equity be filed, seeking the dissolution of unlawful monopolization of transportation in New England territory now sought to be mantained by the New York, New Haven and Hartford Railroad Company, and that the criminal aspects of the case be laid before a Grand Jury.

WOODROW WILSON.

THE WHITE HOUSE, July 21, 1914.

[EDITORIAL NOTE: *The suit was begun October 13, 1915, and ended January 10, 1916, in the acquittal of six defendants and a disagreement of the jury as to the guilt or innocence of the other five.*]

WILSON'S SPECIAL MESSAGE ON PROVISIONS FOR ADDITIONAL REVENUE

(Delivered before Congress in Joint Session September 4, 1914.)

Gentlemen of the Congress:

I come to you to-day to discharge a duty which I wish with all my heart I might have been spared; but it is a very clear duty, and therefore I perform it without hesitation or apology. I come to ask very earnestly that additional revenue be provided for the Government.

During the month of August there was, as compared with the corresponding month of last year, a falling off of $10,-629,538 in the revenues collected from customs. A continuation of this decrease in the same proportion throughout the current fiscal year would probably mean a loss of customs revenues of from sixty to one hundred millions. I need not tell you to what this falling off is due. It is due, in chief part, not to the reductions recently made in the customs duties, but to the great decrease in importations; and that is due to the extraordinary extent of the industrial area affected by the present war in Europe. Conditions have arisen which no man foresaw; they affect the whole world of commerce and economic production; and they must be faced and dealt with.

It would be very unwise to postpone dealing with them. Delay in such a matter and in the particular circumstances in which we now find ourselves as a nation might involve consequences of the most embarrassing and deplorable sort, for which I, for one, would not care to be responsible. It would be very dangerous in the present circumstances to create a moment's doubt as to the strength and sufficiency of the Treasury of the United States, its ability to assist, to steady, and sustain the financial operations of the country's business. If the Treasury is known, or even thought, to be weak, where will be our peace of mind? The whole industrial activity of the country would be chilled and demoralized. Just now the peculiarly difficult financial problems of the moment are being successfully dealt with, with great self-possession and good sense and very sound judgment; but they are only in process of being worked out. If the process of solution is to be completed, no one must be given reason to doubt the solidity and adequacy of the Treasury of the Government which stands behind the whole method by which our difficulties are being met and handled.

The Treasury itself could get along for a considerable period, no doubt, without immediate resort to new sources of taxation. But at what cost to the business of the community? Approximately $75,000,000, a large part of the present Treasury balance, is now on deposit with national banks distributed throughout the country. It is deposited, of course, on call. I need not point out to you what the probable consequences of inconvenience and distress and confusion would be if the diminishing income of the Treasury should make it necessary rapidly to withdraw these deposits. And yet without additional revenue that plainly might become necessary, and the time when it became necessary could not be controlled or determined by the convenience of the business of the country. It would have to be determined by the operations and necessities of the Treasury itself. Such risks are not necessary and ought not to be run. We can not too scrupulously or carefully safeguard a financial situation which is at best, while war continues in Europe, difficult and abnormal. Hesitation and delay are the worst forms of bad policy under such conditions.

And we ought not to borrow. We ought to resort to taxation, however we may regret the necessity of putting additional temporary burdens on our people. To sell bonds would be to make a most untimely and unjustifiable demand on the money market; untimely, because this is manifestly not the time to withdraw working capital from other uses to pay the Government's bills; unjustifiable, because unnecessary. The country is able to pay any just and reasonable taxes without distress. And to every other form of borrowing, whether for long periods or for short, there is the same objection. These are not the circumstances, this is at this particular moment and in this particular exigency not the market, to borrow large sums of money. What we are seeking is to ease and assist every financial transaction, not to add a single additional embarrassment to the situation. The people of this country are both intelligent and profoundly patriotic. They are ready to meet the present conditions in the right way and to support the Government with generous self-denial. They know and understand, and will be intolerant only of those who dodge responsibility or are not frank with them.

The occasion is not of our own making. We had no part in making it. But it is here. It affects us as directly and palpably almost as if we were participants in the circumstances which gave rise to it. We must accept the inevitable with calm judgment and unruffled spirits, like men accustomed to deal with the unexpected, habituated to take care of themselves, masters of their own affairs and their own fortunes. We shall pay the bill, though we did not deliberately incur it.

In order to meet every demand upon the Treasury without delay or peradventure and in order to keep the Treasury strong, unquestionably strong, and strong throughout the present anxieties, I respectfully urge that an additional revenue of $100,000,000 be raised through internal taxes devised in your wisdom to meet the emergency. The only suggestion I take the liberty of making is that such sources of revenue be chosen as will begin to yield at once and yield with a certain and constant flow.

I can not close without expressing the confidence with which I approach a Congress, with regard to this or any other matter, which has shown so untiring a devotion to public duty, which has responded to the needs of the Nation throughout a long season despite inevitable fatigue and personal sacrifice, and so large a proportion of whose Members have devoted their whole time and energy to the business of the country.

Wilson's Second Annual Message

(Delivered before Congress in Joint Session December 8, 1914.)

Gentlemen of the Congress:

The session upon which you are now entering will be the closing session of the Sixty-third Congress, a Congress, I venture to say, which will long be remembered for the great body of thoughtful and constructive work which it has done, in loyal response to the thought and needs of the country. I should like in this address to review the notable record and try to make adequate assessment of it; but no doubt we stand too near the work that has been done and are ourselves too much part of it to play the part of historians toward it.

Our program of legislation with regard to the regulation of business is now virtually complete. It has been put forth, as we intended, as a whole, and leaves no conjecture as to what is to follow. The road at last lies clear and firm before business. It is a road which it can travel without fear or embarrassment. It is the road to ungrudged, unclouded success. In it every honest man, every man who believes that the public interest is part of his own interest, may walk with perfect confidence.

Moreover, our thoughts are now more of the future than of the past. While we have worked at our tasks of peace the circumstances of the whole age have been altered by war. What we have done for our own land and our own people we did with the best that was in us, whether of character or of intelligence, with sober enthusiasm and a confidence in the principles upon which we were acting which sustained us at every step of the difficult undertaking; but it is done. It has passed from our hands. It is now an established part of the legislation of the country. Its usefulness, its effects will disclose themselves in experience. What chiefly strikes us now, as we look about us during these closing days of a year which will be forever memorable in the history of the world, is that we face new tasks, have been facing them these six months, must face them in the months to come,—face them without partisan feeling, like men who have forgotten everything but a common duty and the fact that we are representatives of a great people whose thought is not of us but of what America owes to herself and to all mankind in such circumstances as these upon which we look amazed and anxious.

War has interrupted the means of trade not only but also the processes of production. In Europe it is destroying men and resources wholesale and upon a scale unprecedented and appalling. There is reason to fear that the time is near, if it be not already at hand, when several of the countries of Europe will find it difficult to do for their people what they have hitherto been always easily able to do,—many essential and fundamental things. At any rate, they will need our help and our manifold services as they have never needed them before; and we should be ready, more fit and ready than we have ever been.

It is of equal consequence that the nations whom Europe has usually supplied with innumerable articles of manufacture and commerce of which they are in constant need and without which their economic development halts and stands still can now get only a small part of what they formerly imported and eagerly look to us to supply their all but empty markets. This is particularly true of our own neighbors, the States, great and small, of Central and South America. Their lines of trade have hitherto run chiefly athwart the seas, not to our ports but to the ports of Great Britain and of the older continent of Europe. I do not stop to inquire why, or to make any comment on probable causes. What interests us just now is not the explanation but the fact, and our duty and opportunity in the presence of it. Here are markets which we must supply, and we must find the means of action. The United States, this great people for whom we speak and act, should be ready, as never before, to serve itself and to serve mankind; ready with its resources, its energies, its forces of production, and its means of distribution.

It is a very practical matter, a matter of ways and means. We have the resources, but are we fully ready to use them? And, if we can make ready what we have, have we the means at hand to distribute it? We are not fully ready; neither have we the means of distribution. We are willing, but we are not fully able. We have the wish to serve and to serve greatly, generously; but we are not prepared as we should be. We are not ready to mobilize our resources at once. We are not prepared to use them immediately and at their best, without delay and without waste.

To speak plainly, we have grossly erred in the way in which we have stunted and hindered the development of our merchant marine. And now, when we need ships, we have not got them. We have year after year debated, without end or conclusion, the best policy to pursue with regard to the use of the ores and forests and water powers of our national domain in the rich States of the West, when we should have acted; and they are still locked up. The key is still turned upon them, the door shut fast at which thousands of vigorous men, full of initiative, knock clamorously for admittance. The water power of our navigable streams outside the national domain also, even in the eastern States, where we have worked and planned for generations, is still not used as it might be, because we will and we won't; because the laws we have made do not intelligently balance encouragement against restraint. We withhold by regulation.

I have come to ask you to remedy and correct these mistakes and omissions, even at this short session of a Congress which would certainly seem to have done all the work that could reasonably be expected of it. The time and the circumstances are extraordinary, and so must our efforts be also.

Fortunately, two great measures, finely conceived, the one to unlock, with proper safeguards, the resources of the national domain, the other to encourage the use of the navigable waters outside that domain for the generation of power, have already passed the House of Representatives and are ready for immediate consideration and action by the Senate. With the deepest earnestness I urge their prompt passage. In them both we turn our backs upon hesitation and makeshift and formulate a genuine policy of use and conservation, in the best sense of those words. We owe the one measure not only to the people of that great western country for whose free and systematic development, as it seems to me, our legislation has done so little, but also to the people of the Nation as a whole; and we as clearly owe the other in fulfillment of our repeated promises that the water power of the country should in fact as well as in name be put at the disposal of great industries which can make economical and profitable use of it, the rights of the public being adequately guarded the while, and monopoly in the use prevented. To have begun such measures and not completed them would indeed mar the record of this great Congress very seriously. I hope and confidently believe that they will be completed.

And there is another great piece of legislation which awaits and should receive the sanction of the Senate: I mean the bill which gives a larger measure of self-government to the people of the Philippines. How better, in this time of anxious questioning and perplexed policy, could we show our confidence in the principles of liberty, as the sources as well as the expression of life, how better could we demonstrate our own self-possession and steadfastness in the courses of justice and disinterestedness than by thus going calmly forward to fulfill our promises to a dependent people, who will now look more anxiously than ever to see whether we have indeed the liberality, the unselfishness, the courage, the faith we have boasted and professed. I can not believe that the Senate will let this great measure of constructive justice await the action of another Congress. Its passage would nobly crown the record of these two years of memorable labor.

But I think that you will agree with me that this does not complete the toll of our duty. How are we to carry our goods to the empty markets of which I have spoken if we have not the ships? How are we to build up a great trade if we have not the certain and constant means of transportation upon which all profitable and useful commerce depends? And how are we to get the ships if we wait for the trade to develop without them? To correct th many mistakes by which we have discouraged and all bu destroyed the merchant marine of the country, to retrac the steps by which we have, it seems almost deliberately withdrawn our flag from the seas, except where, here an there, a ship of war is bidden carry it or some wanderin yacht displays it, would take a long time and involve man detailed items of legislation, and the trade which we ough immediately to handle would disappear or find other chan nels while we debated the items.

The case is not unlike that which confronted us whe our own continent was to be opened up to settlement an industry, and we needed long lines of railway, extende means of transportation prepared beforehand, if develop ment was not to lag intolerably and wait interminably. W lavishly subsidized the building of trancontinental rail roads. We look back upon that with regret now, becaus the subsidies led to many scandals of which we are ashamed but we know that the railroads had to be built, and if w had it to do over again we should of course build them, bu in another way. Therefore I propose another way of pro viding the means of transportation, which must precede not tardily follow, the development of our trade with ou neighbor states of America. It may seem a reversal of th natural order of things, but it is true, that the routes o trade must be acually opened—by many ships and regula sailings and moderate charges—before streams of merchan dise will flow freely and profitably through them.

Hence the pending shipping bill, discussed at the las session but as yet passed by neither House. In my judg ment such legislation is imperatively needed and can no wisely be postponed. The Government must open these gates of trade, and open them wide; open them before it is altogether profitable to open them, or altogether reason able to ask private capital to open them at a venture. It is not a question of the Government monopolizing the field

It should take action to make it certain that transportation at reasonable rates will be promptly provided, even where the carriage is not at first profitable; and then, when the carriage has become sufficiently profitable to attract and engage private capital, and engage it in abundance, the Government ought to withdraw. I very earnestly hope that the Congress will be of this opinion, and that both Houses will adopt this exceedingly important bill.

The great subject of rural credits still remains to be dealt with, and it is a matter of deep regret that the difficulties of the subject have seemed to render it impossible to complete a bill for passage at this session. But it can not be perfected yet, and therefore there are no other constructive measures the necessity for which I will at this time call your attention to; but I would be negligent of a very manifest duty were I not to call the attention of the Senate to the fact that the proposed convention for safety at sea awaits its confirmation and that the limit fixed in the convention itself for its acceptance is the last day of the present month. The conference in which this convention originated was called by the United States; the representatives of the United States played a very influential part indeed in framing the provisions of the proposed convention; and those provisions are in themselves for the most part admirable. It would hardly be consistent with the part we have played in the whole matter to let it drop and go by the board as if forgotten and neglected. It was ratified in May last by the German Government and in August by the Parliament of Great Britain. It marks a most hopeful and decided advance in international civilization. We should show our earnest good faith in a great matter by adding our own acceptance of it.

There is another matter of which I must make special mention, if I am to discharge my conscience, lest it should escape your attention. It may seem a very small thing. It affects only a single item of appropriation. But many human lives and many great enterprises hang upon it. It is the matter of making adequate provision for the survey and charting of our coasts. It is immediately pressing and exigent in connection with the immense coast line of Alaska, a coast line greater than that of the United States themselves, though it is also very important indeed with regard to the older coasts of the continent. We can not use our great Alaskan domain, ships will not ply thither, if those coasts and their many hidden dangers are not thoroughly surveyed and charted. The work is incomplete at almost every point. Ships and lives have been lost in threading what were supposed to be well-known main channels. We have not provided adequate vessels or adequate machinery for the survey and charting. We have used old vessels that were not big enough or strong enough and which were so nearly unseaworthy that our inspectors would not have allowed private owners to send them to sea. This is a matter which, as I have said, seems small, but is in reality very great. Its importance has only to be looked into to be appreciated.

Before I close may I say a few words upon two topics, much discussed out of doors, upon which it is highly important that our judgments should be clear, definite and steadfast?

One of these is economy in government expenditures. The duty of economy is not debatable. It is manifest and imperative. In the appropriations we pass we are spending the money of the great people whose servants we are,—not our own. We are trustees and responsible stewards in the spending. The only thing debatable and upon which we should be careful to make our thought and purpose clear is the kind of economy demanded of us. I assert with the greatest confidence that the people of the United States are not jealous of the amount their Government costs if they are sure that they get what they need and desire for the outlay, that the money is being spent for objects of which they approve, and that it is being applied with good business sense and management.

Governments grow, piecemeal, both in their tasks and in the means by which those tasks are to be performed, and very few Governments are organized, I venture to say, as wise and experienced business men would organize them if they had a clean sheet of paper to write upon. Certainly the Government of the United States is not. I think that it is generally agreed that there should be a systematic reorganization and reassembling of its parts so as to secure greater efficiency and effect considerable savings in expense. But the amount of money saved in that way would, I believe, though no doubt considerable in itself, running, it may be, into the millions, be relatively small,—small, I mean, in proportion to the total necessary outlays of the Government. It would be thoroughly worth effecting, as every saving would, great or small. Our duty is not altered by the scale of the saving. But my point is that the people of the United States do not wish to curtail the activities of this Government; they wish, rather, to enlarge them; and with every enlargement, with the mere growth, indeed, of the country itself, there must come, of course, the inevitable increase of expense. The sort of economy we ought to practice may be effected, and ought to be effected, by a careful study and assessment of the tasks to be performed; and the money spent ought to be made to yield the best possible returns in efficiency and achievement. And, like good stewards, we should so account for every dollar of our appropriations as to make it perfectly evident what it was spent for and in what way it was spent.

It is not expenditure but extravagance that we should fear being criticized for; not paying for the legitimate enterprises and undertakings of a great Government whose people command what it should do, but adding what will benefit only a few or pouring money out for what need not have been undertaken at all or might have been postponed or better and more economically conceived and carried out. The Nation is not niggardly; it is very generous. It will chide us only if we forget for whom we pay money out and whose money it is we pay. These are large and general standards, but they are not very difficult of application to particular cases.

The other topic I shall take leave to mention goes deeper into the principles of our national life and policy. It is the subject of national defense.

It can not be discussed without first answering some very searching questions. It is said in some quarters that we are not prepared for war. What is meant by being prepared? Is it meant that we are not ready upon brief notice to put a nation in the field, a nation of men trained to arms? Of course we are not ready to do that; and we shall never be in time of peace so long as we retain our present political principles and institutions. And what is it that it is suggested we should be prepared to do? To defend ourselves against attack? We have always found means to do that, and shall find them whenever it is necessary without calling our people away from their necessary tasks to render compulsory military service in times of peace.

Allow me to speak with great plainness and directness upon this great matter and to avow my convictions with deep earnestness. I have tried to know what America is, what her people think, what they are, what they most cherish and hold dear. I hope that some of their finer passions are in my own heart,—some of the great conceptions and desires which gave birth to this Government and which have made the voice of this people a voice of peace and hope and liberty among the peoples of the world, and that, speaking my own thoughts, I shall, at least in part, speak theirs also, however faintly and inadequately, upon this vital matter.

We are at peace with all the world. No one who speaks

counsel based on fact or drawn from a just and candid interpretation of realities can say that there is reason to fear that from any quarter our independence or the integrity of our territory is threatened. Dread of the power of any other nation we are incapable of. We are not jealous of rivalry in the fields of commerce or of any other peaceful achievement. We mean to live our own lives as we will; but we mean also to let live. We are, indeed, a true friend to all the nations of the world, because we threaten none, covet the possessions of none, desire the overthrow of none. Our friendship can be accepted and is accepted without reservation, because it is offered in a spirit and for a purpose which no one need ever question or suspect. Therein lies our greatness. We are the champions of peace and of concord. And we should be very jealous of this distinction which we have sought to earn. Just now we should be particularly jealous of it, because it is our dearest present hope that this character and reputation may presently, in God's providence, bring us an opportunity such as has seldom been vouchsafed any nation, the opportunity to counsel and obtain peace in the world and reconciliation and a healing settlement of many a matter that has cooled and interrupted the friendship of nations. This is the time above all others when we should wish and resolve to keep our strength by self-possession, our influence by preserving our ancient principles of action.

From the first we have had a clear and settled policy with regard to military establishments. We never have had, and while we retain our present principles and ideals we never shall have, a large standing army. If asked, Are you ready to defend yourselves? we reply, Most assuredly, to the utmost; and yet we shall not turn America into a military camp. We will not ask our young men to spend the best years of their lives making soldiers of themselves. There is another sort of energy in us. It will know how to declare itself and make itself effective should occasion arise. And especially when half the world is on fire we shall be careful to make our moral insurance against the spread of the conflagration very definite and certain and adequate indeed.

Let us remind ourselves, therefore, of the only thing we can do or will do. We must depend in every time of national peril, in the future as in the past, not upon a standing army, nor yet upon a reserve army, but upon a citizenry trained and accustomed to arms. It will be right enough, right American policy, based upon our accustomed principles and practices, to provide a system by which every citizen who will volunteer for the training may be made familiar with the use of modern arms, the rudiments of drill and maneuver, and the maintenance and sanitation of camps. We should encourage such training and make it a means of discipline which our young men will learn to value. It is right that we should provide it not only, but that we should make it as attractive as possible, and so induce our young men to undergo it at such times as they can command a little freedom and can seek the physical development they need, for mere health's sake, if for nothing more. Every means by which such things can be stimulated is legitimate, and such a method smacks of true American ideas. It is right, too, that the National Guard of the States should be developed and strengthened by every means which is not inconsistent with our obligations to our own people or with the established policy of our Government. And this, also, not because the time or occasion specially calls for such measures, but because it should be our constant policy to make these provisions for our national peace and safety.

More than this carries with it a reversal of the whole history and character of our polity. More than this, proposed at this time, permit me to say, would mean merely that we had lost our self-possession, that we had been thrown off our balance by a war with which we have nothing to do, whose causes can not touch us, whose very existence affords us opportunities of friendship and disinterested service which should make us ashamed of any thought of hostility or fearful preparation for trouble. This is assuredly the opportunity for which a people and a government like ours were raised up, the opportunity not only to speak but actually to embody and exemplify the counsels of peace and amity and the lasting concord which is based on justice and fair and generous dealing.

A powerful navy we have always regarded as our proper and natural means of defense; and it has always been of defense that we have thought, never of aggression or of conquest. But who shall tell us now what sort of navy to build? We shall take leave to be strong upon the seas, in the future as in the past; and there will be no thought of offense or of provocation in that. Our ships are our natural bulwarks. When will the expert tell us just what kind we should construct—and when will they be right for ten years together, if the relative efficiency of craft of different kinds and uses continues to change as we have seen it change under our very eyes in these last few months?

But I turn away from the subject. It is not new. There is no new need to discuss it. We shall not alter our attitude toward it because some amongst us are nervous and excited. We shall easily and sensibly agree upon a policy of defense. The question has not changed its aspects because the times are not normal. Our policy will not be for an occasion. It will be conceived as a permanent and settled thing, which we will pursue at all seasons, without haste and after a fashion perfectly consistent with the peace of the world, the abiding friendship of states, and the unhampered freedom of all with whom we deal. Let there be no misconception. The country has been misinformed. We have not been negligent of national defense. We are not unmindful of the great responsibility resting upon us. We shall learn and profit by the lesson of every experience and every new circumstance; and what is needed will be adequately done.

I close, as I began, by reminding you of the great tasks and duties of peace which challenge our best powers and invite us to build what will last, the tasks to which we can address ourselves now and at all times with free-hearted zest and with all the finest gifts of constructive wisdom we possess. To develop our life and our resources; to supply our own people, and the people of the world as their need arises, from the abundant plenty of our fields and our marts of trade; to enrich the commerce of our own States and of the world with the products of our mines, our farms, and our factories, with the creations of our thought and the fruits of our character,—this is what will hold our attention and our enthusiasm steadily, now and in the years to come, as we strive to show in our life as a nation what liberty and the inspirations of an emancipated spirit may do for men and for societies, for individuals, for states, and for mankind.

Wilson's Jackson Day Address at Indianapolis, January 8, 1915

[In which he praises the Democratic party and ridicules everything Republican. Here we find President Wilson in his lightest vein. In this address, also, he declared, regarding Mexican factions, that "so far as my influence goes while I am President nobody shall interfere with them."]

Governor Ralston, Ladies and Gentlemen:

You have given me a most royal welcome, for which I thank you from the bottom of my heart. It is rather lonely living in Washington. I have been confined for two years at hard labor, and even now I feel that I am simply out on parole. You notice that one of the most distinguished members of the United States Senate is here to see that I go back. And yet, with sincere apologies to the Senate and

House of Representatives, I want to say that I draw more inspiration from you than I do from them. They, like myself, are only servants of the people of the United States. Our sinews consist in your sympathy and support, and our renewal comes from contact with you and with the strong movements of public opinion in the country. . . .

But I have come here on Jackson Day. If there are Republicans present, I hope they will feel the compelling influences of such a day. There was nothing mild about Andrew Jackson; that is the reason I spoke of the "compelling influences" of the day. Andrew Jackson was a forthright man who believed everything he did believe in fighting earnest. And really, ladies and gentlemen, in public life that is the only sort of man worth thinking about for a moment. If I was not ready to fight for everything I believe in, I would think it my duty to go back and take a back seat. I like, therefore, to breathe the air of Jackson Day. I like to be reminded of the old militant hosts of Democracy which I believe have come to life again in our time. The United States had almost forgotten that it must keep its fighting ardor in behalf of mankind when Andrew Jackson became President; and you will notice that whenever the United States forgets its ardor for mankind it is necessary that a Democrat should be elected President.

The trouble with the Republican party is that it has not had a new idea for thirty years. I am not speaking as a politician; I am speaking as an historian. I have looked for new ideas in the records and I have not found any proceeding from the Republican ranks. They have had leaders from time to time who suggested new ideas, but they never did anything to carry them out. I suppose there was no harm in their talking, provided they could not do anything. Therefore, when it was necessary to say that we had talked about things long enough which it was necessary to do, and the time had come to do them, it was indispensable that a Democrat should be elected President.

I would not speak with disrespect of the Republican party. I always speak with great respect of the past. The past was necessary to the present, and was a sure prediction of the future. The Republican party is still a covert and refuge for those who are afraid, for those who want to consult their grandfathers about everything. You will notice that most of the advice taken by the Republican party is taken from gentlemen old enough to be grandfathers, and that when they claim that a reaction has taken place, they react to the re-election of the oldest members of their party. They will not trust the youngsters. They are afraid the youngsters may have something up their sleeve. . . .

My friends, what I particularly want you to observe is this, that politics in this country does not depend any longer upon the regular members of either party. There are not enough regular Republicans in this country to take and hold national power; and I must immediately add there are not enough regular Democrats in this country to do it, either. This country is guided and its policy is determined by the independent voter; and I have come to ask you how we can best prove to the independent voter that the instrument he needs is the Democratic party, and that it would be hopeless for him to attempt to use the Republican party. I do not have to prove it; I admit it.

What seems to me perfectly evident is this: That if you made a rough reckoning, you would have to admit that only about one-third of the Republican party is progressive; and you would also have to admit that about two-thirds of the Democratic party is progressive. Therefore, the independent progressive voter finds a great deal more company in the Democratic ranks than in the Republican ranks. . . .

What I want to point out to you—and I believe that this is what the whole country is beginning to perceive—is this, that there is a larger body of men in the regular ranks of the Democratic party who believe in the progressive policies of our day and mean to see them carried forward and perpetuated than there is in the ranks of the Republican party. How can it be otherwise, gentlemen? The Democratic party, and only the Democratic party, has carried out the policies which the progressive people of this country have desired. There is not a single great act of this present great Congress which has not been carried out in obedience to the public opinion of America; and the public opinion of America is not going to permit any body of men to go backward with regard to these great matters.

Let me instance a single thing: I want to ask the business men here present if this is not the first January in their recollection that did not bring a money stringency for the time being, because of the necessity of paying out great sums of money by way of dividends and the other settlements which come at the first of the year? I have asked the bankers if that happened this year, and they say, "No; it did not happen; it could not happen under the Federal Reserve Act." We have emancipated the credits of this country; and is there anybody here who will doubt that the other policies that have given guaranty to this country that there will be free competition are policies which this country will never allow to be reversed? I have taken a long time, ladies and gentlemen, to select the Federal Trade Commission, because I wanted to choose men and be sure that I had chosen men who would be really serviceable to the business men of this country, great as well as small, the rank and the file. These things have been done and will never be undone. They were talked about and talked about with futility until a Democratic Congress attempted and achieved them.

But the Democratic party is not to suppose that it is done with the business. The Democratic party is still on trial. The Democratic party still has to prove to the independent voters of the country not only that it believes in these things, but that it will continue to work along these

lines and that it will not allow any enemy of these thing
to break its ranks. This country is not going to use an
party that can not do continuous and consistent teamwork
If any group of men should dare to break the solidarity c
the Democratic team for any purpose or from any motiv
theirs will be a most unenviable notoriety and a respons
bility which will bring deep bitterness to them. The onl
party that is serviceable to a nation is a party that ca
hold absolutely together and march with the discipline an
with the zest of a conquering host.

I am not saying these things because I doubt that th
Democratic party will be able to do this, but because I be
lieve that as leader for the time being of that party I ca
promise the country that it will do these things. I know m
colleagues at Washington; I know their spirit and their pur
pose; and I know that they have the same emotion, the sam
high emotion of public service, that I hope I have.

I want at this juncture to pay my tribute of respect an
of affectionate admiration for the two great Democrati
Senators from the State of Indiana. I have never had t
lie awake nights wondering what they were going to dc
And the country is not going to trouble itself, ladies an
gentlemen, to lie awake nights and wonder what men ar
going to do. If they have to do that, they will choose othe
men. Teamwork all the time is what they are going to de
mand of us, and that is our individual as well as our col
lective responsibility. That is what Jackson stands for
If a man will not play with the team, then he does no
belong to the team. You see, I have spent a large part o
my life in college and I know what a team means when
see it; and I know what the captain of a team must hav
if he is going to win. So it is no idle figure of speecl
with me.

Now, what is their duty? You say, "Hasn't this Con
gress carried out a great program?" Yes, it has carriec
out a great program. It has had the most remarkabl

record that any Congress since the Civil War has had; and I say since the Civil War because I have not had time to think about those before the Civil War. But we are living at an extraordinary moment. The world has never been in the condition that it is in now, my friends. Half the world is on fire. Only America among the great powers of the world is free to govern her own life; and all the world is looking to America to serve its economic need. And while this is happening what is going on?

Do you know, gentlemen, that the ocean freight rates have gone up in some instances to ten times their ordinary figure? and that the farmers of the United States, those who raise grain and those who raise cotton—these things that are absolutely necessary to the world as well as to ourselves—can not get their due profit out of the great prices that they are willing to pay for these things on the other side of the sea, because practically the whole profit is eaten up by the extortionate charges for ocean carriage? In the midst of this the Democrats propose a temporary measure of relief in a shipping bill. The merchants and the farmers of this country must have ships to carry their goods. Just at the present moment there is no other way of getting them through the instrumentality that is suggested in the shipping bill. I hear it said in Washington on all hands that the Republicans in the United States Senate mean to talk enough to make the passage of that bill impossible. These self-styled friends of business, these men who say the Democratic party does not know what to do for business, are saying that the Democrats shall do nothing for business. I challenge them to show their right to stand in the way of the release of American products to the rest of the world! Who commissioned them—a minority, a lessening minority? (For they will be in a greater minority in the next Senate than in this.) You know it is the peculiarity of that great body that it has rules of procedure which make it possible for a minority to defy the

Nation; and these gentlemen are now seeking to defy th
Nation and prevent the release of American products t
the suffering world which needs them more than it eve
needed them before. Their credentials as friends of busi
ness and friends of America will be badly discredited i
they succeed. If I were speaking from a selfish, partisa
point of view, I could wish nothing better than that the
should show their true colors as partisans and succeed. Bu
I am not quite so malevolent as that. Some of them ar
misguided; some of them are blind; most of them are igno
rant. I would rather pray for them than abuse them. Th
great voice of America ought to make them understan
what they are said to be attempting now really means.
have to say "are said to be attempting," because they d
not come and tell me that they are attempting them. I d
not know why. I would express my opinion of them i
parliamentary language, but I would express it, I hope, n
less plainly because couched in the terms of courtesy. Thi
country is bursting its jacket, and they are seeing to it tha
the jacket is not only kept tight but is riveted with steel

The Democratic party does know how to serve busines
in this country, and its future program is a program o
service. We have cleared the decks. We have laid th
lines now upon which business that was to do the countr
harm shall be stopped and an economic control which wa
intolerable shall be broken up. We have emancipate
America, but America must do something with her freedom.
There are great bills pending in the United States Senate
just now that have been passed by the House of Representatives, which are intended as constructive measures in
behalf of business—one great measure which will make
available the enormous water powers of this country for
the industry of it; another bill which will unlock the resources of the public domain which the Republicans, desiring to save, locked up so that nobody could use them.

The reason I say the Republicans have not had a new

idea in thirty years is that they have not known how to do anything except sit on the lid. If you can release the steam so that it will drive great industries, it is not necessary to sit on the lid. What we are trying to do in the great conservation bill is to carry out for the first time in the history of the United States a system by which the great resources of this country can be used instead of being set aside so that no man can get at them. I shall watch with a great deal of interest what the self-styled friends of business try to do to those bills. Do not misunderstand me. There are some men on that side of the Chamber who understand the value of these things and are standing valiantly by them, but they are a small minority. The majority that is standing by them is on our side of the Chamber, and they are the friends of America.

But there are other things which we have to do. Sometimes when I look abroad, my friends, and see the great mass of struggling humanity on this continent, it goes very much to my heart to see how many men are at a disadvantage and are without guides and helpers. Don't you think it would be a pretty good idea for the Democratic party to undertake a systematic method of helping the workingmen of America? There is one very simple way in which they can help the workingmen. If you were simply to establish a great Federal employment bureau, it would do a vast deal. By the Federal agencies which spread over this country men could be directed to those parts of the country, to those undertakings, to those tasks where they could find profitable employment. The labor of this country needs to be guided from opportunity to opportunity. We proved it the other day. We were told that in two States of the Union 30,000 men were needed to gather the crops. We suggested in a Cabinet meeting that the Department of Labor should have printed information about this in such form that it could be posted up in the post offices all over the United States, and that the Department of Labor should get in touch with the labor departments of the States, so that notice could go out from them, and their cooperation obtained. What was the result? Those 30,000 men were found and were sent to the places where they got profitable employment. I do not know any one thing that has happened in my administration that made me feel happier than that—that the job and the man had been brought together. It will not cost a great deal of money and it will do a great deal of service if the United States were to undertake to do such things systematically and all the year round; and I for my part hope that it will do that. If I were writing an additional plank for a Democratic platform, I would put that in.

There is another thing that needs very much to be done. I am not one of those who doubt either the industry or the learning or the integrity of the courts of the United States, but I do know that they have a very antiquated way of doing business. I do know that the United States in its judicial procedure is many decades behind every other civilized Government in the world, and I say that it is an immediate and an imperative call upon us to rectify that, because the speediness of justice, the inexpensiveness of justice, the ready access to justice, is the greater part of justice itself. . . .

Then there is something else. The Democrats have heard the Republicans talking about the scientific way in which to handle a tariff, though the Republicans have never given any exhibition of a knowledge of how to handle it scientifically. If it is scientific to put additional profits into the hands of those who are already getting the greater part of the profits, then they have been exceedingly scientific. It has been the science of selfishness; it has been the science of privilege. That kind of science I do not care to know anything about except enough to stop it. But if by scientific treatment of the tariff they mean adjustment to the actual trade conditions of America and the world, then I am with them; and I want to call their attention—for though they voted for it they apparently have not noticed it—to the fact that the bill which creates the new Trade Commission does that very thing. We were at pains to see that it was put in there. That commission is authorized and empowered to inquire into and report to Congress not only upon all the conditions of trade in this country, but upon the conditions of trade, the cost of manufacture, the cost of transportation—all the things that enter into the question of the tariff—in foreign countries and into all those questions of foreign combinations which affect international trade between Europe and the United States. It has the full powers which will guide Congress in the scientific treatment of questions of international trade. Being by profession a schoolmaster, I am glad to point that out to the class of uninstructed Republicans, though I have not always taught in the primary grade.

At every turn the things that the progressive Republicans have proposed that were practicable, the Democrats either have done or are immediately proposing to do. If that is not our bill of particulars to satisfy the independent voters of the country, I would like to have one produced. There are things that the Progressive program contained which we, being constitutional lawyers, happened to know can not be done by the Congress of the United States. That is a detail which they seem to have overlooked. But so far as they can be done by State legislatures, I, for one, speaking for one Democrat, am heartily in favor of their being done. . . .

Just before I came away from Washington I was going over some of the figures of the last elections, the elections of November last. The official returns have not all come in yet. I do not know why they are so slow in getting to us, but so far as they have come in they have given me this useful information, that taking the States where Senators were elected, and where Senators were not elected taking the election of Governors, and where Governors were not elected taking the returns for the State legislatures or for the Congressional delegates, the Democrats, reckoning State by State, would, if it had been a presidential year, have had a majority of about eighty in the Electoral College. Fortunately or unfortunately, this is not a presidential year; but the thing is significant to me for this reason. A great many people have been speaking of the Democratic party as a minority party. Well, if it is, it is not so much of a minority party as the Republican, and as between the minorities I think we can claim to belong to the larger minority. The moral of that is merely what I have already been pointing out to you, that neither party in its regular membership has a majority. I do not want to make the independent voter too proud of himself, but I have got to admit that he is our boss; and I am bound to admit that the things that he wants are, so far as I have seen them mentioned, things that I want.

I am not an independent voter, but I hope I can claim to be an independent person, and I want to say this distinctly: I do not love any party any longer than it continues to serve the immediate and pressing needs of America. I have been bred in the Democratic party; I love the Democratic party; but I love America a great deal more than I love the Democratic party; and when the Democratic party thinks that it is an end in itself, then I rise up and dissent. It is a means to an end, and its power depends, and ought to depend, upon its showing that it knows what America needs and is ready to give it what it needs. That is the reason I say to the independent voter you have got us in the palm of your hand. I do not happen to be one of your number, but I recognize your supremacy, because I read the election returns; and I have this ambition, my Democratic friends—I can avow it on Jackson day—I want to make every independent voter in this country a Democrat. It is a little cold and lonely out where he is, because, though he holds the balance of power, he is not the majority, and I want him to come in where it is warm. I want him to come in where there is a lot of good society, good companionship, where there are great emotions. That is what I miss in the Republican party; they do not seem to have any great emotions. They seem to think a lot of things, old things, but they do not seem to have any enthusiasm about anything.

There is one thing I have got a great enthusiasm about, I might almost say a reckless enthusiasm, and that is human liberty. The Governor has just now spoken about watchful waiting in Mexico. I want to say a word about Mexico, or not so much about Mexico as about our attitude towards Mexico. I hold it as a fundamental principle, and so do you, that every people has the right to determine its own form of government; and until this recent revolution in Mexico, until the end of the Diaz reign, eighty per cent. of the people of Mexico never had a "look in" in determining who should be their governors or what their government should be. Now, I am for the eighty per cent! It is none of my business, and it is none of your business, how long they take in determining it. It is none of my business, and it is none of yours, how they go about the business. The country is theirs. The Government is theirs. The liberty, if they can get it, and Godspeed them in getting it, is theirs. And so far as my influence goes while I am President nobody shall interfere with them.

That is what I mean by a great emotion, the great emotion of sympathy. Do you suppose that the American people are ever going to count a small amount of material benefit and advantage to people doing business in Mexico against the liberties and the permanent happiness of the Mexican people? Have not European nations taken as long as they wanted and spilt as much blood as they pleased in settling their affairs, and shall we deny that to Mexico because she is weak? No, I say! I am proud to belong to a strong nation that says, "This country which we could crush shall have just as much freedom in her own affairs as we have." If I am strong, I am ashamed to bully the weak. In proportion to my strength is my pride in withholding that strength from the oppression of another people. And I know when I speak these things, not merely from the generous response with which they have just met from you, but from my long-time knowledge of the American people, that that is the sentiment of this great people. With all due respect to editors of great newspapers, I have to say to them that I seldom take my opinion of the American people from their editorials. When some great dailies, not very far from where I am temporarily residing, thundered with rising scorn at watchful waiting, my confidence was not for a moment shaken. I knew what were the temper and principles of the American people. If I did not at least think I knew, I would emigrate, because I would not be satisfied to stay where I am. There may come a time when the American people will have to judge whether I know what I am talking about or not, but at least for two years more I am free to think that I do, with a great comfort in immunity in the time being.

I feel, my friends, in a very confident mood today. I feel confident that we do know the spirit of the American people, that we do know the program of betterment which it will be necessary for us to undertake, that we do have a very reasonable confidence in the support of the American people. I have been talking with business men recently about the present state of mind of American business. There is nothing the matter with American business except a state of mind. I understand that your chamber of commerce here in Indianapolis is working now upon the motto, "If you are going to buy it, buy it now." That is a perfectly safe maxim to act on. It is just as safe to buy it now as it ever will be, and if you start the buying there will be no end to it, and you will be a seller as well as a buyer. I am just as sure of that as I can be, because I have taken counsel with the men who know. I never was in business and, therefore, I have none of the prejudices of business. I have looked on and tried to see what the interests of the country were in business; I have taken counsel with men who did know, and their counsel is uniform, that all that is needed in America now is to believe in the future; and I can assure you as one of those who speak for the Democratic party that it is perfectly safe to believe in the future. We are so much the friends of business that we were for a little time the enemies of those who were trying to control business. I say "for a little time" because we are now reconciled to them. They have graciously admitted that we had a right to do what we did do, and they have very handsomely said that they were going to play the game.

I believe—I always have believed—that American business men were absolutely sound at heart, but men immersed in business do a lot of things that opportunity offers which in other circumstances they would not do; and I have thought all along that all that was necessary to do was to call their attention sharply to the kind of reforms in business which were needed and that they would acquiesce. Why, I believe they have heartily acquiesced. There is all the more reason, therefore, that, great and small, we should be confident in the future.

And what a future it is, my friends! Look abroad upon the troubled world! Only America at peace! Among all the great powers of the world only America saving her power for her own people! Only America using her great character and her great strength in the interests of peace and of prosperity! Do you not think it likely that the world will some time turn to America and say, "You were right and we were wrong. You kept your head when we lost ours. You tried to keep the scale from tipping, and we threw the whole weight of arms in one side of the scale.

Now, in your self-possession, in your coolness, in your strength, may we not turn to you for counsel and for assistance?" Think of the deep-wrought destruction of economic resources, of life, and of hope that is taking place in some parts of the world, and think of the reservoir of hope, the reservoir of energy, the reservoir of sustenance that there is in this great land of plenty! May we not look forward to the time when we shall be called blessed among the nations, because we succored the nations of the world in their time of distress and of dismay? I for one pray God that that solemn hour may come, and I know the solidity of character and I know the exaltation of hope, I know the big principle with which the American people will respond to the call of the world for this service. I thank God that those who believe in America, who try to serve her people, are likely to be also what America herself from the first hoped and meant to be—the servant of mankind.

Wilson Vetoes Immigration Bill Because of Literacy Test and Restriction of Political Asylum

The White House, January 28, 1915.

To the House of Representatives:

It is with unaffected regret that I find myself constrained by clear conviction to return this bill (H. R. 6060, "An act to regulate the immigation of aliens to and the residence of aliens in the United States") without my signature. Not only do I feel it to be a very serious matter to exercise the power of veto in any case, because it involves opposing the single judgment of the President to the judgment of a majority of both the Houses of the Congress, a step which no man who realizes his own liability to error can take without great hesitation, but also because this particular bill is in so many important respects admirable, well conceived, and desirable. Its enactment into law would undoubtedly enhance the efficiency and improve the methods of handling the important branch of the public service to which it relates. But candor and a sense of duty with regard to the responsibility so clearly imposed upon me by the Constitution in matters of legislation leave me no choice but to dissent.

In two particulars of vital consequence this bill embodies a radical departure from the traditional and long-established policy of this country, a policy in which our people have conceived the very character of their Government to be expressed, the very mission and spirit of the Nation in respect of its relations to the peoples of the world outside their borders. It seeks to all but close entirely the gates of asylum which have always been open to those who could find nowhere else the right and opportunity of constitutional agitation for what they conceived to be the natural and inalienable rights of men; and it excludes those to whom the opportunities of elementary education have been denied, without regard to their character, their purposes, or their natural capacity.

Restrictions like these, adopted earlier in our history as a Nation, would very materially have altered the course and cooled the humane ardors of our politics. The right of political asylum has brought to this country many a man of noble character and elevated purpose who was marked as an outlaw in his own less fortunate land, and who has yet become an ornament to our citizenship and to our public councils. The children and the compatriots of these illustrious Americans must stand amazed to see the representatives of their Nation now resolved, in the fullness of our national strength and at the maturity of our great institutions, to risk turning such men back from our shores without test of quality or purpose. It is difficult for me to believe that the full effect of this feature of the bill was realized when it was framed and adopted, and it is impossible for me to assent to it in the form in which it is here cast.

The literacy test and the tests and restrictions which accompany it constitute an even more radical change in the policy of the Nation. Hitherto we have generously kept our doors open to all who were not unfitted by reason of disease or incapacity for self-support or such personal records and antecedents as were likely to make them a menace to our peace and order or to the wholesome and essential relationships of life. In this bill it is proposed to turn away from tests of character and of quality and impose tests which exclude and restrict; for the new tests here embodied are not tests of quality or of character or of personal fitness, but tests of opportunity. Those who come seeking opportunity are not to be admitted unless they have already had one of the chief of the opportunities they seek, the opportunity of education. The object of such provisions is restriction, not selection.

If the people of this country have made up their minds to limit the number of immigrants by arbitrary tests and so reverse the policy of all the generations of Americans that have gone before them, it is their right to do so. I am their servant and have no license to stand in their way. But I do not believe that they have. I respectfully submit that no one can quote their mandate to that effect. Has any political party ever avowed a policy of restriction in this fundamental matter, gone to the country on it, and been commissioned to control its legislation? Does this bill rest upon the conscious and universal assent and desire of the American people? I doubt it. It is because I doubt it that I make bold to dissent from it. I am willing to abide by the verdict, but not until it has been rendered. Let the platforms of parties speak out upon this policy and the people pronounce their wish. The matter is too fundamental to be settled otherwise.

I have no pride of opinion in this question. I am not foolish enough to profess to know the wishes and ideals of America better than the body of her chosen representatives know them. I only want instruction direct from those whose fortunes, with ours and all men's, are involved.

WOODROW WILSON.

[Just two years later—on January 29, 1917—President Wilson again vetoed an Immigration bill carrying a literacy test. An additional reason then was that exempting those fleeing from religious persecution was likely to lead to international complications. But Congress immediately repassed the bill by large majorities, and the literacy test thus became a law, after having been vetoed by Presidents Cleveland, Taft, and Wilson.]

WILSON'S ADDRESS BEFORE THE AMERICAN ELECTRIC RAILWAY ASSOCIATION, WASHINGTON, JANUARY 29, 1915

[Referring to the beneficent influence the new Federal Trade Commission should exert on "big business"—the era of suspicion passed, the era of confidence entered.]

Mr. President, Ladies and Gentlemen:

It is a real pleasure to me to be here and to look this company in the face. I know how important the interests that you represent are. . . .

It seems to me that I can say with a good deal of confidence that we are upon the eve of a new era of enterprise and of prosperity. Enterprise has been checked in this country for almost twenty years, because men were moving amongst a maze of interrogation points. They did not know what was going to happen to them. All sorts of regulation were proposed, and it was a matter of uncertainty what sort of regulation was going to be adopted. All sorts of charges were made against business, as if business were at default, when most men knew that the great majority of business men were honest, were public-spirited, were intending the right thing, and the many were made afraid because the few did not do what was right.

The most necessary thing, therefore, was for us to agree, as we did by slow stages agree, upon the main particulars of what ought not to be done and then to put our laws in such shape as to correspond with that general judgment. That, I say, was a necessary preliminary not only to a common understanding, but also to a universal coöperation. The great forces of a country like this can not pull separately; they have got to pull together. And except upon a basis of common understanding as to the law and as to the proprieties of conduct, it is impossible to pull together. I, for one, have never doubted that all America was of one principle. I have never doubted that all America believed in doing what was fair and honorable and of good report. But the method, the method of control by law against the small minority that was recalcitrant against these principles, was a thing that it was difficult to determine upon; and it was a very great burden, let me say, to fall upon a particular administration of this Government to have to undertake practically the whole business of final definition. That is what has been attempted by the Congress now about to come to a close. It has attempted the definitions for which the country had been getting ready, or trying to get ready, for half a generation. It will require a period of test to determine whether they have successfully defined them or not; but no one needs to have it proved to him that it was necessary to define them and remove the uncertainties, and that, the uncertainties being removed, common understandings are possible and a universal coöperation.

You, gentlemen, representing these arteries of which I have spoken, that serve to release the forces of communities and serve, also, to bind community with community, are surely in a better position than the men perhaps of any other profession to understand how communities constitute units—how even a nation constitutes a unit; and that what is detrimental and hurtful to a part you, above all men, ought to know is detrimental to all. You can not demoralize some of the forces of a community without being in danger of demoralizing all the forces of a community. Your interest is not in the congestion of life, but in the release of life. Your interest is not in isolation, but in union, the union of parts of this great country, so that every energy in those parts will flow freely and with full force from county to county throughout the whole nation.

What I have come to speak of this afternoon is this unity of our interest, and I want to make some—I will not say "predictions," but to use a less dangerous though bigger word—prognostications. I understand that there is among the medical profession diagnosis and prognosis. I dare say the prognosis is more difficult than the diagnosis, since it has to come first; and not being a physician, I have all the greater courage in the prognosis. I have noticed all my life that I could speak with the greatest freedom about those things that I did not understand; but there are some things that a man is bound to try to think out whether he fully comprehends them or not. The thought of no single man can comprehend the life of a great Nation like this, and yet men in public life upon whom the burden of guidance is laid must attempt to comprehend as much of it as they can. Their strength will lie in common counsel; their strength will lie in taking counsel of as many informed persons as possible in each department with which they have to deal; but some time or other the point will come when they have to make a decision based upon a prognosis. We have had to do that in attempting the definitions of law which have been attempted by this Congress, and now it is necessary for us, in order to go forward with the confident spirit with which I believe we can go forward, to look ahead and see the things that are likely to happen.

In the first place, I feel that the mists and miasmic airs of suspicion that have filled the business world have now been blown away. I believe that we have passed the era of suspicion and have come into the era of confidence. Knowing the elements we have to deal with, we can deal with them; and with that confidence of knowledge we can have confidence of enterprise. That enterprise is going to mean this: Nobody is henceforth going to be afraid of or suspicious of any business merely because it is big. If my judgment is correct, nobody has been suspicious of any business merely because it was big; but they have been suspicious whenever they thought that the bigness was being used to take an unfair advantage. We all have to admit that it is easier for a big fellow to take advantage of you than for a little fellow to take advantage of you; therefore, we instinctively watch the big fellow with a little closer scrutiny than we watch the little fellow. But, bond having been given for the big fellow, we can sleep o'nights. Bond having been given that he will keep the peace, we do not have to spend our time and waste our energy watching him. The conditions of confidence being established, nobody need think that if he is taller than the rest anybody is going to throw a stone at him simply because he is a favorable target—always provided there is fair dealing and real service.

Because the characteristic of modern business, gentlemen, is this: The number of cases in which men do business on their own individual, private capital is relatively small in our day. Almost all the greater enterprises are done on what is, so far as the managers of that business are concerned, other people's money. That is what a joint-stock company means. It means, "Won't you lend us your resources to conduct this business and trust us, a little group of managers, to see that you get honest and proper returns for your money?" and no man who manages a joint-stock company can know for many days together, without fresh inquiry, who his partners are, because the stock is constantly changing hands, and the partners are seldom the same people for long periods together. Which amounts to saying that, inasmuch as you are using the money of everybody who chooses to come in, your responsibility is to everybody who has come in or who may come in. That is simply another way of saying that your business is, so far forth, a public business, and you owe it to the public to take them into your confidence in regard to the way in which it is conducted.

The era of private business in the sense of business conducted with the money of the partners—I mean of the managing partners—is practically passed, not only in this country, but almost everywhere. Therefore, almost all business has this direct responsibility to the public in general: We owe a constant report to the public, whose money we are constantly asking for in order to conduct the business itself. Therefore, we have got to trade not only on our efficiency, not only on the service that we render, but on the confidence that we cultivate. There is a new atmosphere for business. The oxygen that the lungs of modern business takes in is the oxygen of the public confidence, and if you have not got that, your business is essentially paralyzed and asphyxiated.

I take it that we are in a position now to come to a common understanding, knowing that only a common understanding will be the stable basis of business, and that what we want for business hereafter is the same kind of liberty that we want for the individual. The liberty of the individual is limited with the greatest sharpness where his actions come into collision with the interests of the community he lives in. My liberty consists in a sort of parole. Society says to me, "You may do what you please until you do something that is in violation of the common understanding, of the public interest; then your parole is forfeited. We will take you into custody. We will limit your activities. We will penalize you if you use this thing that you call your liberty against our interest." Business does not want, and ought not to ask for, more liberty than the individual has; and I have always in my own thought summed up individual liberty, and business liberty, and every other kind of liberty, in the phrase that is common in the sporting world, "A free field and no favor."

There have been times—I will not specify them, but there have been times—when the field looked free, but when there were favors received from the managers of the course; when there were advantages given; inside tracks accorded; practices which would block the other runners; rules which would exclude the amateur who wanted to get in. That may be a free field, but there is favor, there is partiality, there is preference, there is covert advantage taken of somebody, and while it looks very well from the grandstand, there are men whom you can find who were not allowed to get in to the track and test their powers against the other men who were racing for the honors of the day.

I think it is a serviceable figure. It means this: That you are not going to be barred from the contest because you are big and strong, and you are not going to be penalized because you are big and strong, but you are going to be made to observe the rules of the track and not get in anybody's way except as you can keep ahead of him by having more vigor and skill than he has. When we get that understanding, that we are all sports, and that we are not going to ask for, not only, but we are not going to condescend to take, advantage of anything that does not belong to us, then the atmosphere will clear so that it will seem as if the sun had never shone as it does that day. It is the spirit of true sportsmanship that ought to get into everything, and men who, when they get beaten that way, squeal do not deserve our pity. . . .

VILSON'S ADDRESS BEFORE THE UNITED STATES CHAMBER OF COMMERCE, WASHINGTON, FEBRUARY 3, 1915

[The war in Europe, then ending its sixth month, had already egun to increase enormously the foreign trade of the United tates. It had also, however, brought limitations of markets. The 'resident here began to urge that American business should proprly seek new foreign fields.]

Ir. President, Ladies and Gentlemen:

I feel that it is hardly fair to you for me to come in in his casual fashion among a body of men who have been eriously discussing great questions, and it is hardly fair o me, because I come in cold, not having had the advanage of sharing the atmosphere of your deliberations and atching the feeling of your conference. Moreover, I hardly now just how to express my interest in the things you are ndertaking. . . .

I have asked myself before I came here today, what relaion you could bear to the Government of the United States nd what relation the Government could bear to you?

There are two aspects and activities of the Government vith which you will naturally come into most direct conact. The first is the Government's power of inquiry, sysematic and disinterested inquiry, and its power of scienific assistance. You get an illustration of the latter, for xample, in the Department of Agriculture. Has it ocurred to you, I wonder, that we are just upon the eve of time when our Department of Agriculture will be of nfinite importance to the whole world? There is a shortge of food in the world now. That shortage will be much nore serious a few months from now than it is now. It is ecessary that we should plant a great deal more; it is ecessary that our lands should yield more per acre than hey do now; it is necessary that there should not be a plow r a spade idle in this country if the world is to be fed. And the methods of our farmers must feed upon the scienific information to be derived from the State departments of agriculture, and from that taproot of all, the Unite States Department of Agriculture. The object and use o that department is to inform men of the latest development and disclosures of science with regard to all the processes b which soils can be put to their proper use and their fertilit made the greatest possible. Similarly with the Bureau o Standards. It is ready to supply those things by which yo can set norms, you can set bases, for all the scientific pro cesses of business.

I have a great admiration for the scientific parts of th Government of the United States, and it has amazed m that so few men have discovered them. Here in these de partments are quiet men, trained to the highest degree o skill, serving for a petty remuneration along lines that ar infinitely useful to mankind; and yet in some cases the waited to be discovered until this Chamber of Commerc of the United States was established. Coming to this city officers of that association found that there were here thing that were infinitely useful to them and with which th whole United States ought to be put into communication.

The Government of the United States is very properl a great instrumentality of inquiry and information. On thing we are just beginning to do that we ought to hav done long ago: We ought long ago to have had our Burea of Foreign and Domestic Commerce. We ought long ag to have sent the best eyes of the Government out into th world to see where the opportunities and openings of Ameri can commerce and American genius were to be found— men who were not sent out as the commercial agents of an particular set of business men in the United States, but wh were eyes for the whole business community. . . .

We are just beginning to do, systematically and scien tifically, what we ought long ago to have done, to emplo the Government of the United States to survey the worl in order that American commerce might be guided.

But there are other ways of using the Government of th

United States, ways that have long been tried, though not always with conspicuous success or fortunate results. You can use the Government of the United States by influencing its legislation. That has been a very active industry, but it has not always been managed in the interest of the whole people. It is very instructive and useful for the Government of the United States to have such means as you are ready to supply for getting a sort of consensus of opinion which proceeds from no particular quarter and originates with no particular interest. Information is the very foundation of all right action in legislation. . . .

If we on the outside cannot understand the thing and cannot get advice from the inside, then we will have to do it with the flat hand and not with the touch of skill and discrimination. Isn't that true? Men on the inside of business know how business is conducted and they cannot complain if men on the outside make mistakes about business if they do not come from the inside and give the kind of advice which is necessary.

The trouble has been that when they came in the past—for I think the thing is changing very rapidly—they came with all their bristles out; they came on the defensive; they came to see, not what they could accomplish, but what they could prevent. They did not come to guide; they came to block. That is of no use whatever to the general body politic. What has got to pervade us like a great motive power is that we cannot, and must not, separate our interests from one another, but must pool our interests. A man who is trying to fight for his single hand is fighting against the community and not fighting with it. There are a great many dreadful things about war, as nobody needs to be told in this day of distress and of terror, but there is one thing about war which has a very splendid side, and that is the consciousness that a whole nation gets that they must all act as a unit for a common end. And when peace is as handsome as war there will be no war. When men,

I mean, engage in the pursuits of peace in the same spirit of self-sacrifice and of conscious service of the community with which, at any rate, the common soldier engages in war, then shall there be wars no more. You have moved the vanguard for the United States in the purposes of this association just a little nearer that ideal. That is the reason I am here, because I believe it.

There is a specific matter about which I, for one, want your advice. Let me say, if I may say it without disrespect, that I do not think you are prepared to give it right away. You will have to make some rather extended inquiries before you are ready to give it. What I am thinking of is competition in foreign markets as between the merchants of different nations.

I speak of the subject with a certain degree of hesitation, because the thing farthest from my thought is taking advantage of nations now disabled from playing their full part in that competition, and seeking a sudden selfish advantage because they are for the time being disabled. Pray believe me that we ought to eliminate all that thought from our minds and consider this matter as if we and the other nations now at war were in the normal circumstances of commerce.

There is a normal circumstance of commerce in which we are apparently at a disadvantage. Our anti-trust laws are thought by some to make it illegal for merchants in the United States to form combinations for the purpose of strengthening themselves in taking advantage of the opportunities of foreign trade. That is a very serious matter for this reason: There are some corporations, and some firms for all I know, whose business is great enough and whose resources are abundant enough to enable them to establish selling agencies in foreign countries; to enable them to extend the long credits which in some cases are necessary in order to keep the trade they desire; to enable them, in other words, to organize their business in foreign territory in a way which the smaller man cannot afford to do. His business has not grown big enough to permit him to establish selling agencies. The export commission merchant, perhaps, taxes him a little too highly to make that an available competitive means of conducting and extending his business.

The question arises, therefore, how are the smaller merchants, how are the younger and weaker corporations going to get a foothold as against the combinations which are permitted and even encouraged by foreign governments in this field of competition? There are governments which, as you know, distinctly encourage the formation of great combinations in each particular field of commerce in order to maintain selling agencies and to extend long credits, and to use and maintain the machinery which is necessary for the extension of business; and American merchants feel that they are at a very considerable disadvantage in contending against that. The matter has been many times brought to my attention, and I have each time suspended judgment. I want to be shown this: I want to be shown how such a combination can be made and conducted in a way which will not close it against the use of everybody who wants to use it. A combination has a tendency to exclude new members. When a group of men get control of a good thing, they do not see any particular point in letting other people into the good thing. What I would like very much to be shown, therefore, is a method of coöperation which is not a method of combination. Not that the two words are mutually exclusive, but we have come to have a special meaning attached to the word "combination." Most of our combinations have a safety lock, and you have to know the combination to get in. I want to know how these coöperative methods can be adopted for the benefit of everybody who wants to use them, and I say frankly if I can be shown that, I am for them. If I can not be shown that, I am against them. I hasten to add that I hopefully expect I *can* be shown that.

You, as I have just now intimated, probably can not show it to me offhand, but by the methods which you have the means of using you certainly ought to be able to throw a vast deal of light on the subject. . . .

WILSON'S ADDRESS AT A MEETING OF THE ASSOCIATED PRESS, NEW YORK, APRIL 20, 1915

[In which he pleads for "America First."]

Mr. President, Gentlemen of the Associated Press, Ladies and Gentlemen: I am deeply gratified by the generous reception you have accorded me. It makes me look back with a touch of regret to former occasions when I have stood in this place and enjoyed a greater liberty than is granted me to-day. There have been times when I stood in this spot and said what I really thought, and I can not help praying that those days of indulgence may be accorded me again. I have come here to-day, of course, somewhat restrained by a sense of responsibility which I cannot escape. For I take the Associated Press very seriously. I know the enormous part that you play in the affairs not only of this country but of the world. You deal in the raw material of opinion and, if my convictions have any validity, opinion ultimately governs the world.

It is, therefore, of very serious things that I think as I face this body of men. I do not think of you, however, as members of the Associated Press. I do not think of you as men of different parties or of different racial derivations or of different religious denominations. I want to talk to you as to my fellow citizens of the United States, for there are serious things which as fellow citizens we ought to consider. The times behind us, gentlemen, have been difficult enough; the times before us are likely to be more difficult still, because, whatever may be said about the present condition of the world's affairs, it is clear that they are drawing rapidly to a climax, and at the climax the test will come, not only for the nations engaged in the present colossal struggle—it will come to them, of course—but the test will come for us particularly.

Do you realize that, roughly speaking, we are the only great Nation at present disengaged? I am not speaking, of course, with disparagement of the greatness of those nations in Europe which are not parties to the present war, but I am thinking of their close neighborhood to it. I am thinking how their lives much more than ours touch the very heart and stuff of the business, whereas we have rolling between us and those bitter days across the water 3,000 miles of cool and silent ocean. Our atmosphere is not yet charged with those disturbing elements which must permeate every nation of Europe. Therefore, is it not likely that the nations of the world will some day turn to us for the cooler assessment of the elements engaged? I am not now thinking so preposterous a thought as that we should sit in judgment upon them—no nation is fit to sit in judgment upon any other nation—but that we shall some day have to assist in reconstructing the processes of peace. Our resources are untouched; we are more and more becoming by the force of circumstances the mediating Nation of the world in respect of its finance. We must make up our minds what are the best things to do and what are the best ways to do them. We must put our money, our energy, our enthusiasm, our sympathy into these things, and we must have our judgments prepared and our spirits chastened against the coming of that day.

So that I am not speaking in a selfish spirit when I say that our whole duty, for the present at any rate, is summed up in this motto, "America first." Let us think of America before we think of Europe, in order that America may be fit to be Europe's friend when the day of tested friendship comes. The test of friendship is not now sympathy with the one side or the other, but getting ready to help both sides when the struggle is over. The basis of neutrality, gentlemen, is not indifference; it is not self-interest. The basis of neutrality is sympathy for mankind. It is fairness, it is good will, at bottom. It is impartiality of spirit and of judgment. I wish that all of our fellow citizens could realize that. There is in some quarters a disposition to create distempers in this body politic. Men are even uttering slanders against the United States, as if to excite her. Men are saying that if we should go to war upon either side there would be a divided America—an abominable libel of ignorance! America is not all of it vocal just now. It is vocal in spots, but I, for one, have a complete and abiding faith in that great silent body of Americans who are not standing up and shouting and expressing their opinions just now, but are waiting to find out and support the duty of America. I am just as sure of their solidity and of their loyalty and of their unanimity, if we act justly, as I am that the history of this country has at every crisis and turning point illustrated this great lesson.

We are the mediating Nation of the world. I do not mean that we undertake not to mind our own business and to mediate where other people are quarreling. I mean the word in a broader sense. We are compounded of the nations of the world; we mediate their blood, we mediate their traditions, we mediate their sentiments, their tastes, their passions; we are ourselves compounded of those things. We are, therefore, able to understand all nations; we are able to understand them in the compound, not separately, as partisans, but unitedly as knowing and comprehending and embodying them all. It is in that sense that I mean that America is a mediating Nation. The opinion of America, the action of America, is ready to turn, and free to turn, in any direction. Did you ever reflect upon how almost every other nation has through long centuries been headed in one direction? That is not true of the United States. The United States has no racial momentum. It has no history back of it which makes it run all its energies and all its ambitions in one particular direction. And America is particularly free in this, that she has no hampering ambitions as a world power. We do not want a foot of anybody's territory. If we have been obliged by circumstances, or have considered ourselves to be obliged by circumstances, in the past, to take territory which we otherwise would not have thought of taking, I believe I am right in saying that we have considered it our duty to administer that territory, not for ourselves but for the people living in it, and to put this burden upon our consciences—not to think that this thing is ours for our use, but to regard ourselves as trustees of the great business for those to whom it does really belong, trustees ready to hand it over to the cestui que trust at any time when the business seems to make that possible and feasible. That is what I mean by saying we have no hampering ambitions. We do not want anything that does not belong to us. Is not a nation in that position free to serve other nations, and is not a nation like that ready to form some part of the assessing opinion of the world?

My interest in the neutrality of the United States is not the petty desire to keep out of trouble. To judge by my experience, I have never been able to keep out of trouble. I have never looked for it, but I have always found it. I do not want to walk around trouble. If any man wants a scrap that is an interesting scrap and worth while, I am his man. I warn him that he is not going to draw me into the scrap for his advertisement, but if he is looking for trouble that is the trouble of men in general and I can help a little, why, then, I am in for it. But I am interested in neutrality because there is something sc much greater to do than fight; there is a distinction wait-ing for this Nation that no nation has ever yet got. Tha is the distinction of absolute self-control and self-mastery Whom do you admire most among your friends? The irri-table man? The man out of whom you can get a "rise" without trying? The man who will fight at the drop o the hat, whether he knows what the hat is dropped fo or not? Don't you admire and don't you fear, if yo have to contest with him, the self-mastered man wh watches you with calm eye and comes in only when yo have carried the thing so far that you must be disposed of That is the man you respect. That is the man who, yo know, has at bottom a much more fundamental and ter-rible courage than the irritable, fighting man. Now, covet for America this splendid courage of reserve mora force, and I wanted to point out to you gentlemen simpl this:

There is news and news. There is what is called new from Turtle Bay that turns out to be falsehood, at an rate in what it is said to signify, but which, if you coul get the Nation to believe it true, might disturb our equi-librium and our self-possession. We ought not to deal i stuff of that kind. We ought not to permit that sort o thing to use up the electrical energy of the wires, becaus its energy is malign, its energy is not of the truth, it energy is of mischief. It is possible to sift truth. I hav known some things to go out on the wires as true whe there was only one man or one group of men who could hav told the originators of that report whether it was true o not, and they were not asked whether it was true or not fo fear it might not be true. That sort of report ought nc to go out over the wires. There is generally, if not alway somebody who knows whether the thing is so or not, an in these days, above all other days, we ought to take pa ticular pains to resort to the one small group of men, c to the one man if there be but one, who knows whether those things are true or not. The world ought to know the truth; the world ought not at this period of unstable equilibrium to be disturbed by rumor, ought not to be disturbed by imaginative combinations of circumstances, or, rather, by circumstances stated in combination which do not belong in combination. You gentlemen, and gentlemen engaged like you, are holding the balances in your hand. This unstable equilibrium rests upon scales that are in your hands. For the food of opinion, as I began by saying, is the news of the day. I have known many a man to go off at a tangent on information that was not reliable. Indeed, that describes the majority of men. The world is held stable by the man who waits for the next day to find out whether the report was true or not.

We cannot afford, therefore, to let the rumors of irresponsible persons and origins get into the atmosphere of the United States. We are trustees for what I venture to say is the greatest heritage that any nation ever had, the love of justice and righteousness and human liberty. For, fundamentally, those are the things to which America is addicted and to which she is devoted. There are groups of selfish men in the United States, there are coteries, where sinister things are purposed, but the great heart of the American people is just as sound and true as it ever was. And it is a single heart; it is the heart of America. It is not a heart made up of sections selected out of other countries.

What I try to remind myself of every day when I am almost overcome by perplexities, what I try to remember, is what the people at home are thinking about. I try to put myself in the place of the man who does not know all the things that I know and ask myself what he would like the policy of this country to be. Not the talkative man, not the partisan man, not the man who remembers first that he is a Republican or a Democrat, or that his parents were

German or English, but the man who remembers first that the whole destiny of modern affairs centers largely upon his being an American first of all. If I permitted myself to be a partisan in this present struggle, I would be unworthy to represent you. If I permitted myself to forget the people who are not partisans, I would be unworthy to be your spokesman. I am not sure that I am worthy to represent you, but I do claim this degree of worthiness—that before everything else I love America.

Wilson's Address to Several Thousand Foreign-Born Citizens, After Naturalization Ceremonies, at Philadelphia, May 10, 1915

[Three days earlier the *Lusitania* had been sunk by a German submarine; and three days later a note was dispatched to Berlin demanding disavowal. But in his speech the President made no specific reference to the crisis—although his declaration that a man may be "too proud to fight," and a nation so right that it does not need to use force, was widely understood to have a direct bearing on the submarine controversy. This address and one similar in scope, which will be found on page 290, were occasioned by an aroused interest on the part of aliens in American citizenship because of controversies with belligerent European governments over neutral rights.]

Mr. Mayor, Fellow-Citizens:

It warms my heart that you should give me such a reception; but it is not of myself that I wish to think tonight, but of those who have just become citizens of the United States.

This is the only country in the world which experiences this constant and repeated rebirth. Other countries depend upon the multiplication of their own native people. This country is constantly drinking strength out of new sources by the voluntary association with it of great bodies of strong men and forward-looking women out of other lands. And so by the gift of the free will of independent people

you brought some of it with you. A man does not go out to seek the thing that is not in him. A man does not hope for the thing that he does not believe in, and if some of us have forgotten what America believed in, you, at any rate, imported in your own hearts a renewal of the belief. That is the reason that I, for one, make you welcome. If I have in any degree forgotten what America was intended for, I will thank God if you will remind me. I was born in America. You dreamed dreams of what America was to be, and I hope you brought the dreams with you. No man that does not see visions will ever realize any high hope or undertake any high enterprise. Just because you brought dreams with you, America is more likely to realize dreams such as you brought. You are enriching us if you come expecting us to be better than we are.

See, my friends, what that means. It means that Americans must have a consciousness different from the consciousness of every other nation in the world. I am not saying this with even the slightest thought of criticism of other nations. You know how it is with a family. A family gets centered on itself if it is not careful and is less interested in the neighbors than it is in its own members. So a nation that is not constantly renewed out of new sources is apt to have the narrowness and prejuice of a family; whereas, America must have this consciousness, that on all sides it touches elbows and touches hearts with all the nations of mankind. The example of America must be a special example. The example of America must be the example not merely of peace because it will not fight, but of peace because peace is the healing and elevating influence of the world and strife is not. There is such a thing as a man being too proud to fight. There is such a thing as a nation being so right that it does not need to convince others by force that it is right.

You have come into this great Nation voluntarily seeking something that we have to give, and all that we have to give is this: We cannot exempt you from work. No man is exempt from work anywhere in the world. We cannot exempt you from the strife and the heartbreaking burden of the struggle of the day—that is common to mankind everywhere; we cannot exempt you from the loads that you must carry. We can only make them light by the spirit in which they are carried. That is the spirit of hope, it is the spirit of liberty, it is the spirit of justice.

When I was asked, therefore, by the Mayor and the committee that accompanied him to come up from Washington to meet this great company of newly admitted citizens, I could not decline the invitation. I ought not to be away from Washington, and yet I feel that it has renewed my spirit as an American to be here. In Washington men tell you so many things every day that are not so, and I like to come and stand in the presence of a great body of my fellow-citizens, whether they have been my fellow-citizens a long time or a short time, and drink, as it were, out of the common fountains with them and go back feeling what you have so generously given me—the sense of your support and of the living vitality in your hearts of the great ideals which have made America the hope of the world.

President Wilson's Address at the Pan-American Financial Conference, Washington, May 24, 1915

[The development of trade between North and South America—both as a temporary substitute for the uncertain markets of warring Europe and as a permanent asset—had been widely urged. Many and serious were the technical difficulties cited by those in a position to know. To eliminate some of these, and to obtain mutual knowledge of commercial and financial methods, the Secretary of the Treasury (W. G. McAdoo) called a conference of Pan-American bankers and business men. Delegates came from eighteen of the American republics.]

Mr. Chairman, Gentlemen of the American Republics, Ladies and Gentlemen:

The part that falls to me this morning is a very simple one, but a very delightful one. It is to bid you a very hearty welcome indeed to this conference. The welcome is the more hearty because we are convinced that a conference like this will result in the things that we most desire. I am sure that those who have this conference in charge have already made plain to you its purpose and its spirit. Its purpose is to draw the American Republics together by bonds of common interest and of mutual understanding; and we comprehend, I hope, just what the meaning of that is. There can be no sort of union of interest if there is a purpose of exploitation by any one of the parties to a great conference of this sort. The basis of successful commercial intercourse is common interest, not selfish interest. It is an actual interchange of services and of values: it is based upon reciprocal relations and not selfish relations. It is based upon those things upon which all successful economic intercourse must be based, because selfishness breeds suspicion; suspicion, hostility; and hostility, failure. We are not, therefore, trying to make use of each other, but we are trying to be of use to one another.

It is very surprising to me, it is even a source of mortification, that a conference like this should have been so long delayed, that it should never have occurred before, that it should have required a crisis of the world to show the Americas how truly they were neighbors to one another. If there is any one happy circumstance, gentlemen, arising out of the present distressing condition of the world, it is that it has revealed us to one another: it has shown us what it means to be neighbors. And I cannot help harboring the hope, the very high hope, that by this commerce of minds with one another, as well as commerce in goods, we may show the world in part the path to peace. It would be a very great thing if the Americas could add to the distinction which they already wear this of showing the way to peace, to permanent peace.

The way to peace for us, at any rate, is manifest. It is the kind of rivalry which does not involve aggression. It is the knowledge that men can be of the greatest service to one another, and nations of the greatest service to one another, when the jealousy between them is merely a jealousy of excellence, and when the basis of their intercourse is friendship. There is only one way in which we wish to take advantage of you and that is by making better goods, by doing the things that we seek to do for each other better, if we can, than you do them, and so spurring you on, if we might, by so handsome a jealousy as that to excel us. I am so keenly aware that the basis of personal friendship is this competition in excellence, that I am perfectly certain that this is the only basis for the friendship of nations—this handsome rivalry, this rivalry in which there is no dislike, this rivalry in which there is nothing but the hope of a common elevation in great enterprises which we can undertake in common.

There is one thing that stands in our way among others—for you are more conversant with the circumstances than I am; the thing I have chiefly in mind is the physical lack of means of communication, the lack of vehicles—the lack of ships, the lack of established routes of trade—the lack of those things which are absolutely necessary if we are to have true commercial and intimate commercial relations with one another; and I am perfectly clear in my judgment that if private capital cannot soon enter upon the adventure of establishing these physical means of communication, the government must undertake to do so. We cannot indefinitely stand apart and need each other for the lack of what can easily be supplied, and if one instrumentality cannot supply it, then another must be found which will supply it. We cannot know each other unless we see each other; we cannot deal with each other unless we communicate with each other. So soon as we communicate and are upon a familiar footing of intercourse, we shall understand one another, and the bonds between the Americas will be such bonds that no influence that the world may produce in the future will ever break them.

If I am selfish for America, I at least hope that my selfishness is enlightened. The selfishness that hurts the other party is not enlightened selfishness. If I were acting upon a mere ground of selfishness, I would seek to benefit the other party and so tie him to myself; so that even if you were to suspect me of selfishness, I hope you will also suspect me of intelligence and of knowing the only safe way for the establishment of the things which we covet, as well as the establishment of the things which we desire and which we would feel honored if we could earn and win.

I have said these things because they will perhaps enable you to understand how far from formal my welcome to this body is. It is a welcome from the heart, it is a welcome from the head; it is a welcome inspired by what I hope are the highest ambitions of those who live in these two great continents, who seek to set an example to the world in freedom of institutions, freedom of trade, and intelligence of mutual service.

President Wilson's Address to the Daughters of the American Revolution, Washington, October 11, 1915

(On the Spirit of America)

Madam President and Ladies and Gentlemen:

There is a very great thrill to be had from the memories of the American Revolution, but the American Revolution was a beginning, not a consummation, and the duty laid upon us by that beginning is the duty of bringing the things then begun to a noble triumph of completion. For it seems to me that the peculiarity of patriotism in America is that it is not a mere sentiment. It is an active principle of conduct. It is something that was born into the world, not to please it, but to regenerate it. It is something that was born into the world to replace systems that had preceded it and to bring men out upon a new plane of privilege. The glory of the men whose memories you honor and perpetuate is that they saw this vision, and it was a vision of the future. It was a vision of great days to come when a little handful of three million people upon the borders of a single sea should have become a great multitude of free men and women spreading across a great continent, dominating the shores of two oceans, and sending West as well as East the influences of individual freedom. . . .

The American Revolution was the birth of a nation; it was the creation of a great free republic based upon traditions of personal liberty which theretofore had been confined to a single little island, but which it was purposed should spread to all mankind. And the singular fascination of American history is that it has been a process of constant re-creation, of making over again in each generation the thing which was conceived at first. You know how peculiarly necessary that has been in our case, because America has not grown by the mere multiplication of the original stock. It is easy to preserve tradition with continuity of blood; it is easy in a single family to remember the origins of the race and the purposes of its organization; but it is not so easy when that race is constantly being renewed and augmented from other sources, from stocks that did not carry or originate the same principles.

So from generation to generation strangers have had to be indoctrinated with the principles of the American family, and the wonder and the beauty of it all has been that the infection has been so generously easy. For the principles of liberty are united with the principles of hope. Every individual, as well as every Nation, wishes to realize the best thing that is in him, the best thing that can be conceived out of the materials of which his spirit is constructed. It has happened in a way that fascinates the imagination that we have not only been augmented by additions from outside, but that we have been greatly stimulated by those additions. Living in the easy prosperity of a free people, knowing that the sun had always been free to shine upon us and prosper our undertakings, we did not realize how hard the task of liberty is and how rare the privilege of liberty is; but men were drawn out of every climate and out of every race because of an irresistible attraction of their spirits to the American ideal. They thought of America as lifting, like that great statue in the harbor of New York, a torch to light the pathway of men to the things that they desire, and men of all sorts and conditions struggled toward that light and came to our shores with an eager desire to realize it, and a hunger for it such as some of us no longer felt, for we were as if satiated and satisfied and were indulging ourselves after a fashion that did not belong to the ascetic devotion of the early devotees of those great principles. Strangers came to remind us of what we had promised ourselves and through ourselves had promised mankind. . . .

Now we have come to a time of special stress and test. There never was a time when we needed more clearly to conserve the principles of our own patriotism than this present time. The rest of the world from which our politics were drawn seems for the time in the crucible and no man can predict what will come out of that crucible. We stand apart, unembroiled, conscious of our own principles, conscious of what we hope and purpose, so far as our powers permit, for the world at large, and it is necessary that we should consolidate the American principle. Every political action, every social action, should have for its object in America at this time to challenge the spirit of America; to ask that every man and woman who thinks first of America should rally to the standards of our life. There have been some among us who have not thought first of America, who have thought to use the might of America in some matter not of America's origination. They have forgotten that the first duty of a nation is to express its own individual principles in the action of the family of nations and not to seek to aid and abet any rival or contrary ideal.

Neutrality is a negative word. It is a word that does not express what America ought to feel. America has a heart and that heart throbs with all sorts of intense sympathies, but America has schooled its heart to love the things that America believes in and it ought to devote itself only to the things that America believes in; and, believing that America stands apart in its ideals, it ought not to allow itself to be drawn, so far as its heart is concerned, into anybody's quarrel. Not because it does not understand the quarrel, not because it does not in its head assess the merits of the controversy, but because America had promised the world to stand apart and maintain certain principles of action which are grounded in law and in justice. We are not trying to keep out of trouble; we are trying to preserve the foundations upon which peace can be rebuilt. Peace can be rebuilt only upon the ancient and accepted principles of international law, only upon those things which remind nations of their duties to each other, and, deeper than that, of their duties to mankind and to humanity.

America has a great cause which is not confined to the American continent. It is the cause of humanity itself. I do not mean in anything that I say even to imply a judgment upon any nation or upon any policy, for my object here this afternoon is not to sit in judgment upon anybody but ourselves and to challenge you to assist all of us who are trying to make America more than ever conscious of her own principles and her own duty. I looked forward to the necessity in every political agitation in the years which are immediately at hand of calling upon every man to declare himself, where he stands. Is it America first or is it not?

We ought to be very careful about some of the impressions that we are forming just now. There is too general an impression, I fear, that very large numbers of our fellow-citizens born in other lands have not entertained with sufficient intensity and affection the American ideal. But the number of such is, I am sure, not large. Those who would seek to represent them are very vocal, but they are not very influential. Some of the best stuff of America has come out of foreign lands, and some of the best stuff in America is in the men who are naturalized citizens of the United States. I would not be afraid upon the test of "America first" to take a census of all the foreign-born citizens of the United States, for I know that the vast majority of them came here because they believed in America; and their belief in America has made them better citizens than some people who were born in America. They can say that they have bought this privilege with a great price. They have left their homes, they have left their kindred, they have broken all the nearest and dearest ties of human life in order to come to a new land, take a new rootage, begin a new life, and so by self-sacrifice express their confidence in a new principle; whereas, it cost us none of these things. We were born into this privilege; we were rocked and cradled in it; we did nothing to create it; and it is, therefore, the greater duty on our part to do a great deal to enhance it and preserve it. I am not deceived as to the balance of opinion among the foreign-born citizens of the United States, but I am in a hurry for an opportunity to have a line-up and let the men who are thinking first of other countries stand on one side and all those that are for America first, last, and all the time on the other side. . . .

President Wilson Outlines the Administration's Program of Preparedness for National Defense

(Address at the Manhattan Club, New York City, November 4, 1915)

[Editorial Note: *The submarine controversy with Germany—for diplomatic notes* *see pages beginning with 155**—had long before this passed through several acute phases; and the President had frankly altered his views regarding an immediate and radical strengthening of the nation's means for defense. He had called upon Secretary Garrison, of the War Department, and Secretary Daniels, of the Navy, to prepare plans for submission to Congress. A month before the session began, when he was to make formal recommendations, the President made public the Administration's program, in the following address:*]

Mr. Toastmaster and Gentlemen:

I shall assume that here around the dinner table on this memorable occasion our talk should properly turn to the wide and common interests which are most in our thoughts, whether they be the interests of the community or of the nation.

A year and a half ago our thought would have been almost altogether of great domestic questions. They are many and of vital consequence. We must and shall address ourselves to their solution with diligence, firmness, and self-possession, notwithstanding we find ourselves in the midst of a world disturbed by great disaster and ablaze with terrible war; but our thought is now inevitably of new things about which formerly we gave ourselves little concern. We are thinking now chiefly of our relations with the rest of the world—not our commercial relations—about those we have thought and planned always—but about our political relations, our duties as an individual and independent force in the world to ourselves, our neighbors, and the world itself.

Our principles are well known. It is not necessary to avow them again. We believe in political liberty and founded our great government to obtain it, the liberty of men and of peoples—of men to choose their own lives and of peoples to choose their own allegiance. Our ambition, also, all the world has knowledge of. It is not only to be free and prosperous ourselves, but also to be the friend and thoughtful partisan of those who are free or who desire freedom the world over. If we have had aggressive purposes and covetous ambitions, they were the fruit of our thoughtless youth as a nation and we have put them aside. We shall, I confidently believe, never again take another foot of territory by conquest. We shall never in any circumstances seek to make an independent people subject to our dominion; because we believe, we passionately believe, in the right of every people to choose their own allegiance and be free of masters altogether. For ourselves we wish nothing but the full liberty of self-development; and with ourselves in this great matter we associate all the peoples of our own hemisphere. We wish not only for the United States but for them the fullest freedom of independent growth and of action, for we know that throughout this hemisphere the same aspirations are everywhere being worked out, under diverse conditions but with the same impulse and ultimate object.

All this is very clear to us and will, I confidently predict, become more and more clear to the whole world as the great processes of the future unfold themselves. It is with a full consciousness of such principles and such ambitions that we are asking ourselves at the present time what our duty is with regard to the armed force of the Nation. Within a year we have witnessed what we did not believe possible, a great European conflict involving many of the greatest nations of the world. The influences of a great war are everywhere in the air. All Europe is embattled. Force everywhere speaks out with a loud and imperious voice in a titanic struggle of governments, and from one end of our own dear country to the other men are asking one another what our own force is, how far we are prepared to maintain ourselves against any interference with our national action or development.

In no man's mind, I am sure, is there even raised the question of the wilful use of force on our part against any nation or any people. No matter what military or naval force the United States might develop, statesmen throughout the whole world might rest assured that we were gathering that force, not for attack in any quarter, not for aggression of any kind, not for the satisfaction of any political or international ambition, but merely to make sure of our own security. We have it in mind to be prepared, not for war, but only for defense; and with the thought constantly in our minds that the principles we hold most dear can be achieved by the slow processes of history only in the kindly and wholesome atmosphere of peace, and not by the use of hostile force. The mission of America in the world is essentially a mission of peace and good will among men. She has become the home and asylum of men of all creeds and races. Within her hospitable borders they have found homes and congenial associations and freedom and a wide and cordial welcome, and they have become part of the bone and sinew and spirit of America itself. America has been made up out of the nations of the world and is the friend of the nations of the world.

But we feel justified in preparing ourselves to vindicate our right to independent and unmolested action by making the force that is in us ready for assertion.

And we know that we can do this in a way that will be itself an illustration of the American spirit. In accordance with our American traditions we want and shall work for only an army adequate to the constant and legitimate uses of times of international peace. But we do want to feel that there is a great body of citizens who have received at least the most rudimentary and necessary forms of military training; that they will be ready to form themselves into a fighting force at the call of the nation; and that the nation has the munitions and supplies with which to equip them without delay should it be necessary to call them into action. We wish to supply them with the training they need, and we think we can do so without calling them at any time too long away from their civilian pursuits.

It is with this idea, with this conception, in mind that the plans have been made which it will be my privilege to lay before the Congress at its next session. That plan calls for only such an increase in the regular Army of the United States as experience has proved to be required for the performance of the necessary duties of the Army in the Philippines, in Hawaii, in Porto Rico, upon the borders of the United States, at the coast fortifications, and at the military posts of the interior. For the rest, it calls for the training within the next three years of a force of 400,000 citizen soldiers to be raised in annual contingents of 133,-000, who would be asked to enlist for three years with the colors and three years on furlough, but who during their three years of enlistment with the colors would not be organized as a standing force but would be expected merely to undergo intensive training for a very brief period of each year. Their training would take place in immediate association with the organized units of the regular Army. It would have no touch of the amateur about it, neither would it exact of the volunteers more than they could give in any one year from their civilian pursuits.

And none of this would be done in such a way as in the slightest degree to supersede or subordinate our present serviceable and efficient National Guard. On the contrary, the National Guard itself would be used as part of the instrumentality by which training would be given the citizens who enlisted under the new conditions, and I should hope and expect that the legislation by which all this would be accomplished would put the National Guard itself upon a better and more permanent footing than it has ever been before, giving it not only the recognition which it deserves, but a more definite support from the national government and a more definite connection with the military organization of the nation.

What we all wish to accomplish is that the forces of the nation should indeed be part of the nation and not a separate professional force, and the chief cost of the system would not be in the enlistment or in the training of the men, but in the providing of ample equipment in case it should be necessary to call all forces into the field.

Moreover, it has been American policy time out of mind to look to the Navy as the first and chief line of defense. The Navy of the United States is already a very great and efficient force. Not rapidly, but slowly, with careful attention, our naval force has been developed until the Navy of the United States stands recognized as one of the most efficient and notable of the modern time. All that is needed in order to bring it to a point of extraordinary force and efficiency as compared with the other navies of the world is that we should hasten our pace in the policy we have long been pursuing, and that chief of all we should have a definite policy of development, not made from year to year but looking well into the future and planning for a definite consummation. We can and should profit in all that we do by the experience and example that have been made obvious to us by the military and naval events of the actual present. It is not merely a matter of building battleships and cruisers and submarines, but also a matter of making sure that we shall have the adequate equipment of men and munitions and supplies for the vessels we build and intend to build. Part of our problem is the problem of what I may call the mobilization of the resources of the nation at the proper time if it should ever be necessary to mobilize them for national defense. We shall study efficiency and adequate equipment as carefully as we shall study the number and size of our ships, and I believe that the plans already in part made public by the Navy Department are plans which the whole nation can approve with rational enthusiasm.

No thoughtful man feels any panic haste in this matter. The country is not threatened from any quarter. She stands in friendly relations with all the world. Her resources are known and her self-respect and her capacity to care for her own citizens and her own rights. There is no fear amongst us. Under the new-world conditions we have become thoughtful of the things which all reasonable men consider necessary for security and self-defense on the part of every nation confronted with the great enterprise of human liberty and independence. That is all.

Is the plan we propose sane and reasonable and suited to the needs of the hour? Does it not conform to the ancient traditions of America? Has any better plan been proposed than this programme that we now place before the country? In it there is no pride of opinion. It represents the best professional and expert judgment of the country. But I am not so much interested in programmes as I am in safeguarding at every cost the good faith and honor of the country. If men differ with me in this vital matter, I shall ask them to make it clear how far and in what way they are interested in making the permanent interests of the country safe against disturbance.

In the fulfillment of the programme I propose I shall ask for the hearty support of the country, of the rank and file of America, of men of all shades of political opinion. For my position in this important matter is different from that of the private individual who is free to speak his own thoughts and to risk his own opinions in this matter. We are here dealing with things that are vital to the life of America itself. In doing this I have tried to purge my heart of all personal and selfish motives. For the time being, I speak as the trustee and guardian of a nation's rights, charged with the duty of speaking for that nation in matters involving her sovereignty—a nation too big and generous to be exacting and yet courageous enough to defend its rights and the liberties of its people wherever assailed or invaded. I would not feel that I was discharging the solemn obligation I owe the country were I not to speak in terms of deepest solemnity of the urgency and necessity of preparing ourselves to guard and protect the rights and privileges of our people, our sacred heritage of the fathers who struggled to make us an independent nation.

The only thing within our own borders that has given us grave concern in recent months has been that voices have been raised in America professing to be the voices of Americans which were not indeed and in truth American, but which spoke alien sympathies, which came from men who loved other countries better than they loved America, men who were partisans of other causes than that of America and had forgotten that their chief and only allegiance was to the great government under which they live. These voices have not been many, but they have been loud and very clamorous. . . . . The chief thing necessary is that the real voice of the nation should sound forth unmistakably and in majestic volume, in the deep unison of a common, unhesitating national feeling. . . .

Wilson's Third Annual Message

(Delivered before Congress in Joint Session, December 7, 1915.)

[The President here makes his formal recommendations looking toward preparedness for national defense. Vast naval increases were ultimately granted by Congress, but the "absolutely imperative" proposal of a citizen army was not pressed for passage—a fact which was in part responsible for the resignation of the Secretary of War, Mr. Garrison, on February 10, 1916. The President's remarks about Mexico refer to the withdrawal of American troops from Vera Cruz in November, 1914, and to the recognition of the Carranza government in October, 1915. Three months after this message to Congress occurred the Villa raid on Columbus, N. M.]

Gentlemen of the Congress: Since I last had the privilege of addressing you on the state of the Union the war of nations on the other side of the sea, which had then only begun to disclose its portentous proportions, has extended its threatening and sinister scope until it has swept within its flame some portion of every quarter of the globe, not excepting our own hemisphere, has altered the whole face of international affairs, and now presents a prospect of reorganization and reconstruction such as statesmen and peoples have never been called upon to attempt before.

We have stood apart, studiously neutral. It was our manifest duty to do so. Not only did we have no part or interest in the policies which seem to have brought the conflict on; it was necessary, if a universal catastrophe was to be avoided, that a limit should be set to the sweep of destructive war and that some part of the great family of nations should keep the processes of peace alive, if only to prevent collective economic ruin and the breakdown throughout the world of the industries by which its populations are fed and sustained. It was manifestly the duty of the self-governed nations of this hemisphere to redress, if possible, the balance of economic loss and confusion in the other, if they could do nothing more. In the day of

much of which to purge itself and so little sympathy from any outside quarter in the radical but necessary process. We will aid and befriend Mexico, but we will not coerce her; and our course with regard to her ought to be sufficient proof to all America that we seek no political suzerainty or selfish control.

The moral is, that the states of America are not hostile rivals, but coöperating friends, and that their growing sense of community of interest, alike in matters political and in matters economic, is likely to give them a new significance as factors in international affairs and in the political history of the world. It presents them as in a very deep and true sense a unit in world affairs, spiritual partners, standing together because thinking together, quick with common sympathies and common ideals. Separated they are subject to all the cross-currents of the confused politics of a world of hostile rivalries; united in spirit and purpose they cannot be disappointed of their peaceful destiny.

This is Pan-Americanism. It has none of the spirit of empire in it. It is the embodiment, the effectual embodiment, of the spirit of law and independence and liberty and mutual service.

A very notable body of men recently met in the City of Washington, at the invitation and as the guests of this Government, whose deliberations are likely to be looked back to as marking a memorable turning point in the history of America. They were representative spokesmen of the several independent states of this hemisphere and were assembled to discuss the financial and commercial relations of the republics of the two continents which nature and political fortune have so intimately linked together. I earnestly recommend to your perusal the reports of their proceedings and of the actions of their committees. You will get from them, I think, a fresh conception of the ease and intelligence and advantage with which Americans of both continents may draw together in practical cooperation and of what the material foundations of this hopeful partnership of interest must consist,—of how we should build them and of how necessary it is that we should hasten their building.

There is, I venture to point out, an especial significance just now attaching to this whole matter of drawing the Americas together in bonds of honorable partnership and mutual advantage because of the economic readjustments which the world must inevitably witness within the next generation, when peace shall have at last resumed its healthful tasks. In the performance of these tasks I believe the Americas to be destined to play their parts together. I am interested to fix your attention on this prospect now because unless you take it within your view and permit the full significance of it to command your thought I can not find the right light in which to set forth the particular matter that lies at the very front of my whole thought as I address you to-day. I mean national defense.

No one who realily comprehends the spirit of the great people for whom we are appointed to speak can fail to perceive that their passion is for peace, their genius best displayed in the practice of the arts of peace. Great democracies are not belligerent. They do not seek or desire war. Their thought is of individual liberty and of the free labor that supports life and the uncensored thought that quickens it. Conquest and dominion are not in our reckoning, or agreeable to our principles. But just because we demand unmolested development and the undisturbed government of our own lives upon our own principles of right and liberty, we resent, from whatever quarter it may come, the aggression we ourselves will not practice. We insist upon security in prosecuting our self-chosen lines of national development. We do more than that. We demand it also for others. We do not confine our enthusiasm for individual liberty and free national development to the incidents and movements of affairs which affect only ourselves. We feel it wherever there is a people that tries to walk in these difficult paths of independence and right. From the first we have made common cause with all partisans of liberty on this side of the sea, and have deemed it as important that our neighbors should be free from all outside domination as that we ourselves should be; have set America aside as a whole for the uses of independent nations and political freemen.

Out of such thoughts grow all our policies. We regard war merely as a means of asserting the rights of a people against aggression. And we are as fiercely jealous of coercive or dictatorial power within our own nation as of aggression from without. We will not maintain a standing army except for uses which are as necessary in times of peace as in times of war; and we shall always see to it that our military peace establishment is no larger than is actually and continuously needed for the uses of days in which no enemies move against us. But we do believe in a body of free citizens ready and sufficient to take care of themselves and of the governments which they have set up to serve them. In our constitutions themselves we have commanded that "the right of the people to keep and bear arms shall not be infringed," and our confidence has been that our safety in times of danger would lie in the rising of the nation to take care of itself, as the farmers rose at Lexington.

But war has never been a mere matter of men and guns. It is a thing of disciplined might. If our citizens are ever to fight effectively upon a sudden summons, they must know how modern fighting is done, and what to do when the summons comes to render themselves immediately available and immediately effective. And the government must be their servant in this matter, must supply them with the training they need to take care of themselves and of it. The military arm of their government, which they will not allow to direct them, they may properly use to serve them

shall be carried out; but it does make definite and explicit a programme which has heretofore been only implicit, held in the minds of the Committees on Naval Affairs and disclosed in the debates of the two Houses but nowhere formulated or formally adopted. It seems to me very clear that it will be to the advantage of the country for the Congress to adopt a comprehensive plan for putting the navy upon a final footing of strength and efficiency and to press that plan to completion within the next five years. We have always looked to the navy of the country as our first and chief line of defense; we have always seen it to be our manifest course of prudence to be strong on the seas. Year by year we have been creating a navy which now ranks very high indeed among the navies of the maritime nations. We should now definitely determine how we shall complete what we have begun, and how soon.

The programme to be laid before you contemplates the construction within five years of ten battleships, six battle-cruisers, ten scout-cruisers, fifty destroyers, fifteen fleet submarines, eighty-five coast submarines, four gunboats, one hospital ship, two ammunition ships, two fuel-oil ships, and one repair ship. It is proposed that of this number we shall the first year provide for the construction of two battleships, two battle-cruisers, three scout-cruisers, fifteen destroyers, five fleet submarines, twenty-five coast submarines, two gunboats, and one hospital ship; the second year, two battleships, one scout-cruiser, ten destroyers, four submarines, fifteen coast submarines, one gunboat, and one fuel-oil ship; the third year, two battleships, one battle-cruiser, two scout-cruisers, five destroyers, two fleet submarines, and fifteen coast submarines; the fourth year, two battleships, two battle-cruisers, two scout-cruisers, ten destroyers, two fleet submarines, fifteen coast submarines, one ammunition ship, and one fuel-oil ship; and the fifth year, two battleships, one battle-cruiser, two scout-cruisers, ten destroyers, two fleet submarines, fifteen coast submarines, one gunboat, one ammunition ship, and one repair ship.

The Secretary of the Navy is asking also for the immediate addition to the personnel of the navy of seven thousand five hundred sailors, twenty-five hundred apprentice seamen, and fifteen hundred marines. This increase would be sufficient to care for the ships which are to be completed within the fiscal year 1917 and also for the number of men which must be put in training to man the ships which will be completed early in 1918. It is also necessary that the number of midshipmen at the Naval Academy at Annapolis should be increased by at least three hundred in order that the force of officers should be more rapidly added to; and authority is asked to appoint, for engineering duties only, approved graduates of engineering colleges, and for service in the aviation corps a certain number of men taken from civil life.

If this full programme should be carried out we should have built or building in 1921, according to the estimates of survival and standards of classification followed by the General Board of the Department, an effective navy consisting of twenty-seven battleships, of the first line, six battle-cruisers, twenty-five battleships of the second line, ten armored cruisers, thirteen scout-cruisers, five first-class cruisers, three second-class cruisers, ten third-class cruisers, one hundred and eight destroyers, eighteen fleet submarines, one hundred and fifty-seven coast submarines, six monitors, twenty gunboats, four supply ships, fifteen fuel ships, four transports, three tenders to torpedo vessels, eight vessels of special types, and two ammunition ships. This would be a navy fitted to our needs and worthy of our traditions.

But armies and instruments of war are only part of what has to be considered if we are to provide for the supreme matter of national self-sufficiency and security in all its aspects. There are other great matters which will be thrust upon our attention whether we will or not. There is, for example, a very pressing question of trade and shipping involved in this great problem of national adequacy. It is necessary for many weighty reasons of national efficiency and development that we should have a great merchant marine. The great merchant fleet we once used to make us rich, that great body of sturdy sailors who used to carry our flag into every sea, and who were the pride and often the bulwark of the nation, we have almost driven out of existence by inexcusable neglect and indifference and by a hopelessly blind and provincial policy of so-called economic protection. It is high time we repaired our mistake and resumed our commercial independence on the seas.

For it is a question of independence. If other nations go to war or seek to hamper each other's commerce, our merchants, it seems, are at their mercy, to do with as they please. We must use their ships, and use them as they determine. We have not ships enough of our own. We can not handle our own commerce on the seas. Our independence is provincial, and is only on land and within our own borders. We are not likely to be permitted to use even the ships of other nations in rivalry of their own trade, and are without means to extend our commerce even where the doors are wide open and our goods desired. Such a situation is not to be endured. It is of capital importance not only that the United States should be its own carrier on the seas and enjoy the economic independence which only an adequate merchant marine would give it, but also that the American hemisphere as a whole should enjoy a like independence and self-sufficiency, if it is not to be drawn into the tangle of European affairs. Without such independence the whole question of our political unity and self-determination is very seriously clouded and complicated indeed.

Moreover, we can develop no true or effective American

policy without ships of our own,—not ships of war, but ships of peace, carrying goods and carrying much more; creating friendships and rendering indispensable services to all interests on this side the water. They must move constantly back and forth between the Americas. They are the only shuttles that can weave the delicate fabric of sympathy, comprehension, confidence, and mutual dependence in which we wish to clothe our policy of America for Americans.

The task of building up an adequate merchant marine for America private capital must ultimately undertake and achieve, as it has undertaken and achieved every other like task amongst us in the past, with admirable enterprise, intelligence, and vigor; and it seems to me a manifest dictate of wisdom that we should promptly remove every legal obstacle that may stand in the way of this much-to-be-desired revival of our old independence and should facilitate in every possible way the building, purchase, and American registration of ships. But capital cannot accomplish this great task of a sudden. It must embark upon it by degrees, as the opportunities of trade develop. Something must be done at once; done to open routes and develop opportunities where they are as yet undeveloped; done to open the arteries of trade where the currents have not yet learned to run,—especially between the two American continents, where they are, singularly enough, yet to be created and quickened; and it is evident that only the government can undertake such beginnings and assume the initial financial risks. When the risk has passed and private capital begins to find its way in sufficient abundance into these new channels, the government may withdraw. But it can not omit to begin. It should take the first steps, and should take them at once. Our goods must not lie piled up at our ports and stored upon side-tracks in freight cars which are daily needed on the roads; must not be left without means of transport to any foreign quarter. We must not await the permission of foreign ship-owners and foreign governments to send them where we will.

With a view to meeting these pressing necessities of our commerce and availing ourselves at the earliest possible moment of the present unparalleled opportunity of linking the two Americas together in bonds of mutual interest and service, an opportunity which may never return again if we miss it now, proposals will be made to the present Congress for the purchase or construction of ships to be owned and directed by the government similar to those made to the last Congress, but modified in some essential particulars. I recommend these proposals to you for your prompt acceptance with the more confidence because every month that has elapsed since the former proposals were made has made the necessity for such action more and more manifestly imperative. This need was then foreseen; it is now acutely felt and everywhere realized by those for whom trade is waiting but who can find no conveyance for their goods. I am not so much interested in the particulars of the programme as I am in taking immediate advantage of the great opportunity which awaits us if we will but act in this emergency. In this matter, as in all others, a spirit of common counsel should prevail, and out of it should come an early solution of this pressing problem.

There is another matter which seems to me to be very intimately associated with the question of national safety and preparation for defense. That is our policy towards the Philippines and the people of Porto Rico. Our treatment of them and their attitude towards us are manifestly of the first consequence in the development of our duties in the world and in getting a free hand to perform those duties. We must be free from every unnecessary burden or embarrassment; and there is no better way to be clear of embarrassment than to fulfil our promises and promote the interests of those dependent on us to the utmost. Bills for the alteration and reform of the government of the Philippines and for rendering fuller political justice to the people of Porto Rico were submitted to the sixty-third Congress. They will be submitted also to you. I need not particularize their details. You are most of you already familiar with them. But I do recommend them to your early adoption with the sincere conviction that there are few measures you could adopt which would more serviceably clear the way for the great policies by which we wish to make good, now and always, our right to lead in enterprises of peace and good will and economic and political freedom.

The plans for the armed forces of the nation which I have outlined, and for the general policy of adequate preparation for mobilization and defense, involve of course very large additional expenditures of money,—expenditures which will considerably exceed the estimated revenues of the government. It is made my duty by law, whenever the estimates of expenditure exceed the estimates of revenue, to call the attention of the Congress to the fact and suggest any means of meeting the deficiency that it may be wise or possible for me to suggest. I am ready to believe that it would be my duty to do so in any case; and I feel particularly bound to speak of the matter when it appears that the deficiency will arise directly out of the adoption by the Congress of measures which I myself urge it to adopt. Allow me, therefore, to speak briefly of the present state of the Treasury and of the fiscal problems which the next year will probably disclose.

On the thirtieth of June last there was an available balance in the general fund of the Treasury of $104,170,-105.78. The total estimated receipts for the year 1916, on the assumption that the emergency revenue measure passed by the last Congress will not be extended beyond its present limit, the thirty-first of December, 1915, and that the present duty of one cent per pound on sugar will be discontinued after the first of May, 1916, will be $670,365,500. The balance of June last and these estimated revenues come, therefore, to a grand total of $774,535,605.78. The total estimated disbursements for the present fiscal year, including twenty-five millions for the Panama Canal, twelve millions for probable deficiency appropriations, and fifty thousand dollars for miscellaneous debt redemptions, will be $753,891,000; and the balance in the general fund of the Treasury will be reduced to $20,644,605.78. The emergency revenue act, if continued beyond its present time limitation, would produce, during the half year then remaining, about forty-one millions. The duty of one cent per pound on sugar, if continued, would produce during the two months of the fiscal year remaining after the first of May, about fifteen millions. These two sums, amounting together to fifty-six millions, if added to the revenues of the second half of the fiscal year, would yield the Treasury at the end of the year an available balance of $76,644,-605.78.

The additional revenues required to carry out the programme of military and naval preparation of which I have spoken would, as at present estimated, be for the fiscal year 1917, $93,800,000. Those figures, taken with the figures for the present fiscal year which I have already given, disclose our financial problem for the year 1917. Assuming that the taxes imposed by the emergency revenue act and the present duty on sugar are to be discontinued, and that the balance at the close of the present fiscal year will be only $20,644,605.78, that the disbursements for the Panama Canal will again be about twenty-five millions, and that the additional expenditures for the army and navy are authorized by the Congress, the deficit in the general fund of the Treasury on the thirtieth of June, 1917, will be nearly two hundred and thirty-five millions. To this sum at least fifty millions should be added to represent a safe working balance for the Treasury, and twelve millions to include the usual deficiency estimates in 1917; and these additions would make a total deficit of some two hundred and ninety-seven millions. If the present taxes should be continued throughout this year and the next, however, there would be a balance in the Treasury of some seventy-six and a half millions at the end of the present fiscal year and a deficit at the end of the next year of only some fifty millions, or, reckoning in sixty-two millions for deficiency appropriations and a safe Treasury balance at the end of the year, a total deficit of some one hundred and twelve millions. The obvious moral of the figures is that it is a plain counsel of prudence to continue all of the present taxes or their equivalents, and confine ourselves to the problem of providing one hundred and twelve millions of new revenue rather than two hundred and ninety-seven millions.

How shall we obtain the new revenue? We are frequently reminded that there are many millions of bonds which the Treasury is authorized under existing law to sell to reimburse the sums paid out of current revenues for the construction of the Panama Canal; and it is true that bonds to the amount of approximately $222,000,000 are now available for that purpose. Prior to 1913 $134,631,980 of these bonds had actually been sold to recoup the expenditures at the Isthmus; and now constitute a considerable item of the public debt. But I, for one, do not believe that the people of this country approve of postponing the payment of their bills. Borrowing money is short-sighted finance. It can be justified only when permanent things are to be accomplished which many generations will certainly benefit by and which it seems hardly fair that a single generation should pay for. The objects we are now proposing to spend money for cannot be so classified, except in the sense that everything wisely done may be said to be done in the interest of posterity as well as in our own. It seems to me a clear dictate of prudent statesmanship and frank finance that in what we are now, I hope, about to undertake we should pay as we go. The people of the country are entitled to know just what burdens of taxation they are to carry, and to know from the outset, now. The new bills should be paid by internal taxation.

To what sources, then, shall we turn? This is so peculiarly a question which the gentlemen of the House of Representatives are expected under the Constitution to propose an answer to that you will hardly expect me to do more than discuss it in very general terms. We should be following an almost universal example of modern governments if we were to draw the greater part or even the whole of the revenues we need from the income taxes. By somewhat lowering the present limits of exemption and the figure at which the surtax shall begin to be imposed, and by increasing, step by step throughout the present graduation, the surtax itself, the income taxes as at present apportioned would yield sums sufficient to balance the books of the Treasury at the end of the fiscal year 1917 without anywhere making the burden unreasonably or oppressively heavy. The precise reckonings are fully and accurately set out in the report of the Secretary of the Treasury which will be immediately laid before you.

And there are many additional sources of revenue which can justly be resorted to without hammering the industries of the country or putting any too great charge upon individual expenditure. A tax of one cent per gallon on gasoline and naphtha would yield, at the present estimated production, $10,000,000; a tax of fifty cents per horsepower on automobiles and internal explosion engines, $15,000,000; a stamp tax on bank cheques, probably $18,000,000; a tax of twenty-five cents per ton on pig iron, $10,000,000; a tax of twenty-five cents per ton on fabricated iron and steel probably $10,000,000. In a country of great industries like this it ought to be easy to distribute the burdens of taxation without making them anywhere bear too heavily or too exclusively upon any one set of persons or undertakings. What is clear is, that the industry of this generation should pay the bills of this generation.

I have spoken to you to-day, Gentlemen, upon a single theme, the thorough preparation of the nation to care for its own security and to make sure of entire freedom to play the impartial rôle in this hemisphere and in the world which we all believe to have been providentially assigned to it. I have had in my mind no thought of any immediate or particular danger arising out of our relations with other nations. We are at peace with all the nations of the world, and there is reason to hope that no question in controversy between this and other Governments will lead to any serious breach of amicable relations, grave as some differences of attitude and policy have been and may yet turn out to be. I am sorry to say that the gravest threats against our national peace and safety have been uttered within our own borders. There are citizens of the United States, I blush to admit, born under other flags but welcomed under our generous naturalization laws to the full freedom and opportunity of America, who have poured the poison of disloyalty into the very arteries of our national life; who have sought to bring the authority and good name of our Government into contempt, to destroy our industries wherever they thought it effective for their vindictive purposes to strike at them, and to debase our policies to the uses of foreign intrigue. Their number is not great as compared with the whole number of those sturdy hosts by which our nation has been enriched in recent generations out of virile foreign stocks; but it is great enough to have brought deep disgrace upon us and to have made it necessary that we should promptly make use of processes of law by which we may be purged of their corrupt distempers. America never witnessed anything like this before. It never dreamed it possible that men sworn into its own citizenship, men drawn out of great free stocks such as supplied some of the best and strongest elements of that little, but how heroic, nation that in a high day of old staked its very life to free itself from every entanglement that had darkened the fortunes of the older nations and set up a new standard here, —that men of such origins and such free choices of allegiance would ever turn in malign reaction against the Government and people who had welcomed and nurtured them and seek to make this proud country once more a hotbed of European passion. A little while ago such a thing would have seemed incredible. Because it was incredible we made no preparation for it. We would have been almost ashamed to prepare for it, as if we were suspicious of ourselves, our own comrades and neighbors! But the ugly and incredible thing has actually come about and we are without adequate federal laws to deal with it. I urge you to enact such laws at the earliest possible moment and feel that in doing so I am urging you to do nothing less than save the honor and self-respect of the nation. Such creatures of passion, disloyalty, and anarchy must be crushed out. They are not many, but they are infinitely malignant, and the hand of our power should close over them at once. They have formed plots to destroy property, they have entered into conspiracies against the neutrality of the Government, they have sought to pry into every confidential transaction of the Government in order to serve interests alien to our own. It is possible to deal with these things very effectually. I need not suggest the terms in which they may be dealt with.

I wish that it could be said that only a few men, misled by mistaken sentiments of allegiance to the governments under which they under which they were born, had been guilty of disturbing the self-possession and misrepresenting the temper and principles of the country during these days of terrible war, when it would seem that every man who was truly an American would instinctively make it his duty and his pride to keep the scales of judgment even and prove himself a partisan of no nation but his own. But it cannot. There are some men among us, and many resident abroad who, though born and bred in the United States and calling themselves Americans, have so forgotten themselves and their honor as citizens as to put their passionate sympathy with one or the other side in the great European conflict above their regard for the peace and dignity of the United States. They also preach and practice disloyalty. No laws, I suppose, can reach corruptions of the mind and heart; but I should not speak of others without also speaking of these and expressing the even deeper humiliation and scorn which every self-possessed and thoughtfully patriotic American must feel when he thinks of them and of the discredit they are daily bringing upon us.

While we speak of the preparation of the nation to make sure of her security and her effective power we must not fall into the patent error of supposing that her real strength comes from armaments and mere safeguards of written law. It comes, of course, from her people, their energy, their success in their undertakings, their free opportunity to use the natural resources of our great home land and of the lands outside our continental borders which look to us for protection, for encouragement, and for assistance in their development; from the organization and freedom and vitality of our economic life. The domestic questions which engaged the attention of the last Congress are more vital to the nation in this its time of test than at any other time. We can not adequately make ready for any trial of our strength unless we wisely and promptly direct the force of our laws into these all-important fields of domestic action. A matter which it seems to me we should have very much at heart is the creation of the right instrumentalities by which to mobilize our economic resources in any time of national necessity. I take it for granted that I do not need your authority to call into sympathetic consultation with the directing officers of the army and navy men of recognized leadership and ability from among our citizens who are thoroughly familiar, for example, with the transportation facilities of the country and therefore competent to advise how they may be coördinated when the need arises, those who can suggest the best way in which to bring about prompt coöperation among the manufacturers of the country, should it be necessary, and those who could assist to bring the technical skill of the country to the aid of the Government in the solution of particular problems of defense. I only hope that if I should find it feasible to constitute such an advisory body the Congress would be willing to vote the small sum of money that would be needed to defray the expenses that would probably be necessary to give it the clerical and administrative machinery with which to do serviceable work.

What is more important is, that the industries and resources of the country should be available and ready for mobilization. It is the more imperatively necessary, therefore, that we should promptly devise means for doing what we have not yet done: that we should give intelligent federal aid and stimulation to industrial and vocational education, as we have long done in the large field of our agricultural industry; that, at the same time that we safeguard and conserve the natural resources of the country we should put them at the disposal of those who will use them promptly and intelligently, as was sought to be done in the admirable bills submitted to the last Congress from its committees on the public lands, bills which I earnestly recommend in principle to your consideration; that we should put into early operation some provision for rural credits which will add to the extensive borrowing facilities already afforded the farmer by the Reserve Bank Act, adequate instrumentalities by which long credits may be obtained on land mortgages; and that we should study more carefully than they have hitherto been studied the right adaptation of our economic arrangements to changing conditions.

Many conditions about which we have repeatedly legislated are being altered from decade to decade, it is evident, under our very eyes, and are likely to change even more rapidly and more radically in the days immediately ahead of us, when peace has returned to the world and the nations of Europe once more take up their tasks of commerce and industry with the energy of those who must bestir themselves to build anew. Just what these changes will be no one can certainly foresee or confidently predict. There are no calculable, because no stable, elements in the problem. The most we can do is to make certain that we have the necessary instrumentalities of information constantly at our service so that we may be sure that we know exactly what we are dealing with when we come to act, if it should be necessary to act at all. We must first certainly know what it is that we are seeking to adapt ourselves to. I may ask the privilege of addressing you more at length on this important matter a little later in your session.

In the meantime may I make this suggestion? The transportation problem is an exceedingly serious and pressing one in this country. There has from time to time of late been reason to fear that our railroads would not much longer be able to cope with it successfully, as at present equipped and coördinated. I suggest that it would be wise to provide for a commission of inquiry to ascertain by a thorough canvass of the whole question whether our laws as at present framed and administered are as serviceable as they might be in the solution of the problem. It is obviously a problem that lies at the very foundation of our efficiency as a people. Such an inquiry ought to draw out every circumstance and opinion worth considering and we need to know all sides of the matter if we mean to do anything in the field of federal legislation.

No one, I am sure, would wish to take any backward step. The regulation of the railways of the country by federal commission has had admirable results and has fully justified the hopes and expectations of those by whom the policy of regulation was originally proposed. The question is not what should we undo? It is, whether there is anything else we can do that will supply us the effective means, in the very process of regulation, for bettering the conditions under which the railroads are operated and for making them more useful servants of the country as a whole. It seems to me that it might be the part of wisdom, therefore, before further legislation in this field is attempted, to look at the whole problem of coördination and efficiency in the full light of a fresh assessment of circumstance and opinion, as a guide to dealing with the several parts of it.

For what we are seeking now, what in my mind is the single thought of this message, is national efficiency and security. We serve a great nation. We should serve it in the spirit of its peculiar genius. It is the genius of common men for self-government, industry, justice, liberty and peace. We should see to it that it lacks no instrument, no facility or vigor of law, to make it sufficient to play its part with energy, safety, and assured success. In this we are no partisans but heralds and prophets of a new age.

Wilson's Addresses on Middle Western Tour, Urging Preparedness for National Defense, January 27 to February 3, 1916

[Editorial Note: *Congress had been in session nearly two months without definite accomplishment, and the President undertook this speaking trip to urge citizens to "back him up" in demands for national defense. He confessed his own change of mind since his message to Congress in December, 1914, and his purpose "to go out and tell my fellow countrymen that new circumstances have arisen which make it absolutely necessary that this country should prepare herself, not for war, but for adequate national defense." He went as far west as Kansas, delivering*

But, gentlemen, there is something that the American people love better than they love peace. They love the principles upon which their political life is founded. They are ready at any time to fight for the vindication of their character and of their honor. They will not at any time seek the contest, but they will at no time cravenly avoid it; because if there is one thing that the individual ought to fight for, and that the Nation ought to fight for, it is the integrity of its own convictions. We can not surrender our convictions. I would rather surrender territory than surrender those ideals which are the staff of life of the soul itself. . . .

Perhaps when you learned, as I dare say you did learn beforehand, that I was expecting to address you on the subject of preparedness, you recalled the address which I made to Congress something more than a year ago, in which I said that this question of military preparedness was not a pressing question. But more than a year has gone by since then and I would be ashamed if I had not learned something in fourteen months. The minute I stop changing my mind with the change of all the circumstances of the world, I will be a back number.

There is another thing about which I have changed my mind. A year ago I was not in favor of a tariff board, and I will tell you why. Then the only purpose of a tariff board was to keep alive an unprofitable controversy. If you set up any board of inquiry whose purpose it is to keep business disturbed and to make it always an open question what you are going to do about the public policy of the Government, I am opposed to it; and the very men who were dinning it into our ears that what business wanted was to be let alone were, many of them, men who were insisting that we should stir up a controversy which meant that we could not let business alone. There is a great deal more opinion vocal in this world than is consistent with logic. But the circumstances of the present time are these: There is going on in the world under our eyes an economic revolution. No man understands that revolution; no man has the elements of it clearly in his mind. No part of the business of legislation with regard to international trade can be undertaken until we do understand it; and members of Congress are too busy, their duties are too multifarious and distracting to make it possible within a sufficiently short space of time for them to master the change that is coming. . . .

What I am trying to impress upon you now is that the circumstances of the world to-day are not what they were yesterday, or ever were in any of our yesterdays. And it is not certain what they will be to-morrow. I can not tell you what the international relations of this country will be to-morrow, and I use the word literally; and I would not dare keep silent and let the country suppose that to-morrow was certain to be as bright as to-day. America will never be the aggressor, America will always seek to the last point at which her honor is involved to avoid the things which disturb the peace of the world; but America does not control the circumstances of the world, and we must be sure that we are faithful servants of those things which we love, and are ready to defend them against every contingency that may affect or impair them.

And, as I was saying a moment ago, we must seek the means which are consistent with the principles of our lives. It goes without saying, though apparently it is necessary to say it to some excited persons, that one thing that this country never will endure is a system that can be called militarism. But militarism consists in this, gentlemen: It consists in preparing a great machine whose only use is for war and giving it no use upon which to expend itself. Men who are in charge of edged tools and bidden to prepare them for exact and scientific use grow very impatient if they are not permitted to use them, and I do not believe that the creation of such an instrument is an insurance of peace. I believe that it involves the danger of all the impulses that skillful persons have to use the things that they know how to use.

But we do not have to do that. America is always going to use her Army in two ways. She is going to use it for the purposes of peace, and she is going to use it as a nucleus for expansion into those things which she does believe in, namely, the preparation of her citizens to take care of themselves. There are two sides to the question of preparation; there is not merely the military side, there is the industrial side; and the ideal which I have in mind is this: We ought to have in this country a great system of industrial and vocational education under Federal guidance and with Federal aid, in which a very large percentage of the youth of this country will be given training in the skillful use and application of the principles of science in manufacture and business; and it will be perfectly feasible and highly desirable to add to that and combine with it such a training in the mechanism and care and use of arms, in the sanitation of camps, in the simpler forms of maneuver and organization, as will make these same men at one and the same time industrially efficient and immediately serviceable for national defense. The point about such a system will be that its emphasis will lie on the industrial and civil side of life, and that, like all the rest of America, the use of force will only be in the background and as the last resort. Men will think first of their families and their daily work, of their service in the economic ranks of the country, of their efficiency as artisans, and only last of all of their serviceability to the Nation as soldiers and men at arms. That is the ideal of America.

But, gentlemen, you can not create such a system overnight; you cannot create such a system rapidly. It has got to be built up, and I hope it will be built up, by slow and effective stages; and there is much to be done in the meantime. We must see to it that a sufficient body of citizens is given the kind of training which will make them efficient now if called into the field in case of necessity. It is discreditable to this country, gentlemen, for this is a country full of intelligent men, that we should have exhibited to the world the example we have sometimes exhibited to it, of stupid and brutal waste of force. Think of asking men who can be easily trained to come into the field, crude, ignorant, inexperienced, and merely furnishing the stuff for camp fever and the bullets of the enemy. The sanitary experience of our Army in the Spanish-American War was merely an indictment of America's indifference to the manifest lessons of experience in the matter of ordinary, careful preparation. We have got the men to waste, but God forbid that we should waste them. Men who go as efficient instruments of national honor into the field afford a very handsome spectacle indeed. Men who go in crude and ignorant boys only indict those in authority for stupidity and neglect. So it seems to me that it is our manifest duty to have a proper citizen reserve.

I am not forgetting our National Guard. I have had the privilege of being governor of one of our great States, and there I was brought into association with what I am glad to believe is one of the most efficient portions of the National Guard of the Nation. I learned to admire the men, to respect the officers, and to believe in the National Guard; and I believe that it is the duty of Congress to do very much more for the National Guard than it has ever done heretofore. I believe that that great arm of our national defense should be built up and encouraged to the utmost; but, you know, gentlemen, that under the Constitution of the United States the National Guard is under the direction of more than twoscore States; that it is not permitted to the National Government directly to have a voice in its development and organization; and that only upon occasion of actual invasion has the President of the United States the right to ask those men to leave their respective States. I, for my part, am afraid, though some gentlemen differ with me, that there is no way in which that force can be made a direct resource as a national reserve under national authority.

What we need is a body of men trained in association with units of the Army, and a body of men organized under the immediate direction of the national authority, a body of men subject to the immediate call to arms of the national authority, and yet men not put into the ranks of the Regular Army; men left to their tasks of civil life, men supplied with equipment and training, but not drawn away from the peaceful pursuits which have made America great and must keep her great. I am not a partisan of any one plan. I have had too much experience to think that it is right to so say that the plan that I propose is the only plan that will work, because I have a shrewd suspicion that there may be other plans that will work. What I am after, and what every American ought to insist upon, is a body of at least half a million trained citizens who will serve under conditions of danger as an immediately available national reserve. . . .

At Pittsburgh, Pa., January 29, 1916.

(The Western Preparedness Tour)

Mr. Chairman, Ladies and Gentlemen:

I am conscious of a sort of truancy in being absent from my duties in Washington, and yet it did seem to me to be clearly the obligation laid upon me by the office to which I have been chosen that, as your servant and representative, I should come and report to you upon the progress of public affairs. . . .

You know that there is a multitude of voices upon the question of national defense, and I, for my part, am not inclined to criticize any of the views that have been put forth upon this important subject, because if there is one thing we love more than another in the United States, it is that every man should have the privilege, unmolested and uncriticized, to utter the real convictions of his mind. . . .

What is it that we want to defend? You do not need to have me answer that question for you; it is your own thought. We want to defend the life of this Nation against any sort of interference. We want to maintain the equal right of this Nation as against the action of all other nations, and we wish to maintain the peace and unity of the Western Hemisphere. Those are great things to defend, and in their defense sometimes our thought must take a great sweep, even beyond our own borders. Do you never stop to reflect just what it is that America stands for? If she stands for one thing more than another, it is for the sovereignty of self-governing peoples, and her example, her assistance, her encouragement, has thrilled two continents in this Western World with all the fine impulses which have built up human liberty on both sides of the water. She stands, therefore, as an example of independence, as an example of free institutions, and as an example of disinterested international action in the maintenance of justice. These are very great things to defend, and wherever they are attacked America has at least the duty of example, has at least the duty of such action as it is possible for her with self-respect to take, in order that these things may not be neglected or thrust on one side. . . .

I am not going before audiences like this to go into the details of the programme which has been proposed to the Congress of the United States, because, after all, the details do not make any difference. I believe in one plan; others may think that an equally good plan can be substituted, and I hope my mind is open to be convinced that it can; but what I am convinced of and what we are all working for is that there should be provided, not a great militant force in this country, but a great reserve of adequate and available force which can be called on upon occasion. I have proposed that we should be supplied with at least half a million men accustomed to handle arms and to live in camps; and that is a very small number as compared with the gigantic proportions of modern armies. Therefore, it seems to me that no man can speak of proposals like that as if they pointed in the direction of militarism. . . .

For I am proposing something more than what is temporary. It is my conception that as the Government of the United States has done a great deal, though even yet probably not enough, to promote agricultural education in this country, it ought to do a great deal to promote industrial education in this country, and that along with thoroughgoing industrial and vocational training it is perfectly feasible to instruct the youth of the land in the mechanism and use of arms, in the sanitation of camps, in the more rudimentary principles and practices of modern warfare, and so not to bring about occasions such as we have sometimes brought about, when upon a sudden danger youngsters were summoned by the proclamation of the President out of every community, who came crude and green and raw into the service of their country—infinitely willing but also wholly unfitted for the great physical task which was ahead of them. No nation should waste its youth like that. A nation like this should be ashamed to use an inefficient instrument when it can make its instrument efficient for everything that it needs to employ it for, and can do it along with the magnifying and ennobling and quickening of the tasks of peace.

But we have to create the schools and develop the schools to do these things, and we can not at present wait for this slow process. We must go at once to the task of training a very considerable body of men to the use of arms and the life of camps, and we can do so upon one condition, and one condition only. The test, ladies and gentlemen, of what we are proposing is not going to be the action of Congress; it is going to be the response of the country. It is going to be the volunteering of the men to take the training and the willingness of their employers to see to it that no obstacle is put in the way of their volunteering. It will be up to the young men of this country and to the men who employ them; then, and not till then, we shall know how far it is true that America wishes to prepare itself for national defense—not a matter of sentiment, but a matter of hard practice.

Are the men going to come out, and are those who employ them going to facilitate their coming out? I for one believe that they will. There are many selfish influences at work in this country, as in every other; but when it comes to the large view America can produce the substance of patriotism as abundantly as any other country under God's sun. I have no anxiety along those lines, and I have no anxiety along the lines of what Congress is going to do. You elect men to Congress who have opinions, and it is not strange that they should have differing opinions. I am not jealous of debate. If what I propose can not stand debate, then something ought to be substituted for it which can. And I am not afraid that it is going to be all debate. I am not afraid that nothing is going to come out of it. I am not afraid that we shall fail to get out of it the most substantial and satisfactory results. Certainly when I talk a great deal myself I am not going to be jealous of the other man's having a chance to talk also. We are talking, I take it, in order to get at the very final analysis of the case, the final proof and demonstration of what we ought to do.

My own feeling, ladies and gentlemen, is that it is a pity that this is a campaign year. I hope, with the chairman of the meeting, that the question of national preparation for defense will not by anybody be drawn into campaign uses or partisan aspects. There are many differences between Democrats and Republicans, honest differences of opinion and of conviction, but Democrats do not differ from Republicans upon the question of the Nation's safety, and no man ought to draw this thing into controversy in order to make party or personal profit out of it. I am ready to acknowledge that men on the other side politically are just as deeply and just as intelligently interested in this question as I am, of course, and I shall be ashamed of any friends of mine who may take any different view of it.

I want you to realize just what is happening, not in America, but in the rest of the world. It is very hard to describe it briefly. It is very hard to describe it in quiet phrases. The world is on fire, and there is tinder everywhere. The sparks are liable to drop anywhere, and somewhere there may be material which we can not prevent from bursting into flame. The influence of passion is everywhere abroad in the world. It is not strange that men see red in such circumstances. What a year ago was incredible has now happened and the world is so in the throes of this titanic struggle that no part of it is unaffected.

You know what is happening. You know that by a kind of improvidence which should be very uncharacteristic of America we have neglected for several generations to provide the means to carry our own commerce on the seas, and, therefore, being dependent upon other nations for the most part to carry our commerce, we are dependent upon other nations now for the movement of our commerce when other nations are caught in the grip of war. So that every natural impulse of our peaceful life is embarrassed and impeded by the circumstances of the time, and wherever there is contact there is apt to be friction. Wherever the ordinary rules of commerce at sea and of international relationship are thrust aside or ignored, there is danger of the more critical kind of controversy. Where nations are engaged as many nations are now engaged, they are peculiarly likely to be stubbornly steadfast in the pursuit of the purpose which is the main purpose of the moment; and so, while we move among friends, we move among friends who are preoccupied, preoccupied with an exigent matter which is foreign to our own life, foreign to our own policy, but which nevertheless inevitably affects our own life and our own policy. While a year ago it seemed impossible that a struggle upon so great a scale should last a whole twelvemonth, it has now lasted a year and a half and the end is not yet, and all the time things have grown more and more difficult to handle.

It fills me with a very strange feeling sometimes, my fellow citizens, when it seems to be implied that I am not the friend of peace. If these gentlemen could have sat with me reading the dispatches and handling the questions which arise every hour of the twenty-four, they would have known how infinitely difficult it had been to maintain the peace and they would have believed that I was the friend of peace. But I also know the difficulties, the real dangers, dangers not about things that I can handle, but about things that the other parties handle and I can not control.

It amazes me to hear men speak as if America stood alone in the world and could follow her own life as she pleased. We are in the midst of a world that we did not make and can not alter; its atmospheric and physical conditions are the conditions of our own life also, and therefore, as your responsible servant, I must tell you that the dangers are infinite and constant. I should feel that I was guilty of an unpardonable omission if I did not go out and tell my fellow countrymen that new circumstances have arisen which make it absolutely necessary that this country should prepare herself, not for war, not for anything that smacks in the least of aggression, but for adequate national defense. . . .

What I want you to do is this: I do not want you merely to listen to speeches. I want you to make yourselves vocal. I want you to let everybody who comes within earshot of it know that you are a partisan for the adequate preparation of the United States for national defense. I have come to ask you not merely to go home and say, "The President seems to be a good fellow and to mean what he says"; I want you to go home determined that within the whole circle of your influence the President, not as a partisan, but as the representative of the national honor, shall be backed up by the whole force that is in the Nation. . . .

At Cleveland, Ohio, January 29, 1916.

(The Western Preparedness Tour)

Mr. President and Fellow Citizens:

I suppose that from the first America has had one peculiar and particular mission in the world. Other nations have grown rich, my fellow citizens, other nations have been as powerful as we in material resources in comparison with the other nations of the world, other nations have built up empires and exercised dominion; we are not peculiar in any of these things, but we are peculiar in this, that from the first we have dedicated our force to the service of justice and righteousness and peace. We have said: "Our chief interest is not in the rights of property, but in the rights of men; our chief interest is in the spirits of men that they might be free, that they might enjoy their lives unmolested so long as they observed the just rules of the game, that they might deal with their fellowmen with their heads erect the subjects and servants of no man; the servants only of the principles upon which their lives rested." And America has done more than care for her own people and think of her own fortunes in these great matters. She has said ever since the time of President Monroe that she was the champion of the freedom and the separate sovereignty of peoples throughout the Western Hemisphere. She is trustee for these ideals and she is pledged, deeply and permanently pledged, to keep these momentous promises.

She not only, therefore, must play her part in keeping this conflagration from spreading to the people of the

United States; she must also keep this conflagration from spreading on this side of the sea. These are matters in which our very life and our whole pride are embedded and rooted, and we can never draw back from them. And I, my fellow citizens, because of the extraordinary office with which you have intrusted me, must, whether I will or not, be your responsible spokesman in these great matters. It is my duty, therefore, when impressions are deeply borne in upon me with regard to the national welfare to speak to you with the utmost frankness about them, and that is the errand upon which I have come away from Washington.

For my own part, I am sorry that these things fall within the year of a national political campaign. They ought to have nothing whatever to do with politics. The man who brings partisan feeling into these matters and seeks partisan advantage by means of them is unworthy of your confidence. I am sorry that upon the eve of a campaign we should be obliged to discuss these things, for fear they might run over into the campaign and seem to constitute a part of it. Let us forget that this is a year of national elections. That is neither here nor there. The thing to do now is for all men of all parties to think along the same lines and do the same things and forget every difference that may have divided them.

And what ought they to do? In the first place, they ought to tell the truth. There have been some extraordinary exaggerations both of the military weakness and the military strength of this country. Some men tell you that we have no means of defense and others tell you that we have sufficient means of defense, and neither statement is true. Take, for example, the matter of our coast defenses. It is obvious to every man that they are of the most vital importance to the country. Such coast defenses as we have are strong and admirable, but we have not got coast defenses in enough places. Their quality is admirable, but their quantity is insufficient. The military authorities of this country have not been negligent; they have sought adequate appropriations from Congress, and in most instances have obtained them, so far as we saw the work in hand that it was necessary to do, and the work that they have done in the use of these appropriations has been admirable and skillful work. Do not let anybody deceive you into supposing that the Army of the United States, so far as it has had opportunity, is in any degree unworthy of your confidence.

And the Navy of the United States. You have been told that it is the second in strength in the world. I am sorry to say that experts do not agree with those who tell you that. Reckoning by its actual strength, I believe it to be one of the most efficient navies in the world, but in strength it ranks fourth, not second. You must reckon with the fact that it is necessary that that should be our first arm of defense, and you ought to insist that everything should be done that it is possible for us to do to bring the Navy up to an adequate standard of strength and efficiency.

Where we are chiefly lacking in preparation is on land and in the number of men who are ready to fight. Not the number of fighting men, but the number of men who are ready to fight. Some men are born troublesome, some men have trouble thrust upon them, and other men acquire trouble. I think I belong to the second class. But the characteristic desire of America is not that she should have a great body of men whose chief business is to fight, but a great body of men who know how to fight and are ready to fight when anything that is dear to the Nation is threatened. You might have what we have, millions of men who had never handled arms of war, who are mere material for shot and powder if you put them in the field, and America would be ashamed of the inefficiency of calling such men to defend the Nation. What we want is to associate in training with the Army of the United States men who will volunteer for a sufficient length of time every year to get a rudimentary acquaintance with arms, a rudimentary skill in handling them, a rudimentary acquaintance with camp life, a rudimentary acquaintance with military drill and discipline; and we ought to see to it that we have men of that sort in sufficient number to constitute an initial army when we need an army for the defense of the country.

I have heard it stated that there are probably several million men in this country who have received a sufficient amount of military drill either here or in the countries in which they were born and from which they have come to us. Perhaps there are, nobody knows, because there is no means of counting them; but if there are so many, they are not obliged to come at our call; we do not know who they are. That is not military preparation. Military preparation consists in the existence of such a body of men known to the Federal authorities, organized provisionally by the Federal authorities, and subject by their own choice and will to the immediate call of the Federal authorities.

We have no such body of men in the United States except the National Guard. Now, I have a very great respect for the National Guard. I have been associated with one section of that guard in one of the great States of the Union, and I know the character of the officers and the quality of the men, and I would trust them unhesitatingly both for skill and for efficiency, but the whole National Guard of the United States falls short of 130,000 men. It is characterized by a very great variety of discipline and efficiency as between State and State, and it is by the Constitution itself put under authority of more than two score State executives. The President of the United States has not the right to call on these men except in the case of actual invasion, and, therefore, no matter how skillful they are, no matter how ready they are, they are not the instruments for immediate National use. I believe that the Congress of the United States ought to do, and that it will do, a great deal more for the National Guard than it ever has done, and everything ought to be done to make it a model military arm.

But that is not the arm that we are immediately interested in. We are interested in making certain that there are men all over the United States prepared, equipped, and ready to go out at the call of the National Government upon the shortest possible notice. You will ask me, "Why do you say the shortest possible notice?" Because, gentlemen, let me tell you very solemnly you can not afford to postpone this thing. I do not know what a single day may bring forth. I do not wish to leave you with the impression that I am thinking of some particular danger; I merely want to leave you with this solemn impression, that I know that we are daily treading amidst the most intricate dangers, and that the dangers that we are treading amongst are not of our making and are not under our control, and that no man in the United States knows what a single week or a single day or a single hour may bring forth. These are solemn things to say to you, but I would be unworthy of my office if I did not come out and tell you with absolute frankness just exactly what I understand the situation to be.

I do not wish to hurry the Congress of the United States. These things are too important to be put through without very thorough sifting and debate and I am not in the least jealous of any of the searching processes of discussion. That is what free people are for, to understand what they are about and to do what they wish to do only if they understand what they are about. But it is impossible to discuss the details of plans in great bodies, unorganized bodies, of men like this audience, for example. All that I can do in this presence is to tell you what I know of the necessities of the case, and to ask you to stand back of the executive authorities of the United States in urging upon those who make our laws as early and effective action as possible.

America is not afraid of anybody. I know that I express your feeling and the feeling of all our fellow citizens when I say that the only thing I am afraid of is not being ready to perform my duty. I am afraid of the danger of shame; I am afraid of the danger of inadequacy; I am afraid of the danger of not being able to express the great character of this country with tremendous might and effectiveness whenever we are called upon to act in the field of the world's affairs.

For it is character we are going to express, not power merely. The United States is not in love with the aggressive use of power. It despises the aggressive use of power. There is not a foot of territory belonging to any other nation which this Nation covets or desires. There is not a privilege which we ourselves enjoy that we would dream of denying any other nation in the world. If there is one thing that the American people love and believe in more than another it is peace and all the handsome things that belong to peace. I hope that you will bear me out in saying that I have proved that I am a partisan of peace. I would be ashamed to be belligerent and impatient when the fortunes of my whole country and the happiness of all my fellow countrymen were involved. But I know that peace is not always within the choice of the Nation, and I want to remind you, and remind you very solemnly, of the double obligation you have laid upon me. I know you have laid it upon me because I am constantly reminded of it in conversation, by letter, in editorial, by means of every voice that comes to me out of the body of the Nation. You have laid upon me this double obligation: "We are relying upon you, Mr. President, to keep us out of this war, but we are relying upon you, Mr. President, to keep the honor of the Nation unstained."

Do you not see that a time may come when it is impossible to do both of these things? Do you not see that if I am to guard the honor of the Nation, I am not protecting it against itself, for we are not going to do anything to stain the honor of our own country. I am protecting it against things that I cannot control, the action of others. And where the action of others may bring us I cannot foretell. You may count upon my heart and resolution to keep you out of the war, but you must be ready if it is necessary that I should maintain your honor. That is the only thing a real man loves about himself. Some men who are not real men love other things about themselves, but the real man believes that his honor is dearer than his life; and a nation is merely all of us put together, and the Nation's honor is dearer than the Nation's comfort and the Nation's peace and the Nation's life itself. . . .

At Milwaukee, Wis., January 31, 1916.

(The Western Preparedness Tour)

Mr. Chairman and Fellow Citizens:

I need not inquire whether the citizens of Milwaukee and Wisconsin are interested in the subject of my errand. The presence of this great body in this vast hall sufficiently attests your interest, but I want at the outset to remove a misapprehension that I fear may exist in your mind. There is no sudden crisis; nothing new has happened; I am not out upon this errand because of any unexpected situation. I have come to confer with you upon a matter upon which it would, in any circumstances, be necessary for us to confer when all the rest of the world is on fire and our own house is not fireproof. Everywhere the atmosphere of the world is thrilling with the passion of a disturbance such as the world has never seen before, and it is wise, in the words just uttered by your chairman, that we should see that our own house is set in order and that everything is done to make certain that we shall not suffer by the general conflagration.

There were some dangers to which this Nation seemed

at the outset of the war to be exposed, which, I think I can say with confidence, are now passed and overcome. America has drawn her blood and her strength out of almost all the nations of the world. It is true of a great many of us that there lies deep in our hearts the recollection of an origin which is not American. We are aware that our roots, our traditions, run back into other national soils. There are songs that stir us; there are some far-away historical recollections which engage our affections and stir our memories. We can not forget our forbears; we can not altogether ignore the fact of our essential blood relationship; and at the outset of this war it did look as if there were a division of domestic sentiment which might lead us to some errors of judgment and some errors of action; but I, for one, believe that danger is passed. . . .

I have at no time supposed that the men whose voices seemed to contain the threat of division amongst us were really uttering the sentiments even of those whom they pretended to represent. I for my part have no jealousy of family sentiment. I have no jealousy of that deep affection which runs back through long lineage. It would be a pity if we forget the fine things that our ancestors have done. But I also know the magic of America; I also know the great principles which thrill men in the singular body politic to which we belong in the United States. I know the impulses which have drawn men to our shores. They have not come idly; they have not come without conscious purpose to be free; they have not come without voluntary desire to unite themselves with the great nation on this side of the sea; and I know that whenever the test comes every man's heart will be first for America. It was principle and affection and ambition and hope that drew men to these shores, and they are not going to forget the errand upon which they came and allow America, the home of their refuge and hope, to suffer by any forgetfulness on their part. And so the trouble makers have shot their bolt, and it has been ineffectual. Some of them have been vociferous; all of them have been exceedingly irresponsible. Talk was cheap, and that was all it cost them. They did not have to do anything. But you will know without my telling you that the man who for the time being you have charged with the duties of President of the United States must talk with a deep sense of responsibility, and he must remember, above all things else, the fine traditions of his office which some men seem to have forgotten. There is no precedent in American history for any action of aggression on the part of the United States or for any action which might mean that America is seeking to connect herself with the controversies on the other side of the water. Men who seek to provoke us to such action have forgotten the traditions of the United States, but it behooves those with whom you have entrusted office to remember the traditions of the United States and to see to it that the actions of the Government are made to square with those traditions. . . .

Our thoughts are concentrated upon our own affairs and our own relations to the rest of the world, but the thoughts of the men who are engaged in this struggle are concentrated upon the struggle itself, and there is daily and hourly danger that they will feel themselves constrained to do things which are absolutely inconsistent with the rights of the United States. They are not thinking of us. I am not criticizing them for not thinking of us. I dare say if I were in their place neither would I think of us. They believe that they are struggling for the lives and honor of their nations, and that if the United States puts its interests in the path of this great struggle, she ought to know beforehand that there is danger of very serious misunderstanding and difficulty. So that the very uncalculating unpremeditated, one might almost say accidental, course of affairs, may touch us to the quick at any moment, and I want you to realize that, standing in the midst of these difficulties, I feel that I am charged with a double duty of the utmost difficulty. In the first place, I know that you are depending upon me to keep this Nation out of the war. So far I have done so, and I pledge you my word that, God helping me, I will if it is possible. But you have laid another duty upon me. You have bidden me see to it that nothing stains or impairs the honor of the United States, and that is a matter not within my control; that depends upon what others do, not upon what the Government of the United States does. Therefore, there may at any moment come a time when I can not preserve both the honor and the peace of the United States. Do not exact of me an impossible and contradictory thing, but stand ready and insistent that everybody who represents you should stand ready to provide the necessary means for maintaining the honor of the United States.

I sometimes think that it is true that no people ever went to war with another people. Governments have gone to war with one another. Peoples, so far as I remember, have not, and this is a government of the people, and this people is not going to choose war. But we are not dealing with people; we are dealing with Governments. We are dealing with Governments now engaged in a great struggle, and therefore we do not know what a day or an hour will bring forth. All that we know is the character of our own duty. We do not want the question of peace and war, or the conduct of war, entrusted too entirely to our Government. We want war, if it must come, to be something that springs out of the sentiments and principles and actions of the people themselves; and it is on that account that I am counseling the Congress of the United States not to take the advice of those who recommend that we should have, and have very soon, a great standing Army, but, on the contrary, to see to it that the citizens of this country are so trained and that the military equipment is so sufficiently provided for them that when they choose they can take up arms and defend themselves.

The Constitution of the United States makes the President the Commander-in-Chief of the Army and Navy of the Nation, but I do not want a big Army subject to my personal command. If danger comes, I want to turn to you and the rest of my fellow countrymen and say, "Men, are you ready?" and I know what the response will be. I know that there will spring up out of the body of the Nation a great host of free men, and I want those men not to be mere targets for shot and shell. I want them to know something of the arms they have in their hands. I want them to know something about how to guard against the diseases that creep into camps, where men are unaccustomed to live. I want them to know something of what the orders mean that they will be under when they enlist under arms for the Government of the United States. I want them to be men who can comprehend and easily and intelligently step into the duty of national defense. That is the reason that I am urging upon the Congress of the United States at any rate the beginnings of a system by which we may give a very considerable body of our fellow citizens the necessary training. . . .

It is being very sedulously spread abroad in this country that the impulse back of all this is the desire of men who make the materials of warfare to get money out of the Treasury of the United States. I wish the people that say that could see meetings like this. Did you come here for that purpose? Did you come here because you are interested to see some of your fellow citizens make money out of the present situation? Of course you did not. I am ready to admit that probably the equipment of those men whom we are training will have to be bought from somebody, and I know that if the equipment is bought, it will have to be paid for; and I dare say somebody will make some money out of it. It is also true, ladies and gentlemen, that there are men now, a great many men, in the belligerent countries who are growing rich out of the sale of the materials needed by the armies of those countries. If the Government itself does not manufacture everything that an army needs, somebody has got to make money out of it, and I for my part have been urging the Congress of the United States to make the necessary preparations by which the Government can manufacture armor plate and munitions, so that, being in the business itself and having the ability to manufacture all it needs, if it is put upon a business basis, it can at any rate keep the price that it pays within moderate and reasonable limits. The Government of the United States is not going to be imposed upon by anybody, and you may rest assured, therefore, that while I believe you prefer that private capital and private initiative should bestir themselves in these matters, it is also possible, and I assure you that it is most likely, that the Government of the United States will have adequate means of controlling this matter very thoroughly indeed. There need be no fear on that side. Let nobody suppose that this is a money-making agitation. I would for one be ashamed to be such a dupe as to be engaged in it if it had any suspicion of that about it, but I am not as innocent as I look; and I believe that I can say for my colleagues in Washington that they are just as watchful in such matters as you would desire them to be.

And there is another misapprehension that I do not wish you to entertain. Do not suppose that there is any new or sudden or recent inadequacy on the part of this Government in respect of preparation for national defense. I have heard some gentlemen say that we had no coast defenses worth talking about. Coast defenses are not nowadays advertised, you understand, and they are not visible to the naked eye, so that if you passed them and nothing exploded, you would not know they were there. The coast defenses of the United States, while not numerous enough, are equipped in the most modern and efficient fashion. You are told that there has been some sort of neglect about the Navy. There has not been any sort of neglect about the Navy. We have been slowly building up a Navy which in quality is second to no navy in the world. The only thing it lacks is quantity. In size it is the fourth navy in the world, though I have heard it said by some gentlemen in this very region that it was the second. In fighting force, though not in quality, it is reckoned by experts to be the fourth in rank in the world; and yet when I go on board those ships and see their equipment and talk with their officers I suspect that they could give an account of themselves which would raise them above the fourth class. It reminds me of that very quaint saying of the old darky preacher, "The Lord says unto Moses, come fourth, and he came fifth and lost the race." But I think this Navy would not come fourth in the race, but higher.

What we are proposing now is not the sudden creation of a Navy, for we have a splendid Navy, but the definite working out of a program by which within five years we shall bring the Navy to a fighting strength which otherwise might have taken eight or ten years; along exactly the same lines of development that have been followed and followed diligently and intelligently for at least a decade past. There is no sudden panic, there is no sudden change of plan; all that has happened is that we now see that we ought more rapidly and more thoroughly than ever before to do the things which have always been characteristic of America. For she has always been proud of her Navy and has always been addicted to the principle that her citizenship must do the fighting on land. We are working out American principle a little faster, because American pulses are beating a little faster, because the world is in a whirl, because there are incalculable elements of trouble abroad which we cannot control or alter. I would be derelict to the duty which you have laid upon me if I did not tell you that it was absolutely necessary to carry out our principles in this matter now and at once. . . .

Woodrow Wilson

At Chicago, Ill., January 31, 1916.

(The Western Preparedness Tour)

Mr. Chairman and Fellow Citizens:

A year ago, though the war in Europe had then been six months in progress, I take it it would have seemed incredible to all of us that the storm should continue to gather in intensity instead of spending its force. I suppose that twelve months ago no one could have predicted the extraordinary way in which the violence of the struggle has increased from month to month; and the difficulties involved by reason of that war have also increased beyond all calculation. A year ago it did seem as if America might rest secure without very great anxiety and take it for granted that she would not be drawn into this terrible maelstrom, but those first six months was merely the beginning of the struggle. Another year has been added, and now no man can confidently say whether the United States will be drawn into the struggle or not. Therefore, it is absolutely necessary that we should take counsel together as to what it is necessary that we should do. . . .

Have you not realized how all the world seems to have been constantly conscious from the beginning of this struggle that America was, so to say, the only audience before whom this terrible plot was being worked out; how everybody engaged in the struggle has seemed to turn to America for moral judgments concerning it; how each side in the titanic struggle has appealed to us to adjudge their enemies in the wrong; how there has been no tragical turn in the course of events that America has not been called on for some sort of protest or expression of opinion? And so those of us who are charged with the responsibility of affairs have realized very intensely that there was a certain sense in which America was looked to to keep even the balance of the whole world's thought.

And America was called upon to do something very much more than that even; profoundly difficult, if not impossible, though that be, she was called upon to assert in times of war the standards of times of peace. There is an old saying that the laws are silent in the presence of war. Alas, yes; not only the civil laws of individual nations but also apparently the law that governs the relation of nations with one another must at times fall silent and look on in dumb impotency. And yet it has been assumed throughout this struggle that the great principles of international law and of international comity had not been suspended, and the United States, as the greatest and most powerful of the disengaged nations, has been looked to to hold high the standards which should govern the relationship of nations to each other.

I know that on the other side of the water there has been a great deal of cruel misjudgment with regard to the reasons why America has remained neutral. Those who look at us at a distance, my fellow citizens, do not feel the strong pulses of ideal principle that are in us. They do not feel the conviction of America, that her mission is a mission of peace, and that righteousness can be maintained as a standard in the midst of arms. They do not realize that back of all our energy by which we have built up great material wealth and created great material power we are a body of idealists, much more ready to lay down our lives for a thought than for a dollar. They suppose, some of them, that we are holding off because we can make money while others are dying, the most cruel misunderstanding that any nation has ever had to face; so wrong that it seems almost useless to try to correct it, because it shows that the very fundamentals of our life are not comprehended and understood.

I need not tell you, my fellow citizens, that we have not held off from this struggle from motives of self-interest, unless it be considered self-interest to maintain our position as the trustees of the moral judgment of the world. We have believed, and I believe, that we can serve even the nations at war better by remaining at peace and holding off from this contest than we could possibly serve them in any other way. Your interest, your sympathy, your affections may be engaged on the one side or the other, but no matter which side they are engaged on it is your duty even to your affections in this great affair to stand off and not let this Nation be drawn into the war. Somebody must keep the great stable foundations of the life of nations untouched and undisturbed. Somebody must keep the great economic processes of the world of business alive. Somebody must see to it that we stand ready to repair the enormous damage and the incalculable losses which will ensue from this war, and which it is hardly credible could be repaired if every great nation in the world were drawn into the contest. Do you realize how nearly it has come about that every great nation in the world has been drawn in? The flame has touched even our own continent by drawing in our Canadian neighbors to the north of us, and, except for the South American Continent, there is not one continent upon the whole surface of the world to which this flame has not spread; and when I see some of my fellow citizens spread tinder where the sparks are falling, I wonder what their ideal of Americanism is. . . .

Look at the task that is assigned to the United States, to assert the principles of law in a world in which the principles of law have broken down—not the technical principles of law, but the essential principles of right dealing and humanity as between nation and nation. Law is a very complicated term. It includes a great many things that do not engage our affections, but at the basis of the things that we are now dealing with lie the deepest affections of the human heart, the love of life, the love of righteousness, the love of fair dealing, the love of those things that are just and of good report. The things that are rooted in our very spirit are the stuff of the law that I am talking about now.

We may have to assert these principles of right and of humanity at any time. What means are available? What force is at the disposal of the United States to assert these things? The force of opinion? Opinion, I am sorry to say, my fellow citizens, did not bring this war on, and I am afraid that opinion can not stay its progress. This war was brought on by rulers, not by the people; and I thank God that there is no man in America who has the authority to bring war on without the consent of the people. No man for many a year yet can trace the real sources of this war, but this thing we know, that opinion did not bring it on and that the force of opinion, at any rate the force of American opinion, is not going to stop it.

I admire the hopeful confidence of those of our fellow citizens who believe that American opinion can stop it, but, being somewhat older than some of them, and having run through a rather wide gamut of experience, I am prevented from sharing their hopeful optimism. I would not belittle the influences of opinion, least of all the influences of American opinion—it is very influential—but it will not stop this overwhelming flood. And, if not the force of opinion, what force has America available to stop the flood from overflowing her own fair area?

We have one considerable arm of force, a very considerable arm of force, namely, the splendid Navy of the United States. I am told by the experts, to whose judgment I must defer in these matters, that the Navy of the United States, in respect of its enumerated force, ranks only fourth among the navies of the world. I indulge myself in the opinion that in quality it ranks very much higher than fourth place. The United States has never been negligent of its Navy, despite what some gentlemen may say; least of all has it been negligent in recent years. Three years ago there were 182 vessels in commission in that Navy;

there are now 238. Three dreadnoughts and fifteen subordinate craft will be added within a month or two. There have been added six thousand capable sailors to the ranks of the enlisted men of that Navy. The Congress of the United States in the last three years has poured out more money than was poured out on the average in any previous years in the history of the United States for the maintenance and upbuilding of the United States Navy; has spent forty-four million dollars a year as contrasted with a previous average of not more than thirty-three and a half million. All the subsidiary arms of the service have been built up. Three years ago there were four officers assigned the duty connected with aviation, and they did not have a single available—at any rate usable—craft at their service; now there are thirty-seven airships, 121 commissioned officers, and a large number of non-commissioned officers and a sufficient force of enlisted men in the school of practice at Pensacola; and that is only the beginning, because the Sixty-third Congress, the last Congress, was the first to make a specific appropriation for aviation in connection with the Navy.

We have given to the present fleet of the United States an organization such as it never had before, I am told by Admiral Fletcher, and we have made preparations for immediate war, so far as the Navy is concerned. The trouble is not with the quality or the organization of the existing Navy; it is merely that we have followed plans piecemeal, a little bit at a time, now in this direction, now in that direction; that we have never had a plan thought out to cover a number of years in advance; that we have never set ourselves a definite goal of equipment and set our resolution to attain that goal within a reasonable length of time. The plans that are being proposed to the present Congress, and which the present Congress will adopt, are plans to remedy this piecemeal treatment of the Navy and bring it to its highest point of efficiency by steady plans carried out from month to month and year to year. It is going to cost a good deal of money, and I find that the difficulty with some members of Congress is, not what ought to be done about the Navy, but what they are going to tax in order to get the money. . . .

But what Army have we available? I can tell you, because it has been necessary for us to take care of the patrolling of a very long southern border between us and Mexico. We have not men enough in the United States Army for the routine work of peace, and the increase in the Regular Army that is being proposed to the present Congress is intended only to bring the Regular Army up to an adequate peace establishment. I say that that is all that is being proposed with regard to the Regular Army. The United States has never, my fellow citizens, depended upon the Regular Army to conduct its wars. It has depended upon the Volunteers of the United States, and it has never been disappointed either in their numbers or in their quality. But modern warfare is very different from what warfare used to be. Warfare has changed so within the span of a single life that it is nothing less than brutal to send raw recruits into the trenches and into the field. . . .

What we wish is a definite citizen reserve of men trained to arms to a sufficient extent to make them quickly transformable into a fighting force, organized under the immediate direction of the United States, subject to a definite pledge to serve the United States, and pledged to obey immediately the call of the President when Congress authorizes him to call them to arms. We do not want men to devote the greater part of their time to training in arms. We want men whose occupation and passion and habit is peace, because they are the only men who can carry into the field the spirit of America as contrasted with the spirit of the professional soldier. I would not have you for a moment understand me as detracting from the character and reputation of the professional soldier as we know him in the United States. I have dealt with him; he is as good an American as I am. He has a degree of intelligence and of devotion to his duty which commands my entire admiration. But the spirit of every profession is different from the spirit of the community. . . .

I have been asked by questioning friends in Washington whether I thought a sufficient number of men would volunteer for the training or not. Why, if they did not, it is not the America that you and I know; something has happened. They have said, "Do you suppose that the men who employ young men would give them leave to take this training?" I say, "Certainly I suppose it; I know it." Because I know that the patriotism of America is not a name and an empty boast, but a splendid reality. If they did not do it, I should be ashamed of America, and I never expect to see the day when America gives me the slightest reason to be ashamed of her. I am sorry for the skeptics who believe that the response would not be tremendous; not grudging, but overflowing in its abundant strength. And it is to prove that that we want to try the plans that are before the present Congress.

You will remind me of the great National Guard of the country; but how great is it, ladies and gentlemen? There are one hundred million people in this country and there are only 129,000 men in the National Guard, and those 129,000 men are under the direction, by the constitutional arrangement of our system, of the governments of more than two score States. The President of the United States is not at liberty to call them out of their States except upon the occasion of actual invasion of the territory of the United States. We are not now thinking of invasion of the territory of the United States. That is not what is making us anxious. We are not asking ourselves, "Shall we be prepared to defend our own shores and our own homes?" Is that all that we stand for, to keep the door securely shut against enemies? Certainly not. What of the great trusteeship we have set up for liberty of government and national independence in the whole Western Hemisphere? What of the pledges back of that great principle that has been ours and guided our foreign affairs ever since the day of President Monroe? We stand pledged to see that both the continents of America are left free to be used by their peoples as those peoples choose to use them, under a principle of national popular sovereignty as absolute and unchallenged as our own. And at this very moment, as I am speaking to you, the Americas are drawing together upon that handsome principle of reciprocal respect and reciprocal defense. . . .

At Des Moines, Iowa, February 1, 1916.

(The Western Preparedness Tour)

Mr. Chairman, Your Excellency, and Fellow Citizens:

Some one who does not know our fellow citizens quite as well as he ought to know them told me that there was a certain degree of indifference and lethargy in the Middle West with regard to the defense of the Nation. I said, "I do not believe it, but I am going out to see"; and I have seen. I have seen what I expected to see—great bodies of serious men, great bodies of earnest women, coming together to show their profound interest in the objects of this visit of mine. I know, therefore, that it is my privilege to address those who will realize the spirit of responsibility in which I speak to them.

My fellow citizens, it would be easy, if I permitted myself to do so, to draw a picture of the present situation of the world which would deeply stir your feelings and perhaps deeply excite your apprehension, but you would not think that it was right for your Chief Magistrate to speak any word of excitement whatever. I want you to believe that in what I say to you I am endeavoring as far as extemporaneous speech will permit to weigh every word that

I say. I said a moment ago that you know the errand upon which I have come to you, but do you know the reasons why I have undertaken that errand? There are some very conclusive and imperative reasons. Some of our fellow citizens are seeking to darken counsel upon this great matter; not I hope and believe out of wrong motives, but certainly I believe out of mistaken conceptions of the duty and interest of America.

On the one hand, there is a considerable body of men who are trying to stir the very sort of excitement in this country upon which every true, well-balanced American ought to frown. There are actually men in America who are preaching war, who are preaching the duty of the United States to do what it never would before, seek entanglement in the controversies which have arisen on the other side of the water—abandon its habitual and traditional policy and deliberately engage in the conflict which is now engulfing the rest of the world. I do not know what the standards of citizenship of these gentlemen may be. I only know that I for one can not subscribe to those standards. I believe that I more truly speak the spirit of America when I say that that spirit is a spirit of peace. Why, no voice has ever come to any public man more audibly, more unmistakably, than the voice of this great people has come to me, bearing this impressive lesson, "We are counting upon you to keep this country out of war." And I call you to witness, my fellow countrymen, that I have spent every thought and energy that has been vouchsafed me in order to keep this country out of war. It can not be disclosed now, perhaps it can never be disclosed, how anxious and difficult that task has been, but my heart has been in it. I have not grudged a single burden that has been thrown upon me with that end in view, for I knew that not only my own heart, but the heart of all America, was in the cause of peace.

Yet, my fellow citizens, there are some men amongst

us preaching peace who go much further than I can go. Not further than I can go in the sentiment of peace; not further than truth warrants them in going in interpreting the desire and sentiment of America, but further than I can follow them, further, I believe, than you can follow them, in preaching the doctrine of peace at any price and in any circumstances. There is a price which is too great to pay for peace, and that price can be put in one word. One can not pay the price of self-respect. One can not pay the price of duties abdicated, of glorious opportunities neglected, of character, national character left without vindication and exemplification in action. America has a character as distinct as the character of any individual amongst us. We read that character in every page of her singular and glorious history. It is written in invisible signs which, nevertheless, our spirits can decipher upon the very folds of the flag which is the emblem of our national life.

The gentlemen who are out-and-out pacifists are making one fundamental mistake. That is not a mistake about the sentiments of America, but a mistake about the circumstances of the world. America does not constitute the world. In many of her sentiments and predilections she does not represent or influence the world. The dangers to our peace do not come any longer from within our own borders. I could not have said that a few months ago. Passion was astir in this country. There was a clash of sympathies and a heat of passion which made our air tense and made men hold their breath for fear some of our fellow countrymen would forget that their first loyalty was to America and only their second loyalty to the ancient affections which bound them, and honorably bound them, to some older country and polity. But those dangers have passed. America has regained her self-possession. Men are now ready to feel and to act in common in the great cause of a common national life, and no influence within America is going to disturb the peace of America.

But America can not be an ostrich with its head in the sand. America can not shut itself out from the rest of the world, because all the dangers at this present moment, and they are many, come from her contacts with the rest of the world. Those contacts are going to be largely determined by other nations and not determined by ourselves. I have not come to tell you that there is any danger to our national life from anything that your Government may do or your Congress propose. I have come to tell you that there is danger to our national life from what other nations may do. And let me say, ladies and gentlemen, that I would not speak of other nations in a spirit of criticism. Not only would it not become me to do so, as your spokesman and representative, but I would not be interpreting my real feeling if I did so. Every nation now engaged in the titanic struggle on the other side of the water believes, with an intensity of conviction that can not be exaggerated, that it is fighting for its rights, and in most instances that it is fighting for its life; and we must not be too critical of the men who lead those nations. . . .

What is America expected to do? She is expected to do nothing less than keep law alive while the rest of the world burns. You know that there is no international tribunal, my fellow citizens. I pray God that if this contest have no other result, it will at least have the result of creating an international tribune and producing some sort of joint guarantee of peace on the part of the great nations of the world. But it has not yet done that, and the only thing, therefore, that keeps America out of danger is that to some degree the understandings, the ancient and honorable understandings, of nations with regard to their relations to one another and to the citizens of one another are to some extent still observed and followed. And whenever there is a departure from them, the United States is called upon to intervene, to speak its voice of protest, to speak its voice of insistence.

Do you want it to be only a voice of insistence? Do you want the situation to be such that all that the President can do is to write messages; to utter words of protest? If these breaches of international law which are in daily danger of occurring should touch the very vital interests and honor of the United States, do you wish to do nothing about it? Do you wish to have all the world say that the flag of the United States, which we love, can be stained with impunity? Why, to ask the question is to answer it. I know that there is not a man or a woman in the hearing of my voice who would wish peace at the expense of the honor of the United States. . . .

My fellow citizens, you may be called upon any day to stand behind me to maintain the honor of the United States. And how are you going to do it? There are two ways of doing it. One is the careless, easy-going, wasteful way in which we have done these things hitherto. You say, "There are plenty of fighting men in the United States; there are unexhausted and inexhaustible material resources in the United States; nobody could do more than put us at a disadvantage for a little while." Yes; there are plenty of fighting men in the United States; but do they know how modern war is conducted? Do they know how to guard themselves against disease in the camp? Do they know what the discipline of organization is? Shall we send the whole body of those men who first volunteer to be butchered because they did not know how to make themselves immediately ready for the battlefield and the trench; because they did not know anything about the terrible vicissitudes and disciplines of modern battle?

Why, war has been transformed almost within the memory of men. The mere mustering of volunteers is not war. Mere bodies of men are not an army; and we have neither the men nor the equipment for the men if they should be called out. It would take time to make an army of them —perhaps a fatal length of time—and it would take a long time to provide them with the absolute necessities of warfare. America is not going to sacrifice her youth after that fashion. America is going to prepare for war by preparing citizens who know what war means and how war can be conducted. It is going to increase its standing army up to the point of efficiency for the present uses for which it is needed, and it is going to put back of that army a great body of peaceful men, following their daily pursuits, knowing that their own happiness and the happiness of everybody they love depends upon peace, who, nevertheless, at the call of their country, will know how immediately to make themselves into an army and to come out and face an enemy in a fashion which will show that America can neither be daunted nor taken by surprise. . . .

AT TOPEKA, KANS., FEBRUARY 2, 1916.

(The Western Preparedness Tour)

Mr. Chairman, Your Excellency, Fellow Citizens:

I was told before I came here, and I read in one of your papers this morning, that Kansas was not in sympathy with any policy of preparation for national defense. I do not believe a word of it. I long ago learned to distinguish between editorial opinion and popular opinion. Moreover, having been addicted to books, I happened to have read the history of Kansas, and if there is any place in the world fuller of fight than Kansas I would like to hear of it; any other place fuller of fight on the right lines. Kansas is not looking for trouble, but Kansas has made trouble for everybody that interfered with her liberties or her rights, and if I were to pick out one place which was likely to wince first and get hot first about invasion of the essential principles of American liberty I certainly would look to Kansas among the first places in the country. If Kansas is opposed or has been opposed to the policy of preparation for national defense, it has been only because somebody has misrepresented that policy, and Kansas does not know what it is.

What is the issue? Why, of course, there are some men going about proposing great military establishments for America, but you have not heard anybody connected with the administration who did. You have not heard anybody in any responsible position who could carry his plan out who did. The singular thing about this situation is that the loudest voices have been the irresponsible voices. It is easy to talk and to say what ought to be done when you know that you do not have to do it. Nobody in authority, nobody in a position to lead the policy of the country, has proposed great military armaments, and nobody who really understands the history or shares the spirit of America could or would propose great military establishments for America. But I have heard of men in Kansas who owned their own firearms and knew how to use them, and if there is any place in the Union more than another where you ought to understand what it is to be ready to take care of yourselves, this is the place. All that anybody in authority has proposed is that America should be put in such a position that her free citizens should know how to take care of themselves and their country when the occasion arose.

We have been proposing only a very moderate increase in the standing army of the country because it is already too small for the routine uses of peace. I have not had soldiers enough to patrol the border between here and Mexico. I have not had soldiers enough for the ordinary services of the Army, and there are many things that it has been impossible for me to do which it was my duty to do, because there were not men to do them with. You are not, I am sure, going to be jealous of an increase of the Army merely sufficient to enable the Executive to carry out his constitutional responsibilities. Over and above that we have proposed this, that a sufficient number of men out of the ranks of the civil pursuits of the country should be trained in the use and keeping of arms, in the sanitation of camps, in the maneuvers of the field, and in military organization; to be ready and pledged to be ready, if the call should come upon act of Congress, to unite their force with the little force of the Army itself and make a great multitude of armed men who were ready to vindicate the rights of America.

Is there anything inconsistent with the traditions of Kansas or with the true traditions of America in a proposal like that? The very essence of American tradition is contained in the proposal. Every constitution of every State in the Union forbids the State legislature to abridge the right of its citizens to carry arms. At the very outset the makers of our very institutions realized that the force of the Nation must dwell in the homes of the Nation. I do not mean the moral force merely; I mean the physical force also. They realized that every man must be allowed not only to have a vote, but, if he wanted to, to have a gun too, so that when the voices of peace did not suffice, the voices of force would prevail; knowing that great bodies of men do not use force to usurp their own liberties, but to declare and vindicate their liberties, and that there will be no collusion among free men to upset free institutions; that, whereas cliques and coteries and professional groups may conceive it to be of their interest to interfere with the peaceful life of the country, the general body of citizens would never so conceive it.

What we are asking is this, that the Nation supply arms for those of the Nation who are ready, if occasion should arise, to come to the national defense, and that it should do this without withdrawing them from their pursuits of industry and of peace, in order that America should know that in the fountains from which she always draws her strength there welled up the inexhaustible resources of American manhood. This is not a military policy; this is a policy of adequate preparation for national defense, and any man who represents it in any other light must either be ignorant or is consciously misrepresenting the facts. . . .

The spirit of America would hold any Executive back, would hold any Congress back, from any action that had the least taint of aggression upon it. We are not going to invade any nation's territory. We are not going to covet any nation's possessions. We are not going to invade any nation's rights. But suppose, my fellow countrymen, some nation should invade our rights. What then? What would Kansas think? What would Kansas do then? What would America, speaking by the voice of Kansas or any other State in the Union, think and do then? I have come here to tell you that the difficulties of our foreign policy, the delicate questions of our foreign relationships, do not diminish either in number or in delicacy and difficulty, but, on the contrary, daily increase in number and in intricacy and in danger, and I would be derelict to my duty to you if I did not deal with you in these matters with the utmost candor and tell you what it may be necessary to use the force of the United States to do.

For one thing, it may be necessary to use the force of the United States to vindicate the right of American citizens everywhere to enjoy the protection of international law. There is nothing you would be quicker to blame me for than neglecting to safeguard the rights of Americans, no matter where they might be in the world. There are perfectly clearly marked rights guaranteed by international law which every American is entitled to enjoy, and America is not going to abide the habitual or continued neglect of those rights. Perhaps not being as near the ports as some other Americans, you do not travel as much and you do not realize the infinite number of legitimate errands upon which Americans travel—errands of commerce, errands of relief, errands of business for the Government, errands of every sort which make America useful to the world. Americans do not travel to disturb the world; they travel to quicken the processes of the interchange of life and of goods in the world, and their travel ought not to be impeded by a reckless disregard of international obligation.

There is another thing that we ought to safeguard, and that is our right to sell what we produce in the open neutral markets of the world. Where there is a blockade, we recognize the right to blockade; where there are the ordinary restraints created by a state of war, we ought to recognize those restraints; but the world needs the wheat off of the Kansas fields and off the other great flowering acres of the United States, and we have a right to supply the rest of the world with the products of those fields. We have a right to send food to peaceful populations wherever the conditions of war make it possible to do so under the ordinary rules of international law. We have a right to supply them with our cotton to clothe them. We have a right to supply them with our manufactured products.

We have made some mistakes, my fellow citizens. For several generations past we have so neglected our merchant marine that one of the difficulties we are struggling against has nothing to do with international questions. We have not got the American ships to send the goods in, and we have got to get them. I am going to ask you to follow the fortunes of the so-called shipping bill in the present Congress and make suggestions to your Congressmen as to the absolute necessity of getting your wheat and your other products out of the ports and upon the high seas where they can go, and shall go, under the protection of the laws of the United States.

But that is a mere parenthesis. Aside from that, so far as there are vehicles to carry our trade, we have the right to extend our trade for the assistance of the world. For we have not been selfish in this neutral attitude of ours. I resent the suggestion that we have been selfish, desiring merely to make money. What would happen if there were no great nation disengaged from this terrible struggle? What would happen if every nation were consuming its substance in war? What would happen if no nation stood ready to assist the world with its finances and to supply it with its food? We are more indispensable now to the nations at war by the maintenance of our peace than we could possibly be to either side if we engaged in the war, and therefore there is a moral obligation laid upon us to keep out of this war if possible. But by the same token there is a moral obligation laid upon us to keep free the courses of our commerce and of our finance, and I believe that America stands ready to vindicate those rights.

But there are rights higher than either of those, higher than the rights of individual Americans outside of America, higher and greater than the rights of trade and of commerce. I mean the rights of mankind. We have made ourselves the guarantors of the rights of national sovereignty and of popular sovereignty on this side of the water in both the continents of the Western Hemisphere. You would be ashamed, as I would be ashamed, to withdraw one inch from that handsome guarantee; for it is a handsome guarantee. We have nothing to make by it, unless it be that we are to make friendships by it, and friendships are the best usury of any sort of business. So far as dollars and cents and material advantage are concerned we have nothing to make by the Monroe doctrine. We have nothing to make by allying ourselves with the other nations of the Western Hemisphere in order to see to it that no man from outside, no government from outside, no nation from outside attempts to assert any kind of sovereignty or undue political influence over the peoples of this continent.

America knows that the only thing that sustains the Monroe doctrine and all the inferences that flow from it is her own moral and physical force. The Monroe doctrine is not part of international law. The Monroe doctrine has never been formally accepted by any international agreement. The

Monroe doctrine merely rests upon the statement of the United States that if certain things happen she will do certain things. So, nothing sustains the honour of the United States in respect of these long-cherished and long-admired promises except her own moral and physical force.

Do you know what has interfered more than anything else with the peaceful relations of the United States with the rest of the world? The incredulity of the rest of the world when we have made statement of our sincere unselfishness in these matters! The greatest surprise the world ever had, politically speaking, was when the United States withdrew from Cuba. We said, "We are fighting this war for the sake of the Cubans, and when it is over we are going to turn Cuba over to her own people"; and statesmen in every capital in Europe smiled behind their hand. They said, "What! that great rich island lying directly south of the foot of your own Florida! plant your flag there and then haul it down?" Some Americans even said, "We will never raise the flag of the United States anywhere and then haul it down." And then, when the American people saw that the time had come when her promises were to be fulfilled, down came that fluttering emblem of our sovereignty, and we were more honored in its lowering than we had been in its hoisting. The American people feel the same way about the Philippines, though the rest of the world does not yet believe it. We are trustees for the Filipino people, and just so soon as we feel that they can take care of their own affairs without our direct interference and protection, the flag of the United States will again be honored by the fulfillment of a promise. That flag stands for honor, not for advantage. That flag stands for the rights of mankind, no matter where they be, no matter what their antecedents, no matter what the race involved; it stands for the absolute right to political liberty and free self government, and wherever it stands for the contrary American traditions have begun to be forgotten.

But, my friends, the world does not understand that yet. It has got to have a few more demonstrations like the demonstration in Cuba; it has got to have a few more vindications of the American name. When those vindications have come, I believe that nothing but peace will ever reign between the United States and the nations of the rest of the world. For every man who minds his own business is sure of peace. Every man who respects his own character and observes the rights of others is sure of peace. And every nation that makes right its guide and honor its principle is sure of peace. But until these things are believed of us we must be ready with the hand of force to hold others off from the invasion of any right which we hold sacred.

I have come to you with the utmost confidence that the moment you understood the issue, all differences of party, all differences of individual judgment, all differences of point of view would fall away, and like true Americans we should all stand shoulder to shoulder in a common cause—America first and her vindication the sacred law of our life. For it is only upon the most solemn occasions that I would appeal to you as I have been appealing to-day. The final test of the validity, the strength, the irresistible force of the American ideal, has come. . . .

At Kansas City, Mo., February 2, 1916.

(The Western Preparedness Tour)

Mr. Chairman and Fellow Citizens:

I would not have come away from Washington had I not believed that there was a stronger compulsion of conscience to acquaint you with the state of affairs than there was to remain during this week at the place of guidance. You will know without my describing it to you what the task assigned me has been. It has been the task of keeping the scales so poised from day to day that no man should throw into one scale or the other any makeweight which would imperil the peace of the United States; for I have felt that you were depending upon your Government to keep you out of this turmoil which is disturbing the rest of the world. You are counting upon me to do more than keep you out of trouble, however. You are counting upon me to see to it that the rights of citizens of the United States, wherever they might be, are respected by everybody. You have counted upon me to see that your energies should be released also along the channels of trade in order that you might serve the world as the only Nation disengaged and ready to serve it. You have expected me to see that the rest of the world permitted America thus to express and exercise her human and legitimate energy.

I have come out to ask you what there was behind me in this task. . . . It is necessary, my fellow citizens, that I should ask you this question, because I do not know how long the mere word and insistence of your Government will prevail to maintain your honor and the dignity and power of the Nation. There may come a time—I pray God it may never come, but it may, in spite of everything we do, come upon us, and come of a sudden—when I shall have to ask: "I have had my say; who stands back of me? Where is the force by which the majesty and right of the United States are to be maintained and asserted?" I take it that there may in your own conviction come a time when that might and force must be vindicated and asstered. You are not willing that what your Government says should be ignored.

I have seen editorials written in more than one part of the United States sneering at the number of notes that were being written from the State Department to foreign Governments, and asking, "Why does not the Government act?" And in those same papers I have seen editorials against the preparation to do anything whatever effective if those notes are not regarded. Is that the temper of the United States? It may be the temper of some editorial offices, but it is not the temper of the people of the United States.

I came out upon this errand from Washington, and see what happened. Before I started everybody knew what errand I was bound on. I expected to meet quiet audiences and explain to them the issues of the day, and what did I meet? At every stop of the train multitudes of my fellow citizens crowded out, not to see the President of the United States merely—he is not much to look at—but to declare their ardent belief in the majesty of the Government which he stands for and for the time being represents, and to declare in one fashion or another, if it were only by cheers, that they stood ready to do their duty in the hour of need. I have been thrilled by the experiences of these few days, and I shall go back to Washington and smile at anybody who tells me that the United States is not wide awake. But, gentlemen, crowds at the stations, multitudes in great audience halls, cheers for the Government, the display—the ardent display, as from the heart—of the emblem of our Nation, the Stars and Stripes, only express the spirit of the Nation; they do not express the organized force of the Nation. And while I know, and knew before I left Washington, what the spirit of the people was, I have come out to ask them what their organization is and what they intend to make it.

Modern wars are not won by mere numbers. They are not won by mere enthusiasm. They are not won by mere national spirit. They are won by the scientific conduct of war, the scientific application of irresistible force. And what is there behind the President of the United States? Well, in the first place, there is a Navy, which, for my part, I am very proud of; a Navy, which for its numbers, ship by ship, man by man, officer by officer, I believe to be the equal of any navy in the world. But look at the great sweep of our coasts. Mind you, this war has engaged all the rest of the world outside of South America and the portion of North America occupied by the United States, and if this flame begins to creep in on us, it may, my fellow citizens, creep in toward both coasts, and here are thousands upon thousands of miles of coast. Do you know that the great sweep from the canal up the coast to Alaska is something like half the circumference of the world? Do you remember the great reaches of sea from the canal up to the St. Lawrence River? Do you know the bays, the inviting harbors, the great cities which cluster upon those coasts? And do you think that a Navy that ranks only fourth in the world in force is enough to defend the coasts and make secure the territory of a great continent like this?

We have been interested in our Navy for a great many years, and we have been slowly building it up to excellent force, but we have done it piecemeal and a little at a time. There has been a party in Congress that was for a little Navy, as well as a party in Congress that was for a big Navy, and it seemed to me a sort of theoretical situation as to whether we wanted a Navy to be proud of or not. No nation ought to wish either an Army or Navy to be proud of, to make a display with, to make a toy of. It is the arm of force which must lie back of every sovereignty in the world, and the Navy of the United States must now be as rapidly as possible brought to a state of efficiency and of numerical strength which will make it practically impregnable to the navies of the world. The fighting force of the Navy now is splendid, and I should expect very great achievements from the fine officers and trained men that constitute it, but it is not big enough; it is not numerous enough; it is incomplete. It must be completed, and what the present administration is proposing is that we limit the number of years to five within which we shall complete a definite program which will make that Navy adequate for the defense of both coasts.

But, on land what stands behind the President, if he should have to act in your behalf to enforce the demands of the United States for respect and right? An Army so small that I have not had men enough to patrol the Mexican border. The Mexican border is a very long border, I admit; it runs the whole southern length of Texas and the whole southern length of New Mexico and Arizona besides, and that is a great strip of noble territory. But what is that single border to the whole extent and coast of the United States? I have not had men enough to prevent bandits from raiding across the border of Mexico into the United States. It has been a very mortifying circumstance indeed. I have been tempted to advise Congress to help Texas build up its little force of Texas Rangers; and now, if you please, because I am asking the Congress to give the Government an Army adequate to the uses of peace, to the uses of the moment, some gentlemen go about and prate of military establishments. They see phantoms, they dream dreams. Militarism in the United States springing out of any of the proposals of this administration is—why, a man must have a very strong imagination indeed to conceive any such nonsense as that! I am not asking, the administration is not asking, to be backed by any bigger standing Army than is necessary for the uses of the moment, but it is asking this:

Do you remember the experiences of the Spanish-American war? That was not much of a war, was it? It did not last very long. . . . What happened? You sent thousands of men to their death because they were ignorant. They did not get any farther than the camps in Florida. They did not get on the water even, much less get to Cuba, and they died in the camps like flies, of all sorts of camp diseases, of all sorts of diseases that come from the ignorance of medical science and camp sanitation. Splendid boys, boys fit, with a little training, to make an invincible army, but sent to their death by miserable disease, the soil of which was ignorance, helpless ignorance. Why, the percentage of our loss in that war by disease in the camp was greater than the percentage of the loss of the Japanese by disease and battle together in their war with Russia.

It is a very mortifying thing. There is not any place in

the world where medical science is more nobly studied or more adequately applied than in the United States, but we poured crude, ignorant, untrained boys into the ranks of those armies and they died before they got sight of an enemy. Do you want to repeat that? And while that is going on what may happen? What sort of disaster may come to you while you are trying to make an army out of absolutely raw material? Why, it seems almost ridiculous to state how little the present administration is asking for. It is asking that you give it something that is not mere raw material out of which to begin to make an army when it is absolutely necessary to make an army. It is asking that five hundred thousand men be asked to volunteer to take a little training every year for three years, not more than two or three months out of the year, in order that when volunteers are called for in the case of war we may have men, at least five hundred thousand of them, who know something about the use of arms, something about the sanitation of camps, something about the organization and discipline of war in the field and in the trenches. That is all that we are asking for at the present time, and if there is any criticism to be made upon it, it is that it is too little, not too much.

There are men in Congress asking, "Can you get the five hundred thousand men? Will they volunteer?" Why, I believe you could get them out of any one State in the Union. You could almost get five thousand of them out of this audience. But, ladies and gentlemen, do not forget that that is not all there is to this problem. Suppose that I knew that back of the insistence of the United States upon its rights was a great navy that ranked first in the world and a body of men trained to arms adequate, at any rate, to fend off any initial disaster to the United States while we were making a greater army ready. That would be only the beginning. There are other things that we have been very much concerned about in Washington and that we are taking steps to attend to. The railroads of this country have never been drawn into the counsels of the Government, never until recently, in such fashion as to make plans for coordinating all of them, to transport troops and transport provisions and transport munitions in such a way as to be the effective arteries of the red blood and energy of the Nation; never until recently, though we are now beginning to do it, for we called the business men and the engineers of the country into counsel to say, "What are the resources of manufacture in this country, and how can we coordinate them and put them into cooperation, so that there will be no waste of time, no duplication of effort, and no failure to get every part of the machinery into operation should we need to use them in times of war?" We are taking counsel with regard to that now; but, mark you, the munitions of war are made in this country almost exclusively near the borders of the country, and for the most part upon the Atlantic seaboard, and any initial disaster to the force of the United States might put the greater part of them, if not all of them, in the possession of an enemy. So that you see the circle of my argument leads right back to the necessity for a force of men who can prevent an initial disaster, so that there will be no first failure, no first invasion, no first disaster.

Did you ever hear more momentous things spoken of than these? Did it ever before occur to you that you must put more than the authority of words into the mouths of men who speak for you? I have been wringing my heart and straining every energy of mind that I have to preserve the honor and integrity and peace of the United States, but think of what must lie at the back of my thought. I know what you want me to do. I would be ashamed if I did not use the utmost powers that are in me to do it. But suppose that some morning I should have to turn to you and say, "Fellow citizens, I have done as much as I can; now I must ask you to back me up with the force of the Nation." And suppose that I should know before I said it that I had not told you what that meant, as I am telling you to-night. Suppose that I had not warned you of what was involved. Suppose that I had not challenged you in a moment of peace to make ready. Do not suppose, however, that I am afraid that it is not going to be done. I would not do the injustice that that implication would involve to the gallant men upon the Hill yonder in Washington who make the laws of the Nation. They are going to do a good deal of debating, but they are going to deliver the goods. Do not misunderstand me; I do not mean that I can oblige them to deliver the goods; they are going to deliver the goods because you want them delivered.

I am a believer not only in some of the men who talk, though not all of them, but also in that vast body of my fellow citizens who do not do any talking. I would a great deal rather listen to the still, small voice that comes out of the great body of the Nation than to all the vocal orators in the land. But there are times when I must come out and say, "Do not let the voice be too small and too still"; when I must come out and say, "Fellow citizens, get up on your hind legs and talk and tell the people who represent you, wherever they are—in your State Capital or in your National Capital—what it is that the Nation desires and demands." The thing that everybody is listening for in a democracy is the tramp, tramp, tramp of the facts and the people. . . .

I am anxious, therefore, my fellow citizens, that you should look at the hot stuff of war before you touch it; that you should be cool; that you should apply your hard business sense to the proposition, "Shall we be caught unaware and do a scientific job like tyros and ignoramuses? Or shall we be ready? Shall we know how to do it, and when it is necessary to do it; shall we do it to the queen's taste?" I know what the answer of America is, but I want it to be unmistakably uttered, and I want it to be uttered now. Because, speaking with all solemnity, I assure you that there is not a day to be lost; not, understand me, because of any new or specially critical matter, but because I can not tell twenty-four hours at a time whether there is going to be trouble or not. And whether there is or not does not depend upon what I do or what I say, or upon what any man in the United States does or says. It depends upon what foreign governments do; what the commanders of ships at sea do; what those in charge of submarines do; what those who are conducting blockades do. Upon the judgment of a score of men, big and little, hang the vital issues of peace or war for the United States. . . .

This month should not go by without something decisive being done by the people of the United States by way of preparation of the arms of self-vindication and defence. . . .

I am going away from here reassured beyond even the hope that I entertained when I came here; and yet I want to beg of you that you do not let the impressions of this hour die with the hour. Let every man and woman in this place go out of here with the feeling that he must concentrate his influence from this moment until the thing is accomplished upon making certain the security and adequacy of national defence. Because, if America suffer, all the world loses its equipoise. Madness has entered into everything, and that serene flag which we have thrown to the breeze upon so many occasions as the beckoning finger of hope to those who believe in the rights of mankind will itself be stained with the blood of battle, and staggering here and there among its foes will lead men to wonder where the star of America has gone and why America has allowed herself to be embroiled when she might have carried that standard serenely forward to the redemption of the affairs of mankind. I beg of you to stand by your Government with your minds as well as your hearts, and let us redeem America by applying our judgments to the wholesome process of national defence.

At St. Louis, Mo., February 3, 1916.

(The Western Preparedness Tour)

Mr. Chairman and Fellow Citizens:

I came into the Middle West to find something, and I found it. I was told in Washington that the Middle West had a different feeling from the portions of the country that lie upon either coast, and that it was indifferent to the question of preparation for national defence. I knew enough of the Middle West of this great continent to know that the men who said that did not know what they were talking about. I knew the spirit of America to dwell as much in this great section of the country as in any other section of it, and I knew that the men of these parts loved the honor and safety of America as much as Americans everywhere love it and are ready to stand by it. I did not come out to find out how you felt or what you thought, but to tell you what was going on. I came out in order that there might be an absolute clarification of the issues which are involved in the questions immediately confronting us, because I, for one, have an absolute faith in the readiness of America to act upon the facts just as soon as America knows what the facts are.

The facts are very easily and briefly stated. What is the situation? The situation is that America is at peace with all the world and desires to remain at peace with all the world. And it is not a shallow peace; it is a genuine peace, based upon some of the most fundamental influences of international intercourse. America is at peace with all the world because she entertains a real friendship for all the nations of the world. It is not, as some have mistakenly supposed, a peace based upon self-interest. It is a peace based upon some of the most generous sentiments that characterize the human heart.

You know, my fellow citizens, that this Nation is a composite Nation. It has a genuine friendship for all the nations of the world because it is drawn from all the nations of the world. The blood of all the great national stocks runs, and runs red and strong, in the veins of America, and America understands what the genuine ties of friendship and affection are. It would tear the heartstrings of America to be at war with any of the great nations of the world. Our peace is not a superficial peace. Our peace is not based upon the mere conveniences of our national life. If great issues were involved which it was our honorable obligation to defend, we should not be at peace, but would plunge into any struggle that was necessary in order to defend the honor and integrity of the Nation; but we believe, my fellow citizens, that we can show our friendship for the world and our devotion to the principles of humanity better and more effectively by keeping out of this struggle than by getting into it. . . .

The danger is not from within, gentlemen; it is from without, and I am bound to tell you that that danger is constant and immediate, not because anything new has happened, not because there has been any change in our international relationships within recent weeks or months, but because the danger comes with every turn of events. Why gentlemen, the commanders of submarines have their instructions, and those instructions are consistent for the most part with the law of nations, but one reckless commander of a submarine, choosing to put his private interpretation upon what his government wishes him to do, might set the world on fire. There are not only governments to deal with, but the servants of governments; there are not only the contacts of politics, but also those infinitely varied contacts which come from the mere movement of mankind, the quiet processes of the everyday world. There are cargoes of cotton on the seas; there are cargoes of wheat on the seas; there are cargoes of manufactured articles on the seas; and every one of those cargoes may be the point of ignition, because every cargo goes into the field of fire, goes where there are flames which no man can control.

I know the spirit of America to be this: We respect other nations and absolutely respect their rights so long as they respect our rights. We do not claim anything for ourselves which they would not in like circumstances claim for themselves. Every statement of right that we have made is grounded upon the previous utterances of their own public men and their own judges. There is no dispute about the rights of nations under the understandings of international law. America has drawn no fine points. America has raised no novel issue. America has merely asserted the rights of her citizens and her Government upon what is written plain upon all the documents of international intercourse. Therefore America is not selfish in claiming her rights; she is merely standing for the rights of mankind when the life of mankind is being disturbed by an unprecedented war between the greatest nations of the world. Some of these days we shall be able to call the statesmen of the older nations to witness that it was we who kept the quiet flame of international principle burning upon its altars while the winds of passion were sweeping every other altar in the world. Some of these days they will look back with gratification upon the steadfast allegiance of the United States to those principles of action which every man loves when his temper is not upset and his judgment not disturbed. . . .

I am ready to make every allowance for both sides; for, having pledged myself, as your chairman has reminded you, to maintain, if it be possible for me to maintain, the peace of the United States, I have thereby pledged myself to think as far as possible from the point of view of the other side as well as from the point of view of America. I want the record of the conduct of this administration to be a record of genuine neutrality and not of pretended neutrality.

You know the circumstances of the time. You know how one group of belligerents is practically shut off by circumstances over which we have no control from the ordinary commerce of the world. You know, therefore, how the spirit of America has not been able to express itself adequately in both directions. But I believe that the people of America are genuinely neutral. I believe that their desire is to stand in unprejudiced judgment upon what is going on; not that they would arrogate to themselves the right to utter rebuking judgment upon any nation, but that they are holding themselves off to assist neither side in what is wrong, and to countenance both sides in what they are doing for the legitimate defense of their national honor.

The fortunate circumstance of America, my fellow countrymen, is that it desires nothing but a free field and no favor. Our security is in the purity of our motives. The minute we get an impure motive we are going to deserve to be insecure. The minute we desire what we have no right to, then we are going to get into trouble and ought to get into trouble. But, my fellow citizens, while we know our own hearts and know our own desires, it does not follow that other nations and other governments understand our purpose and our principle of action. These are days of infinite prejudice and passion, because they are days of war. It is said by an old maxim that amidst war the law is silent. It is also true that amidst war the judgment is silent. Men press forward towards their object with a certain degree of blind recklessness, and they are apt to excite their passion particularly against those who in any way stand in their way. Therefore, this is the situation that I have come to remind you of, for you need merely to have it stated to see it: The peace of the world, including America, depends upon the aroused passion of other nations and not upon the motives of the United States. It is for that reason that I have come to call you to a consciousness of the necessity for preparing this country for anything that may happen.

Here is the choice, and I do not see how any prudent man

could doubt which side of the alternative to take: Either we shall stand still and wait for the necessity for immediate national defence to come and then call for raw volunteers who for the first few months would be impotent as against a trained and experienced enemy, or we shall adopt the ancient American principle that the men of the country shall immediately be made ready to take care of their own Government. You have either got to make the men of this Nation in sufficient number ready to defend the Nation against initial disaster, or you have got to take the risk of initial disaster. Think of the cruelty, think of the stupidity, of putting raw levies of inexperienced men into the modern field of battle! We are not asking for armies; we are asking for a trained citizenship which will act in the spirit of citizenship and not in the spirit of military establishments. If anybody is afraid of a trained citizenship in America he is afraid also of the spirit of America itself. I do not want to command a great army under the authority granted me by the Constitution to be Commander in Chief of the Army and Navy of the United States; I want to command the confidence and support of my fellow citizens.

Of course you will back me up and come to my assistance if I need you, but will you come knowing what you are about, or will you not? Will you come knowing the character of the arms that you carry in your hands, knowing something of the discipline of organization, knowing something of how to take care of yourselves in camp, knowing something of all those things that it is necessary to know so as not to throw human life away? It is handsome, my fellow citizens, to sacrifice human life intelligently for something greater than life itself, but it is not handsome for any cause whatever to throw human life away.

The plans now laid before the Congress of the United States are merely plans not to throw the life of American youth away. Those plans are going to be adopted. I am not jealous and you are not jealous of the details; no man ought to be confident that his judgment is correct about the details; no man ought to say to any legislative body, "You must take my plan or none at all"—that is arrogance and stupidity—but we have the right to insist, and I believe that it will not be necessary to insist, that we get the essential thing; that is to say, a principle, a system, by which we can secure a trained citizenship, so that if it becomes necessary to defend the Nation the first line of defence on land will be an adequate and intelligent line of defence.

I say "on land" because America apparently has never been jealous of armed men if they are only at sea. America also knows that you can not send volunteers to sea unless you want to send them to the bottom. The modern fighting ship, the modern submarine, every instrument of modern naval warfare must be handled by experts. America has never debated or disputed that proposition, and all that we are asking for now is that a sufficient number of experts and a sufficient number of vessels be at our disposal. The vessels we have are manned by experts. There is not a better service in the world than that of the American Navy. But no matter how skilled and capable the officers or devoted the men, they must have ships enough, and we are going to give them ships enough. We have been doing it slowly and leisurely and good-naturedly, as we are accustomed to do everything in times of peace, but now we must get down to business and do it systematically. We must lay down a programme and then steadfastly carry it out and complete it. There are no novelties about the programme. All the lines of it are the lines already established, only drawn out to their legitimate conclusion, and drawn out so that they will be completed within a calculable length of time.

[It will be noticed that President Wilson grew more positive in his own convictions as the speaking tour progressed. He not only pleaded for "a great navy that ranked first in the world" (at Kansas City), and for a volunteer army of 500,000 men "to take a little training every year for three years"; but he also urged haste, for "no man knows what danger a single week or a single day or a single hour may bring forth" (Cleveland address).

A naval program of vast proportions had previously been agreed upon by the Administration, recommended to and ultimately adopted by Congress. But the details of an army system the President left to the legislative body, he finding it impossible to endorse any one of several plans proposed. Congress, after long deliberation, passed a bill federalizing the State militia and *authorizing* an increase in the regular army. The real strength of the armed forces of the United States remained unchanged until the country was drawn into the European War—fourteen months after the President's "preparedness" tour—when a selective conscription system was adopted in order to raise immediately a large army.]

PRESIDENT WILSON AND THE EUROPEAN WAR

[Included in the pages immediately following are the more important of the diplomatic notes which were sent from Washington to European governments, upon matters affecting the interests of neutrals. President Wilson himself guided the foreign policies of the nation; and, although the notes are signed by his Secretary of State—first Mr. Bryan and later Mr. Lansing—they not only express the President's views and decisions, but frequently are from his own pen.]

WILSON ASKS BELLIGERENT NATIONS TO GOVERN THEIR OPERATIONS AND CONDUCT BY THE DECLARATION OF LONDON

[The Declaration of London, laying down the rules that were to govern the signatory Nations in the conduct of war, blockade, definitions of contraband and treatment of neutral shipping, was signed in London February 26, 1909, by the United States, Great Britain, Germany, Austria-Hungary, France, Russia, Italy, Japan, Holland, and Spain. President Wilson sent the following identical note to all the belligerent European Nations as soon as war began:]

DEPARTMENT OF STATE,
WASHINGTON, August 6, 1914, 1 P. M.

Mr. Bryan instructs Mr. Page to inquire whether the British Government is willing to agree that the laws of naval warfare as laid down by the Declaration of London of

1909 shall be applicable to naval warfare during the present conflict in Europe provided that the Governments with whom Great Britain is or may be at war also agree to such application. Mr. Bryan further instructs Mr. Page to state that the Government of the United States believes that an acceptance of these laws by the belligerents would prevent grave misunderstanding which may arise as to the relations between neutral powers and the belligerents. Mr. Bryan adds that it is earnestly hoped that this inquiry may receive favorable consideration.

[August 13 Austria-Hungary replied in the affirmative. August 22 the German government did the same. Great Britain replied that she would adopt "generally the rules of the Declaration, subject to certain modifications." Following this, the British and French governments issued steadily enlarging definitions and lists of contraband and made such other radical modifications of the Declaration, that the United States withdrew its proposal in the following notes:]

DEPARTMENT OF STATE,
WASHINGTON, October 22, 1914.

To Ambassador W. H. Page (London):

Inasmuch as the British Government consider that the conditions of the present European conflict make it impossible for them to accept without modification the Declaration of London, you are requested to inform His Majesty's Government that in the circumstances the Government of the United States feels obliged to withdraw its suggestion that the Declaration of London be adopted as a temporary code of naval warfare to be observed by belligerents and neutrals during the present war; that therefore this Government will insist that the rights and duties of the United States and its citizens in the present war be defined by the existing rules of international law and the treaties of the United States irrespective of the provisions of the Declaration of London; and that this Government reserves to itself the right to enter a protest or demand in each case in which those rights and duties so defined are violated or their free exercise interfered with by the authorities of His Britannic Majesty's Government.

LANSING.

DEPARTMENT OF STATE,
WASHINGTON, October 24, 1914.

To the Ambassadors in Germany and Austria-Hungary:

Referring to Department's August 6, 1 p. m., and Embassy's October 22, relative to the Declaration of London, Mr. Lansing instructs Mr. Gerard to inform the German Government that the suggestion of the department to belligerents as to the adoption of declaration for sake of uniformity as to a temporary code of naval warfare during the present conflict has been withdrawn because some of the belligerents are unwilling to accept the declaration without modifications and that this Government will therefore insist that the rights and duties of the Government and citizens of the United States in the present war be defined by existing rules of international law and the treaties of the United States without regard to the provisions of the declaration and that the Government of the United States reserves to itself the right to enter a protest or demand in every case in which the rights and duties so defined are violated or their free exercise interfered with by the authorities of the belligerent governments.

WILSON'S APPEAL TO THE AMERICAN PEOPLE FOR NEUTRALITY

(A Proclamation—August 19, 1914.)

My Fellow Countrymen:

I suppose that every thoughtful man in America has asked himself, during these last troubled weeks, what influence the European war may exert upon the United States, and I take the liberty of addressing a few words to you in order to point out that it is entirely within our own choice what its effects upon us will be and to urge very earnestly upon you the sort of speech and conduct which will best safeguard the Nation against distress and disaster.

The effect of the war upon the United States will depend upon what American citizens say and do. Every man who really loves America will act and speak in the true spirit of neutrality, which is the spirit of impartiality and fairness and friendliness to all concerned. The spirit of the Nation in this critical matter will be determined largely by what individuals and society and those gathered in public meetings do and say, upon what newspapers and magazines contain, upon what ministers utter in their pulpits, and men proclaim as their opinions on the street.

The people of the United States are drawn from many nations, and chiefly from the nations now at war. It is natural and inevitable that there should be the utmost variety of sympathy and desire among them with regard to the issues and circumstances of the conflict. Some will wish one nation, others another, to succeed in the momentous struggle. It will be easy to excite passion and difficult to allay it. Those responsible for exciting it will assume a heavy responsibility, responsibility for no less a thing than that the people of the United States, whose love of their country and whose loyalty to its Government should unite them as Americans all, bound in honor and affection to think first of her and her interests, may be divided in camps of hostile opinion, hot against each other, involved in the war itself in impulse and opinion if not in action.

Such divisions among us would be fatal to our peace of mind and might seriously stand in the way of the proper performance of our duty as the one great nation at peace, the one people holding itself ready to play a part of impartial mediation and speak the counsels of peace and accommodation, not as a partisan, but as a friend.

I venture, therefore, my fellow countrymen, to speak a solemn word of warning to you against that deepest, most subtle, most essential breach of neutrality which may spring out of partisanship, out of passionately taking sides. The United States must be neutral in fact as well as in name during these days that are to try men's souls. We must be impartial in thought as well as in action, must put a curb upon our sentiments as well as upon every transaction that might be construed as a preference of one party to the struggle before another.

My thought is of America. I am speaking, I feel sure, the earnest wish and purpose of every thoughtful American that this great country of ours, which is, of course, the first in our thoughts and in our hearts, should show herself in this time of peculiar trial a Nation fit beyond others to exhibit the fine poise of undisturbed judgment, the dignity of self-control, the efficiency of dispassionate action; a Nation that neither sits in judgment upon others nor is disturbed in her own counsels and which keeps herself fit and free to do what is honest and disinterested and truly serviceable for the peace of the world.

Shall we not resolve to put upon ourselves the restraints which will bring to our people the happiness and the great and lasting influence for peace we covet for them?

Wilson's Reply to Belligerents' Declarations of Maritime War Zones

[November 3, 1914, Great Britain declared the entire North Sea a war-zone. February 14, 1915, Germany declared the waters surrounding the British Isles and the whole English Channel a war-zone and announced that, in retaliation for Great Britain's violations of maritime rules of war, all enemy merchant vessels found in the zone would be destroyed after February 18. Navigation in the waters north of the Shetland Islands, and in the eastern part of the North Sea, and in a zone thirty miles wide along the Dutch coast was expressly declared as being outside of this danger zone. Neutral vessels were warned that though German submarine commanders had orders to refrain from all violence against neutral shipping, Great Britain's misuse of neutral flags made the conditions dangerous.

In response, the United States sent the following communications to German and Great Britain:]

DEPARTMENT OF STATE,

WASHINGTON, February 10, 1915.

To Ambassador Gerard (Berlin):

Please address a note immediately to the Imperial German Government to the following effect:

The Government of the United States, having had its attention directed to the proclamation of the German Admiralty issued on the fourth of February, that the waters surrounding Great Britain and Ireland, including the whole of the English Channel, are to be considered as comprised within the seat of war; that all enemy merchant vessels found in those waters after the eighteenth instant will be destroyed, although it may not always be possible to save crews and passengers; and that neutral vessels expose themselves to danger within this zone of war because, in view of the misuse of neutral flags said to have been ordered by the British Government on the thirty-first of January and of the contingencies of maritime warfare, it may not be possible always to exempt neutral vessels from attacks intended to strike enemy ships, feels it to be its duty to call the attention of the Imperial German Government, with sincere respect and the most friendly sentiments but very candidly and earnestly, to the very serious possibilities of the course of action apparently contemplated under that proclamation.

The Government of the United States views those possibilities with such grave concern that it feels it to be its privilege, and indeed its duty in the circumstances, to request the Imperial German Government to consider before action is taken the critical situation in respect of the relations between this country and Germany which might arise were the German naval forces, in carrying out the policy foreshadowed in the Admiralty's proclamation, to destroy any merchant vessel of the United States or cause the death of American citizens.

It is of course not necessary to remind the German Government that the sole right of a belligerent in dealing with neutral vessels on the high seas is limited to visit and search, unless a blockade is proclaimed and effectively maintained, which this Government does not understand to be proposed in this case. To declare or exercise a right to attack and destroy any vessel entering a prescribed area of the high seas without first certainly determining its belligerent nationality and the contraband character of its cargo would be an act so unprecedented in naval warfare that this Government is reluctant to believe that the Imperial Government of Germany in this case contemplates it as possible. The suspicion that enemy ships are using neutral flags improperly can create no just presumption that all ships traversing a prescribed area are subject to the same suspicion. It is to determine exactly such questions that this Government understands the right of visit and search to have been recognized.

This Government has carefully noted the explanatory statement issued by the Imperial German Government at the same time with the proclamation of the German Admiralty, and takes this occasion to remind the Imperial German Government very respectfully that the Government of the United States is open to none of the criticisms for unneutral action to which the German Government believe the governments of certain of other neutral nations have laid themselves open; that the Government of the United States has not consented to or acquiesced in any measures which may have been taken by the other belligerent nations in the present war which operate to restrain neutral trade, but has, on the contrary, taken in all such matters a position which warrants it in holding those governments responsible in the proper way for any untoward effects upon American shipping which the accepted principles of international law do not justify; and that it, therefore, regards itself as free in the present instance to take with a clear conscience and upon accepted principles the position indicated in this note.

If the commanders of German vessels of war should act upon the presumption that the flag of the United States was not being used in good faith and should destroy on the high seas an American vessel or the lives of American citizens, it would be difficult for the Government of the United States to view the act in any other light than as an indefensible violation of neutral rights which it would be very hard indeed to reconcile with the friendly relations now so happily subsisting between the two Governments.

If such a deplorable situation should arise, the Imperial German Government can readily appreciate that the Government of the United States would be constrained to hold the Imperial German Government to a strict accountability for such acts of their naval authorities and to take any steps it might be necessary to take to safeguard American lives and property and to secure to American citizens the full enjoyment of their acknowledged rights on the high seas.

The Government of the United States, in view of these considerations, which it urges with the greatest respect and with the sincere purpose of making sure that no misunderstanding may arise and no circumstance occur that might even cloud the intercourse of the two Governments, expresses the confident hope and expectation that the Imperial German Government can and will give assurance that American citizens and their vessels will not be molested by the naval forces of Germany otherwise than by visit and search, though their vessels may be traversing the sea area delimited in the proclamation of the German Admiralty.

It is added for the information of the Imperial Government that representations have been made to His Britannic Majesty's Government in respect to the unwarranted use of the American flag for the protection of British ships.

BRYAN.

DEPARTMENT OF STATE,
WASHINGTON, February 10, 1915.

To Ambassador W. H. Page (London):

The department has been advised of the Declaration of the German Admiralty on February fourth, indicating that the British Government had on January thirty-first explicitly authorized the use of neutral flags on British merchant vessels presumably for the purpose of avoiding recognition by German naval forces. The department's attention has also been directed to reports in the press that the captain of the *Lusitania,* acting upon orders or information received from the British authorities, raised the American flag as his vessel approached the British coasts, in order to escape anticipated attacks by German submarines. To-day's press reports also contain an alleged official statement of the Foreign Office defending the use of the flag of a neutral country by a belligerent vessel in order to escape capture or attack by an enemy.

Assuming that the foregoing reports are true, the Government of the United States, reserving for future consideration the legality and propriety of the deceptive use of the flag of a neutral power in any case for the purpose of avoiding capture, desires very respectfully to point out to His Britannic Majesty's Government the serious consequences which may result to American vessels and American citizens if this practice is continued.

The occasional use of the flag of a neutral or an enemy under the stress of immediate pursuit and to deceive an approaching enemy, which appears by the press reports to be represented as the precedent and justification used to support this action, seems to this Government a very different thing from an explicit sanction by a belligerent government for its merchant ships generally to fly the flag of a neutral power within certain portions of the high seas which are presumed to be frequented with hostile warships. The formal declaration of such a policy of general misuse of a neutral's flag jeopardizes the vessels of the neutral visiting those waters in a peculiar degree by raising the presumption that they are of belligerent nationality regardless of the flag which they may carry.

In view of the announced purpose of the German Admiralty to engage in active naval operations in certain delimited sea areas adjacent to the coasts of Great Britain and Ireland, the Government of the United States would view with anxious solicitude any general use of the flag of the United States by British vessels traversing those waters. A policy such as the one which His Majesty's Government is said to intend to adopt would, if the declaration of the German Admiralty is put in force, it seems clear, afford no protection to British vessels, while it would be a serious and constant menace to the lives and vessels of American citizens.

The Government of the United States, therefore, trusts that His Majesty's Government will do all in their power to restrain vessels of British nationality from the deceptive use of the flag of the United States in the sea area defined in the German declaration, since such practice would greatly endanger the vessels of a friendly power navigating those waters and would even seem to impose upon the Government of Great Britain a measure of responsibility for the loss of American lives and vessels in case of an attack by a German naval force.

Please present a note to Sir Edward Grey in the sense of the foregoing and impress him with the grave concern which this Government feels in the circumstances in regard to the safety of American vessels and lives in the war zone declared by the German Admiralty.

You may add that this Government is making earnest representations to the German Government in regard to the danger to American vessels and citizens if the declaration of the German Admiralty is put into effect.

BRYAN.

THE SECRETARY OF STATE TO AMBASSADOR W. H. PAGE [LONDON]

The same to Ambassador Gerard (Berlin).

DEPARTMENT OF STATE,
WASHINGTON, February 20, 1915.

You will please deliver to Sir Edward Grey the following identic note which we are sending England and Germany:

In view of the correspondence which has passed between this Government and Great Britain and Germany respectively, relative to the Declaration of a war zone by the German Admiralty and the use of neutral flags by British merchant vessels, this Government ventures to express the hope that the two belligerent Governments may, through reciprocal concessions, find a basis for agreement which will relieve neutral ships engaged in peaceful commerce from the great dangers which they will incur in the high seas adjacent to the coasts of the belligerents.

The Government of the United States respectfully suggests that an agreement in terms like the following might be entered into. This suggestion is not to be regarded as in any sense a proposal made by this Government, for it of course fully recognizes that it is not its privilege to propose terms of agreement between Great Britain and Germany, even though the matter be one in which it and the people of the United States are directly and deeply interested. It is merely venturing to take the liberty which it hopes may be accorded a sincere friend desirous of embarrassing neither nation involved and of serving, if it may, the common interests of humanity. The course outlined is offered in the hope that it may draw forth the views and elicit the suggestions of the British and German Governments on a matter of capital interest to the whole world.

Germany and Great Britain to agree:

1. That neither will sow any floating mines, whether upon the high seas or in territorial waters; that neither will plant on the high seas anchored mines except within cannon range of harbors for defensive purposes only; and that all mines shall bear the stamp of the Government planting them and be so constructed as to become harmless if separated from their moorings.

2. That neither will use submarines to attack merchant vessels of any nationality except to enforce the right of visit and search.

3. That each will require their respective merchant vessels not to use neutral flags for the purpose of *disguise or ruse de guerre.*

Germany to agree:

That all importations of food or foodstuffs from the United States (and from such other neutral countries as may ask it) into Germany shall be consigned to agencies to be designated by the United States Government; that these American agencies shall have entire charge and control without interference on the part of the German Government, of the receipt and distribution of such importations, and shall distribute them solely to retail dealers bearing licenses from the German Government entitling them to receive and furnish such food and foodstuffs to noncombatants only; that any violation of the terms of the retailers' licenses shall work a forfeiture of their rights to receive such food and foodstuffs for this purpose; and that such food and foodstuffs will not be requisitioned by the German Government for any purpose whatsoever or be diverted to the use of the armed forces of Germany.

Great Britain to agree:

That food and foodstuffs will not be placed upon the absolute contraband list and that shipments of such commodities will not be interfered with or detained by British authorities if consigned to agencies designated by the United States Government in Germany for the receipt and distribution of such cargoes to licensed German retailers for distribution solely to the noncombatant population.

In submitting this proposed basis of agreement this Government does not wish to be understood as admitting or denying any belligerent or neutral right established by the principles of international law, but would consider the agreement, if acceptable to the interested powers, a *modus vivendi* based upon expediency rather than legal right and as not binding upon the United States either in its present form or in a modified form until accepted by this Government.

BRYAN.

[February 28, 1915, Germany agreed to the suggested rules practically in entirety. March 13, 1915, Great Britain declared that it did not understand from the German reply that submarine practices would be abandoned. The note recited other German offenses against humanity and upheld the British blockade.]

THE SECRETARY OF STATE TO AMBASSADOR PAGE [LONDON]

Same note sent to Ambassador Sharp (Paris).

DEPARTMENT OF STATE,
WASHINGTON, March 5, 1915.

In regard to the recent communications received from the British and French Governments concerning restraints upon commerce with Germany, please communicate with the British foreign office in the sense following:

The difficulty of determining action upon the British and French declarations of intended retaliation upon commerce with Germany lies in the nature of the proposed measures in their relation to commerce by neutrals.

While it appears that the intention is to interfere with and take into custody all ships both outgoing and incoming, trading with Germany, which is in effect a blockade of German ports, the rule of blockade, that a ship attempting to enter or leave a German port regardless of the character of its cargo may be condemned, is not asserted.

The language of the declaration is "the British and

French Governments will, therefore, hold themselves free to detain and take into port ships carrying goods of presumed enemy destination, ownership, or origin. It is not intended to confiscate such vessels or cargoes unless they would otherwise be liable to condemnation."

The first sentence claims a right pertaining only to a state of blockade. The last sentence proposes a treatment of ships and cargoes as if no blockade existed. The two together present a proposed course of action previously unknown to international law.

As a consequence neutrals have no standard by which to measure their rights or to avoid danger to their ships and cargoes. The paradoxical situation thus created should be changed and the declaring powers ought to assert whether they rely upon the rules governing a blockade or the rules applicable when no blockade exists.

The declaration presents other perplexities.

The last sentence quoted indicates that the rules of contraband are to be applied to cargoes detained. The rule covering noncontraband articles carried in neutral bottoms is that the cargoes shall be released and the ships allowed to proceed. This rule can not, under the first sentence quoted, be applied as to destination. What then is to be done with a cargo of noncontraband goods detained under the declaration? The same question may be asked as to conditional contraband cargoes.

The foregoing comments apply to cargoes destined for Germany. Cargoes coming out of German ports present another problem under the terms of the declaration. Under the rules governing enemy exports only goods owned by enemy subjects in enemy bottoms are subject to seizure and condemnation. Yet by the declaration it is purposed to seize and take into port all goods of enemy "ownership and origin." The word "origin" is particularly significant. The origin of goods destined to neutral territory on neutral ships is not and never has been a ground for forfeiture except in case a blockade is declared and maintained. What then would the seizure amount to in the present case except to delay the delivery of the goods? The declaration does not indicate what disposition would be made of such cargoes if owned by a neutral or if owned by an enemy subject. Would a different rule be applied according to ownership? If so, upon what principles of international law would it rest? And upon what rule if no blockade is declared and maintained could the cargo of a neutral ship sailing out of a German port be condemned? If it is not condemned, what other legal course is there but to release it?

While this Government is fully alive to the possibility that the methods of modern naval warfare, particularly in the use of the submarine for both defensive and offensive operations, may make the former means of maintaining a blockade a physical impossibility, it feels that it can be urged with great force that there should be also some limit to "the radius of activity," and especially so if this action by the belligerents can be construed to be a blockade. It would certainly create a serious state of affairs if, for example, an American vessel laden with a cargo of German origin should escape the British patrol in European waters only to be held up by a cruiser off New York and taken into Halifax.

BRYAN.

WILSON'S COMMUNICATIONS TO GREAT BRITAIN ABOUT RESTRAINTS ON TRADE AND HIS NOTE DENOUNCING THE BRITISH NORTH SEA BLOCKADE AS "INEFFECTIVE, ILLEGAL AND INDEFENSIBLE"

[Four and one-half months after the beginning of the European war, Wilson sent the note of December 26, 1914, to Great Britain reciting the grievances of American merchants and declaring that the United States "is reluctantly forced to the conclusion that the present policy of His Majesty's Government toward neutral ships and cargoes exceeds the manifest necessity of a belligerent and constitutes restrictions upon the rights of American citizens on the high seas which are not justified by the rules of international law or required under the principle of self-preservation."

The British replies were long and complicated, citing American trade statistics and alleging precedents established by Federal maritime operations in the Civil War.

March 30, 1915, a second American note answered many of these subtly-argued points and declared that a recent "Order in Council" constituted "a practical assertion of unlimited belligerent rights over neutral commerce, and an almost unqualified denial of the sovereign rights of the nations now at peace."

A correspondence followed, marked by British communications still more complex than the early ones and extremely voluminous. President Wilson finally summed up the American contention in the following comprehensive note, answering British notes of January 7, February 10, June 22, July 23, July 31, August 2 and August 6, 1915.]

DEPARTMENT OF STATE,
WASHINGTON, October 21, 1915.

To Ambassador W. H. Page (London):

I desire that you present a note to Sir Edward Grey in the sense of the following:

This Government has delayed answering the earlier of these notes in the hope that the announced purpose of His Majesty's Government "to exercise their belligerent rights with every possible consideration for the interest of neutrals" and their intention of "removing all causes of avoidable delay in dealing with American cargoes" and of causing "the least possible amount of inconvenience to persons engaged in legitimate trade," as well as their "assurances to the United States Government that they would make it their first aim to minimize the inconveniences" resulting from the "measures taken by the Allied Governments," would in practice not unjustifiably infringe upon the neutral rights of American citizens engaged in trade and commerce. It is, therefore, a matter of regret that this hope has not been realized, but that, on the contrary, interferences with American ships and cargoes destined in good faith to neutral ports and lawfully entitled to proceed have become increasingly vexatious, causing American shipowners and American merchants to complain to this Government of the failure to take steps to prevent an exercise of belligerent power in contravention of their just rights. As the measures complained of proceed directly from orders issued by the British Government, are executed by British authorities, and arouse a reasonable apprehension that, if not resisted, they may be carried to an extent even more injurious to American interests, this Government directs the attention of His Majesty's Government to the following considerations:

[Here followed a denial of the correctness of deductions drawn from trade statistics as to the injury to American foreign trade, and (1) objection to the seizure of cargoes on suspicion, and their detention while the British government looked for evidence to support the suspicion (2) insistence that international usage permitted only a search at sea and not a deviation of vessels from their course in order to carry them into a port for search (3) a denial that American practice in this respect during the Civil War justified the British proceedings (4) denial of the British claim that modern conditions made search at sea impracticable, and a statement from American naval experts that the "facilities for boarding and inspection of modern ships are in fact greater than in former times" (5) objections to a demand for evidence of innocent voyage beyond the papers of the ship and the goods found on board, and a repetition of the American objection to the practice of seizing and detaining ships "on mere suspicion while efforts are made to obtain evidence from extraneous sources to justify the detention." (6) Repudiation of the British claim that the American seizure of the *Bermuda* in the Civil War (a famous case cited frequently by Great Britain) was in any sense similar to the British practices.

The British contention that greatly increased imports of neutral countries adjoining Great Britain's enemies raised a presumption that they were intended for sale to the belligerents, was characterized as not laying down a "just or legal rule of evidence. Such a presumption is too far from the facts and offers too great opportunity for abuse by a belligerent, who could, if the rule were adopted, entirely ignore neutral rights on the high seas and prey with impunity on neutral commerce." On this subject the note continued:]

Great Britain cannot expect the United States to submit to such manifest injustice or to permit the rights of its citizens to be so seriously impaired. . . . When goods are clearly intended to become incorporated in the mass of merchandise for sale in a neutral country, it is an unwarranted and inquisitorial proceeding to detain shipments for examination as to whether those goods are ultimately destined for the enemy's country or use. Whatever may be the conjectural conclusions to be drawn from trade statistics, which, when stated by value, are of uncertain evidence as to quantity, the United States maintains the right to sell goods into the general stock of a neutral country, and denounces as illegal and unjustifiable any attempt of a belligerent to interfere with that right on the ground that it suspects that the previous supply of such goods in the neutral country, which the imports renew or replace, has been sold to an enemy. That is a matter with which the neutral vendor has no concern and which can in no way affect his rights of trade. Moreover, even if goods listed as conditional contraband are destined to an enemy country through a neutral country, that fact is not in itself sufficient to justify their seizure. . . . Relying upon the regard of the British Government for the principles of justice so frequently and uniformly manifested prior to the present war, this Government anticipates that the British Government will instruct their officers to refrain from these vexatious and illegal practices. . . .

The British note of July 23, 1915, appears to confirm the intention indicated in the note of March 15, 1915, to establish a blockade so extensive as to prohibit trade with Germany or Austria-Hungary, even through the ports of neutral countries adjacent to them. Great Britain, however, admits that it should not, and gives assurances that it will not, interfere with trade with the countries contiguous to the territories of the enemies of Great Britain. Nevertheless, after over six months' application of the "blockade" order, the experience of American citizens has convinced the Government of the United States that Great Britain has been unsuccessful in her efforts to distinguish between enemy and neutral trade. Arrangements have been made to create in these neutral countries special consignees, or consignment corporations, with power to refuse shipments and to determine when the state of the country's resources requires the importation of new commodities. American commercial interests are hampered by the intricacies of these arrangements, and many American citizens justly complain that their *bona fide* trade with neutral countries is greatly reduced as a consequence, while others assert that their neutral trade, which amounted annually to a large sum, has been entirely interrupted. . . .

While the United States Government was at first inclined to view with leniency the British measures which were termed in the correspondence but not in the Order in Council of March 11 a "blockade," because of the assurances of the British Government that inconvenience to neutral trade would be minimized, this Government is now forced to the realization that its expectations were based on a misconception of the intentions of the British Government. . . . In the circumstances now developed it feels that it can no longer permit the validity of the alleged blockade to remain unchallenged.

The Declaration of Paris in 1856, which has been universally recognized as correctly stating the rule of international law as to blockade, expressly declares that "blockades, in order to be binding, must be effective; that is to say, maintained by force sufficient really to prevent access to the coast of the enemy. . . .

[Here followed detailed statements that the German coasts were open to trade with the Scandinavian countries, that German naval vessels cruised freely both in the North Sea and the Baltic and took prizes, and that the British Government itself had issued certain orders that showed the ineffectiveness of the blockade. Referring to the incidental blockade of neutral ports, the American note said:]

It is a matter of common knowledge that Great Britain exports and re-exports large quantities of merchandise to

Norway, Sweden, Denmark, and Holland, whose ports, so far as American commerce is concerned, she regards as blockaded. In fact, the British note of August 13 itself indicates that the British exports of many articles, such as cotton, lubricating oil, tobacco, cocoa, coffee, rice, wheat flour, barley, spices, tea, copra, etc., to these countries have greatly exceeded the British exports for the corresponding period of 1914. The note also shows that there has been an important British trade with these countries in many other articles, such as machinery, beef, butter, cotton waste, etc.

Finally, there is no better settled principle of the law of nations than that which forbids the blockade of neutral ports in time of war. The Declaration of London, though not regarded as binding upon the signatories because not ratified by them, has been expressly adopted by the British Government without modification as to blockade in the British Order in Council of October 29, 1914. Article 18 of the Declaration declares specifically that "The blockading forces must not bar access to neutral ports or coasts."

[Here followed citations from authorities and a quotation from Sir Edward Grey's own earlier definitions of blockade, as well as prize court decisions, after which the note said:]

Without mentioning the other customary elements of a regularly imposed blockade, such as notification of the particular coast line invested, the imposition of the penalty of confiscation, etc., which are lacking in the present British "blockade" policy, it need only be pointed out that, measured by the universally conceded tests above set forth, the present British measures cannot be regarded as constituting a blockade in law, in practice, or in effect.

It is incumbent upon the United States Government, therefore, to give the British Government notice that the blockade, which they claim to have instituted under the Order in Council of March 11, cannot be recognized as a legal blockade by the United States.

Since the Government of Great Britain has laid much emphasis on the ruling of the Supreme Court of the United States in the *Springbok* case, that goods of contraband character seized while going to the neutral port of Nassau, though actually bound for the blockaded ports of the south, were subject to condemnation, it is not inappropriate to direct attention to the British view of this case in England prior to the present war, as expressed by Sir Edward Grey in his instructions to the British delegates to the London Conference in 1908:

> It is exceedingly doubtful whether the decision of the Supreme Court was in reality meant to cover a case of blockade running in which no question of contraband arose. Certainly if such was the intention, the decision would *pro tanto* be in conflict with the practice of the British courts. His Majesty's Government sees no reason for departing from that practice, and you should endeavor to obtain general recognition of its correctness.

It may be pointed out also that the circumstances surrounding the *Springbok* case were essentially different from those of the present day. The ports of the Confederate States were effectively blockaded by the naval forces of the United States, though no neutral ports were closed, and a continuous voyage through a neutral port required an all-sea voyage terminating in an attempt to pass the blockading squadron.

[The demand of Great Britain that aggrieved American citizens should seek redress in British prize-courts instead of through diplomatic channels, was refused with the following argument:]

They (the cases) result from acts committed by the British naval authorities upon the high seas, where the jurisdiction over neutral vessels is acquired solely by international law. Vessels of foreign nationality, flying a neutral flag and finding their protection in the country of that flag, are seized without facts warranting a reasonable suspicion that they are destined to blockaded ports of the enemy or that their cargoes are contraband. The officers appear to find their justification in the Orders in Council and regulations of the British Government, in spite of the fact that in many of the present cases the Orders in Council and the regulations are themselves complained of as contrary to international law. Yet the very courts which, it is said, are to dispense justice to dissatisfied claimants are bound by the Orders in Council. . . . How can a tribunal fettered by municipal enactments declare itself emancipated from their restrictions and at liberty to apply the rules of international law with freedom? The very laws and regulations which bind the court are now matters of dispute between the Government of the United States and that of His Britannic Majesty. . . . There is, furthermore, a real and far-reaching injury for which prize courts offer no means of reparation. It is the disastrous effect of the methods of the allied Governments upon the general right of the United States to enjoy its international trade free from unusual and arbitrary limitations imposed by belligerent nations. Unwarranted delay and expense in bringing vessels into port for search and investigation upon mere suspicion has a deterrent effect upon trade ventures, however lawful they may be, which cannot be adequately measured in damages. . . .

There is another ground why American citizens cannot submit their wrongs arising out of undue detentions and seizures to British prize courts for reparation. It is the manner in which British courts obtain jurisdiction of such cases. . . . Municipal regulations in violation of the international rights of another nation cannot be extended to the vessels of the latter on the high seas so as to justify a belligerent nation bringing them into its ports, and, having illegally brought them within its territorial jurisdiction, compelling them to submit to the domestic laws of that nation. Jurisdiction obtained in such a manner is contrary to those principles of justice and equity which all nations should respect. . . . The Government of the

United States has, therefore, viewed with surprise and concern the attempt of His Majesty's Government to confer upon the British prize courts jurisdiction by this illegal exercise of force. . . .

This Government is advised that vessels and cargoes brought in for examination are released only upon condition that costs and expenses incurred in the course of such unwarranted procedure, such as pilotage, unlading costs, etc., be paid by the claimants or on condition that they sign a waiver of right to bring claims against the British Government for these exactions. This Government is loath to believe that such ungenerous treatment will continue to be accorded American citizens by the Government of His Britannic Majesty, but in order that the position of the United States Government may be clearly understood, I take this opportunity to inform Your Excellency that this Government denies that the charges incident to such detentions are rightfully imposed upon innocent trade or that any waiver of indemnity exacted from American citizens under such conditions of duress can preclude them from obtaining redress through diplomatic channels or by whatever other means may be open to them. . . .

I believe it has been conclusively shown that the methods employed by Great Britain to obtain evidence of enemy destination of cargoes bound for neutral ports and to impose a contraband character upon such cargoes are without justification; that the blockade, upon which such methods are partly founded, is ineffective, illegal, and indefensible; that the judicial procedure offered as a means of reparation for an international injury is inherently defective for the purpose; and that in many cases jurisdiction is asserted in violation of the law of nations. The United States, therefore, cannot submit to the curtailment of its neutral rights by these measures, which are admittedly retaliatory, and therefore illegal, in conception and in nature, and intended to punish the enemies of Great Britain for alleged illegalities on their part. The United States might not be in a position to object to them if its interests and the interests of all neutrals were unaffected by them, but, being affected, it cannot with complacence suffer further subordination of its rights to the plea that the exceptional geographic position of the enemies of Great Britain require or justify oppressive and illegal practices.

The Government of the United States desires, therefore, to impress most earnestly upon His Majesty's Government that it must insist that the relations between it and His Majesty's Government be governed, not by a policy of expediency, but by those established rules of international conduct upon which Great Britain in the past has held the United States to account when the latter nation was a belligerent engaged in a struggle for national existence. It is of the highest importance to neutrals not only of the present day but of the future that the principles of international right be maintained unimpaired.

This task of championing the integrity of neutral rights, which have received the sanction of the civilized world against the lawless conduct of belligerents arising out of the bitterness of the great conflict which is now wasting the countries of Europe, the United States unhesitatingly assumes, and to the accomplishment of that task it will devote its energies, exercising always that impartiality which from the outbreak of the war it has sought to exercise in its relations with the warring nations.

ROBERT LANSING.

Wilson's First Note to Germany on Sinking of the "Lusitania"

[May 7, 1915, the Cunard steamship *Lusitania,* bound to England from New York, was torpedoed by a German submarine off Kinsale Head, Ireland, and sank almost immediately, causing the loss of more than 1,000 lives. President Wilson's note was:]

Department of State,
Washington, May 13, 1915.

To Ambassador Gerard:

Please call on the Minister of Foreign Affairs and after reading to him this communication leave with him a copy.

In view of recent acts of the German authorities in violation of American rights on the high seas which culminated in the torpedoing and sinking of the British steamship *Lusitania* on May 7, 1915, by which over 100 American citizens lost their lives, it is clearly wise and desirable that the Government of the United States and the Imperial German Government should come to a clear and full understanding as to the grave situation which has resulted.

The sinking of the British passenger steamer *Falaba* by a German submarine on March 28, through which Leon C. Thrasher, an American citizen, was drowned; the attack on April 28 on the American vessel *Cushing* by a German aeroplane; the torpedoing on May 1 of the American vessel *Gulflight* by a German submarine, as a result of which two or more American citizens met their death; and, finally, the torpedoing and sinking of the steamship *Lusitania,* constitute a series of events which the Government of the United States has observed with growing concern, distress, and amazement.

Recalling the humane and enlightened attitude hitherto assumed by the Imperial German Government in matters of international right, and particularly with regard to the freedom of the seas; having learned to recognize the German views and the German influence in the field of international obligation as always engaged upon the side of justice and humanity; and having understood the instructions of the Imperial German Government to its naval commanders to be upon the same plane of humane action prescribed by the naval codes of other nations, the Government of the United States was loath to believe—it cannot now bring itself to believe—that these acts, so absolutely contrary to the rules, the practices, and the spirit of modern warfare, could have the countenance or sanction of that great Government. It feels it to be its duty, therefore to address the Imperial German Government concerning them with the utmost frankness and in the earnest hope that it is not mistaken in expecting action on the part of the Imperial German Government which will correct the unfortunate impressions which have been created and vindicate once more the position of that Government with regard to the sacred freedom of the seas.

The Government of the United States has been apprised that the Imperial German Government considered them selves to be obliged by the extraordinary circumstance of the present war and the measures adopted by thei adversaries in seeking to cut Germany off from all com merce, to adopt methods of retaliation which go much be yond the ordinary methods of warfare at sea, in the procla mation of a war zone from which they have warned neutra ships to keep away. This Government has already take occasion to inform the Imperial German Government tha it cannot admit the adoption of such measures or such warning of danger to operate as in any degree an abbrevia tion of the rights of American shipmasters or of America citizens bound on lawful errands as passengers on merchar ships of belligerent nationality; and that it must hold th Imperial German Government to a strict accountability fc any infringement of those rights, intentional or incidenta It does not understand the Imperial German Governme to question those rights. It assumes, on the contrary, th the Imperial Government accept, as of course, the rule that the lives of noncombatants, whether they be of neutral citizenship or citizens of one of the nations at war, cannot lawfully or rightfully be put in jeopardy by the capture or destruction of an unarmed merchantman, and recognize also, as all other nations do, the obligation to take the usual precaution of visit and search to ascertain whether a suspected merchantman is in fact of belligerent nationality or is in fact carrying contraband of war under a neutral flag.

The Government of the United States, therefore, desires to call the attention of the Imperial German Government with the utmost earnestness to the fact that the objection to their present method of attack against the trade of their enemies lies in the practical impossibility of employing submarines in the destruction of commerce without disregarding those rules of fairness, reason, justice, and humanity, which all modern opinion regards as imperative. It is practically impossible for the officers of a submarine to visit a merchantman at sea and examine her papers and cargo. It is practically impossible for them to make a prize of her; and, if they cannot put a prize crew on board of her, they cannot sink her without leaving her crew and all on board of her to the mercy of the sea in her small boats. These facts it is understood the Imperial German Government frankly admit. We are informed that in the instances of which we have spoken time enough for even that poor measure of safety was not given, and in at least two of the cases cited not so much as a warning was received. Manifestly submarines cannot be used against merchantmen, as the last few weeks have shown, without an inevitable violation of many sacred principles of justice and humanity.

American citizens act within their indisputable rights in taking their ships and in traveling wherever their legitimate business calls them upon the high seas, and exercise those

Wilson's Second and Third Notes to Germany on Sinking of "Lusitania" and Other Attacks on American Life and Property at Sea

[Germany's reply (May 28, 1915) to the first note was conciliatory but unsatisfactory. It set up the contention that the *Lusitania* had been armed. It alleged also that the rapid sinking was due not to the torpedo, but to the explosion of ammunition. The note asked for permission to reserve a final statement pending the American reply to these and several other points of contention. On June 1 followed Germany's explanation of attacks on the American cargo-steamships *Gulflight* and *Cushing*. The American reply was:]

Department of State,

Washington, June 9, 1915.

To Ambassador Gerard (Berlin):

You are instructed to deliver textually the following note to the Minister of Foreign Affairs:

In compliance with Your Excellency's request I did not fail to transmit to my Government immediately upon their receipt your note of May 28 in reply to my note of May 15, and your supplementary note of June 1, setting forth the conclusions so far as reached by the Imperial German Government concerning the attacks on the American steamers *Cushing* and *Gulflight*. I am now instructed by my Government to communicate the following reply:

The Government of the United States notes with gratification the full recognition by the Imperial German Government, in discussing the cases of the *Cushing* and the *Gulflight*, of the principle of the freedom of all parts of the open sea to neutral ships and the frank willingness of the Imperial German Government to acknowledge and meet its liability where the fact of attack upon neutral ships "which have not been guilty of any hostile act" by German air craft or vessels of war is satisfactorily established; and the Government of the United States will in due course lay before the Imperial German Government, as it requests, full information concerning the attack on the steamer *Cushing.*

With regard to the sinking of the steamer *Falaba,* by which an American citizen lost his life, the Government of the United States is surprised to find the Imperial German Government contending that an effort on the part of a merchantman to escape capture and secure assistance alters the obligation of the officer seeking to make the capture in respect of the safety of the lives of those on board the merchantman, although the vessel had ceased her attempt to escape when torpedoed. These are not new circumstances. They have been in the minds of statesmen and of international jurists throughout the development of naval warfare, and the Government of the United States does not understand that they have ever been held to alter the principles of humanity upon which it has insisted. Nothing but actual forcible resistance or continued efforts to escape by flight when ordered to stop for the purpose of visit on the part of the merchantman has ever been held to forfeit the lives of her passengers or crew. The Government of the United States, however, does not understand that the Imperial German Government is seeking in this case to relieve itself of liability, but only intends to set forth the circumstances which led the commander of the submarine to allow himself to be hurried into the course which he took.

Your Excellency's note, in discussing the loss of American lives resulting from the sinking of the steamship *Lusitania,* adverts at some length to certain information which the Imperial German Government has received with regard to the character and outfit of that vessel, and Your Excellency expresses the fear that this information may not have been brought to the attention of the Government of the United States. It is stated in the note that the *Lusitania* was undoubtedly equipped with masked guns, supplied with trained gunners and special ammunition, transporting troops from Canada, carrying a cargo not permitted under the laws of the United States to a vessel also carrying passengers, and serving, in virtual effect, as an auxiliary to the naval forces of Great Britain. Fortunately, these are matters concerning which the Government of the United States is in a position to give the Imperial German Government official information. Of the facts alleged in Your Excellency's note, if true, the Government of the United States would have been bound to take official cognizance in performing its recognized duty as a neutral power and in enforcing its national laws. It was its duty to see to it that the *Lusitania* was not armed for offensive action, that she was not serving as a transport, that she did not carry a cargo prohibited by the statutes of the United States, and that, if in fact she was a naval vessel of Great Britain, she should not receive clearance as a merchantman; and it performed that duty and enforced its statutes with scrupulous vigilance through its regularly constituted officials. It is able, therefore, to assure the Imperial German Government that it has been misinformed. If the Imperial German Government should deem itself to be in possession of convincing evidence that the officials of the Government of the United States did not perform these duties with thoroughness, the Government of the United States sincerely hopes that it will submit that evidence for consideration.

Whatever may be the contentions of the Imperial German Government regarding the carriage of contraband of war on board the *Lusitania* or regarding the explosion of that material by the torpedo, it need only be said that in the view of this Government these contentions are irrelevant to the question of the legality of the methods used by the German naval authorities in sinking the vessel.

But the sinking of passenger ships involves principles of humanity which throw into the background any special circumstances of detail that may be thought to affect the cases, principles which lift it, as the Imperial German Government will no doubt be quick to recognize and acknowledge, out of the class of ordinary subjects of diplomatic discussion or of international controversy. Whatever be the other facts regarding the *Lusitania,* the principal fact is that a great steamer, primarily and chiefly a conveyance for passengers, and carrying more than a thousand souls who had no part or lot in the conduct of the war, was torpedoed and sunk without so much as a challenge or a warning, and that men, women, and children were sent to their death in circumstances unparalleled in modern warfare. The fact that more than one hundred American citizens were among those who perished made it the duty of the Government of the United States to speak of these things and once more, with solemn emphasis, to call the attention of the Imperial German Government to the grave responsibility which the Government of the United States conceives that it has incurred in this tragic occurrence, and to the indisputable principle upon which that responsibility rests. The Government of the United States is contending for something much greater than mere rights of property or privileges of commerce. It is contending for nothing less high and sacred than the rights of humanity, which every Government honors itself in respecting and which no Government is justified in resigning on behalf of those under its care and authority. Only her actual resistance to capture or refusal to stop when ordered to do so for the purpose of visit could have afforded the commander of the submarine any justification for so much as putting the lives of those on board the ship in jeopardy. This principle the Government of the United States understands the explicit instructions issued on August 3, 1914, by the Imperial German Admiralty to its commanders at sea to have recognized and embodied as do the naval codes of all other nations, and upon it every traveler and seaman had a right to depend. It is upon this principle of humanity as well as upon the law founded upon this principle that the United States must stand.

The Government of the United States is happy to observe that Your Excellency's note closes with the intimation that the Imperial German Government is willing, now as before, to accept the good offices of the United States in an attempt to come to an understanding with the Government of Great Britain by which the character and conditions of the war upon the sea may be changed. The Government of the United States would consider it a privilege thus to serve its friends and the world. It stands ready at any time to convey to either Government any intimation or suggestion the other may be willing to have it convey and cordially invites the Imperial German Government to make use of its services in this way at its convenience. The whole world is concerned in anything that may bring about even a partial accommodation of interests or in any way mitigate the terrors of the present distressing conflict.

In the meantime, whatever arrangement may happily be made between the parties to the war, and whatever may in the opinion of the Imperial German Government have been the provocation or the circumstantial justification for the past acts of its commanders at sea, the Government of the United States confidently looks to see the justice and humanity of the Government of Germany vindicated in all cases where Americans have been wronged or their rights as neutrals invaded.

The Government of the United States therefore very earnestly and very solemnly renews the representations of its note transmitted to the Imperial German Government on the 15th of May, and relies in these representations upon the principles of humanity, the universally recognized understandings of international law, and the ancient friendship of the German nation.

The Government of the United States cannot admit that the proclamation of a war zone from which neutral ships have been warned to keep away may be made to operate as in any degree an abbreviation of the rights either of American shipmasters or of American citizens bound on lawful errands as passengers on merchant ships of belligerent nationality. It does not understand the Imperial German Government to question those rights. It understands it, also, to accept as established beyond question the principle that the lives of noncombatants cannot lawfully or rightfully be put in jeopardy by the capture or destruction of an unresisting merchantman, and to recognize the obligation to take sufficient precaution to ascertain whether a suspected merchantman is in fact of belligerent nationality or is in fact carrying contraband of war under a neutral flag. The Government of the United States therefore deems it reasonable to expect that the Imperial German Government will adopt the measures necessary to put these principles into practice in respect of the safeguarding of American lives and American ships, and asks for assurances that this will be done.

ROBERT LANSING.

[Germany's reply (July 8) was increasingly conciliatory, but remained unsatisfactory on the main issue. It dwelt on Great Britain's illegal blockade and offered to grant complete immunity to passenger ships under the control of the American Government and distinguished by special marks. The American reply was:]

DEPARTMENT OF STATE,

WASHINGON, July 21, 1915.

To Ambassador Gerard (Berlin):

You are instructed to deliver textually the following note to the Minister for Foreign Affairs:

The note of the Imperial German Government, dated the 8th of July, 1915, has received the careful consideration of the Government of the United States, and it regrets to be obliged to say that it has found it very unsatisfactory, because it fails to meet the real differences between the two

Governments and indicates no way in which the accepted principles of law and humanity may be applied in the grave matter in cotroversy, but proposes, on the contrary, arrangements for a partial suspension of those principles which virtually set them aside.

The Government of the United States notes with satisfaction that the Imperial German Government recognizes without reservation the validity of the principles insisted on in the several communications which this Government has addressed to the Imperial German Government with regard to its announcement of a war zone and the use of submarines against merchantmen on the high seas—the principle that the high seas are free, that the character and cargo of a merchantman must first be ascertained before she can lawfully be seized or destroyed, and that the lives of non-combatants may in no case be put in jeopardy unless the vessel resists or seeks to escape after being summoned to submit to examination; for a belligerent act of retaliation is *per se* an act beyond the law, and the defense of an act as retaliatory is an admission that it is illegal.

The Government of the United States is, however, keenly disappointed to find that the Imperial German Government regards itself as in large degree exempt from the obligation to observe these principles, even where neutral vessels are concerned, by what it believes the policy and practice of the Government of Great Britain to be in the present war with regard to neutral commerce. The Imperial German Government will readily understand that the Government of the United States can not discuss the policy of the Government of Great Britain with regard to neutral trade except with that Government itself, and that it must regard the conduct of other belligerent governments as irrelevant to any discussion with the Imperial German Government of what this Government regards as grave and unjustifiable violations of the rights of American citizens by German naval commanders. Illegal and inhuman acts, however justifiable they may be thought to be against an enemy who is believed to have acted in contravention of law and humanity, are manifestly indefensible when they deprive neutrals of their acknowledged rights, particularly when they violate the right to life itself. If a belligerent can not retaliate against an enemy without injuring the lives of neutrals, as well as their property, humanity, as well as justice and a due regard for the dignity of neutral powers, should dictate that the practice be discontinued. If persisted in it would in such circumstances constitute an unpardonable offense against the sovereignty of the neutral nation affected. The Government of the United States is not unmindful of the extraordinary conditions created by this war or of the radical alterations of circumstance and method of attack produced by the use of instrumentalities of naval warfare which the nations of the world can not have had in view when the existing rules of international law were formulated, and it is ready to make every reasonable allowance for these novel and unexpected aspects of war at sea; but it can not consent to abate any essential or fundamental right of its people because of a mere alteration of circumstance. The rights of neutrals in time of war are based upon principle, not upon expediency, and the principles are immutable. It is the duty and obligation of belligerents to find a way to adapt the new circumstances to them.

The events of the past two months have clearly indicated that it is possible and practicable to conduct such submarine operations as have characterized the activity of the Imperial German Navy within the so-called war zone in substantial accord with the accepted practices of regulated warfare. The whole world has looked with interest and increasing satisfaction at the demonstration of that possibility by German naval commanders. It is manifestly possible, therefore, to lift the whole practice of submarine attack above the criticism which it has aroused and remove the chief causes of offense.

In view of the admission of illegality made by the Imperial Government when it pleaded the right of retaliation in defense of its acts, and in view of the manifest possibility of conforming to the established rules of naval warfare, the Government of the United States can not believe that the Imperial Government will longer refrain from disavowing the wanton act of its naval commander in sinking the *Lusitania* or from offering reparation for the American lives lost, so far as reparation can be made for a needless destruction of human life by an illegal act.

The Government of the United States, while not indifferent to the friendly spirit in which it is made, can not accept the suggestion of the Imperial German Government that certain vessels be designated and agreed upon which shall be free on the seas now illegally proscribed. The very agreement would, by implication, subject other vessels to illegal attack and would be a curtailment and therefore an abandonment of the principles for which this Government contends and which in times of calmer counsels every nation would concede as of course.

The Government of the United States and the Imperial German Government are contending for the same great object, have long stood together in urging the very principles, upon which the Government of the United States now so solemnly insists. They are both contending for the freedom of the seas. The Government of the United States will continue to contend for that freedom, from whatever quarter violated, without compromise and at any cost. It invites the practical co-operation of the Imperial German Government at this time when co-operation may accomplish most and this great common object be most strikingly and effectively achieved.

The Imperial German Government expresses the hope that this object may be in some measure accomplished even before the present war ends. It can be. The Government of the United States not only feels obliged to insist upon it, by whomsoever violated or ignored, in the protection of its own citizens, but is also deeply interested in seeing it made practicable between the belligerents themselves, and holds itself ready at any time to act as the common friend who may be privileged to suggest a way.

In the meantime the very value which this Government sets upon the long and unbroken friendship between the people and Government of the United States and the people and Government of the German nation impels it to press very solemnly upon the Imperial German Government the necessity for a scrupulous observance of neutral rights in this critical matter. Friendship itself prompts it to say to the Imperial Government that repetition by the commanders of German naval vessels of acts in contravention of those rights must be regarded by the Government of the United States, when they affect American citizens, as deliberately unfriendly.

LANSING.

GERMANY PROMISES THAT LINERS SHALL NOT BE SUNK WITHOUT WARNING

[Soon after the third note on the submarine issue, Germany conveyed to the United States Government its decision to modify submarine warfare to remove American causes of offense.

August 19, 1915, the White Star liner *Arabic,* bound from Liverpool to New York, was torpedoed and sunk off Fastnet with the loss of some lives, including Americans. August 24, 1915, while the investigation still was unfinished, the German Ambassador in Washington promised full satisfaction. September 1 the German Ambassador informed the State Department officially that before the *Arabic* sinking, and as a result of the American contentions in the *Lusitania* case, German submarine commanders had been instructed to attack no liners without warning. October 5 the Ambassador stated to the American Government that the orders had been made so stringent that a recurrence was out of the question. October 20 Germany forwarded certified copies of the official examination of the submarine's crew. The consensus of these was that while the submarine was sinking a British cargo vessel which she had captured, a large steamship (not known by them at the time to be the *Arabic*,) approached as if to ram. The testimony of the *Arabic's* officers was positively that there had been no intention of attacking the submarine, which they declared had not been seen by them. The testimony also developed the fact that the *Arabic*, which had sighted the sinking cargo steamer first from a distance of about 7 miles, had approached to a distance estimated variously as 3 miles to 1½ miles, and that she began a zig-zag course at a distance of about 4 miles.

October 5 (before these papers reached America) Germany informed the United States that while the submarine commander had believed that the *Arabic* had approached to ram him, the German government did not doubt the good faith of the *Arabic's* officers in their testimony and that, therefore, the attack on the liner was a violation of instructions, that the act was regretted and disavowed, and that indemnity would be paid for the American lives lost. October 20 this declaration was repeated.

November 7 the Italian steamship *Ancona* was sunk by an Austrian submarine in the Mediterranean and on December 6, 1915, President Wilson sent the following note to Austria:]

Wilson's Note to Austria on Ancona Affair

Department of State,
Washington, December 6, 1915.

To Ambassador Penfield (Vienna):

Please deliver a note to the Minister of Foreign Affairs, textually as follows:

Reliable information obtained from American and other survivors who were passengers on the steamship *Ancona* shows that on Nov. 7 a submarine flying the Austro-Hungarian flag fired a solid shot toward the steamship, that thereupon the *Ancona* attempted to escape, but, being overhauled by the submarine, she stopped, that after a brief period and before the crew and passengers were all able to take to the boats the submarine fired a number of shells at the vessel and finally torpedoed and sank her while there were yet many persons on board, and that by gunfire and foundering of the vessel a large number of persons lost their lives or were seriously injured, among whom were citizens of the United States.

The public statement of the Austro-Hungarian Admiralty has been brought to the attention of the Government of the United States and received careful consideration. This statement substantially confirms the principal declaration of the survivors, as it admits that the *Ancona,* after being shelled, was torpedoed and sunk while persons were still on board.

The Austro-Hungarian Government has been advised, through the correspondence which has passed between the United States and Germany, of the attitude of the Government of the United States as to the use of submarines in attacking vessels of commerce, and the acquiescence of Germany in that attitude, yet with full knowledge on the part of the Austro-Hungarian Government of the views of the Government of the United States as expressed in no uncertain terms to the ally of Austria-Hungary, the commander of the submarine which attacked the *Ancona* failed to put in a place of safety the crew and passengers of the vessel which they purposed to destroy because, it is presumed, of the impossibility of taking it into port as a prize of war.

The Government of the United States considers that the commander violated the principles of international law and of humanity by shelling and torpedoing the *Ancona* before the persons on board had been put in a place of safety or even given sufficient time to leave the vessel. The conduct of the commander can only be characterized as wanton slaughter of defenseless noncombatants, since at the time when the vessel was shelled and torpedoed she was not, it appears, resisting or attempting to escape, and no other reason is sufficient to excuse such an attack, not even the possibility of rescue.

The Government of the United States is forced, therefore, to conclude either that the commander of the submarine acted in violation of his instructions or that the Imperial and Royal Government failed to issue instructions to the commanders of its submarines in accordance with the law of nations and the principles of humanity. The Government of the United States is unwilling to believe the latter alternative and to credit the Austro-Hungarian Government with an intention to permit its submarines to destroy the lives of helpless men, women and children. It prefers to believe that the commander of the submarine committed this outrage without authority and contrary to the general or special instructions which he had received.

As the good relations of the two countries must rest upon a common regard for law and humanity, the Government of the United States cannot be expected to do otherwise than to demand that the Imperial and Royal Government denounce the sinking of the *Ancona* as an illegal and indefensible act; that the officer who perpetrated the deed be punished, and that reparation by the payment of an indemnity be made for the citizens of the United States who were killed or injured by the attack on the vessel.

The Government of the United States expects that the Austro-Hungarian Government, appreciating the gravity of the case, will accede to its demand promptly, and it rests this expectation on the belief that the Austro-Hungarian Government will not sanction or defend an act which is condemned by the world as inhumane and barbarous, which is abhorrent to all civilized nations, and which has caused the death of innocent American citizens.

LANSING.

[The Austrian reply was eminently unsatisfactory and asked for more specifications and proofs, but after some irritating correspondence announced that the commander of the submarine had been punished.

March 24, 1916, the British channel steamer *Sussex*, bound from Folkestone, England, to Dieppe, France, was torpedoed and after full investigation the United States sent the following communication to Germany:]

Wilson's Note on Sussex Affair and on General Submarine Warfare Against Merchant Ships

Department of State,
Washington, April 18, 1916.

To Ambassador Gerard (Berlin):

You are instructed to deliver to the Secretary of Foreign Affairs a communication reading as follows:

I did not fail to transmit immediately, by telegraph, to my Government Your Excellency's note of the 10th instant in regard to certain attacks by German submarines, and particularly in regard to the disastrous explosion which on March 24, last, wrecked the French steamship *Sussex* in the English Channel. I have now the honor to deliver, under instruction from my Government, the following reply to Your Excellency:

Information now in the possession of the Government of the United States fully establishes the facts in the case of the *Sussex*, and the inferences which my Government has drawn from that information it regards as confirmed by the circumstances set forth in Your Excellency's note of the 10th instant. On the 24th of March, 1916, at about 2.50 o'clock in the afternoon, the unarmed steamer *Sussex*, with 325 or more passengers on board, among whom were a number of American citizens, was torpedoed while crossing from Folkestone to Dieppe. The *Sussex* had never been armed; was a vessel known to be habitually used only for the conveyance of passengers across the English Channel; and was not following the route taken by troop ships or supply ships. About 80 of her passengers, noncombatants of all ages and sexes, including citizens of the United States, were killed or injured.

A careful, detailed, and scrupulously impartial investigation by naval and military officers of the United States has conclusively established the fact that the *Sussex* was torpedoed without warning or summons to surrender and that

carrying out the policy announced, expressing the hope that the dangers involved, at any rate to neutral vessels, would be reduced to a minimum by the instructions which it had issued to the commanders of its submarines, and assuring the Government of the United States that it would take every possible precaution both to respect the rights of neutrals and to safeguard the lives of noncombatants.

In pursuance of this policy of submarine warfare against the commerce of its adversaries, thus announced and thus entered upon in despite of the solemn protest of the Government of the United States, the commanders of the Imperial Government's undersea vessels have carried on practices of such ruthless destruction which have made it more and more evident as the months have gone by that the Imperial Government has found it impracticable to put any such restraints upon them as it had hoped and promised to put. Again and again the Imperial Government has given its solemn assurances to the Government of the United States that at least passenger ships would not be thus dealt with, and yet it has repeatedly permitted its undersea commanders to disregard those assurances with entire impunity. As recently as February last it gave notice that it would regard all armed merchantmen owned by its enemies as part of the armed naval forces of its adversaries and deal with them as with men-of-war, thus, at least by implication, pledging itself to give warning to vessels which were not armed and to accord security of life to their passengers and crews; but even this limitation their submarine commanders have recklessly ignored.

Vessels of neutral ownership, even vessels of neutral ownership bound from neutral port to neutral port, have been destroyed along with vessels of belligerent ownership in constantly increasing numbers. Sometimes the merchantmen attacked have been warned and summoned to surrender before being fired on or torpedoed; sometimes their passengers and crews have been vouchsafed the poor security of being allowed to take to the ship's boats before the ship was sent to the bottom. But again and again no warning has been given, no escape even to the ship's boats allowed to those on board. Great liners like the *Lusitania* and *Arabic* and mere passenger boats like the *Sussex* have been attacked without a moment's warning, often before they have even become aware that they were in the presence of an armed ship of the enemy, and the lives of noncombatants, passengers, and crew have been destroyed wholesale and in a manner which the Government of the United States can not but regard as wanton and without the slightest color of justification. No limit of any kind has in fact been set to their indiscriminate pursuit and destruction of merchantmen of all kinds and nationalities within the waters which the Imperial Government has chosen to designate as lying within the seat of war. The roll of Americans who have lost their lives upon ships thus attacked and destroyed has grown month by month until the ominous toll has mounted into the hundreds.

The Government of the United States has been very patient. At every stage of this distressing experience of tragedy after tragedy it has sought to be governed by the most thoughtful consideration of the extraordinary circumstances of an unprecedented war and to be guided by sentiments of very genuine friendship for the people and Government of Germany. It has accepted the successive explanations and assurances of the Imperial Government as of course given in entire sincerity and good faith, and has hoped, even against hope, that it would prove to be possible for the Imperial Government so to order and control the acts of its naval commanders as to square its policy with the recognized principles of humanity as embodied in the law of nations. It has made every allowance for unprecedented conditions and has been willing to wait until the facts became unmistakable and were susceptible of only one interpretation.

It now owes it to a just regard for its own rights to say to the Imperial Government that that time has come. It has become painfully evident to it that the position which it took at the very outset is inevitable, namely, the use of submarines for the destruction of an enemy's commerce, is, of necessity, because of the very character of the vessels employed and the very methods of attack which their employment of course involves, utterly incompatible with the principles of humanity, the long-established and incontrovertible rights of neutrals, and the sacred immunities of noncombatants.

If it is still the purpose of the Imperial Government to prosecute relentless and indiscriminate warfare against vessels of commerce by the use of submarines without regard to what the Government of the United States must consider the sacred and indisputable rules of international law and the universally recognized dictates of humanity, the Government of the United States is at last forced to the conclusion that there is but one course it can pursue. Unless the Imperial Government should now immediately declare and effect an abandonment of its present methods of submarine warfare against passenger and freight-carrying vessels, the Government of the United States can have no choice but to sever diplomatic relations with the German Empire altogether. This action the Government of the United States contemplates with the greatest reluctance but feels constrained to take in behalf of humanity and the rights of neutral nations.

LANSING.

[April 19, 1916, the President appeared before Congress and delivered the following address (Special Message):]

WILSON'S ADDRESS TO CONGRESS ON THE SUSSEX AFFAIR

Gentlemen of the Congress:

A situation has arisen in the foreign relations of the

country of which it is my plain duty to inform you very frankly.

It will be recalled that in February, 1915, the Imperial German Government announced its intention to treat the waters surrounding Great Britain and Ireland as embraced within the seat of war and to destroy all merchant ships owned by its enemies that might be found within any part of that portion of the high seas, and that it warned all vessels, of neutral as well as of belligerent ownership, to keep out of the waters it had thus proscribed or else enter them at their peril. The Government of the United States earnestly protested. It took the position that such a policy could not be pursued without the practical certainty of gross and palpable violations of the law of nations, particularly if submarine craft were to be employed as its instruments, inasmuch as the rules prescribed by that law, rules founded upon principles of humanity and established for the protection of the lives of non-combatants at sea, could not in the nature of the case be observed by such vessels. It based its protest on the ground that persons of neutral nationality and vessels of neutral ownership would be exposed to extreme and intolerable risks, and that no right to close any part of the high seas against their use or to expose them to such risks could lawfully be asserted by any belligerent government. The law of nations in these matters, upon which the Government of the United States based its protest, is not of recent origin or founded upon merely arbitrary principles set up by convention. It is based, on the contrary, upon manifest and imperative principles of humanity and has long been established with the approval and by the express assent of all civilized nations.

Notwithstanding the earnest protest of our Government, the Imperial German Government at once proceeded to carry out the policy it had announced. It expressed the hope that the dangers involved, at any rate the dangers to neutral vessels, would be reduced to a minimum by the instructions which it had issued to its submarine commanders, and assured the Government of the United States that it would take every possible precaution both to respect the rights of neutrals and to safeguard the lives of non-combatants.

What has actually happened in the year which has since elapsed has shown that those hopes were not justified, those assurances insusceptible of being fulfilled. In pursuance of the policy of submarine warfare against the commerce of its adversaries, thus announced and entered upon by the Imperial German Government in despite of the solemn protest of this Government, the commanders of German undersea vessels have attacked merchant ships with greater and greater activity, not only upon the high seas surrounding Great Britain and Ireland but wherever they could encounter them, in a way that has grown more and more ruthless, more and more indiscriminate as the months have gone by, less and less observant of restraints of any kind; and have delivered their attacks without compunction against vessels of every nationality and bound upon every sort of errand. Vessels of neutral ownership, even vessels of neutral ownership bound from neutral port to neutral port, have been destroyed along with vessels of belligerent ownership in constantly increasing numbers. Sometimes the merchantman attacked has been warned and summoned to surrender before being fired on or torpedoed; sometimes passengers or crews have been vouchsafed the poor security of being allowed to take to the ship's boats before she was sent to the bottom. But again and again no warning has been given, no escape even to the ship's boats allowed to those on board. What this Government foresaw must happen has happened. Tragedy has followed tragedy on the seas in such fashion, with such attendant circumstances, as to make it grossly evident that warfare of such a sort, if warfare it be, can not be carried on without the most palpable violation of the dictates alike of right and of humanity. Whatever the disposition and intention of the Imperial German Government, it has manifestly proved impossible for it to keep such methods of attack upon the commerce of its enemies within the bounds set by either the reason or the heart of mankind.

In February of the present year the Imperial German Government informed this Government and the other neutral governments of the world that it had reason to believe that the Government of Great Britain had armed all merchant vessels of British ownership and had given them secret orders to attack any submarine of the enemy they might encounter upon the seas, and that the Imperial German Government felt justified in the circumstances in treating all armed merchantmen of belligerent ownership as auxiliary vessels of war, which it would have the right to destroy without warning. The law of nations has long recognized the right of merchantmen to carry arms for protection and to use them to repel attack, although to use them, in such circumstances, at their own risk; but the Imperial German Government claimed the right to set these understandings aside in circumstances which it deemed extraordinary. Even the terms in which it announced its purpose thus still further to relax the restraints it had previously professed its willingness and desire to put upon the operation of its submarines carried the plain implication that at least vessels which were not armed would still be exempt from destruction without warning and that personal safety would be accorded their passengers and crews; but even that limitation, if it was ever practicable to observe it, has in fact constituted no check at all upon the destruction of ships of every sort.

Again and again the Imperial German Government has given this Government its solemn assurances that at least passenger ships would not be thus dealt with, and yet it has again and again permitted its undersea commanders to disregard those assurances with entire impunity. Great liners like the *Lusitania* and the *Arabic* and mere ferry-boats like the *Sussex* have been attacked without a moment's warning, sometimes before they had even become aware that they were in the presence of an armed vessel of the enemy, and the lives of non-combatants, passengers and crew have been sacrificed wholesale, in a manner which the Government of the United States cannot but regard as wanton and without the slightest color of justification. No limit of any kind has in fact been set to the indiscriminate pursuit and destruction of merchantmen of all kinds and nationalities within the waters, constantly extending in area, where these operations have been carried on; and the roll of Americans who have lost their lives on ships thus attacked and destroyed has grown month by month until the ominous toll has mounted into the hundreds.

One of the latest and most shocking instances of this method of warfare was that of the destruction of the French cross channel steamer *Sussex*. It must stand forth, as the sinking of the steamer *Lusitania* did, as so singularly tragical and unjustifiable as to constitute a truly terrible example of the inhumanity of submarine warfare as the commanders of German vessels have for the past twelvemonth been conducting it. If this instance stood alone, some explanation, some disavowal by the German Government, some evidence of criminal mistake or wilful disobedience on the part of the commander of the vessel that fired the torpedo might be sought or entertained; but unhappily it does not stand alone. Recent events make the conclusion inevitable that it is only one instance, even though it be one of the most extreme and distressing instances, of the spirit and method of warfare which the Imperial German Government has mistakenly adopted, and which from the first exposed that Government to the reproach of thrusting all neutral rights aside in pursuit of its immediate objects.

The Government of the United States has been very

patient. At every stage of this distressing experience of tragedy after tragedy in which its own citizens were involved it has sought to be restrained from any extreme course of action or of protest by a thoughtful consideration of the extraordinary circumstances of this unprecedented war, and actuated in all that it said or did by the sentiments of genuine friendship which the people of the United States have always entertained and continue to entertain towards the German nation. It has of course accepted the successive explanations and assurances of the Imperial German Government as given in entire sincerity and good faith, and has hoped, even against hope, that it would prove to be possible for the German Government so to order and control the acts of its naval commanders as to square its policy with the principles of humanity as embodied in the law of nations. It has been willing to wait until the significance of the facts became absolutely unmistakable and susceptible of but one interpretation.

That point has now unhappily been reached. The facts are susceptible of but one interpretation. The Imperial German Government has been unable to put any limits or restraints upon its warfare against either freight or passenger ships. It has therefore become painfully evident that the position which this Government took at the very outset is inevitable, namely, that the use of submarines for the destruction of an enemy's commerce is of necessity, because of the very character of the vessels employed and the very methods of attack which their employment of course involves, incompatible with the principles of humanity, the long established and incontrovertible rights of neutrals, and the sacred immunities of noncombatants.

I have deemed it my duty, therefore, to say to the Imperial German Government that if it is still its purpose to prosecute relentless and indiscriminate warfare against vessels of commerce by the use of submarines, notwithstanding the now demonstrated impossibility of conducting that warfare in accordance with what the Government of the United States must consider the sacred and indisputable rules of international law and the universally recognized dictates of humanity, the Government of the United States is at last forced to the conclusion that there is but one course it can pursue; and that unless the Imperial German Government should now immediately declare and effect an abandonment of its present methods of warfare against passenger and freight carrying vessels this Government can have no choice but to sever diplomatic relations with the Government of the German Empire altogether.

This decision I have arrived at with the keenest regret; the possibility of the action contemplated I am sure all thoughtful Americans will look forward to with unaffected reluctance. But we cannot forget that we are in some sort and by the force of circumstances the responsible spokesman of the rights of humanity, and that we cannot remain silent while those rights seem in process of being swept utterly away in the maelstrom of this terrible war. We owe it to a due regard for our own rights as a nation, to our sense of duty as a representative of the rights of neutrals the world over, and to a just conception of the rights of mankind to take this stand now with the utmost solemnity and firmness.

I have taken it, and taken it in the confidence that it will meet with your approval and support. All sober-minded men must unite in hoping that the Imperial German Government, which has in other circumstances stood as the champion of all that we are now contending for in the interest of humanity, may recognize the justice of our demands and meet them in the spirit in which they are made.

[May 4, 1916, Germany in a long reply informed the American Government that in order to avoid further offense to the United States, it had been decided to limit the use of its effective weapon and the German submarine commanders had been ordered to act only in accordance with the principles of visit and search, and that vessels were not to be sunk without first securing the lives of their occupants unless they attempted to escape or offer resistance. The note concluded with the statement that Germany expected confidently that the United States would demand and insist that the British Government observe the rules of international law. To this the United States replied:]

Wilson's Note Which Closed Submarine Controversy for Nine Months

Department of State,

Washington, May 8, 1916.

To Ambassador Gerard (Berlin):

You are instructed to deliver to the Minister of Foreign Affairs a communication textually as follows:

"The note of the Imperial German Government under date of May 4, 1916, has received careful consideration by the Government of the United States. It is especially noted, as indicating the purpose of the Imperial Government as to the future, that it 'is prepared to do its utmost to confine the operations of the war for the rest of its duration to the fighting forces of the belligerents,' and that it is determined to impose upon all its commanders at sea the limitations of the recognized rules of international law upon which the Government of the United States has insisted. Throughout the months which have elapsed since the Imperial Government announced, on February 4, 1915, its submarine policy, now happily abandoned, the Government of the United States has been constantly guided and restrained by motives of friendship in its patient efforts to bring to an amicable settlement the critical questions arising from that policy. Accepting the Imperial Government's declaration of its abandonment of the policy which has so seriously menaced the good relations between the two countries, the Government of the United States will rely upon a scrupulous execution henceforth of the now altered policy of the Imperial Government, such as will remove the principal danger to an interruption of the good relations existing between the United States and Germany.

"The Government of the United States feels it necessary to state that it takes it for granted that the Imperial German Government does not intend to imply that the maintenance of its newly announced policy is in any way contingent upon the course or result of diplomatic negotiations between the Government of the United States and any other belligerent Government, notwithstanding the fact that certain passages in the Imperial Government's note of the 4th instant might appear to be susceptible of that construction. In order, however, to avoid any possible misunderstanding, the Government of the United States notifies the Imperial Government that it cannot for a moment entertain, much less discuss, a suggestion that respect by German naval authorities for the rights of citizens of the United States upon the high seas should in any way or in the slightest degree be made contingent upon the conduct of any other Government affecting the rights of neutrals and non-combatants. Responsibility in such matters is single, not joint; absolute, not relative."

LANSING.

[EDITORIAL NOTE: *This was the final diplomatic note in the submarine controversy. Germany's pledge that merchant vessels would not be sunk without warning and without saving human lives was observed from May 4, 1916, to January 31, 1917. Then the submarine war was renewed, with increased disregard of neutral rights; and President Wilson abandoned note-writing and severed diplomatic relations.* *See page 356.*]

Wilson's Address Before the League to Enforce Peace, Washington, May 27, 1916

[Editorial Note: *Leagues of individuals who believed it possible to "abolish war," or to "enforce peace," or to establish a "world's court" that would adjudicate international controversies, had long been in existence. Their activities increased as the war in Europe went on year after year, although their proposals were not to become operative until the existing conflict was over. In the following address President Wilson expressed his belief that the United States would be willing to become a partner in any feasible association of nations formed to guarantee territorial integrity and political independence and to prevent hasty wars.*]

When the invitation to be here to-night came to me, I was glad to accept it—not because it offered me an opportunity to discuss the programme of the League—that you will, I am sure, not expect of me—but because the desire of the whole world now turns eagerly, more and more eagerly, towards the hope of peace, and there is just reason why we should take our part in counsel upon this great theme. It is right that I, as spokesman of our Government, should attempt to give expression to what I believe to be the thought and purpose of the people of the United States in this vital matter.

This great war that broke so suddenly upon the world two years ago, and which has swept within its flame so great a part of the civilized world, has affected us very profoundly, and we are not only at liberty, it is perhaps our duty, to speak very frankly of it and of the great interests of civilization which it affects.

With its causes and its objects we are not concerned. The obscure fountains from which its stupendous flood has burst forth we are not interested to search for or explore. But so great a flood, spread far and wide to every quarter of the globe, has of necessity engulfed many a fair province of right that lies very near to us. Our own rights as a Nation, the liberties, the privileges, and the property of our people have been profoundly affected. We are not mere disconnected lookers-on. The longer the war lasts, the more deeply do we become concerned that it should be brought to an end and the world be permitted to resume its normal life and course again. And when it does come to an end we shall be as much concerned as the nations at war to see peace assume an aspect of permanence, give promise of days from which the anxiety of uncertainty shall be lifted, bring some assurance that peace and war shall always hereafter be reckoned part of the common interest of mankind. We are participants, whether we would or not, in the life of the world. The interests of all nations are our own also. We are partners with the rest. What affects mankind is inevitably our affair as well as the affairs of the nations of Europe and of Asia.

One observation on the causes of the present war we are at liberty to make, and to make it may throw some light forward upon the future, as well as backward upon the past. It is plain that this war could have come only as it did, suddenly and out of secret counsels, without warning to the world, without discussion, without any of the deliberate movements of counsel with which it would seem natural to approach so stupendous a contest. It is probable that if it had been foreseen just what would happen, just what alliances would be formed, just what forces arrayed against one another, those who brought the greatest contest on would have been glad to substitute conference for force. If we ourselves had been afforded some opportunity to apprise the belligerents of the attitude which it would be our duty to take, of the policies and practices against which we would feel bound to use all our moral and economic strength, and in certain circumstances even our physical strength also, our own contribution to the counsel which might have averted the struggle would have been considered worth weighing and regarding.

And the lesson which the shock of being taken by surprise in a matter so deeply vital to all the nations of the world has made poignantly clear is, that the peace of the world must henceforth depend upon a new and more wholesome diplomacy. Only when the great nations of the world have reached some sort of agreement as to what they hold to be fundamental to their common interest, and as to some feasible method of acting in concert when any nation or group of nations seeks to disturb those fundamental things, can we feel that civilization is at last in a way of justifying its existence and claiming to be finally established. It is clear that nations must in the future be governed by the same high code of honor that we demand of individuals.

We must, indeed, in the very same breath with which we avow this conviction admit that we have ourselves upon occasion in the past been offenders against the law of diplomacy which we thus forecast; but our conviction is not the less clear, but rather the more clear, on that account. If this war has accomplished nothing else for the benefit of the world, it has at least disclosed a great moral necessity and set forward the thinking of the statesmen of the world by a whole age. Repeated utterances of the leading statesmen of most of the great nations now engaged in war have made it plain that their thought has come to this, that the principle of public right must henceforth take precedence over the individual interests of particular nations, and that the nations of the world must in some way band themselves together to see that that right prevails as against any sort of selfish aggression; that henceforth alliance must not be set up against alliance, understanding against understanding, but that there must be a common agreement for a common object, and that at the heart of that common object must lie the inviolable rights of peoples and of mankind. The nations of the world have become each other's neighbors. It is to their interest that they should understand each other. In order that they may understand each other, it is imperative that they should agree to cooperate in a common cause, and that they should so act that the guiding principle of that common cause shall be even-handed and impartial justice.

This is undoubtedly the thought of America. This is what we ourselves will say when there comes proper occasion to say it. In the dealings of nations with one another arbitrary force must be rejected and we must move forward to the thought of the modern world, the thought of which peace is the very atmosphere. That thought constitutes a chief part of the passionate conviction of America.

We believe these fundamental things: First, that every people has a right to choose the sovereignty under which they shall live. Like other nations, we have ourselves no doubt once and again offended against that principle when for a little while controlled by selfish passion, as our franker historians have been honorable enough to admit; but it has become more and more our rule of life and action. Second, that the small states of the world have a right to enjoy the same respect for their sovereignty and for their territorial integrity that great and powerful nations expect and insist upon. And, third, that the world has a right to be free from every disturbance of its peace that has its origin in aggression and disregard of the rights of peoples and nations.

So sincerely do we believe in these things that I am sure that I speak the mind and wish of the people of America when I say that the United States is willing to become a partner in any feasible association of nations formed in order to realize these objects and make them secure against violation.

There is nothing that the United States wants for itself that any other nation has. We are willing, on the contrary, to limit ourselves along with them to a prescribed course of duty and respect for the rights of others which will check any selfish passion of our own, as it will check any aggressive impulse of theirs.

If it should ever be our privilege to suggest or initiate a movement for peace among the nations now at war, I am sure that the people of the United States would wish their Government to move along these lines: First, such a settlement with regard to their own immediate interests as the belligerents may agree upon. We have nothing material of any kind to ask for ourselves, and are quite aware that we are in no sense or degree parties to the present quarrel. Our interest is only in peace and its future guarantees. Second, an universal association of the nations to maintain the inviolate security of the highway of the seas for the common and unhindered use of all the nations of the world, and to prevent any war begun either contrary to treaty covenants or without warning and full submission of the causes to the opinion of the world—a virtual guarantee of territorial integrity and political independence.

But I did not come here, let me repeat, to discuss a programme. I came only to avow a creed and give expression to the confidence I feel that the world is even now upon the eve of a great consummation, when some common force will be brought into existence which shall safeguard right as the first and most fundamental interest of all peoples and all governments, when coercion shall be summoned not to the service of political ambition or selfish hostility, but to the service of a common order, a common justice, and a common peace. God grant that the dawn of that day of frank dealing and of settled peace, concord, and cooperation may be near at hand!

WILSON'S ADDRESS BEFORE THE PRESS CLUB, NEW YORK, JUNE 30, 1916

[An informal talk on the Mexican crisis. The American Punitive Expedition—sent across the border in March, in a vain attempt to catch the bandit Villa—had been attacked by Mexican Government troops at Carrizal, and the National Guard had been ordered to the border to assist the Regular Army. Rumors of armed intervention in Mexico were insistent.]

I realize that I have done a very imprudent thing; I have come to address this thoughtful company of men without any preparation whatever. . . . As a matter of fact, I have been absorbed by the responsibilities which have been so frequently referred to here to-night, and that preoccupation has made it impossible for me to forecast even what you would like to hear me talk about. . . .

Mr. Colby said something that was among the few things I had forecast to say myself. He said that there are certain things which really it is useless to debate, because they go as a matter of course.

Of course it is our duty to prepare this Nation to take care of its honor and of its institutions. Why debate any part of that, except the detail, except the plan itself, which is always debatable?

Of course it is the duty of the Government, which it will never overlook, to defend the territory and people of this country. It goes without saying that it is the duty of the administration to have constantly in mind with the utmost sensitiveness every point of national honor.

But, gentlemen, after you have said and accepted these obvious things your program of action is still to be formed. When will you act and how will you act?

The easiest thing is to strike. The brutal thing is the impulsive thing. No man has to think before he takes aggressive action; but before a man really conserves the honor by realizing the ideals of the Nation he has to think exactly what he will do and how he will do it.

Do you think the glory of America would be enhanced by a war of conquest in Mexico? Do you think that any act of violence by a powerful nation like this against a weak and distracted neighbor would reflect distinction upon the annals of the United States?

Do you think that it is our duty to carry self-defense to the point of dictation in the affairs of another people? The ideals of America are written plain upon every page of American history.

And I want you to know how fully I realize whose servant I am. I do not own the Government of the United States, even for the time being. I have no right in the use of it to express my own passions.

I have no right to express my own ambitions for the development of America if those ambitions are not coincident with the ambitions of the Nation itself.

And I have constantly to remind myself that I am not the servant of those who wish to enhance the value of their Mexican investments, but that I am the servant of the rank and file of the people of the United States.

I get a great many letters, my fellow citizens, from important and influential men in this country, but I get a great many other letters. I get letters from unknown men, from humble women, from people whose names have never been heard and will never be recorded, and there is but one prayer in all of these letters: "Mr. President, do not allow anybody to persuade you that the people of this country want war with anybody."

I got off a train yesterday, and as I was bidding good-by to the engineer he said, in an undertone, "Mr. President, keep out of Mexico." And if one man has said that to me a thousand have said it to me as I have moved about the country.

If I have opportunity to engage them further in conversation, they say, "Of course, we know that you can not govern the circumstances of the case altogether, and it may be necessary, but for God's sake do not do it unless it is necessary."

I am for the time being the spokesman of such people, gentlemen. I have not read history without observing that the greatest forces in the world and the only permanent forces are the moral forces.

We have the evidence of a very competent witness, namely, the first Napoleon, who said that as he looked back in the last days of his life upon so much as he knew of human history he had to record the judgment that force had never accomplished anything that was permanent.

Force will not accomplish anything that is permanent, I venture to say, in the great struggle which is now going on on the other side of the sea. The permanent things will be accomplished afterwards, when the opinion of mankind is brought to bear upon the issues, and the only thing that will hold the world steady is this same silent, insistent, all-powerful opinion of mankind.

Force can sometimes hold things steady until opinion has time to form, but no force that was ever exerted, except in response to that opinion, was ever a conquering and predominant force.

I think the sentence in American history that I myself am proudest of is that in the introductory sentences of the Declaration of Independence, where the writers say that a due respect for the opinion of mankind demands that they state the reasons for what they are about to do.

I venture to say that a decent respect for the opinion of mankind demanded that those who started the present European war should have stated their reasons; but they did not pay any heed to the opinion of mankind, and the reckoning will come when the settlement comes.

So, gentlemen, I am willing, no matter what my personal fortunes may be, to play for the verdict of mankind. Personally, it will be a matter of indifference to me what the verdict on the 7th of November is, provided I feel any degree of confidence that when a later jury sits I shall get their judgment in my favor. Not in my favor personally—what difference does that make?—but in my favor as an honest and conscientious spokesman of a great nation.

Wilson's Addresses at the Salesmanship Congress, Detroit, July 10, 1916

[Continuing his plea, made in earlier addresses, for expansion of American foreign trade, and commending recent legislation enacted by Congress.]

Mr. Chairman, Ladies, and Gentlemen:

It is with a great deal of gratification that I find myself facing so interesting and important a company as this. You will readily understand that I have not come here to make an elaborate address, but I have come here to express my interest in the objects of this great association, and to congratulate you on the opportunities which are immediately ahead of you in handling the business of this country.

These are days of incalculable change, my fellow citizens. It is impossible for anybody to predict anything that is certain, in detail, with regard to the future either of this country or of the world in the large movements of business; but one thing is perfectly clear, and that is that the United States will play a new part, and that it will be a part of unprecedented opportunity and of greatly increased responsibility.

The United States has had a very singular history in respect of its business relationships with the rest of the world. I have always believed, and I think you have always believed, that there is more business genius in the United States than anywhere else in the world; and yet America has apparently been afraid of touching too intimately the great processes of international exchange. America, of all countries in the world, has been timid; has not until recently, has not until within the last two or three years, provided itself with the fundamental instrumentalities for playing a large part in the trade of the world. America, which ought to have had the broadest vision of any nation, has raised up an extraordinary number of provincial thinkers, men who thought provincially about business, men who thought that the United States was not ready to take her competitive part in the struggle for the peaceful conquest of the world. For anybody who reflects philosophically upon the history of this country, that is the most amazing fact about it.

But the time for provincial thinkers has gone by. We must play a great part in the world whether we choose it or not. Do you know the significance of this single fact, that within the last year or two we have, speaking in large terms, ceased to be a debtor nation and become a creditor nation? We have more of the surplus gold of the world than we ever had before, and our business hereafter is to be to lend and to help and to promote the great peaceful enterprises of the world. We have got to finance the world in some important degree, and those who finance the world must understand it and rule it with their spirits and with their minds. We can not cabin and confine ourselves any longer, and so I said that I came here to congratulate you upon the great rôle that lies ahead of you to play. This is a salesmanship congress, and hereafter salesmanship will have to be closely related in its outlook and scope to statesmanship, to international statesmanship. It will have to be touched with an intimate comprehension of the conditions of business and enterprise throughout the round globe, because America will have to place her goods by running her intelligence ahead of her goods. No amount of mere push, no amount of mere bustling, or, to speak in the western language, no amount of mere rustling, no amount of mere active enterprise, will suffice.

There have been two ways of doing business in the world outside of the lands in which the great manufactures have been made. One has been to try to force the tastes of the manufacturing country on the country in which the markets were being sought, and the other way has been to study the tastes and needs of the countries where the markets were being sought and suit your goods to those tastes and needs; and the latter method has beaten the former method. If you are going to sell carpets, for example, in India, you have got to have as good taste as the Indians in the patterns of the carpets, and that is going some. If you are going to sell things in tropical countries, they must, rather obviously, be different from those which you sell in cold and arctic countries. You cannot assume that the rest of the world is going to wear or use or manufacture what you wear and use and manufacture. Your raw materials must be the raw materials that they need, not the raw materials that you need. Your manufactured goods must be the manufactured goods which they desire, not those which other markets have desired. So your business will keep pace with your knowledge, not of yourself and of your manufacturing processes, but of them and of their commercial needs. That is statesmanship, because that is relating your international activities to the conditions which exist in other countries.

If we can once get what some gentlemen are so loath to give us, a merchant marine! The trouble with some men is that they are slow in their minds. They do not see; they do not know the need, and they will not allow you to point it out to them. If we can once get in a position to deliver our own goods, then the goods that we have to deliver will be adjusted to the desires of those to whom we deliver them, and all the world will welcome America in the great field of commerce and manufacture.

I was trying to expound in another place the other day the long way and the short way to get together. The long way is to fight. I hear some gentlemen say that they want to help Mexico, and the way they propose to help her is to overwhelm her with force. That is the long way to help Mexico as well as the wrong way. After the fighting you have a nation full of justified suspicion and animated by well-founded hostility and hatred, and then will you help them? Then will you establish cordial business relationships with them? Then will you go in as neighbors and enjoy their confidence? On the contrary, you will have shut every door as if it were of steel against you. What makes Mexico suspicious of us is that she does not believe as yet that we want to serve her. She believes that we want to possess her, and she has justification for the belief in the way in which some of our fellow-citizens have tried to exploit her privileges and possessions. For my part, I will not serve the ambitions of these gentlemen, but I will try to serve all America, so far as intercourse with Mexico is concerned, by trying to serve Mexico herself. There are some things that are not debatable. Of course, we have to defend our border. That goes without saying. Of course, we must make good our own sovereignty, but we must respect the sovereignty of Mexico. I am one of those—I have sometimes suspected that there were not many of them—who believe, absolutely believe, the Virginia Bill of Rights, which was the model of the old bill of rights, which says that a people has a right to do anything they please with their own country and their own government. I am old-fashioned enough to believe that, and I am going to stand by that belief. (That is for the benefit of those gentlemen who wish to butt in.)

Now, I use that as an illustration, my fellow citizens. What do we all most desire when the present tragical confusion of the world's affairs is over? We desire permanent peace, do we not? Permanent peace can grow in only one soil. That is the soil of actual good will, and good will can not exist without mutual comprehension.

This, then, my friends, is the simple message that I bring you. Lift your eyes to the horizons of business; do not look too close at the little processes with which you are concerned, but let your thoughts and your imaginations run abroad throughout the whole world, and with the inspiration of the thought that you are Americans and are meant to carry liberty and justice and the principles of humanity wherever you go, go out and sell goods that will make the world more comfortable and more happy, and convert them to the principles of America.

[A later address the same day, at luncheon]

Mr. Chairman, Ladies and Gentlemen:

I am glad to find myself in Detroit and face to face with the men who have played the principal part in giving it distinction throughout the country and throughout the world. Looking about among you, I see that it is true in this matter, as in others, that the only men fit for such a job are young men and men who never grow old. There is the liveliness of youth in the eyes even of those of you who have shared with me the painful parting with the hirsute appendage. . . . I have always been inclined to believe that the business of the world was best understood by those men who were in the struggle for maintenance not only, but for success. The man who knows the strength of the tide is the man who is swimming against it, not the man who is floating with it. The man who is immersed in the beginnings of business, who is trying to get his foothold, who is trying to get other men to believe in him and lend him money and trust him to make profitable use of that money, is the man who knows what the business conditions in the United States are, and I would rather take his counsel as to what ought to be done for business than the counsel of any established captain of industry. The captain of industry is looking backward and the other man is looking forward. The conditions of business change with every generation; change with every decade; are now changing at an almost breathless pace, and the men who have made good are not feeling the tides as the other men are feeling them. . . .

So I invite your thoughts, in what I sincerely believe to be an entirely nonpartisan spirit, to the democracy of business. An act was recently passed in Congress that some of the most intelligent business men of this country earnestly opposed—men whom I knew, men whose character I trusted, men whose integrity I absolutely believed in. I refer to the Federal Reserve Act, by which we intended to take, and succeeded in taking credit out of the control of a small number of men and making it available to everybody who had real commercial assets, and the very men who opposed that act, and opposed it conscientiously, now admit that it saved the country from a ruinous panic when the stress of war came on, and that it is the salvation of every average business man who is in the midst of the tides that I have been trying to describe. . . .

The suspicion is beginning to dawn in many quarters that the average man knows the business necessities of the country just as well as the extraordinary man does. I believe in the ordinary man. If I did not believe in the ordinary man I would move out of a democracy and, if I found an endurable monarchy, I would live in it. The very conception of America is based upon the validity of the judgments of the average man, and I call you to witness that there have not been many catastrophes in American history. I call you to witness that the average judgments of the voters of the United States have been sound judgments. I call you to witness that this great impulse of the common opinion has been a lifting impulse, and not a depressing impulse. What is the object of associations like that which is gathered here to-day, this Salesmanship Congress? The moral of it is that a few men can not determine the interests of a large body of men, and that the only way to determine them and advance them is to have a representative assembly chosen by themselves get together and take common counsel regarding them. . . .

I never went into a committee of any kind upon any important public matter, or private matter so far as that is concerned, that I did not come out with an altered judgment and knowing much more about the matter than when I went in; and not only knowing much more, but knowing that the common judgment arrived at was better than I could have suggested when I went in. That is the universal experience of candid men. If it were not so, there would be no object in congresses like this. Yet whenever we attempt legislation, we find ourselves in this case: We are not in the presence of the many who can counsel wisely, but we are in the presence of the few who counsel too narrowly, and the means by which we have been trying to break away from that is not by excluding these gentlemen who constituted the narrow circles of advice, but by associating them with hundreds of thousands of their fellow citizens.

I have had some say that I was not accessible to them, and when I inquired into it I found they meant that I did not personally invite them. They did not know how to come without being invited, and they did not care to come if they came upon the same terms with everybody else, knowing that everybody else was welcome whom I had the time to confer with.

Am I telling you things unobserved by you? Do you not know that these things are true? And do you not believe with me that the affairs of the Nation can be better conducted upon the basis of general counsel than upon the basis of special counsel? Men are colored and governed by their occupations and their surroundings and their habits. If I wanted to change the law radically, I would not consult a lawyer. If I wanted to change business methods radically, I would not consult a man who had made a conspicuous success by using the present methods that I wanted to change. Not because I would distrust these men, but because I would know that they would not change their thinking over night, that they would have to go through a long process of reacquaintance with the circumstances of the time, the new circumstances of the time, before they could be converted to my point of view. You get a good deal more light on the street than you do in the closet. You get a good deal more light by keeping your ears open among the rank and file of your fellow citizens than you do in any private conference whatever. I would rather hear what the men are talking about on the trains and in the shops and by the fireside than hear anything else, because I want guidance and I know I could get it there, and what I am constantly asking is that men should bring me that counsel, because I am not privileged to determine things independently of this counsel. I am your servant, not your ruler.

One thing that we are now trying to convert the small circles to that the big circles are already converted to is that this country needs a merchant marine and ought to get one. I have found that I had a great deal more resistance when I tried to help business than when I tried to interfere with it. I have had a great deal more resistance of counsel, of special counsel, when I tried to alter the things that are established than when I tried to do anything else. We call ourselves a liberal nation, whereas, as a matter of fact, we are one of the most conservative nations in the world. If you want to make enemies, try to change something. You know why it is. To do things today exactly the way you did them yesterday saves thinking. It does not cost you anything. You have acquired the habit; you know the routine; you do not have to plan anything, and it frightens you with a hint of exertion to learn that you will have to do it a different way to-morrow. Until I became a college teacher, I used to think that the young men were radical, but college boys are the greatest conservatives I ever tackled in my life, largely because they have associated too much with their fathers. What you have to do with them is to take them up upon some visionary height and show them the map of the world as it is. Do not let them see their father's factory. Do not let them see their father's countinghouse. Let them see the great valleys teeming with laborious people. Let them see the great struggle of men in realms they never dreamed of. Let them see the great emotional power that is in the world, the great ambitions, the great hopes, the great fears. Give them some picture of mankind, and then their father's business and every other man's business will begin to fall into place. They will see that it is an item and not the whole thing; and they will sometimes see that the item is not properly related to the whole, and what they will get interested in will be to relate the item to the whole, so that it will form part of the force, and not part of the impediment.

This country, above every country in the world, gentlemen, is meant to lift; it is meant to add to the forces that improve. It is meant to add to everything that betters the world, that gives it better thinking, more honest endeavor, a closer grapple of man with man, so that we will all be pulling together like one irresistible team in a single harness. That is the reason why it seemed wise to substitute for the harsh processes of the law, which merely lays its hand on your shoulder after you have sinned and threatens you with punishment, some of the milder and more helpful processes of counsel. That is the reason the Federal Trade Commission was established—so that men would have some place where they could take counsel as to what the law was and what the law permitted; and also take counsel as to whether the law itself was right and advice had not better be taken as to its alteration. The processes of counsel are only the processes of accommodation, not the processes of punishment. Punishment retards but it does not lift up. Punishment impedes but it does not improve. And we ought to substitute for the harsh processes of the law, wherever we can, the milder and gentler and more helpful processes of counsel.

It has been a very great grief to some of us, year after year, year after year, to see a fundamental thing like the fiscal policy of the Government with regard to duties on imports made a football of politics. Why, gentlemen, party politics ought to have nothing to do with the question of what is for the benefit of the business of the United States, and that is the reason we ought to have a tariff commission, and, I may add, are going to have a tariff commission. But, then, gentlemen, the trouble will be upon me. The provision as it stands makes it obligatory upon me not to choose more than half the commission from any one political party. The bill does not undertake to say how many political parties there are. That just now is a delicate question. But I am forbidden to take more than two of the same variety, and yet the trouble about that is I would like to find men for that commission who were of no one of the varieties. I would like to find men who would find out the circumstances of American business, particularly as it changes and is going to change with perplexing rapidity in the years immediately ahead of us, without any regard whatever to the interest of any party whatever, so that we should be able to legislate upon the facts and upon the large economic aspects of those facts without stopping to think which party it was going to hurt and which party it was going to benefit. But almost everybody in this country wears a label of some kind, and under the law I suppose I will have to turn them around and see how they are labeled, how they are branded; and that is going to be a very great blow to my spirit and a very great test of my judgment. I hope, after the results are achieved, you will judge me leniently, because my desire would be not to have a bipartisan but an absolutely nonpartisan commission of men who really applied the tests of scientific analysis of the facts and no other tests whatever to the conclusions that they arrived at. . . .

I believe that Americans can manufacture goods better than anybody else; that they can sell goods as honestly as anybody else; that they can find out the conditions and meet the conditions of foreign business better than anybody else, and I want to see them given a chance right away, and they will be whether I want them to be or not. We have been trying to get ready for it. The national banks of the United States, until the recent Currency Act, were held back by the very terms of the law under which they operated from some of the most important international transactions. To my mind that is one of the most amazing facts of our commercial history. The Congress of the United States was not willing that the national banks should have a latch-key and go away from home. They were afraid they would not know how to get back under cover, and banks from other countries had to establish branches where American bankers were doing business, to take care of some of the most important processes of international exchange. That is nothing less than amazing, but it is not necessary any longer. It never was necessary; it was only thought to be necessary by some eminently provincial statesmen. We are done with provincialism in the statesmanship of the United States, and we have got to have a view now and a horizon as wide as the world itself. And when I look around upon an alert company like this, it seems to me in my imagination they are almost straining at the leash. They are waiting to be let loose upon this great race that is now going to challenge our abilities. For my part, I shall look forward to the result with absolute and serene confidence, because the spirit of the United States is an international spirit, if we conceive it right. This is not the home of any particular race of men. This is not the home of any particular set of political traditions. This is a home the doors of which have been opened from the first to mankind, to everybody who loved liberty, to everybody whose ideal was equality of opportunity, to everybody whose heart was moved by the fundamental instincts and sympathies of humanity. That is America, and now it is as if the nations of the world, sampled and united here, were in their new union and new common understanding turning about to serve the world with all the honest processes of business and of enterprise. I am happy that I should be witnessing the dawn of the day when America is indeed to come into her own.

President Wilson's Address on Citizenship

(At a Citizenship Convention, Washington, July 13, 1916)

[For a long period before the war in Europe, the tide of emigration toward the United States had grown ever stronger. The census of 1910 showed 6,646,000 foreign-born adult male residents. As the war progressed there was much talk about some of these so-called "hyphenated" Americans; and many thousands had awakened in them a desire to complete the formalities of obtaining American citizenship. This is the third of President Wilson's addresses on citizenship and "America First"—see also pages 108 and 114.]

Mr. Chairman, Ladies and Gentlemen:

I have come here for the simple purpose of expressing my very deep interest in what these conferences are intended to attain. It is not fair to the great multitudes of hopeful men and women who press into this country from other countries that we should leave them without that friendly and intimate instruction which will enable them very soon after they come to find out what America is like at heart and what America is intended for among the nations of the world.

I believe that the chief school that these people must attend after they get here is the school which all of us attend, which is furnished by the life of the communities in which we live and the nation to which we belong. It has been a very touching thought to me sometimes to think of the hopes which have drawn these people to America. I have no doubt that many a simple soul has been thrilled by that great statue standing in the harbor of New York and seeming to lift the light of liberty for the guidance of the feet of men; and I can imagine that they have expected here something ideal in the treatment that they will receive, something ideal in the laws which they would have to live under, and it has caused me many a time to turn upon myself the eye of examination to see whether there burned in me the true light of the American spirit which they expected to find here. It is easy, my fellow-citizens, to communicate physical lessons, but it is very difficult to communicate spiritual lessons. America was intended to be a spirit among the nations of the world, and it is the purpose of conferences like this to find out the best way to introduce the newcomers to this spirit, and by that very interest in them to enhance and purify in ourselves the thing that ought to make America great and not only ought to make her great, but ought to make her exhibit a spirit unlike any other nation in the world. . . .

So my interest in this movement is as much an interest in ourselves as in those whom we are trying to Americanize, because if we are genuine Americans they cannot avoid the infection; whereas, if we are not genuine Americans, there will be nothing to infect them with, and no amount of teaching, no amount of exposition of the Constitution—which I find very few persons understand—no amount of dwelling upon the idea of liberty and of justice will accomplish the object we have in view, unless we ourselves illustrate the idea of justice and of liberty. My interest in this movement is, therefore, a two-fold interest. I believe it will assist us to become self-conscious in respect of the fundamental ideas of American life.

When you ask a man to be loyal to a government, if he comes from some foreign countries, his idea is that he is expected to be loyal to a certain set of persons like a ruler or a body set in authority over him, but that is not the American idea. Our idea is that he is to be loyal to certain objects in life, and that the only reason he has a President and a Congress and a Governor and a State Legislature and courts is that the community shall have instrumentalities by which to promote those objects. It is a coöperative organization expressing itself in this Constitution, expressing itself in these laws, intending to express itself in the exposition of those laws by the courts; and the idea of America is not so much that men are to be restrained and punished by the law as instructed and guided by the law. . . . The object of the law is that there, written upon these pages, the citizen should read the record of the experience of this state and nation; what they have concluded it is necessary for them to do because of the life they have lived and the things that they have discovered to be elements in that life.

So that we ought to be careful to maintain a government at which the immigrant can look with the closest scrutiny and to which he should be at liberty to address this question: "You declare this to be a land of liberty and of equality and of justice; have you made it so by your law?" We ought to be able in our schools, in our night schools and in every other method of instructing these people, to show them that that has been our endeavor. We cannot conceal from them long the fact that we are just as human as any other nation, that we are just as selfish, that there are just as many mean people amongst us as anywhere else, that there are just as many people here who want to take advantage of other people as you can find in other countries, just as many cruel people, just as many people heartless when it comes to maintaining and promoting their own interest; but you can show that our object is to get these people in harmless and see to it that they do not do any damage and are not allowed to indulge the passions which would bring injustice and calamity at last upon a nation whose object is spiritual and not material.

America has built up a great body of wealth. America has become, from the physical point of view, one of the most powerful nations in the world, a nation which if it took the pains to do so, could build that power up into one of the most formidable instruments in the world, one of the most formidable instruments of force, but which has no other idea than to use its force for ideal objects and not for self-aggrandizement.

We have been disturbed recently, my fellow-citizens, by certain symptoms which have showed themselves in our body politic. Certain men—I have never believed a great number—born in other lands, have in recent months thought more of those lands than they have of the honor and interest of the government under which they are now living. They have even gone so far as to draw apart in spirit and in organization from the rest of us to accomplish some special object of their own. I am not here going to utter any criticism of these people, but I want to say this, that such a thing as that is absolutely incompatible with the fundamental idea of loyalty, and that loyalty is not a self-pleasing virtue. I am not bound to be loyal to the United States to please myself. I am bound to be loyal to the United States because I live under its laws and am its citizen, and whether it hurts me or whether it benefits me, I am obliged to be loyal. Loyalty means nothing unless it has at its heart the absolute principle of self-sacrifice. Loyalty means that you ought to be ready to sacrifice every interest that you have, and your life itself, if your country calls upon you to do so, and that is the sort of loyalty which ought to be inculcated into these newcomers, that they are not to be loyal only so long as they are pleased, but that, having once entered into this sacred relationship, they are bound to be loyal whether they are pleased or not; and that loyalty which is merely self-pleasing is only self-indulgence and selfishness. No man has ever risen to the real stature of spiritual manhood until he has found that it is finer to serve somebody else than it is to serve himself.

These are the conceptions which we ought to teach the newcomers into our midst, and we ought to realize that the life of every one of us is part of the schooling, and that we cannot preach loyalty unless we set the example, that we cannot profess things with any influence upon others unless we practice them also. This process of Americanization is going to be a process of self-examination, a process of purification, a process of rededication to the things which America represents and is proud to represent. And it takes a great deal more courage and steadfastness, my fellow-citizens, to represent ideal things than to represent anything else.

Wilson's Special Address (Message) on the Threatened Railroad Strike and the Eight-Hour Law

(Delivered before Congress in Special Session, August 29, 1916)

Gentlemen of the Congress:

I have come to you to seek your assistance in dealing with a very grave situation which has arisen out of the demand of the employees of the railroads engaged in freight train service that they be granted an eight-hour working day, safeguarded by payment for an hour and a half of service for every hour of work beyond the eight.

The matter has been agitated for more than a year. The

public has been made familiar with the demands of the men and the arguments urged in favor of them, and even more familiar with the objections of the railroads and their counter demand that certain privileges now enjoyed by their men and certain bases of payment worked out through many years of contest be reconsidered, especially in their relation to the adoption of an eight-hour day. The matter came some three weeks ago to a final issue and resulted in a complete deadlock between the parties. The means provided by law for the mediation of the controversy failed and the means of arbitration for which the law provides were rejected. The representatives of the railway executives proposed that the demands of the men be submitted in their entirety to arbitration, along with certain questions of readjustment as to pay and conditions of employment which seemed to them to be either closely associated with the demands or to call for reconsideration on their own merits; the men absolutely declined arbitration, especially if any of their established privileges were by that means to be drawn again in question. The law in the matter put no compulsion upon them. The four hundred thousand men from whom the demands proceeded had voted to strike if their demands were refused; the strike was imminent; it has since been set for the fourth of September next. It affects the men who man the freight trains on practically every railway in the country. The freight service throughout the United States must stand still until their places are filled, if, indeed, it should prove possible to fill them at all. Cities will be cut off from their food supplies, the whole commerce of the nation will be paralyzed, men of every sort and occupation will be thrown out of employment, countless thousands will in all likelihood be brought, it may be, to the very point of starvation, and a tragical national calamity brought on, to be added to the other distresses of the time, because no basis of accommodation or settlement has been found.

Just so soon as it became evident that mediation under the existing law had failed and that arbitration had been rendered impossible by the attitude of the men, I considered it my duty to confer with the representatives of both the railways and the brotherhoods, and myself offer mediation, not as an arbitrator, but merely as spokesman of the nation, in the interest of justice, indeed, and as a friend of both parties, but not as judge, only as the representative of one hundred millions of men, women, and children who would pay the price, the incalculable price, of loss and suffering should these few men insist upon approaching and concluding the matters in controversy between them merely as employers and employees, rather than as patriotic citizens of the United States looking before and after and accepting the larger responsibility which the public would put upon them.

It seemed to me, in considering the subject-matter of the controversy, that the whole spirit of the time and the preponderant evidence of recent economic experience spoke for the eight-hour day. It has been adjudged by the thought and experience of recent years a thing upon which society is justified in insisting as in the interest of health, efficiency, contentment, and a general increase of economic vigor. The whole presumption of modern experience would, it seemed to me, be in its favor, whether there was arbitration or not, and the debatable points to settle were those which arose out of the acceptance of the eight-hour day rather than those which affected its establishment. I therefore, proposed that the eight-hour day be adopted by the railway managements and put into practice for the present as a substitute for the existing ten-hour basis of pay and service; that I should appoint, with the permission of the Congress, a small commission to observe the results of the change, carefully studying the figures of the altered operating costs, not only, but also the conditions of labor under which the men worked and the operation of their existing agreements with the railroads, with instructions to report the facts as they found them to the Congress at the earliest possible day, but without recommendation; and that, after the facts had been thus disclosed, an adjustment should in some orderly manner be sought of all the matters now left unadjusted between the railroad managers and the men.

These proposals were exactly in line, it is interesting to note, with the position taken by the Supreme Court of the United States when appealed to to protect certain litigants from the financial losses which they confidently expected if they should submit to the regulation of their charges and of their methods of service by public legislation. The Court has held that it would not undertake to form a judgment upon forecasts, but could base its action only upon actual experience; that it must be supplied with facts, not with calculations and opinions, however scientifically attempted. To undertake to arbitrate the question of the adoption of an eight-hour day in the light of results merely estimated and predicted would be to undertake an enterprise of conjecture. No wise man could undertake it, or, if he did undertake it, could feel assured of his conclusions.

I unhesitatingly offered the friendly services of the administration to the railway managers to see to it that justice was done the railroads in the outcome. I felt warranted in assuring them that no obstacle of law would be suffered to stand in the way of their increasing their revenues to meet the expenses resulting from the change so far as the development of their business and of their administrative efficiency did not prove adequate to meet them. The public and the representatives of the public, I felt justified in assuring them, were disposed to nothing but justice in such cases and were willing to serve those who served them.

The representatives of the brotherhoods accepted the plan; but the representatives of the railroads declined to accept it. In the face of what I cannot but regard as the practical certainty that they will be ultimately obliged to accept the eight-hour day by the concerted action of organized labor, backed by the favorable judgment of society, the representatives of the railway management have felt justified in declining a peaceful settlement which would engage all the forces of justice, public and private, on their side to take care of the event. They fear the hostile influence of shippers, who would be opposed to an increase of freight rates (for which, however, of course, the public itself would pay); they apparently feel no confidence that the Interstate Commerce Commission could withstand the objections that would be made. They do not care to rely upon the friendly assurances of the Congress or the President. They have thought it best that they should be forced to yield, if they must yield, not by counsel, but by the suffering of the country. While my conferences with them were in progress, and when to all outward appearance those conferences had come to a standstill, the representatives of the brotherhoods suddenly acted and set the strike for the fourth of September.

The railway managers based their decision to reject my counsel in this matter upon their conviction that they must at any cost to themselves or to the country stand firm for the principle of arbitration which the men had rejected. I based my counsel upon the indisputable fact that there was no means of obtaining arbitration. The law supplied none; earnest efforts at mediation had failed to influence the men in the least. To stand firm for the principle of arbitration and yet not get arbitration seemed to me futile and something more than futile, because it involved incalculable distress to the country and consequences in some respects worse than those of war, and that in the midst of peace.

I yield to no man in firm adherence, alike of conviction and of purpose, to the principle of arbitration in industrial disputes; but matters have come to a sudden crisis in this particular dispute and the country had been caught unprovided with any practicable means of enforcing that conviction in practice (by whose fault we will not now stop to inquire). A situation had to be met whose elements and fixed conditions were indisputable. The practical and patriotic course to pursue, as it seemed to me, was to secure immediate peace by conceding the one thing in the demands of the men which society itself and any arbitrators who represented public sentiment were most likely to approve, and immediately lay the foundations for securing arbitration with regard to everything else involved. The event has confirmed that judgment.

I was seeking to compose the present in order to safeguard the future; for I wished an atmosphere of peace and friendly cooperation in which to take counsel with the representatives of the nation with regard to the best means for providing, so far as it might prove possible to provide, against the recurrence of such unhappy situations in the future—the best and most practicable means of securing calm and fair arbitration of all industrial disputes in the days to come. This is assuredly the best way of vindicating a principle, namely, having failed to make certain of its observance in the present, to make certain of its observance in the future.

But I could only propose. I could not govern the will of others who took an entirely different view of the circumstances of the case, who even refused to admit the circumstances to be what they have turned out to be.

Having failed to bring the parties to this critical controversy to an accommodation, therefore, I turn to you, deeming it clearly our duty as public servants to leave nothing undone that we can do to safeguard the life and interests of the nation. In the spirit of such a purpose, I earnestly recommend the following legislation:

First, immediate provision for the enlargement and administrative reorganization of the Interstate Commerce

Commission along the lines embodied in the bill recently passed by the House of Representatives and now awaiting action by the Senate; in order that the Commission may be enabled to deal with the many great and various duties now devolving upon it with a promptness and thoroughness which are with its present constitution and means of action practically impossible.

Second, the establishment of an eight-hour day as the legal basis alike of work and of wages in the employment of all railway employees who are actually engaged in the work of operating trains in interstate transportation.

Third, the authorization of the appointment by the President of a small body of men to observe the actual results in experience of the adoption of the eight-hour day in railway transportation alike for the men and for the railroads; its effects in the matter of operating costs, in the application of the existing practices and agreements to the new conditions, and in all other practical aspects, with the provision that the investigators shall report their conclusions to the Congress at the earliest possible date, but without recommendation as to legislative action; in order that the public may learn from an unprejudiced source just what actual developments have ensued.

Fourth, explicit approval by the Congress of the consideration by the Interstate Commerce Commission of an increase of freight rates to meet such additional expenditures by the railroads as may have been rendered necessary by the adoption of the eight-hour day and which have not been offset by administrative readjustments and economies, should the facts disclosed justify the increase.

Fifth, an amendment of the existing federal statute which provides for the mediation, conciliation, and arbitration of such controversies as the present by adding to it a provision that in case the methods of accommodation now provided for should fail, a full public investigation of the merits of every such dispute shall be instituted and completed before a strike or lockout may lawfully be attempted.

And, sixth, the lodgement in the hands of the Executive of the power, in case of military necessity, to take control of such portions and such rolling stock of the railways of the country as may be required for military use and to operate them for military purposes, with authority to draft into the military service of the United States such train crews and administrative officials as the circumstances require for their safe and efficient use.

This last suggestion I make because we cannot in any circumstances suffer the nation to be hampered in the essential matter of national defense. At the present moment circumstances render this duty particularly obvious. Almost the entire military force of the nation is stationed upon the Mexican border to guard our territory against hostile raids. It must be supplied, and steadily supplied, with whatever it needs for its maintenance and efficiency. If it should be necessary for purposes of national defense to transfer any portion of it upon short notice to some other part of the country, for reasons now unforeseen, ample means of transportation must be available, and available without delay. The power conferred in this matter should be carefully and explicitly limited to cases of military necessity, but in all such cases it should be clear and ample.

There is one other thing we should do if we are true champions of arbitration. We should make all arbitral awards judgments by record of a court of law in order that their interpretation and enforcement may lie, not with one of the parties to the arbitration, but with an impartial and authoritative tribunal.

These things I urge upon you, not in haste or merely as a means of meeting a present emergency, but as permanent and necessary additions to the law of the land, suggested, indeed, by circumstances we had hoped never to see, but imperative as well as just, if such emergencies are to be prevented in the future. I feel that no extended argument is needed to commend them to your favorable consideration. They demonstrate themselves. The time and the occasion only give emphasis to their importance. We need them now and we shall continue to need them.

[EDITORIAL NOTE: In response to this Address, Congress passed the Adamson bill, and the President signed it on September 3. It enacted into law only two of the recommendations—the eight-hour day and the authorization of a commission to study the matter and report to Congress. The eight-hour law provides for a standard eight-hour work day for railway train employees, and for payment for overtime at not less than the pro-rata rate. The railway employees had demanded time and one-half for all overtime. The opposition contended that the effect of the law was not to shorten hours of work, but rather to increase wages. The statute was, however, upheld by the Supreme Court, by a 5 to 4 decision.]

WILSON ACCEPTS HIS RENOMINATION

(Address delivered at Long Branch, N. J., September 2, 1916.)

[EDITORIAL NOTE: *President Wilson and Vice-President Marshall had been renominated by acclamation in the Democratic National Convention at St. Louis, on June 15, 1916. Five days earlier the Republican National Convention at Chicago had chosen Charles Evans Hughes, of New York, for President, and Charles Warren Fairbanks, of Indiana, for Vice-President.*

The formal notification ceremonies were held at the President's summer home. United States Senator Ollie M. James, of Kentucky, made the notification speech.]

Senator James, Gentlemen of the Notification Committee, Fellow-Citizens:

I cannot accept the leadership and responsibility which the National Democratic Convention has again, in such generous fashion, asked me to accept without first expressng my profound gratitude to the party for the trust it eposes in me after four years of fiery trial in the midst f affairs of unprecedented difficulty, and the keen sense f added responsibility with which this honour fills (I had lmost said burdens) me as I think of the great issues of ational life and policy involved in the present and imme- iate future conduct of our Government. I shall seek, as have always sought, to justify the extraordinary confi- ence thus reposed in me by striving to purge my heart nd purpose of every personal and of every misleading arty motive and devoting every energy I have to the serv- ice of the nation as a whole, praying that I may continue have the counsel and support of all forward-looking men every turn of the difficult business.

For I do not doubt that the people of the United States ill wish the Democratic Party to continue in control of e Government. They are not in the habit of rejecting ose who have actually served them for those who are aking doubtful and conjectural promises of service. Least all are they likely to substitute those who promised to nder them particular services and proved false to that omise for those who have actually rendered those very rvices.

Boasting is always an empty business, which pleases no- dy but the boaster, and I have no disposition to boast what the Democratic Party has accomplished. It has erely done its duty. It has merely fulfilled its explicit omises. But there can be no violation of good taste in lling attention to the manner in which those promises ve been carried out or in adverting to the interesting ct that many of the things accomplished were what the position party had again and again promised to do but d left undone. Indeed that is manifestly part of the siness of this year of reckoning and assessment. There no means of judging the future except by assessing the st. Constructive action must be weighed against destructive comment and reaction. The Democrats either have or have not understood the varied interests of the country. The test is contained in the record.

What is that record? What were the Democrats called into power to do? What things had long waited to be done, and how did the Democrats do them? It is a record of extraordinary length and variety, rich in elements of many kinds, but consistent in principle throughout and susceptible of brief recital.

The Republican party was put out of power because of failure, practical failure and moral failure; because it had served special interests and not the country at large; because, under the leadership of its preferred and established guides, of those who still make its choices, it had lost touch with the thoughts and the needs of the nation and was living in a past age and under a fixed illusion, the illusion of greatness. It had framed tariff laws based upon a fear of foreign trade, a fundamental doubt as to American skill enterprise, and capacity, and a very tender regard for the profitable privileges of those who had gained control of domestic markets and domestic credits; and yet had enacted anti-trust laws which hampered the very things they meant to foster, which were stiff and inelastic, and in part unintelligible. It had permitted the country throughout the long period of its control to stagger from one financial crisis to another under the operation of a national banking law of its own framing which made stringency and panic certain and the control of the larger business operations of the country by the bankers of a few reserve centres inevitable; had made as if it meant to reform the law but had faint-heartedly failed in the attempt, because it could not bring itself to do the one thing necessary to make the reform genuine and effectual, namely, break up the control of small groups of bankers. It had been oblivious, or indifferent, to the fact that the farmers, upon whom the country depends for its food and in the last analysis for its prosperity, were without standing in the matter of commercial credit, without the protection of standards in their market transactions, and without systematic knowledge of the markets themselves; that the labourers of the country, the great army of men who man the industries it was professing to father and promote, carried their labour as a mere commodity to market, were subject to restraint by novel and drastic process in the courts, were without assurance of compensation for industrial accidents, without federal assistance in accommodating labour disputes, and without national aid or advice in finding the places and the industries in which their labour was most needed. The country had no national system of road construction and development. Little intelligent attention was paid to the army, and not enough to the navy. The other republics of America distrusted us, because they found that we thought first of the profits of American investors and only as an afterthought of impartial justice and helpful friendship. Its policy was provincial in all things; its purposes were out of harmony with the temper and purpose of the people and the timely development of the nation's interests.

So things stood when the Democratic Party came into power. How do they stand now? Alike in the domestic field and in the wide field of the commerce of the world, American business and life and industry have been set free to move as they never moved before.

The tariff has been revised, not on the principle of repelling foreign trade, but upon the principle of encouraging it, upon something like a footing of equality with our own in respect of the terms of competition, and a Tariff Board has been created whose function it will be to keep the relations of American with foreign business and industry under constant observation, for the guidance alike of our business men and of our Congress. American energies are now directed towards the markets of the world.

The laws against trusts have been clarified by definition,

with a view to making it plain that they were not directed against big business but only against unfair business and the pretense of competition where there was none; and a Trade Commission has been created with powers of guidance and accommodation which have relieved business men of unfounded fears and set them upon the road of hopeful and confident enterprise.

By the Federal Reserve Act the supply of currency at the disposal of active business has been rendered elastic, taking its volume, not from a fixed body of investment securities, but from the liquid assets of daily trade; and these assets are assessed and accepted, not by distant groups of bankers in control of unavailable reserves, but by bankers at the many centres of local exchange who are in touch with local conditions everywhere.

Effective measures have been taken for the re-creation of an American merchant marine and the revival of the American carrying trade indispensable to our emancipation from the control which foreigners have so long exercised over the opportunities, the routes, and the methods of our commerce with other countries.

The Interstate Commerce Commission has been reorganized to enable it to perform its great and important functions more promptly and more efficiently. We have created, extended and improved the service of the parcels post.

So much we have done for business. What other party has understood the task so well or executed it so intelligently and energetically? What other party has attempted it at all? The Republican leaders, apparently, know of no means of assisting business but "protection." How to stimulate it and put it upon a new footing of energy and enterprise they have not suggested.

For the farmers of the country we have virtually created commercial credit, by means of the Federal Reserve Act and the Rural Credits Act. They now have the standing of other business men in the money market. We have successfully regulated speculation in "futures" and established standards in the marketing of grains. By an intelligent Warehouse Act we have assisted to make the standard crops available as never before both for systematic marketing and as a security for loans from the banks. We have greatly added to the work of neighborhood demonstration on the farm itself of improved methods of cultivation, and, through the intelligent extension of the functions of the Department of Agriculture, have made it possible for the farmer to learn systematically where his best markets are and how to get at them.

The workingmen of America have been given a veritable emancipation, by the legal recognition of a man's labour as part of his life, and not a mere marketable commodity; by exempting labour organizations from processes of the courts which treated their members like fractional parts of mobs and not like accessible and responsible individuals; by releasing our seamen from involuntary servitude; by making adequate provision for compensation for industrial accidents; by providing suitable machinery for mediation and conciliation in industrial disputes; and by putting the Federal Department of Labor at the disposal of the workingman when in search of work.

We have effected the emancipation of the children of the country by releasing them from hurtful labour. We have instituted a system of national aid in the building of highroads such as the country has been feeling after for a century. We have sought to equalize taxation by means of an equitable income tax. We have taken the steps that ought to have been taken at the outset to open up the resources of Alaska. We have provided for national defense upon a scale never before seriously proposed upon the responsibility of an entire political party. We have driven the tariff lobby from cover and obliged it to substitute solid argument for private influence.

This extraordinary recital must sound like a platform, a list of sanguine promises; but it is not. It is a record of promises made four years ago and now actually redeemed in constructive legislation.

These things must profoundly disturb the thoughts and confound the plans of those who have made themselves believe that the Democratic Party neither understood nor was ready to assist the business of the country in the great enterprises which it is its evident and inevitable destiny to undertake and carry through. The breaking up of the lobby must especially disconcert them; for it was through the lobby that they sought and were sure they had found the heart of things. The game of privilege can be played successfully by no other means.

This record must equally astonish those who feared that the Democratic Party had not opened its heart to comprehend the demands of social justice. We have in four years come very near to carrying out the platform of the Progressive Party as well as our own; for we also are progressives.

There is one circumstance connected with this programme which ought to be very plainly stated. It was resisted at every step by the interests which the Republican Party had catered to and fostered at the expense of the country, and these same interests are now earnestly praying for a reaction which will save their privileges,—for the restoration of their sworn friends to power before it is too late to recover what they have lost. They fought with particular desperation and infinite resourcefulness the reform of the banking and currency system, knowing that to be the citadel of their control; and most anxiously are they hoping and planning for the amendment of the Federal Reserve Act by the concentration of control in a single bank which the old familiar group of bankers can keep under their eye and direction. But while the "big men" who used to write the tariffs and command the assistance of the Treasury have been hostile,—all but a few with vision,—the average business man knows that he has been delivered, and that the fear that was once every day in his heart, that the men who controlled credit and directed enterprise from the committee rooms of Congress would crush him, is there no more, and will not return,—unless the party that consulted only the "big men" should return to power,—the party of masterly inactivity and cunning resourcefulness in standing pat to resist change.

The Republican Party is just the party that *cannot* meet the new conditions of a new age. It does not know the way and it does not wish new conditions. It tried to break away from the old leaders and could not. They still select its candidates and dictate its policy, still resist change, still hanker after the old conditions, still know no methods of encouraging business but the old methods. When it changes its leaders and its purposes and brings its ideas up to date it will have the right to ask the American people to give it power again; but not until then. A new age, an age of revolutionary change, needs new purposes and new ideas.

In foreign affairs we have been guided by principles clearly conceived and consistently lived up to. Perhaps they have not been fully comprehended because they have hitherto governed international affairs only in theory, not in practice. They are simple, obvious, easily stated, and fundamental to American ideals.

We have been neutral not only because it was the fixed and traditional policy of the United States to stand aloof from the politics of Europe and because we had had no part either of action or of policy in the influences which brought on the present war, but also because it was manifestly our duty to prevent, if it were possible, the indefinite extension of the fires of hate and desolation kindled by that terrible conflict and seek to serve mankind by reserving our strength and our resources for the anxious and difficult days of restoration and healing which must follow, when peace will have to build its house anew.

The rights of our own citizens of course became involved: that was inevitable. Where they did this was our guiding principle: that property rights can be vindicated by claims for damages when the war is over, and no modern nation can decline to arbitrate such claims; but the fundamental rights of humanity cannot be. The loss of life is irreparable. Neither can direct violations of a nation's sovereignty await vindication in suits for damages. The nation that violates these essential rights must expect to be checked and called to account by direct challenge and resistance. It at once makes the quarrel in part our own. These are plain principles and we have never lost sight of them or departed from them, whatever the stress or the perplexity of circumstance or the provocation to hasty resentment. The record is clear and consistent throughout and stands distinct and definite for anyone to judge who wishes to know the truth about it.

The seas were not broad enough to keep the infection of the conflict out of our own politics. The passions and intrigues of certain active groups and combinations of men amongst us who were born under foreign flags injected the poison of disloyalty into our own most critical affairs, laid violent hands upon many of our industries, and subjected us to the shame of divisions of sentiment and purpose in which America was contemned and forgotten. It is part of the business of this year of reckoning and settlement to speak plainly and act with unmistakable purpose in rebuke of these things, in order that they may be forever hereafter impossible. I am the candidate of a party, but I am above all things else an American citizen. I neither seek the favour nor fear the displeasure of that small alien element amongst us which puts loyalty to any foreign power before loyalty to the United States.

While Europe was at war our own continent, one of our

own neighbours, was shaken by revolution. In that matter, too, principle was plain and it was imperative that we should live up to it if we were to deserve the trust of any real partisan of the right as free men see it. We have professed to believe, and we do believe, that the people of small and weak states have the right to expect to be dealt with exactly as the people of big and powerful states would be. We have acted upon that principle in dealing with the people of Mexico.

Our recent pursuit of bandits into Mexican territory was no violation of that principle. We ventured to enter Mexican territory only because there were no military forces in Mexico that could protect our border from hostile attack and our own people from violence, and we have committed there no single act of hostility or interference even with the sovereign authority of the Republic of Mexico herself. It was a plain case of the violation of our own sovereignty which could not wait to be vindicated by damages and for which there was no other remedy. The authorities of Mexico were powerless to prevent it.

Many serious wrongs against the property, many irreparable wrongs against the persons, of Americans have been committed within the territory of Mexico herself during this confused revolution, wrongs which could not be effectually checked so long as there was no constituted power in Mexico which was in a position to check them. We could not act directly in that matter ourselves without denying Mexicans the right to any revolution at all which disturbed us and making the emancipation of her own people await our own interest and convenience.

For it is their emancipation that they are seeking,—blindly, it may be, and as yet ineffectually, but with profound and passionate purpose and within their unquestionable right, apply what true American principle you will,—any principle that an American would publicly avow. The people of Mexico have not been suffered to own their own country or direct their own institutions. Outsiders, men out of other nations and with interests too often alien to their own, have dictated what their privileges and opportunities should be and who should control their land, their lives, and their resources,—some of them Americans, pressing for things they could never have got in their own country. The Mexican people are entitled to attempt their liberty from such influences; and so long as I have anything to do with the action of our great Government I shall do everything in my power to prevent anyone standing in their way. I know that this is hard for some persons to understand; but it is not hard for the plain people of the United States to understand. It is hard doctrine only for those who wish to get something for themselves out of Mexico. There are men, and noble women, too, not a few, of our own people, thank God! whose fortunes are invested in great properties in Mexico who yet see the case with true vision and assess its issues with true American feeling. The rest can be left for the present out of the reckoning until this enslaved people has had its day of struggle towards the light. I have heard no one who was free from such influences propose interference by the United States with the internal affairs of Mexico. Certainly no friend of the Mexican people has proposed it.

The people of the United States are capable of great sympathies and a noble pity in dealing with problems of this kind. As their spokesman and representative, I have tried to act in the spirit they would wish me show. The people of Mexico are striving for the rights that are fundamental to life and happiness,—fifteen million oppressed men, overburdened women, and pitiful children in virtual bondage in their own home of fertile lands and inexhaustible treasure! Some of the leaders of the revolution may often have been mistaken and violent and selfish, but the revolution itself was inevitable and is right. The unspeakable Huerta betrayed the very comrades he served, traitorously overthrew the government of which he was a trusted part, impudently spoke for the very forces that had driven his people to the rebellion with which he had pretended to sympathize. The men who overcame him and drove him out represent at least the fierce passion of reconstruction which lies at the very heart of liberty; and so long as they represent, however imperfectly, such a struggle for deliverance, I am ready to serve their ends when I can. So long as the power of recognition rests with me the Government of the United States will refuse to extend the hand of welcome to any one who obtains power in a sister republic by treachery and violence. No permanency can be given the affairs of any republic by a title based upon intrigue and assassination. I declared that to be the policy of this Administration within three weeks after I assumed the presidency. I here again vow it. I am more interested in the fortunes of oppressed men and pitiful women and children than in any property rights whatever. Mistakes I have no doubt made in this perplexing business, but not in purpose or object.

More is involved than the immediate destinies of Mexico and the relations of the United States with a distressed and distracted people. All America looks on. Test is now being made of us whether we be sincere lovers of popular liberty or not and are indeed to be trusted to respect national sovereignty among our weaker neighbours. We have undertaken these many years to play big brother to the republics of this hemisphere. This is the day of our test whether we mean, or have ever meant, to play that part for our own benefit wholly or also for theirs. Upon the outcome of that test (its outcome in their minds, not in ours) depends every relationship of the United States with Latin America, whether in politics or in commerce and enterprise. These are great issues and lie at the heart of the gravest tasks of the future, tasks both economic and political and very intimately inwrought with many of the most vital of the new issues of the politics of the world. The republics of America have in the last three years been drawing together in a new spirit of accommodation, mutual understanding, and cordial cooperation. Much of the politics of the world in the years to come will depend upon their relationships with one another. It is a barren and provincial statesmanship that loses sight of such things!

The future, the immediate future, will bring us squarely face to face with many great and exacting problems which will search us through and through whether we be able and ready to play the part in the world that we mean to play. It will not bring us into their presence slowly, gently, with ceremonious introduction, but suddenly and at once, the moment the war in Europe is over. They will be new problems, most of them; many will be old problems in a new setting and with new elements which we have never dealt with or reckoned the force and meaning of before. They will require for their solution new thinking, fresh courage and resourcefulness, and in some matters radical reconsiderations of policy. We must be ready to mobilize our resources alike of brains and of materials.

It is not a future to be afraid of. It is, rather, a future to stimulate and excite us to the display of the best powers that are in us. We may enter it with confidence when we are sure that we understand it,—and we have provided ourselves already with the means of understanding it.

Look first at what it will be necessary that the nations of the world should do to make the days to come tolerable and fit to live and work in; and then look at our part in what is to follow and our own duty of preparation. For we must be prepared both in resources and in policy.

There must be a just and settled peace, and we here in America must contribute the full force of our enthusiasm and of our authority as a nation to the organization of that peace upon world-wide foundations that cannot easily be shaken. No nation should be forced to take sides in any quarrel in which its own honour and integrity and the fortunes of its own people are not involved; but no nation can any longer remain neutral as against any wilful disturbance of the peace of the world. The effects of war can no longer be confined to the areas of battle. No nation stands wholly apart in interest when the life and interests of all nations are thrown into confusion and peril. If hopeful and generous enterprise is to be renewed, if the healing and helpful arts of life are indeed to be revived when peace comes again, a new atmosphere of justice and friendship must be generated by means the world has never tried before. The nations of the world must unite in joint guarantees that whatever is done to disturb the whole world's life must first be tested in the court of the whole world's opinion before it is attempted.

These are the new foundations the world must build for itself, and we must play our part in the reconstruction, generously and without too much thought of our separate interests. We must make ourselves ready to play it intelligently, vigorously and well.

One of the contributions we must make to the world's peace is this: We must see to it that the people in our insular possessions are treated in their own lands as we would treat them here, and make the rule of the United States mean the same thing everywhere,—the same justice, the same consideration for the essential rights of men.

Besides contributing our ungrudging moral and practical support to the establishment of peace throughout the world we must actively and intelligently prepare ourselves to do our full service in the trade and industry which are to sustain and develop the life of the nations in the days to come.

We have already been provident in this great matter and supplied ourselves with the instrumentalities of prompt adjustment. We have created, in the Federal Trade Commission, a means of inquiry and of accommodation in the field of commerce which ought both to coordinate the enterprises of our traders and manufacturers and to remove the barriers of misunderstanding and of a too technical interpretation of the law. In the new Tariff Commission we have added another instrumentality of observation and adjustment which promises to be immediately serviceable. The Trade Commission substitutes counsel and accommodation for the harsher processes of legal restraint, and the Tariff Commission ought to substitute facts for prejudices and theories. Our exporters have for some time had the advantage of working in the new light thrown upon foreign markets and opportunities of trade by the intelligent inquiries and activities of the Bureau of Foreign and Domestic Commerce which the Democratic Congress so wisely created in 1912. The tariff Commission completes the machinery by which we shall be enabled to open up our legislative policy to the facts as they develop.

We can no longer indulge our traditional provincialism. We are to play a leading part in the world drama whether we wish it or not. We shall lend, not borrow; act for ourselves, not imitate or follow; organize and initiate, not peep about merely to see where we may get in.

We have already formulated and agreed upon a policy of law which will explicitly remove the ban now supposed to rest upon cooperation amongst our exporters in seeking and securing their proper place in the markets of the world. The field will be free, the instrumentalities at hand. It will only remain for the masters of enterprise amongst us to act in energetic concert, and for the Government of the United States to insist upon the maintenance throughout the world of those conditions of fairness and of even-handed justice in the commercial dealings of the nations with one another upon which, after all, in the last analysis, the peace and ordered life of the world must ultimately depend.

At home also we must see to it that the men who plan and develop and direct our business enterprises shall enjoy definite and settled conditions of law, a policy accommodated to the freest progress. We have set the just and necessary limits. We have put all kinds of unfair competition under the ban and penalty of the law. We have barred monopoly. These fatal and ugly things being excluded, we must now quicken action and facilitate enterprise by every just means within our choice. There will be peace in the business world, and, with peace, revived confidence and life.

We ought both to husband and to develop our natural resources, our mines, our forests, our water power. I wish we could have made more progress than we have made in this vital matter; and I call once more, with the deepest earnestness and solicitude, upon the advocates of a careful and provident conservation, on the one hand, and the advocates of a free and inviting field for private capital, on the other, to get together in a spirit of genuine accommodation and agreement and set this great policy forward at once.

We must hearten and quicken the spirit and efficiency of labour throughout our whole industrial system by everywhere and in all occupations doing justice to the labourer, not only by paying a living wage but also by making all the conditions that surround labour what they ought to be. And we must do more than justice. We must safeguard life and promote health and safety in every occupation in which they are threatened or imperilled. That is more than justice, and better, because it is humanity and economy.

We must coordinate the railway systems of the country for national use, and must facilitate and promote their development with a view to that coordination and to their better adaptation as a whole to the life and trade and defense of the nation. The life and industry of the country can be free and unhampered only if these arteries are open, efficient, and complete.

Thus shall we stand ready to meet the future as circumstance and international policy effect their unfolding, whether the changes come slowly or come fast and without preface.

I have not spoken explicitly, Gentlemen, of the platform adopted at St. Louis; but it has been implicit in all that I have said. I have sought to interpret its spirit and meaning. The people of the United States do not need to be assured now that that platform is a definite pledge, a practical programme. We have proved to them that our promises are made to be kept.

We hold very definite ideals. We believe that the energy and initiative of our people have been too narrowly coached and superintended; that they should be set free, as we have set them free, to disperse themselves throughout the nation; that they should not be concentrated in the hands of a few powerful guides and guardians, as our opponents have again and again, in effect if not in purpose, sought to concentrate them. We believe, moreover,—who that looks about him now with comprehending eye can fail to believe?—that the day of Little Americanism, with its narrow horizons, when methods of "protection" and industrial nursing were the chief study of our provincial statesmen, are past and gone and that a day of enterprise has at last dawned for the United States whose field is the wide world.

We hope to see the stimulus of that new day draw all America, the republics of both continents, on to a new life and energy and initiative in the great affairs of peace. We are Americans for Big America, and rejoice to look forward to the days in which America shall strive to stir the world without irritating it or drawing it on to new antagonisms, when the nations with which we deal shall at last come to see upon what deep foundations of humanity and justice our passion for peace rests, and when all mankind shall look npon our great people with a new sentiment of admiration, friendly rivalry and real affection, as upon a people who, though keen to succeed, seeks always to be at once generous and just and to whom humanity is dearer than profit or selfish power.

Upon this record and in the faith of this purpose we go to the country.

President Wilson's Address on Lincoln

(At the Formal Acceptance of the Lincoln Memorial, Built Over the Log-Cabin Birthplace at Hodgenville, Ky., September 4, 1916)

No more significant memorial could have been presented to the nation than this. It expresses so much of what is singular and noteworthy in the history of the country; it suggests so many of the things that we prize most highly in our life and in our system of government. How eloquent this little house within this shrine is of the vigor of democracy! There is nowhere in the land any home so remote, so humble, that it may not contain the power of mind and heart and conscience to which nations yield and history submits its processes. Nature pays no tribute to aristocracy, subscribes to no creed of caste, renders fealty to no monarch or master of any name or kind. Genius is no snob. It does not run after titles or seek by preference the high circles of society. It affects humble company as well as great. It pays no special tribute to universities or learned societies or conventional standards of greatness, but serenely chooses its own comrades, its own haunts, its own cradle even, and its own life of adventure and of training. Here is proof of it. This little hut was the cradle of one of the great sons of men, a man of singular, delightful, vital genius who presently emerged upon the great stage of the nation's history, gaunt, shy, ungainly, but dominant and majestic, a natural ruler of men, himself inevitably the central figure of the great plot. No man can explain this, but every man can see how it demonstrates the vigor of democracy, where every door is open, in every hamlet and countryside, in city and wilderness alike, for the ruler to emerge when he will and claim his leadership in the free life. Such are the authentic proofs of the validity and vitality of democracy.

Here, no less, hides the mystery of democracy. Who shall guess this secret of nature and providence and a free polity? Whatever the vigor and vitality of the stock from which he sprang, its mere vigor and soundness do not explain where this man got his great heart that seemed to comprehend all mankind in its catholic and benignant sympathy, the mind that sat enthroned behind those brooding, melancholy eyes, whose vision swept many an horizon which those about him dreamed not of, that mind that comprehended what it had never seen, and understood the language of affairs with the ready ease of one to the manner born—or that nature which seemed in its varied richness to be the familiar of men of every way of life. This is the sacred mystery of democracy, that its richest fruits spring up out of soils which no man has prepared and in circumstances amidst which they are the least expected. This is a place alike of mystery and of reassurance.

It is likely that in a society ordered otherwise than our own Lincoln could not have found himself or the path of fame and power upon which he walked serenely to his death. In this place it is right that we should remind ourselves of the solid and striking facts upon which our faith in democracy is founded. Many another man besides Lincoln has served the nation in its highest places of counsel and of action whose origins were as humble as his. Though the greatest example of the universal energy, richness, stimulation, and force of democracy, he is only one example among many. The permeating and all-pervasive virtue of the freedom which challenges us in America to make the most of every gift and power we possess every page of our history serves to emphasize and illustrate. Standing here in this place, it seems almost the whole of the stirring story.

Here Lincoln had his beginnings. Here the end and consummation of that great life seem remote and a bit incredible. And yet there was no break anywhere between beginning and end, no lack of natural sequence anywhere. Nothing really incredible happened. Lincoln was unaffectedly as much at home in the White House as he was here. Do you share with me the feeling, I wonder, that he was permanently at home nowhere? It seems to me that in the case of a man—I would rather say of a spirit—like Lincoln the question *where* he was is of little significance, that it is always *what* he was that really arrests our thought and takes hold of our imagination. It is the spirit always that is sovereign. Lincoln, like the rest of us, was put through the discipline of the world—a very rough and exacting discipline for him, an indispensable discipline for every man who would know what he is about in the midst of the world's affairs; but his spirit got only its schooling there. It did not derive its character or its vision from the experiences which brought it to its full revelation. The test of every American must always be, not where he is, but what he is. That, also, is of the essence of democracy, and is the moral of which this place is most gravely expressive.

We would like to think of men like Lincoln and Washington as typical Americans, but no man can be typical who is so unusual as these great men were. It was typical of American life that it should produce such men with supreme indifference as to the manner in which it produced them, and as readily here in this hut as amidst the little circle of cultivated gentlemen to whom Virginia owed so much in leadership and example. And Lincoln and Washington were typical Americans in the use they made of their genius. But there will be few such men at best, and we will not look into the mystery of how and why they come. We will only keep the door open for them always, and a hearty welcome—after we have recognized them.

I have read many biographies of Lincoln; I have sought out with the greatest interest the many intimate stories that are told of him, the narratives of nearby friends, the sketches at close quarters, in which those who had the privilege of being associated with him have tried to depict for us the very man himself "in his habit as he lived;" but I have nowhere found a real intimate of Lincoln's. I nowhere get the impression in any narrative or reminiscence that the writer had in fact penetrated to the heart of his mystery, or that any man could penetrate to the heart of it. That brooding spirit had no real familiars. I get the impression that it never spoke out in complete self-revelation, and that it could not reveal itself completely to anyone. It was a very lonely spirit that looked out from underneath those shaggy brows and comprehended men without fully communing with them, as if, in spite of all its genial efforts at comradeship, it dwelt apart, saw its visions of duty where no man looked on. There is a very holy and very terrible isolation for the conscience of every man who seeks to read the destiny in affairs for others as well as for himself, for a nation as well as for individuals. That privacy no man can intrude upon. That lonely search of the spirit for the right perhaps no man can assist. This strange child of the cabin kept company with invisible things, was born into no intimacy but that of its own silently assembling and deploying thoughts.

I have come here today, not to utter a eulogy on Lincoln; he stands in need of none, but to endeavor to interpret the meaning of this gift to the nation of the place of his birth and origin. Is not this an altar upon which we may forever keep alive the vestal fire of democracy as upon a shrine at which some of the deepest and most sacred hopes of mankind may from age to age be rekindled? For these hopes must constantly be rekindled, and only those who live can rekindle them. The only stuff that can retain the life-giving heat is the stuff of living hearts. And the hopes of mankind cannot be kept alive by words merely, by constitutions and doctrines of right and codes of liberty. The object of democracy is to transmute these into the life and action of society, the self-denial and self-sacrifice of heroic men and women willing to make their lives an embodiment of right and service and enlightened purpose. The commands of democracy are as imperative as its privileges and opportunities are wide and generous. Its compulsion is upon us. It will be great and lift a great light for the guidance of the nations only if we are great and carry that light high for the guidance of our own feet. We are not worthy to stand here unless we ourselves be in deed and in truth real democrats and servants of mankind, ready to give our very lives for the freedom and justice and spiritual exaltation of the great nation which shelters and nurtures us.

Wilson's Address at the Woman Suffrage Convention, Atlantic City, N. J., September 8, 1916

[The movement for woman suffrage had made great advances within recent years; and in the approaching election women were to vote in twelve States—seven more than in the previous Presidential contest. Mr. Hughes, the Republican candidate, had given unqualified approval of the suffrage movement, but President Wilson had displeased one faction by adhering to a belief that suffrage was a question each State should settle for itself. Thus he had supported woman suffrage in his own State of New Jersey, but had refused to support a movement for the adoption of a woman suffrage amendment to the Federal Constitution.]

Madam President, Ladies of the Association:

The astonishing thing about the movement which you represent is, not that it has grown so slowly, but that it has grown so rapidly. No doubt for those who have been a long time in the struggle, like your honored president, it seems a long and arduous path that has been trodden, but when you think of the cumulating force of this movement in recent decades, you must agree with me that it is one of the most astonishing tides in modern history. Two generations ago, no doubt Madam President will agree with me in saying, it was a handful of women who were fighting this cause. Now it is a great multitude of women who are fighting it.

And there are some interesting historical connections which I would like to attempt to point out to you. One of the most striking facts about the history of the United States is that at the outset it was a lawyers' history. Almost all of the questions to which America addressed itself, say a hundred years ago, were legal questions, were questions of method, not questions of what you were going to do with your Government, but questions of how you were going to constitute your Government—how you were going to balance the powers of the States and the Federal Government, how you were going to balance the claims of property against the processes of liberty, how you were going to make your governments up so as to balance the parts against each other so that the legislature would check the executive, and the executive the legislature, and the courts both of them put together. The whole conception of government when the United States became a Nation was a mechanical conception of government, and the mechanical conception of government which underlay it was the Newtonian theory of the universe. If you pick up the Federalist, some parts of it read like a treatise on astronomy instead of a treatise on government. They speak of the centrifugal and the centripetal forces, and locate the President somewhere in a rotating system. The whole thing is a calculation of power and an adjustment of parts. There was a time when nobody but a lawyer could know enough to run the Government of the United States, and a distinguished English publicist once remarked, speaking of the complexity of the American Government, that it was no proof of the excellence of the American Constitution that it had been successfully operated, because the Americans could run any constitution. But there have been a great many technical difficulties in running it.

And then something happened. A great question arose in this country which, though complicated with legal elements, was at bottom a human question, and nothing but a question of humanity. That was the slavery question. And is it not significant that it was then, and then for the first time, that women became prominent in politics in America? Not many women; those prominent in that day were so few that you can name them over in a brief catalogue, but, nevertheless, they then began to play a part in writing, not only, but in public speech, which was a very novel part for women to play in America. After the Civil War had settled some of what seemed to be the most difficult legal questions of our system, the life of the Nation began not only to unfold, but to accumulate. Life in the United States was a comparatively simple matter at the time of the Civil War. There was none of that underground struggle which is now so manifest to those who look only a little way beneath the surface. The pressure of low wages, the agony of obscure and unremunerated toil, did not exist in America in anything like the same proportions that they exist now.

And as our life has unfolded and accumulated, as the contacts of it have become hot, as the populations have assembled in the cities and the cool spaces of the country have been supplanted by the feverish urban areas, the whole nature of our political questions has been altered. They have ceased to be legal questions. They have more and more become social questions, questions with regard to the relations of human beings to one another—not merely their legal relations, but their moral and spiritual relations to one another. This has been most characteristic of

American life in the last few decades, and as these questions have assumed greater and greater prominence, the movement which this association represents has gathered cumulative force. So that, if anybody asks himself, "What does this gathering force mean," if he knows anything about the history of the country, he knows that it means something that has not only come to stay, but has come with conquering power.

I get a little impatient sometimes about the discussion of the channels and methods by which it is to prevail. It is going to prevail, and that is a very superficial and ignorant view of it which attributes it to mere social unrest. It is not merely because the women are discontented. It is because the women have seen visions of duty, and that is something which we not only cannot resist, but, if we be true Americans, we do not wish to resist. America took its origin in visions of the human spirit, in aspirations for the deepest sort of liberty of the mind and of the heart, and as visions of that sort come up to the sight of those who are spiritually minded in America, America comes more and more into her birthright and into the perfection of her development.

So that what we have to realize in dealing with forces of this sort is that we are dealing with the substance of life itself. I have felt as I sat here tonight the wholesome contagion of the occasion. Almost every other time that I ever visited Atlantic City, I came to fight somebody. I hardly know how to conduct myself when I have not come to fight against anybody, but with somebody. I have come to suggest, among other things, that when the forces of nature are steadily working and the tide is rising to meet the moon, you need not be afraid that it will not come to its flood. We feel the tide; we rejoice in the strength of it; and we shall not quarrel in the long run as to the method of it. Because, when you are working with masses of men and organized bodies of opinion, you have got to carry the organized body along. The whole art and practice of government consists, not in moving individuals, but in moving masses. It is all very well to run ahead and beckon, but, after all, you have got to wait for the body to follow. I have not come to ask you to be patient, because you have been, but I have come to congratulate you that there was a force behind you that will beyond any peradventure be triumphant, and for which you can afford a little while to wait.

President Wilson's Address on the Relation of the United States to the Business of the World

(Delivered before the Grain Dealers' Association, Baltimore, September 25, 1916)

Mr. Chairman, Ladies and Gentlemen:

It is a matter of sincere gratification to me that I can come and address an association of this sort, and yet I feel that there is a certain drawback to the present occasion. That drawback consists of the fact that it occurs in the midst of a political campaign. Nothing so seriously interrupts or interferes with the sober and sincere consideration of public questions as a political campaign. I want to say to you at the outset that I believe in *party* action, but that I have a supreme contempt for *partisan* action; that I believe that it is necessary for men to concert measures together in organized coöperation by party, but that whenever party feeling touches any one of the passions that work against the general interest, it is altogether to be condemned. Therefore, I feel that on occasions like this we should divest ourselves of the consciousness that we are in the midst of a political campaign. . . .

What I have come to say to you today, therefore, I would wish to say in an atmosphere from which all the vapors of passion have been cleared away, for I want to speak to you about the business situation of the world, so far as America is concerned. I am not going to take the liberty of discussing that business situation from the special point of view of your association, because I know that I would be bringing coals to Newcastle. I know that I am speaking to men who understand the relation of the grain business to the business of the world very much better than I do; and I know that it is true that, except under very unusual circumstances such as have existed in the immediate past, the export of grain from this country has been a diminishing part of our foreign commerce rather than an increasing part; that the increase of our own population—the decrease in proportion to that increase, of our production of grains—has been rendering the question of foreign markets less important, though still very important, than it was in past generations, so far as the dealing in grain is concerned. I also remember, however, that we have only begun in this country the process by which the full production of our agricultural acreage is to be obtained. The agricultural acreage of this country ought to produce twice what it is now producing, and under the stimulation and instruction which have recently been characteristic of agricultural development I think we can confidently predict that within, let us say, a couple of decades, the agricultural production of this country will be something like double, whereas, there is no likelihood that the population of this country will be doubled within the same period. You can look forward, therefore, it seems to me, with some degree of confidence to an increasing, and perhaps a rapidly increasing, volume of the products in which you deal.

But, as I have said, I have not come to discuss that. I have come to discuss the general relation of the United States to the business of the world in the decades immediately ahead of us. We have swung out, my fellow citizens, into a new business era in America. I suppose that there is no man connected with your association who does not remember the time when the whole emphasis of American business discussion was laid upon the domestic market. I need not remind you how recently it has happened that our attention has been extended to the markets of the world; much less recently, I need not say, in the matters with which you are concerned than in the other export interests of the country. But it happened that American production, not only in the agricultural field and in mining and in all the natural products of the earth, but also in manufacture, increased in recent years to such a volume that American business burst its jacket. It could not any longer be taken care of within the field of the domestic markets; and when that began to disclose itself as the situation, we also became aware that American business men had not studied foreign markets, that they did not know the commerce of the world, and that they did not have the ships in which to take their proportionate part in the carrying trade of the world; that our merchant marine had sunk to a negligible amount, and that it had sunk to its lowest at the very time when the tide of our exports began to grow in most formidable volume.

One of the most interesting circumstances of our business history is this: The banking laws of the United States—I mean the Federal banking laws—did not put the national banks in a position to do foreign exchange under favorable conditions, and it was actually true that private banks, and sometimes branch banks drawn out of other countries, notably out of Canada, were established at our chief ports to do what American bankers ought to have done. It was as if America was not only unaccustomed to touching all the nerves of the world's business, but was disinclined to touch them, and had not prepared the instrumentality by which it might take part in the great commerce of the round globe. Only in very recent years have we been even studying the problem of providing ourselves with the instrumentalities.

Not until the recent legislation of Congress known as the Federal Reserve Act were the federal banks of this country given the proper equipment through which they could assist American commerce, not only in our own country, but in any part of the world where they chose to set up branch institutions. British banks had been serving British merchants all over the world, German banks had been serving German merchants all over the world, and no national bank of the United States had been serving American merchants anywhere in the world except in the United States. We had, as it were, deliberately refrained from playing our part in the field in which we prided ourselves that we were most ambitious and most expert, the field of manufacture and of commerce. All that is past, and the scene has been changed by the events of the last two years, almost suddenly, and with a completeness that almost daunts the planning mind. Not only when this war is over, but now, America has her place in the world and must take her place in the world of finance and commerce upon a scale that she never dreamed of before.

My dream is that she will take her place in that great field in a new spirit which the world has never seen before; not the spirit of those who would exclude others, but the spirit of those who would excel others. I want to see America pitted against the world, not in selfishness, but in brains. . . .

What instrumentalities have we provided ourselves with in order that we may be equipped with knowledge? There has been an instrumentality in operation for four or five years of which, strangely enough, American business men have only slowly become aware. Some four or five years ago the Congress established, in connection with the department which was then the Department of Commerce and Labor(now the Department of Commerce) a Bureau of Foreign and Domestic Commerce, and one of the advantages which the American Government has derived from that bureau is that it has been able to hire brains for much less than the brains were worth. It is in a way a national discredit to us, my fellow citizens, that we are paying studious men, capable of understanding anything and of conducting any business, just about one-third of what they could command in the field of business; and it is one of the admirable circumstances of American life that they are proud to serve the Government on a pittance. There are such men in the Bureau of Foreign and Domestic Commerce. They have been studying the foreign commerce of this country as it was never studied before, and have been making reports so comprehensive and so thorough that they compare to their great advantage with the reports of any similar bureau of any other government in the world, and I have found to my amazement that some of the best of those reports seem never to have been read. . . .

And then, in addition to that, there was recently created the Federal Trade Commission. It is hard to describe the functions of that commission; all I can say is that it has transformed the Government of the United States from being an antagonist of business into being a friend of business. A few years ago American business men—I think you will corroborate this statement—took up their morning paper with some degree of nervousness to see what the Government was doing to them. I ask you if you take up the morning paper now with any degree of nervousness? And I ask you if you have not found, those of you who have dealt with it all, the Federal Trade Commission to be put there to show you the way in which the Government can help you and not the way in which the Government can hinder you?

But that is not the matter that I am most interested in. It has always been a fiction—I don't know who invented it or why he invented it—that there was a contest between the law and business. There has always been a contest in every government between the law and bad business, and I

there. I for myself despise monopoly, and I have an enthusiasm for coöperation. By coöperation I mean working along with anybody who is willing to work along with you under definite understandings and arrangements which will constitute a sound business programme. There can be no jealousy of that, and if there had been time, I can say with confidence that this bill, which passed the House of Representatives, would have passed the Senate of the United States also. So that any obstacle that ingenious lawyers may find in the anti-trust laws will be removed. . . .

And then there must be coöperation, not only between the Government and the business men, but between business men. Shippers must coöperate, and they ought to be studying right now how to coöperate. There are a great many gentlemen in other countries who can show them how! They ought to look forward, particularly, to caring for this matter, that they have vehicles in which to carry their goods. We must address ourselves immediately and as rapidly as possible to the re-creation of a great American merchant marine. Our present situation is very like this: Suppose that a man who had a great department store did not have any delivery wagons and depended upon his competitors in the same market to deliver his goods to his customers. You know what would happen. They would deliver their own goods first and quickest, and they would deliver yours only if yours were to be delivered upon the routes followed by their wagons. That is an exact picture of what is taking place in our foreign trade at this minute. Foreign vessels carry our goods where they, the foreign vessels, happen to be going, and they carry them only if they have room in addition to what they are carrying for other people. You can not conduct trade that way. That is conducting trade on sufferance. That is conducting trade on an "if you please." That is conducting trade on the basis of service the point of view of which is not your advantage. Therefore, we can not lose any time in getting delivery wagons.

There has been a good deal of discussion about this recently, and it has been said, "The Government must not take any direct part in this. You must let private capital do it," and the reply was, "All right, go ahead." "Oh, but we will not go ahead unless you help us." We said, "Very well, then, we will go ahead, but we will not need your help, because we do not want to compete where you are already doing the carrying business, but where you are not doing the carrying business and it has to be done for some time at a loss. We will undertake to do it at a loss until that route is established, and we will give place to private capital whenever private capital is ready to take the place." That sounds like a very reasonable proposition. "We will carry your goods one way when we have to come back empty the other way and lose money on the voyage, and when there are cargoes both ways and it is profitable to carry them, we shall not insist upon carrying them any longer."

And it is absolutely necessary now to make good our new connections. Our new connections are with the great and rich Republics to the south of us. For the first time in my recollection they are beginning to trust and believe in us and want us, and one of my chief concerns has been to see that nothing was done that did not show friendship and good faith on our part. You know that it used to be the case that if you wanted to travel comfortably in your own person from New York to a South American port, you had to go by way of England or else stow yourself away in some uncomfortable fashion in a ship that took almost as long to go straight, and within whose bowels you got in such a temper before you got there that you did not care whether she got there or not. The great interesting geographical fact to me is that by the opening of the Panama Canal there is a straight line south from New York through the canal to the western coast of South America, which hitherto has been one of the most remote coasts in the world so far as we were concerned. The west coast of

South America is now nearer to us than the eastern coast of South America ever was, though we have the open Atlantic upon which to approach the east coast. Here is the loom all ready upon which to spread the threads which can be worked into a fabric of friendship and wealth such as we have never known before! . . .

We have got to have the knowledge, we have got to have the cooperation, and then back of all that has got to lie what America has in abundance and only has to release, that is to say, the self-reliant enterprise.

There is only one thing I have ever been ashamed of about in America, and that was the timidity and fearfulness of Americans in the presence of foreign competitors. I have dwelt among Americans all my life and am an intense absorbent of the atmosphere of America, and I know by personal experience that there are as effective brains in America as anywhere in the world. An American afraid to pit American business men against any competitors anywhere! Enterprise, the shrewdness which Americans have shown, the knowledge of business which they have shown, all these things are going to make for that peaceful and honorable conquest of foreign markets which is our reasonable ambition. . . .

[EDITORIAL NOTE: *The election on November 7 resulted in the choice of Woodrow Wilson for a second term, with 276 votes in the Electoral College to 255 for Charles E. Hughes, the Republican candidate. In addition to the solid South, the President carried most of the West and several States in the East. The principal Democratic claim for support was that Wilson had "kept us out of war."*]

Wilson's Fourth Annual Address to Congress

(Delivered in Joint Session, December 5, 1916)

Gentlemen of the Congress:

In fulfilling at this time the duty laid upon me by the Constitution of communicating to you from time to time information of the state of the Union and recommending to your consideration such legislative measures as may be judged necessary and expedient I shall continue the practice, which I hope has been acceptable to you, of leaving to the reports of the several heads of the executive departments the elaboration of the detailed needs of the public service and confine myself to those matters of more general public policy with which it seems necessary and feasible to deal at the present session of the Congress.

I realize the limitations of time under which you will necessarily act at this session and shall make my suggestions as few as possible; but there were some things left undone at the last session which there will now be time to complete and which it seems necessary in the interest of the public to do at once.

In the first place, it seems to me imperatively necessary that the earliest possible consideration and action should be accorded the remaining measures of the programme of settlement and regulation which I had occasion to recommend to you at the close of your last session in view of the public dangers disclosed by the unaccommodated difficulties which then existed, and which still unhappily continue to exist, between the railroads of the country and their locomotive engineers, conductors, and trainmen.

I then recommended:

First, immediate provision for the enlargement and administrative reorganization of the Interstate Commerce Commission along the lines embodied in the bill recently passed by the House of Representatives and now awaiting action by the Senate; in order that the Commission may be enabled to deal with the many great and various duties now devolving upon it with a promptness and thoroughness which are, with its present constitution and means of action, practically impossible.

Second, the establishment of an eight-hour day as the legal basis alike of work and of wages in the employment of all railway employees who are actually engaged in the work of operating trains in interstate transportation.

Third, the authorization of the appointment by the President of a small body of men to observe the actual results in experience of the adoption of the eight-hour day in railway transportation alike for the men and for the railroads.

Fourth, explicit approval by the Congress of the consideration by the Interstate Commerce Commission of an increase of freight rates to meet such additional expenditures by the railroads as may have been rendered necessary by the adoption of the eight-hour day and which have not been offset by administrative readjustments and economies, should the facts disclosed justify the increase.

Fifth, an amendment of the existing federal statute which provides for the mediation, conciliation, and arbitration of such controversies as the present by adding to it a provision that, in case the methods of accommodation now provided for should fail, a full public investigation of the merits of every such dispute shall be instituted and completed before a strike or lockout may lawfully be attempted.

And, sixth, the lodgment in the hands of the Executive of the power, in case of military necessity, to take control of such portions and such rolling stock of the railways of the country as may be required for military use and to operate them for military purposes, with authority to draft into the military service of the United States such train crews and administrative officials as the circumstances require for their safe and efficient use.

The second and third of these recommendations the Congress immediately acted on: it established the eight-hour day as the legal basis of work and wages in train service and it authorized the appointment of a commission to observe and report upon the practical results, deeming these the measures most immediately needed; but it postponed action upon the other suggestions until an opportunity should be offered for a more deliberate consideration of them. The fourth recommendation I do not deem it necessary to renew. The power of the Interstate Commerce Commission to grant an increase of rates on the ground referred to is indisputably clear and a recommendation by the Congress with regard to such a matter might seem to draw in question the scope of the Commission's authority or its inclination to do justice when there is no reason to doubt either.

The other suggestions,—the increase in the Interstate Commerce Commission's membership and in its facilities for performing its manifold duties, the provision for full public investigation and assessment of industrial disputes, and the grant to the Executive of the power to control and operate the railways when necessary in time of war or other like public necessity,—I now very earnestly renew.

The necessity for such legislation is manifest and pressing. Those who have entrusted us with the responsibility and duty of serving and safeguarding them in such matters would find it hard, I believe, to excuse a failure to act upon these grave matters or any unnecessary postponement of action upon them.

Not only does the Interstate Commerce Commission now find it practically impossible, with its present membership and organization, to perform its great functions promptly and thoroughly but it is not unlikely that it may presently be found advisable to add to its duties still others equally heavy and exacting. It must first be perfected as an administrative instrument.

The country cannot and should not consent to remain any longer exposed to profound industrial disturbances for lack of additional means of arbitration and conciliatio which the Congress can easily and promptly supply. An all will agree that there must be no doubt as to the powe of the Executive to make immediate and uninterrupted us of the railroads for the concentration of the military forc of the nation wherever they are needed and whenever the are needed.

This is a programme of regulation, prevention, and ad ministrative efficiency which argues its own case in the mer statement of it. With regard to one of its items, the in crease in the efficiency of the Interstate Commerce Commis sion, the House of Representatives has already acted; it action needs only the concurrence of the Senate.

I would hesitate to recommend, and I dare say the Con gress would hesitate to act upon the suggestion should make it, that any man in any occupation should be oblige by law to continue in an employment which he desired t leave. To pass a law which forbade or prevented the in dividual workman to leave his work before receiving th approval of society in doing so would be to adopt a nev principle into our jurisprudence which I take it for grante we are not prepared to introduce. But the proposal tha the operation of the railways of the country shall not b stopped or interrupted by the concerted action of organ ized bodies of men until a public investigation shall hav been instituted which shall make the whole question at issu plain, for the judgment of the opinion of the nation is no to propose any such principle. It is based upon the ver different principle that the concerted action of powerfu bodies of men shall not be permitted to stop the industria processes of the nation, at any rate before the nation shal have had an opportunity to acquaint itself with the merit of the case as between employee and employer, time to form its opinion upon an impartial statement of the merits and opportunity to consider all practicable means of con ciliation or arbitration. I can see nothing in that proposi

on but the justifiable safeguarding by society of the nec-
ssary processes of its very life. There is nothing arbitrary
r unjust in it unless it be arbitrarily and unjustly done.
t can and should be done with a full and scrupulous re-
ard for the interests and liberties of all concerned as well
s for the permanent interests of society itself.

Three matters of capital importance await the action
f the Senate which have already been acted upon by the
Iouse of Representatives: the bill which seeks to extend
reater freedom of combination to those engaged in pro-
noting the foreign commerce of the country than is now
hought by some to be legal under the terms of the laws
gainst monopoly; the bill amending the present organic
aw of Porto Rico; and the bill proposing a more thorough
nd systematic regulation of the expenditure of money in
lections, commonly called the Corrupt Practices Act. I
eed not labor my advice that these measures be enacted
nto law. Their urgency lies in the manifest circumstances
vhich render their adoption at this time not only oppor-
une but necessary. Even delay would seriously jeopard
he interests of the country and of the government.

Immediate passage of the bill to regulate the expendi-
ure of money in elections may seem to be less necessary
han the immediate enactment of the other measures to
vhich I refer; because at least two years will elapse before
nother election in which federal offices are to be filled;
ut it would greatly relieve the public mind if this impor-
ant matter were dealt with while the circumstances and
he dangers to the public morals of the present method of
btaining and spending campaign funds stand clear under
ecent observation and the methods of expenditure can be
rankly studied in the light of present experience; and a
lelay would have the further very serious disadvantage of
ostponing action until another election was at hand and
ome special object connected with it might be thought to
e in the mind of those who urged it. Action can be taken

now with facts for guidance and without suspicion of partisan purpose.

I shall not argue at length the desirability of giving a freer hand in the matter of combined and concerted effort to those who shall undertake the essential enterprise of building up our export trade. That enterprise will presently, will immediately assume, has indeed already assumed, a magnitude unprecedented in our experience. We have not the necessary instrumentalities for its prosecution; it is deemed to be doubtful whether they could be created upon an adequate scale under our present laws. We should clear away all legal obstacles and create a basis of undoubted law for it which will give freedom without permitting unregulated license. The thing must be done now, because the opportunity is here and may escape us if we hesitate or delay.

The argument for the proposed amendments of the organic law of Porto Rico is brief and conclusive. The present laws governing the Island and regulating the rights and privileges of its people are not just. We have created expectations of extended privilege which we have not satisfied. There is uneasiness among the people of the Island and even a suspicious doubt with regard to our intentions concerning them which the adoption of the pending measure would happily remove. We do not doubt what we wish to do in any essential particular. We ought to do it at once.

At the last session of the Congress a bill was passed by the Senate which provides for the promotion of vocational and industrial education which is of vital importance to the whole country because it concerns a matter, too long neglected, upon which the thorough industrial preparation of the country for the critical years of economic development immediately ahead of us in very large measure depends. May I not urge its early and favourable consideration by the House of Representatives and its early enactment into law? It contains plans which affect all interests and all parts of the country, and I am sure that there is no legislation now pending before the Congress whose passage the country awaits with more thoughtful approval or greater impatience to see a great and admirable thing set in the way of being done.

There are other matters already advanced to the stage of conference between the two Houses of which it is not necessary that I should speak. Some practicable basis of agreement concerning them will no doubt be found and action taken upon them.

Inasmuch as this is, Gentlemen, probably the last occasion I shall have to address the Sixty-fourth Congress, I hope that you will permit me to say with what genuine pleasure and satisfaction I have cooperated with you in the many measures of constructive policy with which you have enriched the legislative annals of the country. It has been a privilege to labour in such company. I take the liberty of congratulating you upon the completion of a record of rare serviceableness and distinction.

Wilson's Note to the Belligerent Governments, Suggesting That Respective Peace Terms be Stated

[Editorial Note: *On December* 12, 1916, *Germany had made formal proposal "to enter forthwith into peace negotiations." For more than two years the Teutonic Allies had maintained unbroken their line in France and Belgium, and were then also in possession of Poland, Serbia, Montenegro, and half of the newest belligerent country, Rumania. The Entente Powers each rejected the German peace proposal as insincere, arrogant, and a proof of weakness. President Wilson, however, as head of the leading neutral nation—*

believed the occasion opportune for making certain peace proposals of his own, which he was understood to have formulated some time previously. His note, sent to all the belligerents, is as follows:]

Department of State,

Washington, D. C., Dec. 18, 1916.

The President directs me to send you the following communication to be presented immediately to the Minister of Foreign Affairs of the Government to which you are accredited:

The President of the United States has instructed me to suggest to the [here is inserted a designation of the Government addressed] a course of action with regard to the present war, which he hopes that the Government will take under consideration as suggested in the most friendly spirit, and as coming not only from a friend but also as coming from the representative of a neutral nation whose interests have been most seriously affected by the war and whose concern for its early conclusion arises out of a manifest necessity to determine how best to safeguard those interests if the war is to continue.

[The third paragraph of the note as sent to the four Central Powers—Germany, Austria-Hungary, Turkey, and Bulgaria—is as follows:]

The suggestion which I am instructed to make the President has long had it in mind to offer. He is somewhat embarrassed to offer it at this particular time, because it may now seem to have been prompted by a desire to play a part in connection with the recent overtures of the Central Powers. It has, in fact, been in no way suggested by them in its origin, and the President would have delayed offering it until those overtures had been independently answered but for the fact that it also concerns the questions of peace and may best be considered in connection with other proposals which have the same end in view. The President can only beg that his suggestion be considered entirely on its own merits and as if it had been made in other circumstances.

[The third paragraph of the note as sent to the ten Entente Allies—Great Britain, France, Italy, Japan, Russia, Belgium, Montenegro, Portugal, Rumania, and Serbia—is as follows:]

The suggestion which I am instructed to make the President has long had it in mind to offer. He is somewhat embarrassed to offer it at this particular time, because it may now seem to have been prompted by the recent overtures of the Central Powers. It is, in fact, in no way associated with them in its origin, and the President would have delayed offering it until those overtures had been answered but for the fact that it also concerns the question of peace and may best be considered in connection with other proposals which have the same end in view. The President can only beg that his suggestion be considered entirely on its own merits and as if it had been made in other circumstances.

[Thenceforward the note proceeds identically to all the powers, as follows:]

The President suggests that an early occasion be sought to call out from all the nations now at war such an avowal of their respective views as to the terms upon which the war might be concluded and the arrangements which would be deemed satisfactory as a guaranty against its renewal or the kindling of any similar conflict in the future as would make it possible frankly to compare them. He is indifferent as to the means taken to accomplish this. He would be happy himself to serve, or even to take the initiative in its accomplishment, in any way that might prove acceptable, but he has no desire to determine the method or the instrumentality. One way will be as acceptable to him as another, if only the great object he has in mind be attained.

He takes the liberty of calling attention to the fact that the objects, which the statesmen of the belligerents on both sides have in mind in this war, are virtually the same, as stated in general terms to their own people and to the world. Each side desires to make the rights and privileges of weak peoples and small States as secure against aggression or denial in the future as the rights and privileges of the great and powerful States now at war. Each wishes itself to be made secure in the future, along with all other nations and peoples, against the recurrence of wars like this and against aggression or selfish interference of any kind. Each would be jealous of the formation of any more rival leagues to preserve an uncertain balance of power amid multiplying suspicions; but each is ready to consider the formation of a league of nations to insure peace and justice throughout the world. Before that final step can be taken, however, each deems it necessary first to settle the issues of the present war upon terms which will certainly safeguard the independence, the territorial integrity, and the political and commercial freedom of the nations involved.

In the measures to be taken to secure the future peace of the world the people and Government of the United States are as vitally and as directly interested as the Governments now at war. Their interest, moreover, in the means to be adopted to relieve the smaller and weaker peoples of the world of the peril of wrong and violence is as quick and ardent as that of any other people or Government. They stand ready, and even eager, to cooperate in the accomplishment of these ends, when the war is over, with every influence and resource at their command. But the war must first be concluded. The terms upon which it is to be concluded they are not at liberty to suggest, but the President does feel that it is his right and his duty to point out their intimate interest in its conclusion, lest it should presently be too late to accomplish the greater things which lie beyond its conclusion, lest the situation of neutral nations, now exceedingly hard to endure, be rendered altogether intolerable, and lest, more than all, an injury be done civilization itself which can never be atoned for or repaired.

The President therefore feels altogether justified in suggesting an immediate opportunity for a comparison of views as to the terms which must precede those ultimate arrangements for the peace of the world, which all desire and in which the neutral nations as well as those at war are ready to play their full responsible part. If the contest must continue to proceed toward undefined ends by slow attrition until the one group of belligerents or the other is exhausted; if million after million of human lives must continue to be offered up until on the one side or the other there are no more to offer; if resentments must be kindled that can never cool and despairs engendered from which there can be no recovery, hopes of peace and of the willing concert of free peoples will be rendered vain and idle.

The life of the entire world has been profoundly affected. Every part of the great family of mankind has felt the burden and terror of this unprecedented contest of arms. No nation in the civilized world can be said in truth to stand outside its influence or to be safe against its disturbing effects. And yet the concrete objects for which it is being waged have never been definitively stated.

The leaders of the several belligerents have, as has been said, stated those objects in general terms. But, stated in general terms, they seem the same on both sides. Never yet have the authoritative spokesmen of either side avowed the precise objects which would, if attained, satisfy them and their people that the war had been fought out. The world has been left to conjecture what definitive results, what actual exchange of guaranties, what political or territorial changes or readjustments, what stage of military success, even, would bring the war to an end.

It may be that peace is nearer than we know; that the terms which the belligerents on the one side and on the other would deem it necessary to insist upon are not so irreconcilable as some have feared; that an interchange of views would clear the way at least for conference and make

nation in the high and honourable hope that it might in all that it was and did show mankind the way to liberty. They cannot in honour withold the service to which they are now about to be challenged. They do not wish to withhold it. But they owe it to themselves and to the other nations of the world to state the conditions under which they will feel free to render it.

That service is nothing less than this, to add their authority and their power to the authority and force of other nations to guarantee peace and justice throughout the world. Such a settlement cannot now be long postponed. It is right that before it comes this Government should frankly formulate the conditions upon which it would feel justified in asking our people to approve its formal and solemn adherence to a League for Peace. I am here to attempt to state those conditions.

The present war must first be ended; but we owe it to candour and to a just regard for the opinion of mankind to say that, so far as our participation in guarantees of future peace is concerned, it makes a great deal of difference in what way and upon what terms it is ended. The treaties and agreements which bring it to an end must embody terms which will create a peace that is worth guaranteeing and preserving, a peace that will win the approval of mankind, not merely a peace that will serve the several interests and immediate aims of the nations engaged. We shall have no voice in determining what those terms shall be, but we shall, I feel sure, have a voice in determining whether they shall be made lasting or not by the guarantees of a universal covenant, and our judgment upon what is fundamental and essential as a condition precedent to permanency should be spoken now, not afterwards when it may be too late.

No covenant of coöperative peace that does not include the peoples of the New World can suffice to keep the future safe against war; and yet there is only one sort of peace that the peoples of America could join in guaranteeing.

The elements of that peace must be elements that engage the confidence and satisfy the principles of the American governments, elements consistent with their political faith and with the practical convictions which the peoples of America have once for all embraced and undertaken to defend.

I do not mean to say that any American government would throw any obstacle in the way of any terms of peace the governments now at war might agree upon, or seek to upset them when made, whatever they might be. I only take it for granted that mere terms of peace between the belligerents will not satisfy even the belligerents themselves. Mere agreements may not make peace secure. It will be absolutely necessary that a force be created as a guarantor of the permanency of the settlement so much greater than the force of any nation now engaged or any alliance hitherto formed or projected that no nation, no probable combination of nations could face or withstand it. If the peace presently to be made is to endure, it must be a peace made secure by the organized major force of mankind.

The terms of the immediate peace agreed upon will determine whether it is a peace for which such a guarantee can be secured. The question upon which the whole future peace and policy of the world depends is this: Is the present war a struggle for a just and secure peace, or only for a new balance of power? If it be only a struggle for a new balance of power, who will guarantee, who can guarantee, the stable equilibrium of the new arrangement? Only a tranquil Europe can be a stable Europe. There must be, not a balance of power, but a community of power; not organized rivalries, but an organized common peace.

Fortunately we have received very explicit assurances on this point. The statesmen of both of the groups of nations now arrayed against one another have said, in terms that could not be misinterpreted, that it was no part

a right comity of arrangement no nation need be shut away from free access to the open paths of the world's commerce.

And the paths of the sea must alike in law and in fact be free. The freedom of the seas is the *sine qua non* of peace, equality, and coöperation. No doubt a somewhat radical reconsideration of many of the rules of international practice hitherto thought to be established may be necessary in order to make the seas indeed free and common in practically all circumstances for the use of mankind, but the motive for such changes is convincing and compelling. There can be no trust or intimacy between the peoples of the world without them. The free, constant, unthreatened intercourse of nations is an essential part of the process of peace and of development. It need not be difficult either to define or to secure the freedom of the seas if the governments of the world sincerely desire to come to an agreement concerning it.

It is a problem closely connected with the limitation of naval armaments and the coöperation of the navies of the world in keeping the seas at once free and safe. And the question of limiting naval armaments opens the wider and perhaps more difficult question of the limitation of armies and of all programmes of military preparation. Difficult and delicate as these questions are, they must be faced with the utmost candor and decided in a spirit of real accommodation if peace is to come with healing in its wings, and come to stay. Peace cannot be had without concession and sacrifice. There can be no sense of safety and equality among the nations if great preponderating armaments are henceforth to continue here and there to be built up and maintained. The statesmen of the world must plan for peace and nations must adjust and accommodate their policy to it as they have planned for war and made ready for pitiless contest and rivalry. The question of armaments, whether on land or sea, is the most immediately and intensely practical question connected with the future fortunes of nations and of mankind.

I have spoken upon these great matters without reserve and with the utmost explicitness because it has seemed to me to be necessary if the world's yearning desire for peace was anywhere to find free voice and utterance. Perhaps I am the only person in high authority amongst all the peoples of the world who is at liberty to speak and hold nothing back. I am speaking as an individual, and yet I am speaking also, of course, as the responsible head of a great government, and I feel confident that I have said what the people of the United States would wish me to say. May I not add that I hope and believe that I am in effect speaking for liberals and friends of humanity in every nation and of every programme of liberty? I would fain believe that I am speaking for the silent mass of mankind everywhere who have as yet had no place or opportunity to speak their real hearts out concerning the death and ruin they see to have come already upon the persons and the homs they hold most dear.

And in holding out the expectation that the people and Government of the United States will join the other civilized nations of the world in guaranteeing the permanence of peace upon such terms as I have named I speak with the greater boldness and confidence because it is clear to every man who can think that there is in this promise no breach in either our traditions or our policy as a nation, but a fulfilment, rather, of all that we have professed or striven for.

I am proposing, as it were, that the nations should with one accord adopt the doctrine of President Monroe as the doctrine of the world: that no nation should seek to extend its polity over any other nation or people, but that every people should be left free to determine its own polity, its own way of development, unhindered, unthreatened, unafraid, the little along with the great and powerful.

officially condemned should its exercise be attempted. I dare say that these consequences were not in the minds of the proponents of this provision, but the provision separately and in itself renders it unwise for me to give my assent to this legislation in its present form.

WOODROW WILSON.

THE WHITE HOUSE, *January 29, 1917*.

[Immigration legislation was not then a pressing topic; for with the outbreak of war in Europe the number of immigrants admitted into the United States had decreased from 1,200,000 annually to 300,000. Favoring restrictive legislation were those who argued that when war was ended vast numbers would rush to the United States. Opposed to such legislation were many who maintained that a Europe under reconstruction would absorb all the energies of its populations, and others expressed anxiety over the growing scarcity of common labor in the United States.

But Congress was overwhelmingly in favor of the legislation, and the bill was promptly passed over President Wilson's veto. Thus a literacy test was finally imposed on immigrants, in accordance with the recommendations of an Immigration Commission, after vetoes by Presidents Cleveland, Taft, and Wilson.]

WILSON'S ADDRESS TO CONGRESS FOLLOWING GERMANY'S RENEWAL OF SUBMARINE WAR AGAINST MERCHANT SHIPS—AND ANNOUNCING THE SEVERANCE OF DIPLOMATIC RELATIONS

(Delivered in Joint Session, February 3, 1917)

[The diplomatic correspondence which had preceded this crisis will be found in the pages ending with 270.]

Gentlemen of the Congress:

The Imperial German Government on the thirty-first of January announced to this Government and to the governments of the other neutral nations that on and after the first day of February, the present month, it would adopt a policy with regard to the use of submarines against all shipping seeking to pass through certain designated areas of the high seas to which it is clearly my duty to call your attention.

Let me remind the Congress that on the eighteenth of April last, in view of the sinking on the twenty-fourth of March of the cross-channel passenger steamer *Sussex* by a German submarine, without summons or warning, and the consequent loss of the lives of several citizens of the United States who were passengers aboard her, this Government addressed a note to the Imperial German Government in which it made the following declaration:

> If it is still the purpose of the Imperial Government to prosecute relentless and indiscriminate warfare against vessels of commerce by the use of submarines without regard to what the Government of the United States must consider the sacred and indisputable rules of international law and the universally recognized dictates of humanity, the Government of the United States is at last forced to the conclusion that there is but one course it can pursue. Unless the Imperial Government should now immediately declare and effect an abandonment of its present methods of submarine warfare against passenger and freight-carrying vessels, the Government of the United States can have no choice but to sever diplomatic relations with the German Empire altogether.

In reply to this declaration the Imperial German Government gave this Government the following assurance:

> The German Government is prepared to do its utmost to confine the operations of war for the rest of its duration to the fighting forces of the belligerents, thereby also insuring the freedom of the seas, a principle upon which the German Government believes, now as before, to be in agreement with the Government of the United States.
>
> The German Government, guided by this idea, notifies the Government of the United States that the German naval forces have received the following orders: In accordance with the general principles of visit and search and destruction of merchant vessels recognized by international law, such vessels, both within and without the area declared as naval war zone, shall not be sunk without warning and without saving human lives, unless these ships attempt to escape or offer resistance.

"But," it added, "neutrals can not expect that Germany, forced to fight for her existence, shall, for the sake of neutral interest, restrict the use of an effective weapon if her enemy is permitted to continue to apply at will methods of warfare violating the rules of international law. Such a demand would be incompatible with the character of neutrality, and the German Government is convinced that the Government of the United States does not think of making such a demand, knowing that the Government of the United States has repeatedly declared that it is determined to restore the principle of the freedom of the seas, from whatever quarter it has been violated."

To this the Government of the United States replied on the eighth of May, accepting, of course, the assurances given, but adding,

> The Government of the United States feels it necessary to state that it takes it for granted that the Imperial German Government does not intend to imply that the maintenance of its newly announced policy is in any way contingent upon the course or result of diplomatic negotiations between the Government of the United States and any other belligerent Government, notwithstanding the fact that certain passages in the Imperial Government's note of the 4th instant might appear to be susceptible of that construction. In order, however, to avoid any possible misunderstanding, the Government of the United States notifies the Imperial Government that it cannot for a moment entertain, much less discuss, a suggestion that respect by German naval authorities for the rights of citizens of the United States upon the high seas should in any way or in the slightest degree be made contingent upon the conduct of any other Government affecting the rights of neutrals and noncombatants. Responsibility in such matters is single, not joint; absolute, not relative.

To this note of the eighth of May the Imperial German Government made no reply.

On the thirty-first of January, the Wednesday of the present week, the German Ambassador handed to the Secretary of State, along with a formal note, a memorandum which contains the following statement:

> The Imperial Government, therefore, does not doubt that the Government of the United States will understand the situation

thus forced upon Germany by the Entente-Allies' brutal methods of war and by their determination to destroy the Central Powers, and that the Government of the United States will further realize that the now openly disclosed intentions of the Entente-Allies give back to Germany the freedom of action which she reserved in her note addressed to the Government of the United States on May 4, 1916.

Under these circumstances Germany will meet the illegal measures of her enemies by forcibly preventing after February 1, 1917, in a zone around Great Britain, France, Italy, and in the Eastern Mediterranean all navigation, that of neutrals included, from and to England and from and to France, etc., etc. All ships met within the zone will be sunk.

I think that you will agree with me that, in view of this declaration, which suddenly and without prior intimation of any kind deliberately withdraws the solemn assurance given in the Imperial Government's note of the fourth of May, 1916, this Government has no alternative consistent with the dignity and honour of the United States but to take the course which, in its note of the eighteenth of April, 1916, it announced that it would take in the event that the German Government did not declare and effect an abandonment of the methods of submarine warfare which it was then employing and to which it now purposes again to resort.

I have, therefore, directed the Secretary of State to announce to His Excellency the German Ambassador that all diplomatic relations between the United States and the German Empire are severed, and that the American Ambassador at Berlin will immediately be withdrawn; and, in accordance with this decision, to hand to His Excellency his passports.

Notwithstanding this unexpected action of the German Government, this sudden and deeply deplorable renunciation of its assurances, given this Government at one of the most critical moments of tension in the relations of the two governments, I refuse to believe that it is the intention of the German authorities to do in fact what they have warned us they will feel at liberty to do. I cannot bring myself to believe that they will indeed pay no regard to the ancient friendship between their people and our own or to the solemn obligations which have been exchanged between them and destroy American ships and take the lives of American citizens in the wilful prosecution of the ruthless naval programme they have announced their intention to adopt. Only actual overt acts on their part can make me believe it even now.

If this inveterate confidence on my part in the sobriety and prudent foresight of their purpose should unhappily prove unfounded; if American ships and American lives should in fact be sacrificed by their naval commanders in heedless contravention of the just and reasonable understandings of international law and the obvious dictates of humanity, I shall take the liberty of coming again before the Congress, to ask that authority be given me to use any means that may be necessary for the protection of our seamen and our people in the prosecution of their peaceful and legitimate errands on the high seas. I can do nothing less. I take it for granted that all neutral governments will take the same course.

We do not desire any hostile conflict with the Imperial German Government. We are the sincere friends of the German people and earnestly desire to remain at peace with the Government which speaks for them. We shall not believe that they are hostile to us unless and until we are obliged to believe it; and we purpose nothing more than the reasonable defense of the undoubted rights of our people. We wish to serve no selfish ends. We seek merely to stand true alike in thought and in action to the immemorial principles of our people which I sought to express in my address to the Senate only two weeks ago,—seek merely to vindicate our right to liberty and justice and an unmolested life. These are the bases of peace, not war. God grant we may not be challenged to defend them by acts of wilful injustice on the part of the Government of Germany!

Wilson's Address to Congress Requesting Authority to Arm Merchant Ships

(Delivered in Joint Session, February 26, 1917)

Gentlemen of the Congress:

I have again asked the privilege of addressing you because we are moving through critical times during which it seems to me to be my duty to keep in close touch with the Houses of Congress, so that neither counsel nor action shall run at cross purposes between us.

On the third of February I officially informed you of the sudden and unexpected action of the Imperial German Government in declaring its intention to disregard the promises it had made to this Government in April last and undertake immediate submarine operations against all commerce, whether of belligerents or of neutrals, that should seek to approach Great Britain and Ireland, the Atlantic coasts of Europe, or the harbours of the eastern Mediterranean, and to conduct those operations without regard to the established restrictions of international practice, without regard to any considerations of humanity even which might interfere with their object. That policy was forthwith put into practice. It has now been in active execution for nearly four weeks.

Its practical results are not yet fully disclosed. The commerce of other neutral nations is suffering severely, but not, perhaps, very much more severely than it was already suffering before the first of February, when the new policy of the Imperial Government was put into operation. We have asked the cooperation of the other neutral governments to prevent these depredations, but so far none of them has thought it wise to join us in any common course of action. Our own commerce has suffered, is suffering, rather in apprehension than in fact, rather because so many of our ships are timidly keeping to their home ports than because American ships have been sunk.

Two American vessels have been sunk, the *Housatonic* and the *Lyman M. Law.* The case of the *Housatonic,* which was carrying foodstuffs consigned to a London firm, was essentially like the case of the *Fry,* in which, it will be recalled, the German Government admitted its liability for damages, and the lives of the crew, as in the case of the *Fry,* were safeguarded with reasonable care. The case of the *Law,* which was carrying lemon-box staves to Palermo, disclosed a ruthlessness of method which deserves grave condemnation, but was accompanied by no circumstances which might not have been expected at any time in connection with the use of the submarine against merchantmen as the German Government has used it.

In sum, therefore, the situation we find ourselves in with regard to the actual conduct of the German submarine warfare against commerce and its effects upon our own ships and people is substantially the same that it was when I addressed you on the third of February, except for the tying up of our shipping in our own ports because of the unwillingness of our shipowners to risk their vessels at sea without insurance or adequate protection, and the very serious congestion of our commerce which has resulted, a congestion which is growing rapidly more and more serious every day. This in itself might presently accomplish, in effect, what the new German submarine orders were meant to accomplish, so far as we are concerned. We can only say, therefore, that the overt act which I have ventured to hope the German commanders would in fact avoid has not occurred.

But, while this is happily true, it must be admitted that there have been certain additional indications and expressions of purpose on the part of the German press and the German authorities which have increased rather than lessened the impression that, if our ships and our people are spared, it will be because of fortunate circumstances or because the commanders of the German submarines which they may happen to encounter exercise an unexpected discretion and restraint rather than because of the instructions under which those commanders are acting. It would be foolish to deny that the situation is fraught with the gravest possibilities and dangers. No thoughtful man can fail to see that the necessity for definite action may come at any time, if we are in fact, and not in word merely, to defend our elementary rights as a neutral nation. It would be most imprudent to be unprepared.

I cannot in such circumstances be unmindful of the fact that the expiration of the term of the present Congress is immediately at hand, by constitutional limitation; and that it would in all likelihood require an unusual length of time to assemble and organize the Congress which is to succeed it. I feel that I ought, in view of that fact, to obtain from you full and immediate assurance of the authority which I may need at any moment to exercise. No doubt I already possess that authority without special warrant of law, by the plain implication of my constitutional duties and powers; but I prefer, in the present circumstances, not to act upon general implication. I wish to feel that the authority and the power of the Congress are behind me in whatever it may become necessary for me to do. We are jointly the servants of the people and must act together and in their spirit, so far as we can divine and interpret it.

No one doubts what it is our duty to do. We must defend our commerce and the lives of our people in the midst of the present trying circumstances, with discretion but with clear and steadfast purpose. Only the method and the extent remain to be chosen, upon the occasion, if occasion should indeed arise. Since it has unhappily proved impossible to safeguard our neutral rights by diplomatic means against the unwarranted infringements they are suffering at the hands of Germany, there may be no recourse but to *armed* neutrality, which we shall know how to maintain and for which there is abundant American precedent.

It is devoutly to be hoped that it will not be necessary to put armed force anywhere into action. The American people do not desire it, and our desire is not different from theirs. I am sure that they will understand the spirit in which I am now acting, the purpose I hold nearest my heart and would wish to exhibit in everything I do. I am anxious that the people of the nations at war also should understand and not mistrust us. I hope that I need give no further proofs and assurances than I have already given throughout nearly three years of anxious patience that I am the friend of peace and mean to preserve it for America so long as I am able. I am not now proposing or contemplating war or any steps that need lead to it. I merely request that you will accord me by your own vote and definite bestowal the means and the authority to safeguard in practice the right of a great people who are at peace and who are desirous of exercising none but the rights of peace to follow the pursuits of peace in quietness and good will—rights recognized time out of mind by all the civilized nations of the world. No course of my choosing or of theirs will lead to war. War can come only by the wilful acts and aggressions of others.

You will understand why I can make no definite proposals or forecasts of action now and must ask for your supporting authority in the most general terms. The form in which action may become necessary cannot yet be foreseen. I believe that the people will be willing to trust me to act with restraint, with prudence, and in the true spirit of amity and good faith that they have themselves displayed throughout these trying months; and it is in that belief that I request that you will authorize me to supply our merchant ships with defensive arms, should that become necessary, and with the means of using them, and to employ any other instrumentalities or methods that may be necessary and adequate to protect our ships and our people in their legitimate and peaceful pursuits on the seas. I request also that you will grant me at the same time, along with the powers I ask, a sufficient credit to enable me to provide adequate means of protection where they are lacking, including adequate insurance against the present war risks.

I have spoken of our commerce and of the legitimate errands of our people on the seas, but you will not be misled as to my main thought, the thought that lies beneath these phrases and gives them dignity and weight. It is not of material interests merely that we are thinking. It is, rather, of fundamental human rights, chief of all the right of life itself. I am thinking, not only of the rights of Americans to go and come about their proper business by way of the sea, but also of something much deeper, much more fundamental than that. I am thinking of those rights of humanity without which there is no civilization. My theme is of those great principles of compassion and of protection which mankind has sought to throw about human lives, the lives of non-combatants, the lives of men who are peacefully at work keeping the industrial processes of the world quick and vital, the lives of women and children and of those who supply the labour which ministers to their sustenance. We are speaking of no selfish material rights but of rights which our hearts support and whose foundation is that righteous passion for justice upon which all law, all structures alike of family, of state, and of mankind must rest, as upon the ultimate base of our existence and our liberty. I cannot imagine any man with American principles at his heart hesitating to defend these things.

[A bill embodying the President's recommendations was immediately introduced in both houses; but the proposal to confer upon him authority "to employ any other instrumentalities or methods that may be necessary" met with objection, which caused the whole measure to fail of passage during the week that remained before the expiration of the Sixty-fourth Congress on March 4.

Upon the failure of the bill, President Wilson called the Sixty-fifth Congress in special session. Meanwhile the Administration decided that it possessed authority to arm ships for defense.]

WOODROW WILSON'S SECOND INAUGURAL ADDRESS

My Fellow Citizens:

The four years which have elapsed since last I stood in this place have been crowded with counsel and action of the most vital interest and consequence. Perhaps no equal period in our history has been so fruitful of important reforms in our economic and industrial life or so full of significant changes in the spirit and purpose of our political action. We have sought very thoughtfully to set our house in order, correct the grosser errors and abuses of our industrial life, liberate and quicken the processes of our national genius and energy, and lift our politics to a broader view of the people's essential interests. It is a record of singular variety and singular distinction. But I shall not attempt to review it. It speaks for itself and will be of increasing influence as the years go by. This is not the time for retrospect. It is time, rather, to speak our thoughts and purposes concerning the present and the immediate future.

Although we have centered counsel and action with such unusual concentration and success upon the great problems of domestic legislation to which we addressed ourselves four years ago, other matters have more and more forced themselves upon our attention, matters lying outside our own life as a nation and over which we had no control, but which, despite our wish to keep free of them, have drawn us more and more irresistibly into their own current and influence.

It has been impossible to avoid them. They have affected the life of the whole world. They have shaken men everywhere with a passion and an apprehension they never knew before. It has been hard to preserve calm counsel while the thought of our own people swayed this way and that under their influence. We are a composite and cosmopolitan people. We are of the blood of all the nations that are at war. The currents of our thoughts as well as the currents of our trade run quick at all seasons back and forth between us and them. The war inevitably set its mark from the first alike upon our minds, our industries, our commerce, our politics, and our social action. To be indifferent to it or independent of it was out of the question.

And yet all the while we have been conscious that we were not part of it. In that consciousness, despite many divisions, we have drawn closer together. We have been deeply wronged upon the seas, but we have not wished to wrong or injure in return; have retained throughout the consciousness of standing in some sort apart, intent upon an interest that transcended the immediate issues of the war itself. As some of the injuries done us have become intolerable we have still been clear that we wished nothing for ourselves that we were not ready to demand for all mankind—fair dealing, justice, the freedom to live and be at ease against organized wrong.

It is in this spirit and with this thought that we have grown more and more aware, more and more certain that the part we wished to play was the part of those who mean to vindicate and fortify peace. We have been obliged to arm ourselves to make good our claim to a certain minimum of right and of freedom of action. We stand firm in armed neutrality since it seems that in no other way we can demonstrate what it is we insist upon and cannot forego. We may even be drawn on, by circumstances, not by our own purpose or desire, to a more active assertion of our rights as we see them and a more immediate association with the great struggle itself. But nothing will alter our thought or our purpose. They are too clear to be obscured. They are too deeply rooted in the principles of our national life to be altered. We desire neither conquest nor advantage.

We wish nothing that can be had only at the cost of another people. We have always professed unselfish purpose and we covet the opportunity to prove that our professions are sincere.

There are many things still to do at home, to clarify our own politics and give new vitality to the industrial processes of our own life, and we shall do them as time and opportunity serve; but we realize that the greatest things that remain to be done must be done with the whole world for stage and in coöperation with the wide and universal forces of mankind, and we are making our spirits ready for those things. They will follow in the immediate wake of the war itself and will set civilization up again. We are provincials no longer. The tragical events of the thirty months of vital turmoil through which we have just passed have made us citizens of the world. There can be no turning back. Our own fortunes as a nation are involved, whether we would have it so or not.

And yet we are not the less Americans on that account. We shall be the more American if we but remain true to the principles in which we have been bred. They are not the principles of a province or of a single continent. We have known and boasted all along that they were the principles of a liberated mankind. These, therefore, are the things we shall stand for, whether in war or in peace:

That all nations are equally interested in the peace of the world and in the political stability of free peoples, and equally responsible for their maintenance;

That the essential principle of peace is the actual equality of nations in all matters of right or privilege;

That peace cannot securely or justly rest upon an armed balance of power;

That governments derive all their just powers from the consent of the governed and that no other powers should be supported by the common thought, purpose, or power of the family of nations.

That the seas should be equally free and safe for the use of all peoples, under rules set up by common agreement and consent, and that, so far as practicable, they should be accessible to all upon equal terms;

That national armaments should be limited to the necessities of national order and domestic safety;

That the community of interest and of power upon which peace must henceforth depend imposes upon each nation the duty of seeing to it that all influences proceeding from its own citizens meant to encourage or assist revolution in other states should be sternly and effectually suppressed and prevented.

I need not argue these principles to you, my fellow countrymen: they are your own, part and parcel of your own thinking and your own motive in affairs. They spring up native amongst us. Upon this as a platform of purpose and of action we can stand together.

And it is imperative that we should stand together. We are being forged into a new unity amidst the fires that now blaze throughout the world. In their ardent heat we shall, in God's providence, let us hope, be purged of faction and division, purified of the errant humors of party and of private interest, and shall stand forth in the days to come with a new dignity of national pride and spirit. Let each man see to it that the dedication is in his own heart, the high purpose of the Nation in his own mind, ruler of his own will and desire.

I stand here and have taken the high and solemn oath to which you have been audience because the people of the United States have chosen me for this august delegation of power and have by their gracious judgment named me their leader in affairs. I know now what the task means. I realize to the full the responsibility which it involves. I pray God I may be given the wisdom and the prudence to do my duty in the true spirit of this great people. I am their servant and can succeed only as they sustain and guide me by their confidence and their counsel. The thing I shall count upon, the thing without which neither counsel nor action will avail, is the unity of America—an America united in feeling, in purpose, and in its vision of duty, of opportunity, and of service. We are to beware of all men who would turn the tasks and the necessities of the Nation to their own private profit or use them for the building up of private power; beware that no faction or disloyal intrigue break the harmony or embarrass the spirit of our people; beware that our Government be kept pure and incorrupt in all its parts. United alike in the conception of our duty and in the high resolve to perform it in the face of all men, let us dedicate ourselves to the great task to which we must now set our hand. For myself I beg your tolerance, your countenance, and your united aid. The shadows that now lie dark upon our path will soon be dispelled and we shall walk with the light all about us if we be but true to ourselves—to ourselves as we have wished to be known in the counsels of the world and in the thought of all those who love liberty and justice and the right exalted.

WASHINGTON, March 5, 1917

WILSON'S ADDRESS TO CONGRESS ADVISING THAT GERMANY'S COURSE BE DECLARED WAR AGAINST THE UNITED STATES

(Delivered in Joint Session, April 2, 1917)

[The newly elected Congress had been called in special session by President Wilson (see page 365). Neither Democrats nor Republicans had a clear majority in the House, but the Democrats obtained sufficient independent support to establish control. The President appeared in the evening of the first day of the special session, and made the following address:]

Gentlemen of the Congress:

I have called the Congress into extraordinary session because there are serious, very serious, choices of policy to be made, and made immediately, which it was neither right nor constitutionally permissible that I should assume the responsibility of making.

On the third of February last I officially laid before you the extraordinary announcement of the Imperial German Government that on and after the first day of February it was its purpose to put aside all restraints of law or of humanity and use its submarines to sink every vessel that sought to approach either the ports of Great Britain and Ireland or the western coasts of Europe or any of the ports controlled by the enemies of Germany within the Mediterranean. That had seemed to be the object of the German submarine warfare earlier in the war, but since April of last year the Imperial Government had somewhat restrained the commanders of its undersea craft in conformity with its promise then given to us that passenger boats should not be sunk and that due warning would be given to all other vessels which its submarines might seek to destroy, when no resistance was offered or escape attempted, and care taken that their crews were given at least a fair chance to save their lives in their open boats. The precautions taken were meagre and haphazard enough, as was proved in distressing instance after instance in the progress of the cruel and unmanly business, but a certain degree of restraint was observed. The new policy has swept every restriction aside. Vessels of every kind, whatever their flag, their character, their cargo, their destination, their errand, have been ruthlessly sent to the bottom without warning and without thought of help or mercy for those on board, the vessels of friendly neutrals along with those of belligerents. Even hospital ships and ships carrying relief to the sorely bereaved and stricken people of Belgium, though the latter were provided with safe conduct through the proscribed areas by the German Government itself and were distinguished by unmistakable marks of identity, have been sunk with the same reckless lack of compassion or of principle.

I was for a little while unable to believe that such things would in fact be done by any government that had hitherto subscribed to the humane practices of civilized nations. International law had its origin in the attempt to set up some law which would be respected and observed upon the seas, where no nation had right of dominion and where lay the free highways of the world. By painful stage after stage has that law been built up, with meagre enough results, indeed, after all was accomplished that could be accomplished, but always with a clear view, at least, of what the heart and conscience of mankind demanded. This minimum of right the German Government has swept aside under the plea of retaliation and necessity and because it had no weapons which it could use at sea except these which it is impossible to employ as it is employing them without throwing to the winds all scruples of humanity or of respect for the understandings that were supposed to underlie the intercourse of the world. I am not now thinking of the loss of property involved, immense and serious as that is, but only of the wanton and wholesale destruction of the lives of non-combatants, men, women, and children, engaged in pursuits which have always, even in the darkest periods of modern history, been deemed innocent and legitimate. Property can be paid for; the lives of peaceful and innocent people cannot be. The present German submarine warfare against commerce is a warfare against mankind.

It is a war against all nations. American ships have been sunk, American lives taken, in ways which it has stirred us very deeply to learn of, but the ships and people of other neutral and friendly nations have been sunk and overwhelmed in the waters in the same way. There has been no discrimination. The challenge is to all mankind. Each nation must decide for itself how it will meet it. The choice we make for ourselves must be made with a moderation of counsel and a temperateness of judgment befitting our character and our motives as a nation. We must put excited feeling away. Our motive will not be revenge or the victorious assertion of the physical might of the nation, but only the vindication of right, of human right, of which we are only a single champion.

When I addressed the Congress on the twenty-sixth of February last I thought that it would suffice to assert our neutral rights with arms, our right to use the seas against unlawful interference, our right to keep our people safe against unlawful violence. But armed neutrality, it now appears, is impracticable. Because submarines are in effect outlaws when used as the German submarines have been used against merchant shipping, it is impossible to defend ships against their attacks as the law of nations has assumed that merchantmen would defend themselves against privateers or cruisers, visible craft giving chase upon the open sea. It is common prudence in such circumstances, grim necessity indeed, to endeavour to destroy them before they have shown their own intention. They must be dealt with upon sight, if dealt with at all. The German Government denies the right of neutrals to use arms at all within the areas of the sea which it has proscribed, even in the defense of rights which no modern publicist has ever before questioned their right to defend. The intimation is conveyed that the armed guards which we have placed on our merchant ships will be treated as beyond the pale of law and subject to be dealt with as pirates would be. Armed neutrality is ineffectual enough at best; in such circumstances and in the face of such pretensions it is worse than ineffectual; it is likely only to produce what it was meant to prevent; it is practically certain to draw us into the war without either the rights or the effectiveness of belligerents. There is one choice we cannot make, we are incapable of making: we will not choose the path of submission and suffer the most sacred rights of our nation and our people to be ignored or violated. The wrongs against which we now array ourselves are no common wrongs: they cut to the very roots of human life.

With a profound sense of the solemn and even tragical character of the step I am taking and of the grave responsibilities which it involves, but in unhesitating obedience to what I deem my constitutional duty, I advise that the Congress declare the recent course of the Imperial German Government to be in fact nothing less than war against the government and people of the United States; that it formally accept the status of belligerent which has thus been thrust upon it; and that it take immediate steps not only to put the country in a more thorough state of defense but also to exert all its power and employ all its resources to bring the Government of the German Empire to terms and end the war.

What this will involve is clear. It will involve the utmost practicable cooperation in counsel and action with the governments now at war with Germany, and, as incident to that, the extension to those governments of the most liberal financial credits, in order that our resources may so far as possible be added to theirs. It will involve the organization and mobilization of all the material resources of the country to supply the materials of war and serve the incidental needs of the nation in the most abundant and yet the most economical and efficient way possible. It will involve the immediate full equipment of the navy in all respects but particularly in supplying it with the best means of dealing with the enemy's submarines. It will involve the immediate addition to the armed forces of the United States already provided for by law in case of war at least five hundred thousand men, who should, in my opinion, be chosen upon the principle of universal liability to service, and also the authorization of subsequent additional increments of equal force so soon as they may be needed and can be handled in training. It will involve also, of course, the granting of adequate credits to the Government, sustained, I hope, so far as they can equitably be sustained by the present generation, by well conceived taxation.

I say sustained so far as may be equitable by taxation because it seems to me that it would be most unwise to base the credits which will now be necessary entirely on money borrowed. It is our duty, I most respectfully urge, to protect our people so far as we may against the very serious hardships and evils which would be likely to arise out of the inflation which would be produced by vast loans.

In carrying out the measures by which these things are to be accomplished we should keep constantly in mind the wisdom of interfering as little as possible in our own preparation and in the equipment of our own military forces with the duty,—for it will be a very practical duty,—of supplying the nations already at war with Germany with the materials which they can obtain only from us or by our assistance. They are in the field and we should help them in every way to be effective there.

I shall take the liberty of suggesting, through the several executive departments of the Government, for the consideration of your committees, measures for the accomplishment of the several objects I have mentioned. I hope that it will be your pleasure to deal with them as having been framed after very careful thought by the branch of the Government upon which the responsibility of conducting the war and safeguarding the nation will most directly fall.

While we do these things, these deeply momentous things, let us be very clear, and make very clear to all the world what our motives and our objects are. My own thought has not been driven from its habitual and normal course by the unhappy events of the last two months, and I do not believe that the thought of the nation has been altered or clouded by them. I have exactly the same things in mind now that I had in mind when I addressed the Senate on the twenty-second of January last; the same that I had in mind when I addressed the Congress on the third of February and on the twenty-sixth of February. Our object now, as then, is to vindicate the principles of peace and justice in the life of the world as against selfish and autocratic power and to set up amongst the really free and self-governed peoples of the world such a concert of purpose and of action as will henceforth ensure the observance of those principles. Neutrality is no longer feasible or desirable where the peace of the world is involved and the freedom of its peoples, and the menace to that peace and freedom lies in the existence of autocratic governments backed by organized force which is controlled wholly by their will, not by the will of their people. We have seen the last of neutrality in such circumstances. We are at the beginning of an age in which it will be insisted that the same standards of conduct and responsibility for wrong done shall be observed among nations and their governments that are observed among the individual citizens of civilized states.

We have no quarrel with the German people. We have no feeling towards them but one of sympathy and friendship. It was not upon their impulse that their government acted in entering this war. It was not with their previous knowledge or approval. It was a war determined upon as wars used to be determined upon in the old, unhappy days when peoples were nowhere consulted by their rulers and wars were provoked and waged in the interest of dynasties or of little groups of ambitious men who were accustomed to use their fellow men as pawns and tools. Self-governed nations do not fill their neighbour states with spies or set the course of intrigue to bring about some critical posture of affairs which will give them an opportunity to strike and make conquest. Such designs can be successfully worked out only under cover and where no one has the right to ask questions. Cunningly contrived plans of deception or aggression, carried, it may be, from generation to generation, can be worked out and kept from the light only within the privacy of courts or behind the carefully guarded confidences of a narrow and privileged class. They are happily impossible where public opinion commands and insists upon full information concerning all the nation's affairs.

A steadfast concert for peace can never be maintained except by a partnership of democratic nations. No autocratic government could be trusted to keep faith within it or observe its covenants. It must be a league of honour, a partnership of opinion. Intrigue would eat its vitals away; the plottings of inner circles who could plan what they would and render account to no one would be a corruption seated at its very heart. Only free peoples can hold their purpose and their honour steady to a common end and prefer the interests of mankind to any narrow interest of their own.

Does not every American feel that assurance has been added to our hope for the future peace of the world by the wonderful and heartening things that have been happening within the last few weeks in Russia? Russia was known by those who knew it best to have been always in fact democratic at heart, in all the vital habits of her thought, in all the intimate relationships of her people that spoke their natural instinct, their habitual attitude towards life. The autocracy that crowned the summit of her political structure, long as it had stood and terrible as was the reality of its power, was not in fact Russian in origin, character, or purpose; and now it has been shaken off and the great, generous Russian people have been added in all their naive majesty and might to the forces that are fighting for freedom in the world, for justice, and for peace. Here is a fit partner for a League of Honour.

One of the things that has served to convince us that the Prussian autocracy was not and could never be our friend is that from the very outset of the present war it has filled our unsuspecting communities and even our offices of government with spies and set criminal intrigues everywhere afoot against our national unity of counsel, our peace within and without, our industries and our commerce. Indeed it is now evident that its spies were here even before the war began; and it is unhappily not a matter of conjecture but a fact proved in our courts of justice that the intrigues which have more than once come perilously near to disturbing the peace and dislocating the industries of the country have been carried on at the instigation, with the support, and even under the personal direction of official agents of the Imperial Government accredited to the Government of the United States. Even in checking these things and trying to extirpate them we have sought to put the most generous interpretation possible upon them because we knew that their source lay, not in any hostile feeling or purpose of the German people towards us (who were, no doubt, as ignorant of them as we ourselves were), but only in the selfish designs of a Government that did what it pleased and told its people nothing. But they have played their part in serving to convince us at last that that Government entertains no real friendship for us and means to act against our peace and security at its convenience. That it means to stir up enemies against us at our very doors the intercepted note to the German Minister at Mexico City is eloquent evidence.

We are accepting this challenge of hostile purpose because we know that in such a government, following such methods, we can never have a friend; and that in the presence of its organized power, always lying in wait to accomplish we know not what purpose, there can be no assured security for the democratic governments of the world. We are now about to accept gauge of battle with this natural foe to liberty and shall, if necessary, spend the whole force of the nation to check and nullify its pretensions and its power. We are glad, now that we see the facts with no veil of false pretence about them, to fight thus for the ultimate peace of the world and for the liberation of its peoples, the German peoples included: for the rights of nations great and small and the privilege of men everywhere to choose their way of life and of obedience. The world must be made safe for democracy. Its peace must be planted upon the tested foundations of political liberty. We have no selfish ends to serve. We desire no conquest, no dominion. We seek no indemnities for ourselves, no material compensation for the sacrifices we shall freely make. We are but one of the champions of the rights of mankind. We shall be satisfied when those rights have been made as secure as the faith and the freedom of nations can make them.

Just because we fight without rancour and without selfish object, seeking nothing for ourselves but what we shall wish to share with all free peoples, we shall, I feel confident, conduct our operations as belligerents without passion and ourselves observe with proud punctilio the principles of right and of fair play we profess to be fighting for.

I have said nothing of the governments allied with the Imperial Government of Germany because they have not made war upon us or challenged us to defend our right and our honour. The Austro-Hungarian Government has, indeed, avowed its unqualified endorsement and acceptance of the reckless and lawless submarine warfare adopted now without disguise by the Imperial German Government, and it has therefore not been possible for this Government to receive Count Tarnowski, the Ambassador recently accredited to this Government by the Imperial and Royal Government of Austria-Hungary; but that Government has not actually engaged in warfare against citizens of the United States on the seas, and I take the liberty, for the present at least, of postponing a discussion of our relations with the authorities at Vienna. We enter this war only where we are clearly forced into it because there are no other means of defending our rights.

It will be all the easier for us to conduct ourselves as

belligerents in a high spirit of right and fairness because we act without animus, not in enmity towards a people or with the desire to bring any injury or disadvantage upon them, but only in armed opposition to an irresponsible government which has thrown aside all considerations of humanity and of right and is running amuck. We are, let me say again, the sincere friends of the German people, and shall desire nothing so much as the early re-establishment of intimate relations of mutual advantage between us,—however hard it may be for them, for the time being, to believe that this is spoken from our hearts. We have borne with their present government through all these bitter months because of that friendship,—exercising a patience and forbearance which would otherwise have been impossible. We shall, happily, still have an opportunity to prove that friendship in our daily attitude and actions towards the millions of men and women of German birth and native sympathy who live amongst us and share our life, and we shall be proud to prove it towards all who are in fact loyal to their neighbours and to the Government in the hour of test. They are, most of them, as true and loyal Americans as if they had never known any other fealty or allegiance. They will be prompt to stand with us in rebuking and restraining the few who may be of a different mind and purpose. If there should be disloyalty, it will be dealt with with a firm hand of stern repression; but, if it lifts its head at all, it will lift it only here and there and without countenance except from a lawless and malignant few.

It is a distressing and oppressive duty, Gentlemen of the Congress, which I have performed in thus addressing you. There are, it may be, many months of fiery trial and sacrifice ahead of us. It is a fearful thing to lead this great peaceful people into war, into the most terrible and disastrous of all wars, civilization itself seeming to be in the balance. But the right is more precious than peace, and we shall fight for the things which we have always carried nearest our hearts, for democracy, for the right of those who submit to authority to have a voice in their own governments, for the rights and liberties of small nations, for a universal dominion of right by such a concert of free peoples as shall bring peace and safety to all nations and make the world itself at last free. To such a task we can dedicate our lives and our fortunes, everything that we are and everything that we have, with the pride of those who know that the day has come when America is privileged to spend her blood and her might for the principles that gave her birth and happiness and the peace which she has treasured. God helping her, she can do no other.

[The President's recommendation—that "Congress declare the recent course of the Imperiai German Government to be in fact nothing less than war against the government and people of the United States"—was immediately carried out. The address was made on the evening of April 2. On April 4 the Senate adopted the war resolution, by vote of 82 to 6. The House completed its action at 3 a. m. on the morning of April 6, by vote of 373 to 50; and shortly after noon on that day President Wilson attached his signature.]

Proclamation of State of War and of Alien Enemy Regulations, April 6, 1917

Whereas the Congress of the United States in the exercise of the constitutional authority vested in them have resolved, by joint resolution of the Senate and House of Representatives bearing date this day "That the state of war between the United States and the Imperial German Government which has been thrust upon the United States is hereby formally declared:

Whereas it is provided by Section four thousand and sixty-seven of the Revised Statutes, as follows:

Whenever there is declared a war between the United States and any foreign nation or government, or any invasion of predatory incursion is perpetrated, attempted, or threatened against the territory of the United States, by any foreign nation or government, and the President makes public proclamation of the event, all natives, citizens, denizens, or subjects of the hostile nation or government, being males of the age of fourteen years and upwards, who shall be within the United States, and not actually naturalized, shall be liable to be apprehended, restrained, secured, and removed, as alien enemies. The President is authorized, in any such event, by his proclamation thereof, or other public act ,to direct the conduct to be observed, on the part of the United States, toward the aliens who become so liable; the manner and degree of the restraint to which they shall be subject, and in what cases, and upon what security their residence shall be permitted, and to provide for the removal of those who, not being permitted to reside within the United States, refuse or neglect to depart therefrom; and to establish any other regulations which are found necessary in the premises and for the public safety;

Whereas, by Sections four thousand and sixty-eight, four thousand and sixty-nine, and four thousand and seventy, of the Revised Statutes, further provision is made relative to alien enemies;

Now, therefore, I, Woodrow Wilson, President of the United States of America, do hereby proclaim to all whom it may concern that a state of war exists between the United States and the Imperial German Government; and I do specially direct all officers, civil or military, of the United States that they exercise vigilance and zeal in the discharge of the duties incident to such a state of war; and I do, moreover, earnestly appeal to all American citizens that they, in loyal devotion to their country, dedicated from its foundation to the principles of liberty and justice, uphold the laws of the land, and give undivided and willing support to those measures which may be adopted by the constitutional authorities in prosecuting the war to a successful issue and in obtaining a secure and just peace;

And, acting under and by virtue of the authority vested in me by the Constitution of the United States and the said sections of the Revised Statutes, I do hereby further proclaim and direct that the conduct to be observed on the part of the United States towards all natives, citizens, denizens, or subjects of Germany, being males of the age of fourteen years and upwards, who shall be within the United States and not actually naturalized, who for the purpose of this proclamation and under such sections of the Revised Statutes are termed alien enemies, shall be as follows:

All alien enemies are enjoined to preserve the peace towards the United States and to refrain from crime against the public safety, and from violating the laws of the United States and of the States and Territories thereof, and to refrain from actual hostility or giving information, aid or comfort to the enemies of the United States, and to comply strictly with the regulations which are hereby or which may be from time to time promulgated by the President; and so long as they shall conduct themselves in accordance with law, they shall be undisturbed in the peaceful pursuit of their lives and occupations and be accorded the consideration due to all peaceful and law-abiding persons, except so far as restrictions may be necessary for their own protection and for the safety of the United States; and towards such alien enemies as conduct themselves in accordance with law, all citizens of the United States are enjoined to preserve the peace and to treat them with all such friendliness as may be compatible with loyalty and allegiance to the United States

And all alien enemies who fail to conduct themselves as so enjoined, in addition to all other penalties prescribed by law, shall be liable to restraint, or to give security, or to remove and depart from the United States in the manner prescribed by Sections four thousand and sixty-nine and four thousand and seventy of the Revised Statutes, and as prescribed in the regulations duly promulgated by the President;

And pursuant to the authority vested in me, I hereby declare and establish the following regulations, which I find necessary in the premises and for the public safety:

(1) An alien enemy shall not have in his possession, at any time or place, any firearm, weapon, or implement of war, or com-

ponent part thereof, ammunition, maxim or other silencer, bomb or explosive or material used in the manufacture of explosives;

(2) An alien enemy shall not have in his possession at any time or place or use or operate any aircraft or wireless apparatus, or any form of signalling device, or any form of cipher code, or any paper, document or book written or printed in cipher or in which there may be invisible writing.

(3) All property found in the possession of an alien enemy in violation of the foregoing regulations shall be subject to seizure by the United States;

(4) An alien enemy shall not approach or be found within one-half of a mile of any Federal or State fort, camp, arsenal, aircraft station, Government or naval vessel, navy yard, factory, or workshop for the manufacture of munitions of war or of any products for the use of the army or navy;

(5) An alien enemy shall not write, print, or publish any attack or threats against the Government or Congress of the United States, or either branch thereof, or against the measures or policy of the United States, or against the person or property of any person in the military, naval, or civil service of the United States, or of the States or Territories, or of the District of Columbia, or of the municipal governments therein;

(6) An alien enemy shall not commit or abet any hostile act against the United States, or give information, aid, or comfort to its enemies;

(7) An alien enemy shall not reside in or continue to reside in, to remain in, or enter any locality which the President may from time to time designate by Executive Order as a prohibited area in which residence by an alien enemy shall be found by him to constitute a danger to the public peace and safety of the United States, except by permit from the President and except under such limitations or restrictions as the President may prescribe;

(8) An alien enemy whom the President shall have reasonable cause to believe to be aiding or about to aid the enemy, or to be at large to the danger of the public peace or safety of the United States, or to have violated or to be about to violate any of these regulations, shall remove to any location designated by the President by Executive Order, and shall not remove therefrom without a permit, or shall depart from the United States if so required by the President;

(9) No alien enemy shall depart from the United States until he shall have received such permit as the President shall prescribe, or except under order of a court, judge, or justice, under Sections 4069 and 4070 of the Revised Statutes;

(10) No alien enemy shall land in or enter the United States, except under such restrictions and at such places as the President may prescribe;

(11) If necessary to prevent violations of these regulations, all alien enemies will be obliged to register;

(12) An alien enemy whom there may be reasonable cause to believe to be aiding or about to aid the enemy, or who may be at large to the danger of the public peace or safety, or who violates or attempts to violate, or of whom there is reasonable ground to believe that he is about to violate, any regulation duly promulgated by the President, or any criminal law of the United States, or of the States or Territories thereof, will be subject to summary arrest by the United States Marshal, or his deputy, or such other officer as the President shall designate, and to confinement in such penitentiary, prison, jail, military camp, or other place of detention as may be directed by the President.

This proclamation and the regulations herein contained shall extend and apply to all land and water, continental or insular, in any way within the jurisdiction of the United States.

IN WITNESS WHEREOF, *I have hereunto set my hand and caused the seal of the United States to be affixed.*

Done at the City of Washington, this sixth day of April, in the year of our Lord one thousand nine hundred and seventeen, and of the independence of the United States the one hundred and forty-first.

WOODROW WILSON.

WILSON'S ADDRESS TO HIS FELLOW-COUNTRYMEN ON WAYS TO SERVE THE NATION DURING THE WAR

(A Proclamation, April 16, 1917)

My Fellow-Countrymen:

The entrance of our own beloved country into the grim and terrible war for democracy and human rights which has shaken the world creates so many problems of national life and action which call for immediate consideration and settlement that I hope you will permit me to address to you a few words of earnest counsel and appeal with regard to them.

We are rapidly putting our navy upon an efficient war footing and are about to create and equip a great army, but these are the simplest parts of the great task to which we have addressed ourselves. There is not a single selfish element, so far as I can see, in the cause we are fighting for. We are fighting for what we believe and wish to be the rights of mankind and for the future peace and security of the world. To do this great thing worthily and successfully we must devote ourselves to the service without regard to profit or material advantage and with an energy and intelligence that will rise to the level of the enterprise itself. We must realize to the full how great the task is and how many things, how many kinds and elements of capacity and service and self-sacrifice, it involves.

These, then, are the things we must do, and do well, besides fighting,—the things without which mere fighting would be fruitless:

We must supply abundant food for ourselves and for our armies and our seamen not only, but also for a large part of the nations with whom we have now made common cause, in whose support and by whose sides we shall be fighting;

We must supply ships by the hundreds out of our shipyards to carry to the other side of the sea, submarines or no submarines, what will every day be needed there, and abundant materials out of our fields and our mines and our factories with which not only to clothe and equip our own forces on land and sea but also to clothe and support our people for whom the gallant fellows under arms can no longer work, to help clothe and equip the armies with which we are cooperating in Europe, and to keep the looms and manufactories there in raw material; coal to keep the fires going in ships at sea and in the furnaces of hundreds of factories across the sea; steel out of which to make arms and ammunition both here and there; rails for worn-out railways back of the fighting fronts; locomotives and rolling stock to take the place of those every day going to pieces; mules, horses, cattle for labor and for military service; everything with which the people of England and France and Italy and Russia have usually supplied themselves but cannot now afford the men, the materials, or the machinery to make.

It is evident to every thinking man that our industries, on the farms, in the shipyards, in the mines, in the factories, must be made more prolific and more efficient than ever and that they must be more economically managed and better adapted to the particular requirements of our task than they have been; and what I want to say is that the men and the women who devote their thought and their energy to these things will be serving the country and conducting the fight for peace and freedom just as truly and just as effectively as the men on the battlefield or in the trenches. The industrial forces of the country, men and women alike, will be a great national, a great international, Service Army,—a notable and honored host engaged in the service of the nation and the world, the efficient friends and saviors of free men everywhere. Thousands, nay, hundreds of thousands, of men otherwise liable to military service will of right and of necessity be excused from that service and assigned to the fundamental, sustaining work of the fields and factories and mines, and they will be as much part of the great patriotic forces of the nation as the men under fire.

I take the liberty, therefore, of addressing this word to the farmers of the country and to all who work on the farms: The supreme need of our own nation and of the nations with which we are cooperating is an abundance of supplies, and especially of food stuffs. The importance of an adequate food supply, especially for the present year, is superlative. Without abundant food, alike for the armies and the peoples now at war, the whole great enterprise upon which we have embarked will break down and fail. The world's food reserves are low. Not only during the present emergency but for some time after peace shall have come both our own people and a large proportion of the people of Europe must rely upon the harvests in

to correct her unpardonable fault of wastefulness and extravagance. Let every man and every woman assume the duty of careful, provident use and expenditure as a public duty, as a dictate of patriotism which no one can now expect ever to be excused or forgiven for ignoring.

In the hope that this statement of the needs of the nation and of the world in this hour of supreme crisis may stimulate those to whom it comes and remind all who need reminder of the solemn duties of a time such as the world has never seen before, I beg that all editors and publishers everywhere will give as prominent publication and as wide circulation as possible to this appeal. I venture to suggest, also, to all advertising agencies that they would perhaps render a very substantial and timely service to the country if they would give it widespread repetition. And I hope that clergymen will not think the theme of it an unworthy or inappropriate subject of comment and homily from their pulpits.

The supreme test of the nation has come. We must all speak, act, and serve together!

WOODROW WILSON.

PRESIDENT WILSON'S ADDRESS AT DEDICATION OF THE RED CROSS BUILDING, WASHINGTON, MAY 12, 1917

Mr. Chairman, Mr. Secretary, Ladies and Gentlemen:

It gives me a very deep gratification as the titular head of the American Red Cross to accept in the name of that association this significant and beautiful gift, the gift of the Government and of private individuals who have conceived their duty in a noble spirit and upon a great scale. It seems to me that the architecture of the building to which the Secretary of War, Mr. Baker, alluded suggests something very significant. There are few buildings in Washington more simple in their lines and in their ornamentation than the beautiful building we are dedicating this evening. It breathes a spirit of modesty and seems to adorn duty with its proper garment of beauty. It is significant that it should be dedicated to the women who serve to alleviate suffering and comfort those who were in need during our Civil War, because their thoughtful, disinterested, self-sacrificing devotion is the spirit which should always illustrate the services of the Red Cross.

The Red Cross needs at this time more than it ever needed before the comprehending support of the American people and all the facilities which could be placed at its disposal to perform its duties adequately and efficiently. I believe that the American people perhaps hardly yet realize the sacrifices and sufferings that are before them. We thought the scale of our Civil War was unprecedented, but in comparison with the struggle into which we have now entered the Civil War seems almost insignificant in its proportions and in its expenditure of treasure and of blood. And, therefore, it is a matter of the greatest importance that we should at the outset see to it that the American Red Cross is equipped and prepared for the things that lie before it. It will be our instrument to do the works of alleviation and of mercy which will attend this struggle. Of course, the scale upon which it shall act will be greater than the scale of any other duty that it has ever attempted to perform.

It is in recognition of that fact that the American Red Cross has just added to its organization a small body of men whom it has chosen to call its War Council—not because they are to counsel war, but because they are to serve in this special war those purposes of counsel which have become so imperatively necessary. Their first duty will be to raise a great fund out of which to draw the resources for the performance of their duty, and I do not believe that it will be necessary to appeal to the American people to respond to their call for funds, because the heart of this country is in this war, and if the heart of the country is in the war, its heart will express itself in the gifts that will be poured out for these humane purposes.

I say the heart of the country is in this war because it would not have gone into it if its heart had not been prepared for it. It would not have gone into it if it had not first believed that here was an opportunity to express the character of the United States. We have gone in with no special grievance of our own, because we have always said that we were the friends and servants of mankind. We look for no profit. We look for no advantage. We will accept no advantage out of this war. We go because we believe that the very principles upon which the American Republic was founded are now at stake and must be vindicated. In such a contest, therefore, we shall not fail to respond to the call to service that comes through the instrumentality of this particular organization.

And I think it not inappropriate to say this: There will be many expressions of the spirit of sympathy and mercy and philanthropy, and I think that it is very necessary that we should not disperse our activities in those lines too much; that we should keep constantly in view the desire to have the utmost concentration and efficiency of effort, and I hope that most, if not all of the philanthropic activities of this war may be exercised if not through the Red Cross, then through some already-constituted and experienced organization. This is no war for amateurs. This is no war for mere spontaneous impulse. It means grim business on every side of it, and it is the mere counsel of prudence that in our philanthropy, as well as in our fighting, we should act through the instrumentalities already prepared to our hand and already experienced in the tasks which are going to be assigned to them. This should be merely the expression of the practical genius of America itself, and I believe that the practical genius of America will dictate that the efforts in this war in this particular field should be concentrated in experienced hands as our efforts in other fields will be.

There is another thing that is significant and delightful to my thought about the fact that this building should be dedicated to the memory of the women both of the North and of the South. It is a sort of landmark of the unity to which the people have been brought so far as any old question which tore our hearts in days gone by is concerned; and I pray God that the outcome of this struggle may be that every other element of difference amongst us will be obliterated and that some day historians will remember these momentous years as the years which made a single people out of the great body of those who call themselves Americans. The evidences are already many that this is happening. The divisions which were predicted have not occurred and will not occur. The spirit of this people is already united and when effort and suffering and sacrifice have completed the union men will no longer speak of any lines either of race or of association cutting athwart the great body of this nation. So that I feel that we are now beginning the processes which will some day require another beautiful memorial erected to those whose hearts uniting, united America.

[The President's statement that "we have gone in (into the war) with no special grievance of our own" was later clarified by him as meaning that our grievance was the same as that of other neutrals.]

President Wilson's Proclamation of the Selective Draft Act, May 18, 1917

[Editorial Note: *In the President's war address to Congress, on April 2, he had recommended an "immediate addition to the armed forces of the United States . . . chosen upon the principle of universal liability to service." After full debate in both branches—with many members urging that the voluntary system be tried—Congress passed a Selective Draft Act, which President Wilson signed on May 18 and immediately proclaimed as follows:*]

Whereas, Congress has enacted and the President has on the 18th day of May, one thousand nine hundred and seventeen, approved a law, which contains the following provisions:

Section 5.—That all male persons between the ages of 21 and 30, both inclusive, shall be subject to registration in accordance with regulations to be prescribed by the President: And upon proclamation by the President or other public notice given by him or by his direction stating the time and place of such registration, it shall be the duty of all persons of the designated ages, except officers and enlisted men of the regular army, the navy, and the National Guard and Naval Militia while in the service of the United States, to present themselves for and submit to registration under the provisions of this act: And every such person shall be deemed to have notice of the requirements of this act upon the publication of said proclamation or other notice as aforesaid, given by the President or by his direction: And any person who shall willfully fail or refuse to present himself for registration or to submit thereto as herein provided, shall be guilty of a misdemeanor and shall, upon conviction in the District Court of the United States having jurisdiction thereof, be punished by imprisonment for not more than one year, and shall thereupon be duly registered; provided that in the call of the docket precedence shall be given, in courts trying the same, to the trial of criminal proceedings under this act; provided, further, that persons shall be subject to registration as herein provided, who shall have attained their twenty-first birthday and who shall not have attained their thirty-first birthday on or before the day set for the registration; and all persons so registered shall be and remain subject to draft into the forces hereby authorized unless excepted or excused therefrom as in this act provided.

[Here the President also quoted sections of the law relating to the duties of registration officials.]

Now, Therefore, I Woodrow Wilson, President of the United States, do call upon the Governor of each of the several States and Territories, the Board of Commissioners of the District of Columbia, and all officers and agents of the several States and Territories, of the District of Columbia, and the counties and municipalities therein, to perform certain duties in the execution of the foregoing law, which duties will be communicated to them directly in regulations of even date herewith.

And I do further proclaim and give notice to all persons subject to registration in the several States and in the District of Columbia in accordance with the above law, that the time and place of such registration shall be between 7 A. M. and 9 P. M. on the fifth day of June, 1917, at the registration place in the precinct wherein they have their permanent homes. Those who shall have attained their twenty-first birthday and who shall not have attained their thirty-first birthday on or before the day here named are required to register, excepting only officers and enlisted men of the regular army, the navy, the Marine Corps, and the National Guard and Naval Militia, while in the service of the United States, and officers in the Officers' Reserve Corps and enlisted men in the Enlisted Reserve Corps while in active service. In the territories of Alaska, Hawaii, and Porto Rico a day for registration will be named in a later proclamation.

[Here followed detailed instructions for registration of those sick or absent from their counties.]

The Power against which we are arrayed has sought to impose its will upon the world by force. To this end it has increased armament until it has changed the face of war. In the sense in which we have been wont to think of armies, there are no armies in this struggle, there are entire nations armed. Thus, the men who remain to till the soil and man the factories are no less a part of the army that is France than the men beneath the battle flags. It must be so with us. It is not an army that we must shape and train for war; it is a nation.

To this end our people must draw close in one compact front against a common foe. But this cannot be if each man pursues a private purpose. All must pursue one purpose. A nation needs all men; but it needs each man, not in the field that will most pleasure him, but in the endeavor that will best serve the common good. Thus, though a sharpshooter pleases to operate a trip-hammer for the forging of great guns and an expert machinist desires to march with the flag, the nation is being served only when the sharpshooter marches and the machinist remains at his levers.

The whole nation must be a team, in which each man shall play the part for which he is best fitted. To this end, Congress has provided that the nation shall be organized for war by selection; that each man shall be classified for service in the place to which it shall best serve the general good to call him.

The significance of this cannot be overstated. It is a new thing in our history and a landmark in our progress. It is a new manner of accepting and vitalizing our duty to give ourselves with thoughtful devotion to the common purpose of us all. It is in no sense a conscription of the unwilling; it is, rather, selection from a nation which has volunteered in mass. It is no more a choosing of those who shall march with the colors than it is a selection of those who shall serve an equally necessary and devoted purpose in the industries that lie behind the battle line.

The day here named is the time upon which all shall present themselves for assignment to their tasks. It is for that reason destined to be remembered as one of the most conspicuous moments in our history. It is nothing less than the day upon which the manhood of the country shall step forward in one solid rank in defense of the ideals to which this nation is consecrated. It is important to those ideals no less than to the pride of this generation in manifesting its devotion to them, that there be no gaps in the ranks.

It is essential that the day be approached in thoughtful apprehension of its significance, and that we accord to it the honor and the meaning that it deserves. Our industrial need prescribes that it be not made a technical holiday, but the stern sacrifice that is before us urges that it be carried in all our hearts as a great day of patriotic devotion and obligation, when the duty shall lie upon every man, whether he is himself to be registered or not, to see to it that the name of every male person of the designated ages is written on these lists of honor.

In Witness Whereof, I have hereunto set my hand and caused the seal of the United States to be affixed. Done at the City of Washington this 18th day of May in the year of our Lord one thousand nine hundred and seventeen, and of the independence of the United States of America the one hundred and forty-first.

WOODROW WILSON.

By the President:
ROBERT LANSING, Secretary of State.

PRESIDENT WILSON'S OUTLINE OF THE FOOD ADMINISTRATION PROGRAM, MAY 19, 1917

[EDITORIAL NOTE: *In all countries there had been diminishing food supplies due to poor harvests, reduced man power, abnormal consumption by armies, and the creation of vast reserve stores for the military. One of the chief ways in which the United States could help its European Allies was that of furnishing foodstuffs. American farmers had planted increased acreage and Congress was framing legislation to prevent speculation, hoarding, and waste.*]

It is very desirable, in order to prevent misunderstandings or alarms and to assure co-operation in a vital matter, that the country should understand exactly the scope and purpose of the very great powers which I have thought it necessary in the circumstances to ask the Congress to put in my hands with regard to our food supplies. Those powers are very great, indeed, but they are no greater than it has proved necessary to lodge in the other Governments which are conducting this momentous war, and their object is stimulation and conservation, not arbitrary restraint or injurious interference with the normal processes of production. They are intended to benefit and assist the farmer and all those who play a legitimate part in the preparation, distribution, and marketing of foodstuffs.

It is proposed to draw a sharp line of distinction between the normal activities of the Government represented in the Department of Agriculture in reference to food production, conservation, and marketing, on the one hand, and the emergency activities necessitated by the war in reference to the regulation of food distribution and consumption, on the other. All measures intended directly to extend the normal activities of the Department of Agriculture in reference to the production, conservation, and the marketing of farm crops will be administered, as in normal times, through that department, and the powers asked for over distribution and consumption, over exports, imports, prices, purchase, and requisition of commodities, storing, and the like which may require regulation during the war will be placed in the hands of a Commissioner of Food Administration, appointed by the President and directly responsible to him.

The objects sought to be served by the legislation asked for are: Full inquiry into the existing available stocks of foodstuffs and into the costs and practices of the various food-producing and distributing trades; the prevention of all unwarranted hoarding of every kind and of the control of foodstuffs by persons who are not in any legitimate sense producers, dealers, or traders; the requisitioning when necessary for the public use of food supplies and of the equipment necessary for handling them properly; the licensing of wholesome and legitimate mixtures and milling percentages, and the prohibition of the unnecessary or wasteful use of foods.

Authority is asked also to establish prices, but not in order to limit the profits of the farmers, but only to guarantee to them when necessary a minimum price which will insure them a profit where they are asked to attempt new crops and to secure the consumer against extortion by breaking up corners and attempts at speculation, when they occur, by fixing temporarily a reasonable price at which middlemen must sell.

I have asked Mr. Herbert Hoover to undertake this all-important task of food administration. He has expressed his willingness to do so on condition that he is to receive no payment for his services and that the whole of the force under him, exclusive of clerical assistance, shall be employed, so far as possible, upon the same volunteer basis. He has expressed his confidence that this difficult matter of food administration can be successfully accomplished through the voluntary co-operation and direction of legitimate distributers of foodstuffs and with the help of the women of the country.

Although it is absolutely necessary that unquestionable powers shall be placed in my hands, in order to insure the success of this administration of the food supplies of the country, I am confident that the exercise of those powers will be necessary only in the few cases where some small and selfish minority proves unwilling to put the nation's interests above personal advantage, and that the whole country will heartily support Mr. Hoover's efforts by supplying the necessary volunteer agencies throughout the country for the intelligent control of food consumption and securing the co-operation of the most capable leaders of

our available surpluses to their own domestic supply an
of meeting their pressing necessities or deficits. In co
sidering the deficits of food supplies the Government mean
only to fulfill its obvious obligation to assure itself th
neutrals are husbanding their own resources and that ou
supplies will not become available, either directly or i
directly, to feed the enemy.

WOODROW WILSON.

[This first proclamation applied to all countries, but relate
only to fuels, food grains, feed, fertilizers, meats and fats, irc
and steel, arms and ammunition. The second proclamation mac
some additions to the list, and also prohibited the export—to t
enemy and to European neutrals—of practically all articles
commerce. The explanatory statement accompanying the secon
proclamation follows:]

August 27, 1917.

The purpose and effect of this proclamation is not e
port prohibition, but merely export control. It is not th
intention to interfere unnecessarily with our foreign trade
but our own domestic needs must be adequately safeguarde
and there is the added duty of meeting the necessities c
all the nations at war with the Imperial German Goverr
ment.

After these needs are met, it is our wish and intentio
to minister to the needs of the neutral nations as far a
our resources permit. This task will be discharged witl
out other than the very proper qualification that the liber
tion of our surplus products shall not be made the occasio
of benefit to the enemy, either directly or indirectly.

The two lists have been prepared in the interests c
facility and expediency. The first list, applicable to th
enemy and his allies and to the neutral countries of Europ
brings under control practically all articles of commerc
while the second list, applicable to all the other countrie
of the world, makes only a few additions to the list c
commodities controlled by the proclamation of July 9, 191

t is obvious that a closer supervision and control of exorts is necessary with respect to those European neutrals ithin the sphere of hostilities than is required for those ountries further removed.

The establishment of these distinctions will simplify the dministrative processes and enable us to continue our olicy of minimizing the interruption of trade.

No licenses will be necessary for the exportation of coin, ullion, currency and evidences of indebtedness until reuired by regulations to be promulgated by the Secretary f the Treasury in his discretion.

WOODROW WILSON.

[By a proclamation of September 7, the free export of coin, ullion, and currency—permitted in the paragraph above—was also rohibited except under regulations prescribed by the Treasury.]

PRESIDENT WILSON'S MESSAGE TO RUSSIA

Delivered to the Provisional Government on May 26, 1917; made public at Washington on June 9.)

[EDITORIAL NOTE: *This was written two months after he revolution which forced the abdication of Czar Nicholas I (March 15, 1917) and the establishment of a provisional emocratic government. Meanwhile, the Russian peasants, vorkmen, and soldiers—keen to exercise their newly won iberty—had neglected tasks associated with the active rosecution of war; Germany and Austria had made overures for a separate peace; and at best Russia seemed likely o remain for some time an impotent ally. President Wilon sent a special commission to Russia, headed by Elihu Root, and the following note was made public at about the ime of the mission's arrival at Petrograd:*]

In view of the approaching visit of the American delegaion to Russia to express the deep friendship of the Ameri-

tical co-operation that will in effect combine their force to secure peace and justice in the dealings of nations with one another. The brotherhood of mankind must no longer be a fair but empty phrase; it must be given a structure of force and reality. The nations must realize their common life and effect a workable partnership to secure that life against the aggressions of autocratic and self-pleasing power.

For these things we can afford to pour out blood and treasure. For these are the things we have always professed to desire, and unless we pour out blood and treasure now and succeed, we may never be able to unite or show conquering force again in the great cause of human liberty. The day has come to conquer or submit. If the forces of autocracy can divide us they will overcome us; if we stand together, victory is certain and the liberty which victory will secure. We can afford then to be generous, but we cannot afford then or now to be weak or omit any single guarantee of justice and security.

WOODROW WILSON.

PRESIDENT WILSON'S ADDRESS TO CONFEDERATE VETERANS

[At their twenty-seventh annual gathering, Washington, D. C. June 5, 1917—the first Confederate reunion to be held in "the North."]

Mr. Commander, Ladies and Gentlemen:

I esteem it a very great pleasure and a real privilege to extend to the men who are attending this reunion the very cordial greetings of the Government of the United States

I suppose that as you mix with one another you chiefly find these to be days of memory, when your thoughts go back and recall those days of struggle in which your hearts were strained, in which the whole nation seemed in grapple and I dare say that you are thrilled as you remember the heroic things that were then done. You are glad to remember that heroic things were done on both sides, and that men in those days fought in something like the old spirit of chivalric gallantry. There are many memories of the Civil War that thrill along the blood and make one proud to have been sprung of a race that could produce such bravery and constancy; and yet the world does not live on memories. The world is constantly making its toilsome way forward into new and different days, and I believe that one of the things that contributes satisfaction to a reunion like this and a welcome like this is that this is a day of oblivion. There are some things that we have thankfully buried and among them are the great passions of division which once threatened to rend this nation in twain. The passion of admiration we still entertain for the heroic figures of those old days, but the passion of separation, the passion of difference of principle, is gone—gone out of our minds, gone out of our hearts; and one of the things that will thrill this country as it reads of this reunion is that it will read also of a rededication on the part of all of us to the great nation which we serve in common.

These are days of oblivion as well as of memory; for we are forgetting the things that once held us asunder. Not only that, but they are days of rejoicing, because we now at least see why this great nation was kept united, for we are beginning to see the great world purposes which it was meant to serve. Many men, I know, particularly of your own generation, have wondered at some of the dealings of Providence, but the wise heart never questions the dealings of Providence, because the great, long plan as it unfolds has a majesty about it and a definiteness of purpose, an elevation of ideal, which we were incapable of conceiving as we tried to work things out with our own short sight and weak strength. And now that we see ourselves part of a nation united, powerful, great in spirit and in purpose, we know the great ends which God, in His mysterious providence, wrought through our instrumentality, because at the heart of the men of the North and of the South there was the same love of self-government and of liberty, and now we are to be an instrument in the hands of God to see that liberty is made secure for mankind. . . .

As I came along the streets a few minutes ago my heart was full of the thought that this is Registration Day. Will you not support me in feeling that there is some significance in this coincidence, that this day, when I come to welcome you to the national capital, is a day when men young as you were in those old days, when you gathered together to fight, are now registering their names as evidence of this great idea, that in a democracy the duty to serve and the privilege to serve falls upon all alike? There is something very fine, my fellow-citizens, in the spirit of the volunteer, but deeper than the volunteer spirit is the spirit of obligation. There is not a man of us who must not hold himself ready to be summoned to the duty of supporting the great Government under which we live. No really thoughtful and patriotic man is jealous of that obligation. No man who really understands the privilege and the dignity of being an American citizen quarrels for a moment with the idea that the Congress of the United States has the right to call upon whom it will to serve the nation. These solemn lines of young men going to-day all over the Union to places of registration ought to be a signal to the world, to those who dare flout the dignity and honor and rights of the United States, that all her manhood will flock to that standard under which we all delight to serve, and that he who challenges the rights and principles of the United States challenges the united strength and devotion of a nation.

There are not many things that one desires about war, my fellow-citizens, but you have come through war, you know how you have been chastened by it, and there comes a time when it is good for a nation to know that it must sacrifice if need be everything that it has to vindicate the principles which it professes. We have prospered with a sort of heedless and irresponsible prosperity. Now we are going to lay all our wealth, if necessary, and spend all our blood, if need be, to show that we were not accumulating that wealth selfishly, but were accumulating it for the service of mankind. Men all over the world have thought of the United States as a trading and money-getting people, whereas we who have lived at home know the ideals with which the hearts of this people have thrilled; we know the sober convictions which have lain at the basis of our life all the time, and we know the power and devotion which can be spent in heroic ways for the service of those ideals that we have treasured. We have been allowed to become strong in the Providence of God that our strength might be used to prove, not our selfishness, but our greatness, and if there is any ground for thankfulness in a day like this, I am thankful for the privilege of self-sacrifice, which is the only privilege that lends dignity to the human spirit. . . .

Wilson's Flag Day Address

Washington, D. C., June 14, 1917.

[Editorial Note: *As a piece of literary composition and of lofty conception, this speech has been held to take rank with the President's peace address to the Senate on January 22 and his war message to Congress on April 2.*]

My Fellow Citizens:

We meet to celebrate Flag Day because this flag which we honor and under which we serve is the emblem of our unity, our power, our thought and purpose as a nation. It has no other character than that which we give it from generation to generation. The choices are ours. It floats in majestic silence above the hosts that execute those choices, whether in peace or in war. And yet, though silent, it speaks to us—speaks to us of the past, of the men and women who went before us and of the records they wrote upon it. We celebrate the day of its birth; and from its birth until now it has witnessed a great history, has floated on high the symbol of great events, of a great plan of life worked out by a great people. We are about to carry it into battle, to lift it where it will draw the fire of our enemies. We are about to bid thousands, hundreds of thousands, it may be millions, of our men, the young, the strong, the capable men of the nation, to go forth and die beneath it on fields of blood far away—for what? For some unaccustomed thing? For something for which it has never sought the fire before? American armies were never before sent across the seas. Why are they sent now? For some new purpose, for which this great flag has never been carried before, or for some old, familiar, heroic purpose for which it has seen men, its own men, die on every battlefield upon which Americans have borne arms since the Revolution?

These are questions which must be answered. We are Americans. We in our turn serve America, and can serve her with no private purpose. We must use her flag as she has always used it. We are accountable at the bar of history and must plead in utter frankness what purpose it is we seek to serve.

It is plain enough how we were forced into the war. The extraordinary insults and aggressions of the Imperial German Government left us no self-respecting choice but to take up arms in defense of our rights as a free people and of our honor as a sovereign government. The military masters of Germany denied us the right to be neutral. They filled our unsuspecting communities with vicious spies and conspirators and sought to corrupt the opinion of our people in their own behalf. When they found that they could not do that, their agents diligently spread sedition amongst us and sought to draw our own citizens from their allegiance—and some of those agents were men connected with the official Embassy of the German Government itself here in our own capital. They sought by violence to destroy our industries and arrest our commerce. They tried to incite Mexico to take up arms against us and to draw Japan into a hostile alliance with her—and that, not by indirection, but by direct suggestion from the Foreign Office in Berlin. They impudently denied us the use of the high seas and repeatedly executed their threat that they would send to their death any of our people who ventured to approach the coasts of Europe. And many of our own people were corrupted. Men began to look upon their own neighbors with suspicion and to wonder in their hot resentment and surprise whether there was any community in which hostile intrigue did not lurk. What great nation in such circumstances would not have taken up arms? Much as we had desired peace, it was denied us, and not of our own choice. This flag under which we serve would have been dishonored had we withheld our hand.

But that is only part of the story. We know now as clearly as we knew before we were ourselves engaged that we are not the enemies of the German people and that they are not our enemies. They did not originate or desire this hideous war or wish that we should be drawn into it; and we are vaguely conscious that we are fighting their cause, as they will some day see it, as well as our own. They are themselves in the grip of the same sinister power that has now at last stretched its ugly talons out and drawn blood from us. The whole world is at war because the whole world is in the grip of that power and is trying out the great battle which shall determine whether it is to be brought under its mastery or fling itself free.

The war was begun by the military masters of Germany, who proved to be also the masters of Austria Hungary. These men have never regarded nations as peoples, men, women, and children of like blood and frame as themselves, for whom governments existed and in whom governments had their life. They have regarded them merely as serviceable organizations which they could by force or intrigue bend or corrupt to their own purpose. They have regarded the smaller states, in particular, and the peoples who could be overwhelmed by force, as their natural tools and instruments of domination. Their purpose has long been avowed. The statesmen of other nations, to whom that purpose was incredible, paid little attention; regarded what German professors expounded in their classrooms and German writers set forth to the world as the goal of German policy as rather the dream of minds detached from practical affairs, as preposterous private conceptions of German destiny, than as the actual plans of responsible rulers; but the rulers of Germany themselves knew all the while what concrete plans, what well advanced intrigues lay back of what the professors and the writers were saying, and were glad to go forward unmolested, filling the thrones of Balkan states with German princes, putting German officers at the service of Turkey to drill her armies and make interest with her government, developing plans of sedition and rebellion in India and Egypt, setting their fires in Persia. The demands made by Austria upon Servia were a mere single step in a plan which compassed Europe and Asia, from Berlin to Bagdad. They hoped those demands might not arouse Europe, but they meant to press them whether they did or not, for they thought themselves ready for the final issue of arms.

Their plan was to throw a broad belt of German military power and political control across the very center of Europe and beyond the Mediterranean into the heart of Asia; and Austria-Hungary was to be as much their tool and pawn as Servia or Bulgaria or Turkey or the ponderous states of the East. Austria-Hungary, indeed, was to become part of the central German Empire, absorbed and dominated by the same forces and influences that had originally cemented the German states themselves. The dream had its heart at Berlin. It could have had a heart nowhere else! It rejected the idea of solidarity of race entirely. The choice of peoples played no part in it at all. It contemplated binding together racial and political units which could be kept together only by force—Czechs, Magyars, Croats, Serbs, Roumanians, Turks, Armenians—the proud states of Bohemia and Hungary, the stout little commonwealths of the Balkans, the indomitable Turks, the subtle peoples of the East. These peoples did not wish to be united. They ardently desired to direct their own affairs, would be satisfied only by undisputed independence. They could be kept quiet only by the presence or the constant threat of armed men. They would live under a common power only by sheer compulsion and await the day of revolution. But the German military statesmen had reckoned with all that and were ready to deal with it in their own way.

And they have actually carried the greater part of that amazing plan into execution! Look how things stand. Austria is at their mercy. It has acted, not upon its own initiative or upon the choice of its own people, but at Berlin's dictation ever since the war began. Its people now desire peace, but cannot have it until leave is granted from Berlin. The so-called Central Powers are in fact but a single Power. Servia is at its mercy, should its hands be but for a moment freed. Bulgaria has consented to its will, and Roumania is overrun. The Turkish armies, which Germans trained, are serving Germany, certainly not themselves, and the guns of German warships lying in the harbor at Constantinople remind Turkish statesmen every day that they have no choice but to take their orders from Berlin. From Hamburg to the Persian Gulf the net is spread.

Is it not easy to understand the eagerness for peace that has been manifested from Berlin ever since the snare was set and sprung? Peace, peace, peace has been the talk of her Foreign Office for now a year and more; not peace upon her own initiative, but upon the initiative of the nations over which she now deems herself to hold the advantage. A little of the talk has been public, but most of it has been private. Through all sorts of channels it has come to me, and in all sorts of guises, but never with the terms disclosed which the German Government would be willing to accept. That government has other valuable pawns in its hands besides those I have mentioned. It still holds a valuable part of France, though with slowly relaxing grasp, and practically the whole of Belgium. Its armies press close upon Russia and overrun Poland at their will. It cannot go further; it dare not go back. It wishes to close its bargain before it is too late and it has little left to offer for the pound of flesh it will demand.

The military masters under whom Germany is bleeding see very clearly to what point Fate has brought them. If they fall back or are forced back an inch, their power both abroad and at home will fall to pieces like a house of cards. It is their power at home they are thinking about now more than their power abroad. It is that power which is trembling under their very feet; and deep fear has entered their hearts. They have but one chance to perpetuate their military power or even their controlling political influence. If they can secure peace now with the immense advantages still in their hands which they have up to this point apparently gained, they will have justified themselves before the German people; they will have gained by force what they promised to gain by it: an immense expansion of German power, an immense enlargement of German industrial and commercial opportunities. Their prestige will be secure, and with their prestige their political power. If they fail, their people will thrust them aside; a government accountable to the people themselves will be set up in Germany as it has been in England, in the United States, in France, and in all the great countries of the modern time except Germany. If they succeed they are safe and Germany and the world are undone; if they fail Germany is saved and the world will be at peace. If they succeed, America will fall within the menace. We and all the rest of the world must remain armed, as they will remain, and must make ready for the next step in their aggression; if they fail, the world may unite for peace and Germany may be of the union.

Do you not now understand the new intrigue, the intrigue for peace, and why the masters of Germany do not hesitate to use any agency that promises to effect their purpose, the deceit of the nations? Their present particular aim is to deceive all those who throughout the world stand for the rights of peoples and the self-government of nations; for they see what immense strength the forces of justice and of liberalism are gathering out of this war. They are employing liberals in their enterprise. They are using men, in Germany and without, as their spokesmen whom they have hitherto despised and oppressed, using them for their own destruction—socialists, the leaders of labor, the thinkers they have hitherto sought to silence. Let them once succeed and these men, now their tools, will be ground to powder beneath the weight of the great military empire they will have set up; the revolutionists in Russia will be cut off from all succor or co-operation in western Europe and a counter revolution fostered and supported; Germany herself will lose her chance of freedom; and all Europe will arm for the next, the final struggle.

The sinister intrigue is being no less actively conducted in this country than in Russia and in every country in Europe to which the agents and dupes of the Imperial German Government can get access. That government has many spokesmen here, in places high and low. They have learned discretion. They keep within the law. It is opinion they utter now, not sedition. They proclaim the liberal purposes of their masters; declare this a foreign war which can touch America with no danger to either her lands or her institutions; set England at the centre of the stage and talk of her ambition to assert economic dominion throughout the world; appeal to our ancient tradition of isolation in the politics of the nations; and seek to undermine the government with false professions of loyalty to its principles.

But they will make no headway. The false betray themselves always in every accent. It is only friends and partisans of the German Government whom we have already identified who utter these thinly disguised loyalties. The facts are patent to all the world, and nowhere are they more plainly seen than in the United States, where we are accustomed to deal with facts and not with sophistries; and the great fact that stands out above all the rest is that this is a People's War, a war for freedom and justice and self-government amongst all the nations of the world, a war to make the world safe for the peoples who live upon it and have made it their own, the German peoples themselves included; and that with us rests the choice to break through all these hypocrisies and patent cheats and masks of brute force and help set the world free, or else stand aside and let it be dominated a long age through by sheer weight of arms and the arbitrary choices of self-constituted masters, by the nation which can maintain the biggest armies and the most irresistible armaments—a power to which the world has afforded no parallel and in the face of which political freedom must wither and perish.

For us there is but one choice. We have made it. Woe be to the man or group of men that seeks to stand in our way in this day of high resolution when every principle we hold dearest is to be vindicated and made secure for the salvation of the nations. We are ready to plead at the bar of history, and our flag shall wear a new lustre. Once more we shall make good with our lives and fortunes the great faith to which we were born, and a new glory shall shine in the face of our people.

President Wilson's Greeting to France, on Bastile Day, July 14, 1917

On this anniversary of the birth of democracy in France, I offer on behalf of my countrymen and on my own behalf, fraternal greetings as befit the strong ties that unite our peoples, who to-day stand shoulder to shoulder in defense of liberty in testimony of the steadfast purpose of our two countries to achieve victory for the sublime cause of the rights of the people against oppression. The lesson of the Bastile is not lost to the world of free peoples. May the day be near when on the ruins of the dark stronghold of unbridled power and conscienceless autocracy, the nobler structure, upbuilt, like your own great republic, on the eternal foundation of peace and right, shall arise to gladden an enfranchised world.

President Wilson's Welcome to the Special Ambassador from Japan, Viscount Ishii, August 23, 1917

Mr. Ambassador:

It is with a sense of deep satisfaction that I receive from your hand the letters whereby you are accredited as the Ambassador Extraordinary and Plenipotentiary of Japan on special mission to the United States. It is a pleasure to accept through you from your imperial sovereign congratulations on the entrance of the United States into the great conflict which is now raging.

The present struggle is especially characterized by the development of the spirit of co-operation throughout the greater part of the world for the maintenance of the rights of nations and the liberties of individuals. I assure your Excellency that, standing, as our countries now do, associated in this great struggle for the vindication of justice, there will be developed those closer ties of fellowship which must come from the mutual sacrifice of life and property. May the efforts now being exerted by an indigant humanity lead, at the proper time, to the complete establishment of justice and to a peace which will be both permanent and serene.

I trust your Excellency will find your sojourn among us most agreeable and I should be gratified if you would be so good as to make known to his Imperial Majesty my best wishes for his welfare, for that of your wonderful country, and for the happiness of its people.

I am most happy to accord you recognition in your high capacity.

Wilson's Message to the Russian National Council
August 27, 1917

[The path of the new republic had continued to be difficult, and at times it seemed impossible to harmonize the desires of the various elements. Workmen, soldiers, and peasants formed their respective councils; and these and other bodies met at Moscow to establish fundamental principles.]

President of the National Council Assembly, Moscow:

I take the liberty to send to the members of the great council now meeting in Moscow the cordial greetings of their friends, the people of the United States, to express their confidence in the ultimate triumph of ideals of democracy and self-government against all enemies within and without, and to give their renewed assurance of every material and moral assistance they can extend to the Government of Russia in the promotion of the common cause in which the two nations are unselfishly united.

Woodrow Wilson.

President Wilson's Reply to the Pope's Peace Proposals

[Editorial Note: *At the beginning of the fourth year of war, Pope Benedict had addressed an appeal to the belligerents. His suggestions for the basis of a just and durable peace included disarmament, the evacuation of Belgian and French territory, the restitution of German colonies, and the settlement of political and territorial questions—Alsace-Lorraine, Poland, etc.—in a conciliatory spirit for the general welfare. This appeal from the Pope reached Washington on August 15.*]

Washington, D. C., Aug. 27, 1917.

To His Holiness Benedictus XV., Pope:

In acknowledgment of the communication of your Holiness to the belligerent peoples, dated Aug. 1, 1917, the President of the United States requests me to transmit the following reply:

Every heart that has not been blinded and hardened by this terrible war must be touched by this moving appeal of his Holiness the Pope, must feel the dignity and force of the humane and generous motives which prompted it, and must fervently wish that we might take the path of peace he so persuasively points out. But it would be folly to take it if it does not in fact lead to the goal he proposes. Our response must be based upon the stern facts, and upon nothing else. It is not a mere cessation of arms he desires; it is a stable and enduring peace. This agony must not be gone through with again, and it must be a matter of very sober judgment what will insure us against it.

His Holiness in substance proposes that we return to the status quo ante-bellum and that then there be a general condonation, disarmament, and a concert of nations based upon an acceptance of the principle of arbitration; that by a similar concert freedom of the seas be established; and

ment ought to be repaired, but not at the expense of the sovereignty of any people—rather a vindication of the sovereignty both of those that are weak and of those that are strong. Punitive damages, the dismemberment of empires, the establishment of selfish and exclusive economic leagues, we deem inexpedient, and in the end worse than futile, no proper basis for a peace of any kind, least of all for an enduring peace. That must be based upon justice and fairness and the common rights of mankind.

We cannot take the word of the present rulers of Germany as a guarantee of anything that is to endure unless explicitly supported by such conclusive evidence of the will and purpose of the German people themselves as the other peoples of the world would be justified in accepting. Without such guarantees treaties of settlement, agreements for disarmament, covenants to set up arbitration in the place of force, territorial adjustments, reconstitutions of small nations, if made with the German Government, no man, no nation, could now depend on.

We must await some new evidence of the purposes of the great peoples of the Central Powers. God grant it may be given soon and in a way to restore the confidence of all peoples everywhere in the faith of nations and the possibility of a covenanted peace.

ROBERT LANSING,

Secretary of State of the United States of America.

ANNOUNCEMENT OF THE PRICE TO BE PAID FOR WHEAT

[EDITORIAL NOTE: *The Food Administration bill had become a law on August 10, 1917, and the President had appointed Mr. Herbert Hoover as Food Administrator. The first important act of this body—through a committee of prominent citizens headed by President Harry A. Gar-*

field, of Williams College—was to establish a price which the Government would pay for wheat for itself and its Allies. The Government being the largest purchaser, this would tend to set the standard price. Similar committees were to fix prices for other necessities. The President announced the recommendation of the wheat committee:]

Washington, August 30, 1917.

Section 11 of the food act provides, among other things, for the purchase and sale of wheat and flour by the Government, and appropriates money for the purpose. The purchase of wheat and flour for our allies, and to a considerable degree for neutral countries also, has been placed under the control of the Food Administration. I have appointed a committee to determine a fair price to be paid in Government purchases. The price now recommended by that committee—$2.20 per bushel at Chicago for the basic grade—will be rigidly adhered to by the Food Administration.

It is the hope and expectation of the Food Administration, and my own also, that this step will at once stabilize and keep within moderate bounds the price of wheat for all transactions throughout the present crop year, and in consequence the prices of flour and bread also. The food act has given large powers for the control of storage and exchange operations, and these powers will be fully exercised. An inevitable consequence will be that financial dealings can not follow their usual course. Whatever the advantages and disadvantages of the ordinary machinery of trade, it can not function well under such disturbed and abnormal conditions as now exist. In its place the Food Administration now fixes for its purchases a fair price, as recommended unanimously by a committee representative of all interests and all sections, and believes that thereby it will eliminate speculation, make possible the conduct of every operation in the full light of day, maintain the publicly stated price for all, and, through economies made

Appointment of Commission to Adjust Labor Disputes, September 19, 1917

[Editorial Note: *Strikes at large copper mines in Montana and Arizona had continued through several months, endangering the supply for munitions; and a more recent strike of iron and steel workers on the Pacific Coast was halting the great shipbuilding program of the Administration. These strikes involved wage adjustments chiefly.*]

(A Memorandum for the Secretary of Labor)

I am very much interested in the labor situation in the mountain region and on the Pacific Coast. I have listened with attention and concern to the numerous charges of misconduct and injustice that representatives both of employers and of employees have made against each other. I am not so much concerned, however, with the manner in which they have treated each other in the past as I am desirous of seeing some kind of a working arrangement arrived at for the future, particularly during the period of the war, on a basis that will be fair to all parties concerned.

To assist in the accomplishment of that purpose I have decided to appoint a commission to visit the localities where disagreements have been most frequent as my personal representatives. The commission will consist of William B. Wilson, Secretary of Labor; Colonel J. L. Spangler of Pennsylvania, Verner Z. Reed of Colorado, John H. Walker of Illinois, and E. P. Marsh of Washington. Felix Frankfurter of New York will act as Secretary of the commission.

It will be the duty of the commission to visit in each instance the Governor of the State, advising him that they are there as the personal representatives of the President, with a view to lending sympathetic counsel and aid to the State government in the development of a better understanding between laborers and employers, and also themselves to deal with employers and employees in a conciliatory spirit, seek to compose differences and allay misunderstanding, and in any way that may be open to them to show the active interest of the National Government in furthering arrangements just to both sides.

Wherever it is deemed advisable, conferences of employers and employees should be called with the purpose of working out a mutual understanding between them which will insure the continued operation of the industry on conditions acceptable to both sides. The commission should also endeavor to learn the real causes for any discontent which may exist on either side, not by the formal process of public hearings, but by getting into touch with workmen and employers by the more informal process of personal conversation.

I would be pleased to have the commission report to me from time to time such information as may require immediate attention.

WOODROW WILSON.

PRESIDENT WILSON COMMENDS THE WORK OF CONGRESS, OCTOBER 6, 1917

[The new Congress had been called into special session on April 2, to receive the President's war message. It had passed the war resolution, created a system for raising a large army by selective conscription, framed a revenue bill of huge proportions, and adopted other legislation relating to the war.]

The Sixty-fifth Congress, now adjourning, deserves the gratitude and appreciation of a people whose will and purpose I believe it has faithfully expressed. One cannot examine the record of its action without being impressed by its completeness, its courage, and its full comprehension of a great task. The needs of the Army and the Navy have

Two Messages to Brazil, on Occasion of Its Entry Into the War

[The republics of Latin America began to line up against Germany soon after the United States entered the war. From April to December, 1917, Peru, Bolivia, Ecuador, Uruguay, Guatemala, and Costa Rica severed diplomatic relations with the German Government, while Cuba, Panama, and Brazil actually declared war.]

October 30, 1917.

Dr. Wenceslao Braz, President of Brazil, Rio de Janeiro:

Allow me, speaking for the people and the Government of the United States, to say with what genuine pleasure and heartfelt welcome we hail the association with ourselves and the other nations united in war with Germany of the great Republic of Brazil. Her action in this time of crisis binds even closer the bonds of friendship which already united the two Republics.

Woodrow Wilson.

November 15, 1917.

His Excellency the President of Brazil, Rio de Janeiro:

On this anniversary of the independence of Brazil I extend to Your Excellency and the people of your great Republic cordial greetings. The United States has welcomed with applause and admiration the entry of Brazil in the great struggle which confronts us. The day you now celebrate marks your country's achievements of independence. To-day our two countries are engaged in a war for the maintenance of world independence and for the rights of humanity and the life of Democracy. We are both making sacrifices for this common cause. United to Brazil by this strong bond of Democracy and still more by antagonism against a mutual foe, I hope and feel assured that the United States and our sister Republic of South America will at the close of the present conflict stand even closer together in victory.

Woodrow Wilson.

Thanksgiving Proclamation

November 7, 1917

It has long been the honored custom of our people to turn in the fruitful autumn of the year in praise and thanksgiving to Almighty God for His many blessings and mercies to us as a nation. That custom we can follow now even in the midst of the tragedy of a world shaken by war and immeasurable disaster, in the midst of sorrow and great peril, because even amidst the darkness that has gathered about us we can see the great blessings God has bestowed upon us, blessings that are better than mere peace of mind and prosperity of enterprise.

We have been given the opportunity to serve mankind as we once served ourselves in the great day of our Declaration of Independence, by taking up arms against a tyranny that threatened to master and debase men everywhere and joining with other free peoples in demanding for all the nations of the world what we then demanded and obtained for ourselves. In this day of the revelation of our duty not only to defend our own rights as a nation but to defend also the rights of free men throughout the world, there has been vouchsafed us in full and inspiring measure the resolution and spirit of united action. We have been brought to one mind and purpose. A new vigor of common counsel and common action has been revealed in us. We should especially thank God that in such circumstances, in the midst of the greatest enterprise the spirits of men have ever entered upon, we have, if we but observe a reasonable and practicable economy, abundance with which to supply the needs of those associated with us as well as our own. A new light shines about us. The great duties of a new day awaken a new and greater national spirit in us. We shall never again be divided or wonder what stuff we are made of.

And while we render thanks for these things let us pray Almighty God that in all humbleness of spirit we may look

thing that needs to be explained is why Germany started the war. Remember what the position of Germany in the world was—as enviable a position as any nation has ever occupied. The whole world stood at admiration of her wonderful intellectual and material achievements. All the intellectual men of the world went to school to her. As a university man I have been surrounded by men trained in Germany, men who had resorted to Germany because nowhere else could they get such thorough and searching training, particularly in the principles of science and the principles that underlie modern material achievement. Her men of science had made her industries perhaps the most competent industries of the world, and the label "Made in Germany" was a guarantee of good workmanship and of sound material. She had access to all the markets of the world, and every other who traded in those markets feared Germany because of her effective and almost irresistible competition. She had a "place in the sun."

Why was she not satisfied? What more did she want? There was nothing in the world of peace that she did not already have and have in abundance. We boast of the extraordinary pace of American advancement. We show with pride the statistics of the increase of our industries and of the population of our cities. Well, those statistics did not match the recent statistics of Germany. Her old cities took on youth, grew faster than any American cities ever grew. Her old industries opened their eyes and saw a new world and went out for its conquest. And yet the authorities of Germany were not satisfied. You have one part of the answer to the question why she was not satisfied in her methods of competition. There is no important industry in Germany upon which the Government has not laid its hands, to direct it and, when necessity arose, control it; and you have only to ask any man whom you meet who is familiar with the conditions that prevailed before the war in the matter of national competition to find out the methods of competition which the German manufacturer and exporters used under the patronage and support of the Government of Germany. You will find that they were the same sorts of competition that we have tried to prevent by law within our own borders. If they could not sell their goods cheaper than we could sell ours at a profit to themselves they could get a subsidy from the Government which made it possible to sell them cheaper anyhow, and the conditions of competition were thus controlled in large measure by the German Government itself.

But that did not satisfy the German Government. All the while there was lying behind its thought in its dreams of the future a political control which would enable it in the long run to dominate the labor and the industry of the world. They were not content with success by superior achievement; they wanted success by authority. I suppose very few of you have thought much about the Berlin-to-Bagdad Railway. The Berlin-Bagdad Railway was constructed in order to run the threat of force down the flank of the industrial undertakings of half a dozen other countries; so that when German competition came in it would not be resisted too far, because there was always the possibility of getting German armies into the heart of that country quicker than any other armies could be got there.

Look at the map of Europe now! Germany in thrusting upon us again and again the discussion of peace talks about what? Talks about Belgium; talks about northern France; talks about Alsace-Lorraine. Well, those are deeply interesting subjects to us and to them, but they are not talking about the heart of the matter. Take the map and look at it. Germany has absolute control of Austria-Hungary, practical control of the Balkan States, control of Turkey, control of Asia Minor. I saw a map in which the whole thing was printed in appropriate black the other day, and the black stretched all the way from Hamburg to Bagdad —the bulk of German power inserted into the heart of the world. If she can keep that, she has kept all that her dreams contemplated when the war began. If she can keep that, her power can disturb the world as long as she keeps it, always provided, for I feel bound to put this proviso in —always provided the present influences that control the German Government continue to control it. I believe that the spirit of freedom can get into the hearts of Germans and find as fine a welcome there as it can find in any other hearts, but the spirit of freedom does not suit the plans of the Pan-Germans. Power cannot be used with concentrated force against free peoples if it is used by free people.

You know how many intimations come to us from one of the central powers that it is more anxious for peace than the chief central power, and you know that it means that the people in that central power know that if the war ends as it stands they will in effect themselves be vassals of Germany, notwithstanding that their populations are compounded of all the peoples of that part of the world, and notwithstanding the fact that they do not wish in their pride and proper spirit of nationality to be so absorbed and dominated. Germany is determined that the political power of the world shall belong to her. There have been such ambitions before. They have been in part realized, but never before have those ambitions been based upon so exact and precise and scientific a plan of domination.

May I not say that it is amazing to me that any group of persons should be so ill-informed as to suppose, as some groups in Russia apparently suppose, that any reforms planned in the interest of the people can live in the presence of a Germany powerful enough to undermine or overthrow them by intrigue or force? Any body of free men that compounds with the present German Government is compounding for its own destruction. But that is not the whole of the story. Any man in America or anywhere else that supposes that the free industry and enterprise of the world can continue if the Pan-German plan is achieved and

German power fastened upon the world is as fatuous as the dreamers in Russia. What I am opposed to is not the feeling of the pacifists, but their stupidity. My heart is with them, but my mind has a contempt for them. I want peace, but I know how to get it, and they do not.

You will notice that I sent a friend of mine, Col. House, to Europe, who is as great a lover of peace as any man in the world, but I didn't send him on a peace mission yet. I sent him to take part in a conference as to how the war was to be won, and he knows, as I know, that that is the way to get peace if you want it for more than a few minutes.

All of this is a preface to the conference that I have referred to with regard to what we are going to do. If we are true friends of freedom of our own or anybody else's, we will see that the power of this country and the productivity of this country is raised to its absolute maximum, and that absolutely nobody is allowed to stand in the way of it. When I say that nobody is allowed to stand in the way I do not mean that they shall be prevented by the power of the Government but by the power of the American spirit. Our duty, if we are to do this great thing and show America to be what we believe her to be—the greatest hope and energy of the world—is to stand together night and day until the job is finished.

While we are fighting for freedom we must see among other things, that labor is free, and that means a number of interesting things. It means not only that we must do what we have declared our purpose to do, see that the conditions of labor are not rendered more onerous by the war but also that we shall see to it that the instrumentalities by which the conditions of labor are improved are not blocked or checked. That we must do. That has been the matter about which I have taken pleasure in conferring from time to time with your president, Mr. Gompers; and if I may be permitted to do so, I want to express my admiration of his patriotic courage, his large vision, and his statesmanlike sense of what has to be done. I like to lay my mind alongside of a mind that knows how to pull in harness. The horses that kick over the traces will have to be put in corral.

Now, to stand together means that nobody must interrupt the processes of our energy if the interruption can possibly be avoided without the absolute invasion of freedom. To put it concretely, that means this: Nobody has a right to stop the processes of labor until all the methods of conciliation and settlement have been exhausted. And I might as well say right here that I am not talking to you alone. You sometimes stop the courses of labor, but there are others who do the same, and I believe that I am speaking from my own experience not only, but from the experience of others when I say that you are reasonable in a larger number of cases than the capitalists. I am not saying these things to them personally yet, because I have not had a chance, but they have to be said, not in any spirit of criticism, but in order to clear the atmosphere and come down to business. Everybody on both sides has now got to transact business, and a settlement is never impossible when both sides want to do the square and right thing.

Moreover, a settlement is always hard to avoid when the parties can be brought face to face. I can differ from a man much more radically when he is not in the room than I can when he is in the room, because then the awkward thing is he can come back at me and answer what I say. It is always dangerous for a man to have the floor entirely to himself. Therefore, we must insist in every instance that the parties come into each other's presence and there discuss the issues between them and not separately in places which have no communication with each other. I always like to remind myself of a delightful saying of an Englishman of the past generation, Charles Lamb. He stuttered a little bit, and once when he was with a group of friends he spoke very harshly of some man who was not present. One of his friends said: "Why, Charles, I didn't know that you knew so and so." "O-o-oh," he said, "I-I d-d-don't; I-I can't h-h-hate a m-m-man I-I know." There is a great deal of human nature, of very pleasant human nature, in the saying. It is hard to hate a man you know. I may admit, parenthetically, that there are some politicians whose methods I do not at all believe in, but they are jolly good fellows, and if they only would not talk the wrong kind of politics, I would love to be with them.

So it is all along the line, in serious matters and things less serious. We are all of the same clay and spirit, and we can get together if we desire to get together. Therefore, my counsel to you is this: Let us show ourselves Americans by showing that we do not want to go off in separate camps or groups by ourselves, but that we want to cooperate with all other classes and all other groups in the common enterprise which is to release the spirits of the world from bondage. I would be willing to set that up as the final test of an American. That is the meaning of democracy. I have been very much distressed, my fellow citizens, by some of the things that have happened recently. The mob spirit is displaying itself here and there in this country. I have no sympathy with what some men are saying, but I have no sympathy with the men who take their punishment into their own hands; and I want to say to every man who does join such a mob that I do not recognize him as worthy of the free institutions of the United States. There are some organizations in this country whose object is anarchy and the destruction of law, but I would not meet their efforts by making myself partner in destroying the law. I despise and hate their purposes as much as any man, but I respect the ancient processes of justice; and I would be too proud not to see them done justice, however wrong they are.

So I want to utter my earnest protest against any manifestation of the spirit of lawlessness anywhere or in any

grossly obvious and odious to every true American to need to be rehearsed. But I shall ask you to consider again and with a very grave scrutiny our objectives and the measures by which we mean to attain them; for the purpose of discussion here in this place is action, and our action must move straight toward definite ends. Our object is, of course, to win the war; and we shall not slacken or suffer ourselves to be diverted until it is won. But it is worth while asking and answering the question, When shall we consider the war won?

From one point of view it is not necessary to broach this fundamental matter. I do not doubt that the American people know what the war is about and what sort of an outcome they will regard as a realization of their purpose in it. As a Nation we are united in spirit and intention. I pay little heed to those who tell me otherwise. I hear the voices of dissent—who does not? I hear the criticism and the clamor of the noisily thoughtless and troublesome. I also see men here and there fling themselves in impotent disloyalty against the calm, indomitable power of the Nation. I hear men debate peace who understand neither its nature nor the way in which we may attain it with uplifted eyes and unbroken spirits. But I know that none of these speaks for the Nation. They do not touch the heart of anything. They may safely be left to strut their uneasy hour and be forgotten.

But from another point of view I believe that it is necessary to say plainly what we here at the seat of action consider the war to be for and what part we mean to play in the settlement of its searching issues. We are the spokesmen of the American people and they have a right to know whether their purpose is ours. They desire peace by the overcoming of evil, by the defeat once for all of the sinister forces that interrupt peace and render it impossible, and they wish to know how closely our thought runs with theirs and what action we propose. They are impatient with those who desire peace by any sort of compromise—deeply and indignantly impatient—but they will be equally impatient with us if we do not make it plain to them what our objectives are and what we are planning for in seeking to make conquest of peace by arms.

I believe that I speak for them when I say two things: First, that this intolerable Thing of which the masters of Germany have shown us the ugly face, this menace of combined intrigue and force which we now see so clearly as the German power, a Thing without conscience or honor or capacity for covenanted peace, must be crushed, and if it be not utterly brought to an end, at least shut out from the friendly intercourse of the nations; and, second, that when this Thing and its power are indeed defeated and the time comes that we can discuss peace—when the German people have spokesmen whose word we can believe and when those spokesmen are ready in the name of their people to accept the common judgment of the nations as to what shall henceforth be the bases of law and of covenant for the life of the world—we shall be willing and glad to pay the full price for peace, and pay it ungrudgingly. We know what that price will be. It will be full, impartial justice—justice done at every point and to every nation that the final settlement must affect our enemies as well as our friends.

You catch, with me, the voices of humanity that are in the air. They grow daily more audible, more articulate, more persuasive, and they come from the hearts of men everywhere. They insist that the war shall not end in vindictive action of any kind; that no nation or peoples shall be robbed or punished because the irresponsible rulers of a single country have themselves done deep and abominable wrong. It is this thought that has been expressed in the formula "No annexations, no contributions, no punitive indemnities." Just because this crude formula expresses the instinctive judgment as to right of plain men everywhere it has been made diligent use of by the masters of German

And our attitude and purpose with regard to Germany herself are of a like kind. We intend no wrong against the German Empire, no interference with her internal affairs. We should deem either the one or the other absolutely unjustifiable, absolutely contrary to the principles we have professed to live by and to hold most sacred throughout our life as a nation.

The people of Germany are being told by the men whom they now permit to deceive them and to act as their masters that they are fighting for the very life and existence of their Empire, a war of desperate self-defense against deliberate aggression. Nothing could be more grossly or wantonly false, and we must seek by the utmost openness and candor as to our real aims to convince them of its falseness. We are in fact fighting for their emancipation from fear, along with our own—from the fear as well as from the fact of unjust attack by neighbors or rivals or schemers after world empire. No one is threatening the existence or the independence or the peaceful enterprise of the German Empire.

The worst that can happen to the detriment of the German people is this, that if they should still, after the war is over, continue to be obliged to live under ambitious and intriguing masters interested to disturb the peace of the world, men or classes of men whom the other peoples of the world could not trust, it might be impossible to admit them to the partnership of nations which must henceforth guarantee the world's peace. That partnership must be a partnership of peoples, not a mere partnership of governments. It might be impossible, also, in such untoward circumstances, to admit Germany to the free economic intercourse which must inevitably spring out of the other partnerships of a real peace. But there would be no aggression in that; and such a situation, inevitable because of distrust, would in the very nature of things sooner or later cure itself, by processes which would assuredly set in.

The wrongs, the very deep wrongs, committed in this war will have to be righted. That of course. But they cannot and must not be righted by the commission of similar wrongs against Germany and her allies. The world will not permit the commission of similar wrongs as a means of reparation and settlement. Statesmen must by this time have learned that the opinion of the world is everywhere wide awake and fully comprehends the issues involved. No representative of any self-governed nation will dare disregard it by attempting any such covenants of selfishness and compromise as were entered into at the Congress of Vienna. The thought of the plain people here and everywhere throughout the world, the people who enjoy no privilege and have very simple and unsophisticated standards of right and wrong, is the air all governments must henceforth breathe if they would live. It is in the full disclosing light of that thought that all policies must be conceived and executed in this midday hour of the world's life. German rulers have been able to upset the peace of the world only because the German people were not suffered under their tutelage to share the comradeship of the other peoples of the world either in thought or in purpose. They were allowed to have no opinion of their own which might be set up as a rule of conduct for those who exercised authority over them. But the congress that concludes this war will feel the full strength of the tides that run now in the hearts and consciences of free men everywhere. Its conclusions will run with those tides.

All these things have been true from the very beginning of this stupendous war; and I cannot help thinking that if they had been made plain at the very outset the sympathy and enthusiasm of the Russian people might have been once for all enlisted on the side of the allies, suspicion and distrust swept away, and a real and lasting union of purpose effected. Had they believed these things at the very moment of their revolution and had they been confirmed in

punishment; and women as well as men should be included under the terms of the acts placing restraints upon alien enemies. It is likely that as time goes on many alien enemies will be willing to be fed and housed at the expense of the Government in the detention camps, and it would be the purpose of the legislation I have suggested to confine offenders among them in penitentiaries and other similar institutions where they could be made to work as other criminals do.

Recent experience has convinced me that the Congress must go further in authorizing the Government to set limits to prices. The law of supply and demand, I am sorry to say, has been replaced by the law of unrestrained selfishness. While we have eliminated profiteering in several branches of industry it still runs impudently rampant in others. The farmers, for example, complain with a great deal of justice that, while the regulation of food prices restricts their incomes, no restraints are placed upon the prices of most of the things they must themselves purchase; and similar inequities obtain on all sides.

It is imperatively necessary that the consideration of the full use of the water power of the country, and also the consideration of the systematic and yet economical development of such of the natural resources of the country as are still under the control of the Federal Government, should be immediately resumed and affirmatively and constructively dealt with at the earliest possible moment. The pressing need of such legislation is daily becoming more obvious.

The legislation proposed at the last session with regard to regulated combinations among our exporters, in order to provide for our foreign trade a more effective organization and method of coöperation, ought by all means to be completed at this session.

And I beg that the members of the House of Representatives will permit me to express the opinion that it will be impossible to deal in any but a very wasteful and extravagant fashion with the enormous appropriations of the public moneys which must continue to be made, if the war is to be properly sustained, unless the House will consent to return to its former practice of initiating and preparing all appropriation bills through a single committee, in order that responsibility may be centered, expenditures standardized and made uniform, and waste and duplication as much as possible avoided.

Additional legislation may also become necessary before the present Congress again adjourns in order to effect the most efficient co-ordination and operation of the railway and other transportation systems of the country; but to that I shall, if circumstances should demand, call the attention of the Congress upon another occasion.

If I have overlooked anything that ought to be done for the more effective conduct of the war, your own counsels will supply the omission. What I am perfectly clear about is that in the present session of the Congress our whole attention and energy should be concentrated on the vigorous, rapid, and successful prosecution of the great task of winning the war.

We can do this with all the greater zeal and enthusiasm because we know that for us this is a war of high principle, debased by no selfish ambition of conquest or spoliation; because we know, and all the world knows, that we have been forced into it to save the very institutions we live under from corruption and destruction. The purposes of the Central Powers strike straight at the very heart of everything we believe in; their methods of warfare outrage every principle of humanity and of knightly honor; their intrigue has corrupted the very thought and spirit of many of our people; their sinister and secret diplomacy has sought to take our very territory away from us and disrupt the Union of the States. Our safety would be at an end, our honor forever sullied and brought into contempt were we

certain systems of transportation and to utilize the same, to the exclusion as far as may be necessary of other than war traffic thereon, for the transportation of troops, war material and equipment therefor, and for other needful and desirable purposes connected with the prosecution of the war;

Now, therefore, I, Woodrow Wilson, President of the United States, under and by virtue of the powers vested in me by the foregoing resolutions and statute, and by virtue of all other powers thereto enabling, do hereby, through Newton D. Baker, Secretary of War, take possession and assume control at 12 o'clock noon on the twenty-eighth day of December, 1917, of each and every system of transportation and the appurtenances thereof located wholly or in part within the boundaries of the continental United States and consisting of railroads, and owned or controlled systems of coastwise and inland transportation, engaged in general transportation, whether operated by steam or by electric power, including also terminals, terminal companies and terminal associations, sleeping and parlor cars, private cars and private car lines, elevators, warehouses, telegraph and telephone lines, and all other equipment and appurtenances commonly used upon or operated as a part of such rail or combined rail and water systems of transportation—to the end that such systems of transportation be utilized for the transfer and transportation of troops, war material and equipment to the exclusion so far as may be necessary of all other traffic thereon, and that so far as such exclusive use be not necessary or desirable, such systems of transportation be operated and utilized in the performance of such other services as the national interest may require and of the usual and ordinary business and duties of common carriers.

It is hereby directed that the possession, control, operation, and utilization of such transportation systems hereby by me undertaken shall be exercised by and through William G. McAdoo, who is hereby appointed and designated Director General of Railroads. Said Director may perform the duties imposed upon him so long, and to such extent, as he shall determine, through the boards of Directors, receivers, officers, and employes of said systems of transportation. Until and except so far as said Director shall from time to time by general or special orders otherwise provide, the boards of Directors, receivers, officers, and employes of the various transportation systems shall continue the operation thereof in the usual and ordinary course of the business of common carriers in the names of their respective companies.

Until and except so far as said Director shall from time to time otherwise by general or special orders determine, such systems of transportation shall remain subject to all existing statutes and orders of the Interstate Commerce Commission, and to all statutes and orders of regulating commissions of the various States in which said systems or any part thereof may be situated. But any orders, general or special, hereafter made by said Director shall have paramount authority and be obeyed as such.

Nothing herein shall be construed as now affecting the possession, operation, and control of street electric passenger railways, including railways commonly called interurbans, whether such railways be or be not owned or controlled by such railroad companies or systems. By subsequent order and proclamation, if and when it shall be found necessary or desirable, possession, control, or operation may be taken of all or any part of such street railway systems, including subways and tunnels, and by subsequent order and proclamation possession, control, and operation in whole or in part may also be relinquished to the owners thereof of any part of the railroad systems or rail and water systems, possessions and control of which are hereby assumed.

The Director shall, as soon as may be after having as-

To assume control of the vast railway systems of the country is, I realize, a very great responsibility, but to fail to do so in the existing circumstances would have been a much greater. I assumed the less responsibility rather than the weightier.

I am sure that I am speaking the mind of all thoughtful Americans when I say that it is our duty as the representatives of the nation to do everything that it is necessary to do to secure the complete mobilization of the whole resources of America by as rapid and effective means as can be found. Transportation supplies all the arteries of mobilization. Unless it be under a single and unified direction, the whole process of the nation's action is embarrassed.

It was in the true spirit of America, and it was right, that we should first try to effect the necessary unification under the voluntary action of those who were in charge of the great railway properties; and we did try it. The directors of the railways responded to the need promptly and generously. The group of railway executives who were charged with the task of actual coordination and general direction performed their difficult duties with patriotic zeal and marked ability, as was to have been expected, and did, I believe, everything that it was possible for them to do in the circumstances. If I have taken the task out of their hands, it has not been because of any dereliction or failure on their part but only because there were some things which the Government can do and private management cannot. We shall continue to value most highly the advice and assistance of these gentlemen and I am sure we shall not find them withholding it.

It had become unmistakably plain that only under Government administration can the entire equipment of the several systems of transportation be fully and unreservedly thrown into a common service without injurious discrimination against particular properties. Only under Government administration can an absolutely unrestricted and unembarrassed common use be made of all tracks, terminals, terminal facilities and equipment of every kind. Only under that authority can new terminals be constructed and developed without regard to the requirements or limitations of particular roads. But under Government administration all these things will be possible—not instantly, but as fast as practical difficulties, which cannot be merely conjured away, give way before the new management.

The common administration will be carried out with as little disturbance of the present operating organizations and personnel of the railways as possible. Nothing will be altered or disturbed which it is not necessary to disturb. We are serving the public interest and safeguarding the public safety, but we are also regardful of the interest of those by whom these great properties are owned and glad to avail ourselves of the experience and trained ability of those who have been managing them.

It is necessary that the transportation of troops and of war materials, of food and of fuel, and of everything that is necessary for the full mobilization of the energies and resources of the country, should be first considered, but it is clearly in the public interest also that the ordinary activities and the normal industrial and commercial life of the country should be interfered with and dislocated as little as possible, and the public may rest assured that the interest and convenience of the private shipper will be as carefully served and safeguarded as it is possible to serve and safeguard it in the present extraordinary circumstances.

While the present authority of the Executive suffices for all purposes of administration, and while of course all private interests must for the present give way to the public necessity, it is, I am sure you will agree with me, right and necessary that the owners and creditors of the railways, the holders of their stocks and bonds, should receive from the Government an unqualified guarantee that their properties will be maintained throughout the period of Federal control in as good repair and as complete equipment as at present, and that the several roads will receive under Federal management such compensation as is equitable and just alike to their owners and to the general public. I would suggest the average net railway operating income of the three years ending June 30, 1917. I earnestly recommend that these guarantees be given by appropriate legislation, and given as promptly as circumstances permit.

I need not point out the essential justice of such guarantees and their great influence and significance as elements in the present financial and industrial situation of the country. Indeed, one of the strong arguments for assuming control of the railroads at this time is the financial argument.

It is necessary that the values of railway securities should be justly and fairly protected and that the large financial operations every year necessary in connection with the maintenance, operation and development of the roads should, during the period of the war, be wisely related to the financial operations of the Government.

Our first duty is, of course, to conserve the common interest and the common safety and to make certain that nothing stands in the way of the successful prosecution of the great war for liberty and justice, but it is also an obligation of public conscience and of public honor that the private interests we disturb should be kept safe from unjust injury, and it is of the utmost consequence to the Government itself that all great financial operations should be stabilized and co-ordinated with the financial operations of the Government.

No borrowing should run athwart the borrowings of the Federal Treasury, and no fundamental industrial values should anywhere be unnecessarily impaired.

In the hands of many thousands of small investors in the country, as well as in national banks, in insurance companies, in savings banks, in trust companies, in financial agencies of every kind, railway securities, the sum total of which runs up to some ten or eleven thousand millions, constitute a vital part of the structure of credit, and the unquestioned solidity of that structure must be maintained.

The Secretary of War and I easily agreed that, in view of the many complex interests which must be safeguarded and harmonized, as well as because of his exceptional experience and ability in this new field of Governmental action, the Hon. William G. McAdoo was the right man to assume direct administrative control of this new executive task. At our request, he consented to assume the authority and duties of organizer and Director General of the new Railway Administration. He has assumed those duties and his work is in active progress.

It is probably too much to expect that even under the unified railway administration which will now be possible sufficient economies can be effected in the operation of the railways to make it possible to add to their equipment and extend their operative facilities as much as the present extraordinary demands upon their use will render desirable without resorting to the National Treasury for the funds. If it is not possible, it will, of course, be necessary to resort to the Congress for grants of money for that purpose. The Secretary of the Treasury will advise with your committees with regard to this very practical aspect of the matter.

For the present, I suggest only the guarantees I have indicated and such appropriations as are necessary at the outset of this task. I take the liberty of expressing the hope that the Congress may grant these promptly and ungrudgingly. We are dealing with great matters and will, I am sure, deal with them greatly.

Wilson's Address to Congress, Stating the War Aims and Peace Terms of the United States

(Delivered in Joint Session, January 8, 1918)

Gentlemen of the Congress:

Once more, as repeatedly before, the spokesmen of the Central Empires have indicated their desire to discuss the objects of the war and the possible basis of a general peace. Parleys have been in progress at Brest-Litovsk between Russian representatives and representatives of the Central Powers to which the attention of all the belligerents has been invited for the purpose of ascertaining whether it may be possible to extend these parleys into a general conference with regard to terms of peace and settlement.

The Russian representatives presented not only a perfectly definite statement of the principles upon which they would be willing to conclude peace but also an equally definite program of the concrete application of those principles. The representatives of the Central Powers, on their part, presented an outline of settlement which, if much less definite, seemed susceptible of liberal interpretation until their specific program of practical terms was added. That program proposed no concessions at all either to the sovereignty of Russia or to the preferences of the populations with whose fortunes it dealt, but meant, in a word, that the Central Empires were to keep every foot of territory their armed forces had occupied—every province, every city, every point of vantage—as a permanent addition to their territories and their power.

It is a reasonable conjecture that the general principles of settlement which they at first suggested originated with the more liberal statesmen of Germany and Austria, the men who have begun to feel the force of their own people's thought and purpose, while the concrete terms of actual settlement came from the military leaders who have no thought but to keep what they have got. The negotiations have been broken off. The Russian representatives were sincere and in earnest. They cannot entertain such proposals of conquest and domination.

The whole incident is full of significance. It is also full of perplexity. With whom are the Russian representatives dealing? For whom are the representatives of the Central Empires speaking? Are they speaking for the majorities of their respective parliaments or for the minority parties, that military and imperialistic minority which has so far dominated their whole policy and controlled the affairs of Turkey and of the Balkan states which have felt obliged to become their associates in this war?

The Russian representatives have insisted, very justly, very wisely, and in the true spirit of modern democracy, that the conferences they have been holding with the Teutonic and Turkish statesmen should be held within open, not closed, doors, and all the world has been audience, as was desired. To whom have we been listening, then? To those who speak the spirit and intention of the resolutions of the German Reichstag of the 9th of July last, the spirit and intention of the Liberal leaders and parties of Germany, or to those who resist and defy that spirit and intention and insist upon conquest and subjugation? Or are we listening, in fact, to both, unreconciled and in open and hopeless contradiction? These are very serious and pregnant questions. Upon the answer to them depends the peace of the world.

But, whatever the results of the parleys at Brest-Litovsk, whatever the confusions of counsel and of purpose in the utterances of the spokesmen of the Central Empires, they have again attempted to acquaint the world with their objects in the war and have again challenged their adversaries to say what their objects are and what sort of settlement they would deem just and satisfactory. There is no good reason why that challenge should not be responded to, and responded to with the utmost candor. We did not wait for it. Not once, but again and again, we have laid our whole thought and purpose before the world, not in general terms only, but each time with sufficient definition to make it clear what sort of definite terms of settlement must necessarily spring out of them. Within the last week Mr. Lloyd George has spoken with admirable candor and in admirable spirit for the people and Government of Great Britain.

There is no confusion of counsel among the adversaries of the Central Powers, no uncertainty of principle, no vagueness of detail. The only secrecy of counsel, the only lack of fearless frankness, the only failure to make definite statement of the objects of the war, lies with Germany and her allies. The issues of life and death hang upon these definitions. No statesman who has the least conception of his responsibility ought for a moment to permit himself to continue this tragical and appalling outpouring of blood and treasure unless he is sure beyond a peradventure that the objects of the vital sacrifice are part and parcel of the very life of Society and that the people for whom he speaks think them right and imperative as he does.

There is, moreover, a voice calling for these definitions of principle and of purpose which is, it seems to me, more thrilling and more compelling than any of the many moving voices with which the troubled air of the world is filled. It is the voice of the Russian people. They are prostrate and all but helpless, it would seem, before the grim power of Germany, which has hitherto known no relenting and no pity. Their power, apparently, is shattered. And yet their soul is not subservient. They will not yield either in principle or in action. Their conception of what is right, of what is humane and honorable for them to accept, has been stated with a frankness, a largeness of view, a generosity of spirit, and a universal human sympathy which must challenge the admiration of every friend of mankind;

ınd they have refused to compound their ideals or desert ·thers that they themselves may be safe.

They call to us to say what it is that we desire, in what, f in anything, our purpose and our spirit differ from theirs; ınd I believe that the people of the United States would vish me to respond, with utter simplicity and frankness. Whether their present leaders believe it or not, it is our ıeartfelt desire and hope that some way may be opened vhereby we may be privileged to assist the people of Rusia to attain their utmost hope of liberty and ordered peace.

It will be our wish and purpose that the processes of ·eace, when they are begun, shall be absolutely open and hat they shall involve and permit henceforth no secret ınderstandings of any kind. The day of conquest and ıggrandizement is gone by; so is also the day of secret ovenants entered into in the interest of particular governnents and likely at some unlooked-for moment to upset the ·eace of the world. It is this happy fact, now clear to the iew of every public man whose thoughts do not still linger n an age that is dead and gone, which makes it possible ·or every nation whose purposes are consistent with jusice and the peace of the world to avow now or at any ·ther time the objects it has in view.

We entered this war because violations of right had ocurred which touched us to the quick and made the life of ur own people impossible unless they were corrected and he world secure once for all against their recurrence.

What we demand in this war, therefore, is nothing peculır to ourselves. It is that the world be made fit and safe o live in; and particularly that it be made safe for every ›eace-loving nation which, like our own, wishes to live ts own life, determine its own institutions, be assured of ustice and fair dealing by the other peoples of the world s against force and selfish aggression.

All the peoples of the world are in effect partners in this nterest, and for our own part we see very clearly that unless justice be done to others it will not be done to us. The program of the world's peace, therefore, is our program; and that program, the only possible program, as we see it, is this:

1. Open covenants of peace, openly arrived at, after which there shall be no private international understandings of any kind but diplomacy shall proceed always frankly and in the public view.

2. Absolute freedom of navigation upon the seas, outside territorial waters, alike in peace and in war, except as the seas may be closed in whole or in part by international action for the enforcement of international covenants.

3. The removal, so far as possible, of all economic barriers and the establishment of an equality of trade conditions among all the nations consenting to the peace and associating themselves for its maintenance.

4. Adequate guarantees given and taken that national armaments will be reduced to the lowest points consistent with domestic safety.

5. A free, open-minded, and absolutely impartial adjustment of all colonial claims, based upon a strict observance of the principle that in determining all such questions of sovereignty the interests of the populations concerned must have equal weight with the equitable claims of the government whose title is to be determined.

6. The evacuation of all Russian territory and such a settlement of all questions affecting Russia as will secure the best and freest cooperation of the other nations of the world in obtaining for her an unhampered and unembarrassed opportunity for the independent determination of her

own political development and national policy and assure her of a sincere welcome into the society of free nations under institutions of her own choosing; and, more than a welcome, assistance also of every kind that she may need and may herself desire. The treatment accorded Russia by her sister nations in the months to come will be the acid test of their good will, of their comprehension of her needs as distinguished from their own interests, and of their intelligent and unselfish sympathy.

7. Belgium, the whole world will agree, must be evacuated and restored, without any attempt to limit the sovereignty which she enjoys in common with all other free nations. No other single act will serve as this will serve to restore confidence among the nations in the laws which they have themselves set and determined for the government of their relations with one another. Without this healing act the whole structure and validity of international law is forever impaired.

8. All French territory should be freed and the invaded portions restored, and the wrong done to France by Prussia in 1871 in the matter of Alsace-Lorraine, which has unsettled the peace of the world for nearly fifty years, should be righted, in order that peace may once more be made secure in the interest of all.

9. A readjustment of the frontiers of Italy should be effected along clearly recognizable lines of nationality.

10. The peoples of Austria-Hungary, whose place among the nations we wish to see safeguarded and assured, should be accorded the freest opportunity of autonomous development.

11. Rumania, Serbia, and Montenegro should be evacuated; occupied territories restored; Serbia accorded free and secure access to the sea; and the relations of the several Balkan states to one another determined by friendly counsel along historically established lines of allegiance and nationality; and international guarantees of the political and economic independence and territorial integrity of the several Balkan states should be entered into.

12. The Turkish portions of the present Ottoman Empire should be assured a secure sovereignty, but the other nationalities which are now under Turkish rule should be assured an undoubted security of life and an absolutely unmolested opportunity of autonomous development, and the Dardanelles should be permanently opened as a free passage to the ships and commerce of all nations under international guarantees.

13. An independent Polish state should be erected which should include the territories inhabited by indisputably Polish populations, which should be assured a free and secure access to the sea, and whose political and economic independence and territorial integrity should be guaranteed by international covenant.

14. A general association of nations must be formed under specific covenants for the purpose of affording mutual guarantees of political independence and territorial integrity to great and small states alike.

In regard to these essential rectifications of wrong and assertions of right we feel ourselves to be intimate partners of all the governments and peoples associated together against the imperialists. We cannot be separated in interest or divided in purpose. We stand together until the end.

For such arrangements and covenants we are willing to fight and to continue to fight until they are achieved; but only because we wish the right to prevail and desire a just and stable peace such as can be secured only by removing the chief provocations to war, which this program does remove.

We have no jealousy of German greatness, and there is nothing in this program that impairs it. We grudge her no achievement or distinction of learning or of pacific enterprise such as have made her record very bright and very enviable. We do not wish to injure her or to block in any way her legitimate influence or power. We do not wish to fight her either with arms or with hostile arrangements of trade if she is willing to associate herself with us and the other peace-loving nations of the world in covenants of justice and law and fair dealing.

We wish her only to accept a place of equality among the peoples of the world,—the new world in which we now live,—instead of a place of mastery.

Neither do we presume to suggest to her any alteration or modification of her institutions. But it is necessary, we must frankly say, and necessary as a preliminary to any intelligent dealings with her on our part, that we should know whom her spokesmen speak for when they speak to us, whether for the Reichstag majority or for the military party and the men whose creed is imperial domination.

We have spoken now, surely, in terms too concrete to admit of any further doubt or question. An evident principle runs through the whole program I have outlined. It is the principle of justice to all peoples and nationalities, and their right to live on equal terms of liberty and safety with one another, whether they be strong or weak.

Unless this principle be made its foundation no part of the structure of international justice can stand. The people of the United States could act upon no other principle; and to the vindication of this principle they are ready to devote their lives, their honor, and everything that they possess. The moral climax of this the culminating and final war for human liberty has come, and they are ready to put their own strength, their own highest purpose, their own integrity and devotion to the test.

President Wilson's Address to Congress, Analyzing German and Austrian Peace Utterances

(Delivered in Joint Session, February 11, 1918)

Gentlemen of the Congress: On the eighth of January I had the honor of addressing you on the objects of the war as our people conceive them. The Prime Minister of Great Britain had spoken in similar terms on the fifth of January. To these addresses the German Chancellor replied on the tweny-fourth and Count Czernin, for Austria, on the same day. It is gratifying to have our desire so promptly realized that all exchanges of view on this great matter should be made in the hearing of all the world.

Count Czernin's reply, which is directed chiefly to my own address of the eighth of January, is uttered in a very friendly tone. He finds in my statement a sufficiently encouraging approach to the views of his own Government to justify him in believing that it furnishes a basis for a more detailed discussion of purposes by the two Governments. He is represented to have intimated that the views he was expressing had been communicated to me beforehand and that I was aware of them at the time he was uttering them; but in this I am sure he was misunderstood. I had received no intimation of what he intended to say. There was, of course, no reason why he should communicate privately with me. I am quite content to be one of his public audience.

Count von Hertling's reply is, I must say, very vague and very confusing. It is full of equivocal phrases and leads it is not clear where. But it is certainly in a very different tone from that of Count Czernin, and apparently of an opposite purpose. It confirms, I am sorry to say, rather than removes, the unfortunate impression made by what we had learned of the conferences at Brest-Litovsk. His discussion and acceptance of our general principles lead him to no practical conclusions. He refuses to apply them to the substantive items which must constitute the body of any final settlement. He is jealous of international action and of international counsel. He accepts, he says, the principle of public diplomacy, but he appears to insist that it be confined, at any rate in this case, to generalities and that the several particular questions of territory and sovereignty, the several questions upon whose settlement must depend the acceptance of peace by the twenty-three states now engaged in the war, must be discussed and settled, not in general council, but severally by the nations most immediately concerned by interest or neighborhood. He agrees that the seas should be free, but looks askance at any limitation to that freedom by international action in the interest of the common order. He would without reserve be glad to see economic barriers removed between nation and nation, for that could in no way impede the ambitions of the military party with whom he seems constrained to keep on terms. Neither does he raise objection to a limitation of armaments. That matter will be settled of itself, he thinks, by the economic conditions which must follow the war. But the German colonies, he demands, must be returned without debate. He will discuss with no one but the representatives of Russia what disposition shall be made of the people and the lands of the Baltic provinces; with no one but the Government of France the "conditions" under which French territory shall be evacuated; and only with Austria what shall be done with Poland. In the determination of all questions affecting the Balkan states he defers, as I understand him, to Austria and Turkey; and with regard to the agreements to be entered into concerning the non-Turkish peoples of the present Ottoman Empire, to the Turkish authorities themselves. After a settlement all around, effected in this fashion, by individual barter and concession, he would have no objection, if I correctly interpret his statement, to a league of nations which would undertake to hold the new balance of power steady against external disturbance.

It must be evident to everyone who understands what this war has wrought in the opinion and temper of the world that no general peace, no peace worth the infinite sacrifices of these years of tragical suffering, can possibly be arrived at in any such fashion. The method the German Chancellor proposes is the method of the Congress of Vienna. We cannot and will not return to that. What is at stake now is the peace of the world. What we are striving for is a new international order based upon broad and universal principles of right and justice,—no mere peace of shreds and patches. Is it possible that Count von Hertling does not see that, does not grasp it, is in fact living in his thought in a world dead and gone? Has he utterly forgotten the Reichstag Resolutions of the nineteenth of July, or does he deliberately ignore them? They spoke of the conditions of a general peace, not of national aggrandizement or of arrangements between state and state. The peace of the world depends upon the just settlement of each of the several problems to which I adverted in my recent address to the Congress. I, of course, do not mean that the peace of the world depends upon the acceptance of any particular set of suggestions as to the way in which those problems are to be dealt with. I mean only that those problems each and all affect the whole world; that unless they are dealt with in a spirit of unselfish and unbiased justice, with a view to the wishes, the natural connections, the racial aspirations, the security, and the peace of mind of the peoples involved, no permanent peace will have been attained. They cannot be discussed separately or in corners. None of them constitutes a private or separate interest from which the opinion of the world may be shut out. Whatever affects the peace affects mankind, and nothing settled by military force, if settled wrong, is settled at all. It will presently have to be reopened.

Is Count von Hertling not aware that he is speaking in the court of mankind, that all the awakened nations of the world now sit in judgment on what every public man, of whatever nation, may say on the issues of a conflict which has spread to every region of the world? The Reichstag Resolutions of July themselves frankly accepted the decisions of that court. There shall be no annexations, no contributions, no punitive damages. Peoples are not to be handed about from one sovereignty to another by an international conference or an understanding between rivals and antagonists. National aspirations must be respected; peoples may now be dominated and governed only by their own consent. "Self-determination" is not a mere phrase. It is an imperative principle of action, which statesmen will henceforth ignore at their peril. We cannot have general peace for the asking, or by the mere arrangements of a peace conference. It cannot be pieced together out of individual understandings between powerful states. All the parties to this war must join in the settlement of every issue anywhere involved in it; because what we are seeking is a peace that we can all unite to guarantee and maintain and every item of it must be submitted to the common judgment whether it be right and fair, an act of justice, rather than a bargain between sovereigns.

The United States has no desire to interfere in European affairs or to act as arbiter in European territorial disputes.

She would disdain to take advantage of any internal weakness or disorder to impose her own will upon another people. She is quite ready to be shown that the settlements she has suggested are not the best or the most enduring. They are only her own provisional sketch of principles and of the way in which they should be applied. But she entered this war because she was made a partner, whether she would or not, in the sufferings and indignities inflicted by the military masters of Germany, against the peace and security of mankind; and the conditions of peace will touch her as nearly as they will touch any other nation to which is entrusted a leading part in the maintenance of civilization. She cannot see her way to peace until the causes of this war are removed, its renewal rendered as nearly as may be impossible.

This war had its roots in the disregard of the rights of small nations and of nationalities which lacked the union and the force to make good their claim to determine their own allegiances and their own forms of political life. Covenants must now be entered into which will render such things impossible for the future; and those covenants must be backed by the united force of all the nations that love justice and are willing to maintain it at any cost. If territorial settlements and the political relations of great populations which have not the organized power to resist are to be determined by the contracts of the powerful governments which consider themselves most directly affected, as Count von Hertling proposes, why may not economic questions also? It has come about in the altered world in which we now find ourselves that justice and the rights of peoples affect the whole field of international dealing as much as access to raw materials and fair and equal conditions of trade. Count von Hertling wants the essential bases of commercial and industrial life to be safeguarded by common agreement and guarantee, but he cannot expect that to be conceded him if the other matters to be determined by the articles on peace are not handled in the same way as items in the final accounting. He cannot ask the benefit of common agreement in the one field without according it in the other. I take it for granted that he sees that separate and selfish compacts with regard to trade and the essential materials of manufacture would afford no foundation for peace. Neither, he may rest assured, will separate and selfish compacts with regard to provinces and peoples.

Count Czernin seems to see the fundamental elements of peace with clear eyes and does not seek to obscure them. He sees that an independent Poland, made up of all the indisputably Polish peoples who lie contiguous to one another, is a matter of European concern and must of course be conceded; that Belgium must be evacuated and restored, no matter what sacrifices and concessions that may involve; and that national aspirations must be satisfied, even within his own Empire, in the common interest of Europe and mankind. If he is silent about questions which touch the interest and purpose of his allies more nearly than they touch those of Austria only, it must of course be because he feels constrained, I suppose, to defer to Germany and Turkey in the circumstances. Seeing and conceding, as he does, the essential principles involved and the necessity of candidly applying them, he naturally feels that Austria can respond to the purpose of peace as expressed by the United United States with less embarrassment than could Germany. He would probably have gone much farther had it not been for the embarrassments of Austria's alliances and of her dependence upon Germany.

After all, the test of whether it is possible for either government to go any further in this comparison of views is simple and obvious. The principles to be applied are these:

First, that each part of the final settlement must be based upon the essential justice of that particular case and upon such adjustments as are most likely to bring a peace that will be permanent;

Second, that peoples and provinces are not to be bartered about from sovereignty to sovereignty as if they were mere chattels and pawns in a game, even the great game, now forever discredited, of the balance of power; but that

Third, every territorial settlement involved in this war must be made in the interest and for the benefit of the populations concerned, and not as a part of any mere adjustment or compromise of claims amongst rival states; and

Fourth, that all well defined national aspirations shall be accorded the utmost satisfaction that can be accorded them without introducing new or perpetuating old elements of discord and antagonism that would be likely in time to break the peace of Europe and consequently of the world.

A general peace erected upon such foundations can be discussed. Until such a peace can be secured we have no choice but to go on. So far as we can judge, these principles that we regard as fundamental are already everywhere accepted as imperative except among the spokesmen of the military and annexationist party in Germany. If they have anywhere else been rejected, the objectors have not been sufficiently numerous or influential to make their voices audible. The tragical circumstance is that this one party in Germany is apparently willing and able to send millions of men to their death to prevent what all the world now sees to be just.

I would not be a true spokesman of the people of the United States if I did not say once more that we entered this war upon no small occasion, and that we can never turn back from a course chosen upon principle. Our resources are in part mobilized now, and we shall not pause until they are mobilized in their entirety. Our armies are rapidly going to the fighting front, and will go more and more rapidly. Our whole strength will be put into this war of emancipation,—emancipation from the threat and attempted mastery of selfish groups of autocratic rulers,—whatever the difficulties and present partial delays. We are indomitable in our power of independent action and can in no circumstances consent to live in a world governed by intrigue and force. We believe that our own desire for a new international order under which reason and justice and the common interests of mankind shall prevail is the desire of enlightened men everywhere. Without that new order the world will be without peace and human life will lack tolerable conditions of existence and development. Having set our hand to the task of achieving it, we shall not turn back.

I hope that it is not necessary for me to add that no word of what I have said is intended as a threat. That is not the temper of our people. I have spoken thus only that the whole world may know the true spirit of America,—that men everywhere may know that our passion for justice and for self-government is no mere passion of words but a passion which, once set in action, must be satisfied. The power of the United States is a menace to no nation or people. It will never be used in aggression or for the aggrandizement of any selfish interest of our own. It springs out of freedom and is for the service of freedom.

INDEX

INDEX

D

E

INDEX

INDEX

INDEX

NOTABLE PHRASES OF PRESIDENT WILSON

If you think too much about being reëlected, it is very difficult to be worth reëlecting. *Page 30.*

We shall not, I believe, be obliged to alter our policy of watchful waiting. (*Mexico.*) *Page 39.*

I shall not know how to deal with other matters of even greater delicacy and nearer consequence if you do not grant it to me in ungrudging measure. (*Repeal of provision for free tolls for American coastwise ships through Panama Canal.*) *Page 59.*

We must depend . . . not upon a standing army, nor yet upon a reserve army, but upon a citizenry trained and accustomed to arms. *Page 78.*

There is such a thing as a man being too proud to fight. There is such a thing as a nation being so right that it does not need to convince others by force that it is right. *Page 117.*

No man in the United States knows what a single week or a single day or a single hour may bring forth. (*A plea for military preparedness, January, 1916.*) *Page 172.*

There may at any moment come a time when I cannot preserve both the honor and the peace of the United States. *Page 177.*

The United States would be constrained to hold the imperial German Government to a strict accountability. *Page 222.*

The Imperial German Government will not expect the Government of the United States to omit any word or any act necessary to the performance of its sacred duty of maintaining the rights of the United States and its citizens. *Page 243.*

Unless the Imperial Government should now immediately declare and effect an abandonment of its present methods of submarine warfare against passenger and freight-carrying vessels, the Government of the United States can have no choice but to sever diplomatic relations with the German Empire altogether. *Page 262.*

The United States is willing to become a partner in any feasible association of nations formed in order to realize these objects. (*The guarantee of territorial integrity and political independence, and the prevention of hasty wars.*) *Page 274.*

Property rights can be vindicated by claims for damages . . . but the fundamental rights of humanity cannot be. *Page 310.*

So long as the power of recognition rests with me, the Government of the United States will refuse to extend the hand of welcome to anyone who obtains power in a sister republic by treachery and violence. *Page 313.*

It must be a peace without victory. *Page 352.*

I advise that the Congress declare the recent course of the Imperial German Government to be in fact nothing less than war against the government and people of the United States. *Page 376.*

We have no quarrel with the German people. *Page 378.*

The world must be made safe for democracy. *Page 381.*

The right is more precious than peace. *Page 382.*

It is not an army that we must shape and train for war; it is a nation. *Page 393.*

America in this war . . . seeks no material profit or aggrandizement of any kind. She is fighting . . . for the liberation of peoples everywhere from the aggressions of autocratic force. *Page 396.*

The day has come to conquer or submit. *Page 408.*

For us there is but one choice. We have made it. *Page 418.*

Balked, but not defeated, the enemy of four-fifths of the world. (*The German Government.*) *Page 422.*